Transformations

The Anthropology of Children's Play

Transformations

The Anthropology of Children's Play

Helen B. Schwartzman
Institute for Juvenile Research
Chicago, Illinois

PLENUM PRESS · NEW YORK AND LONDON

Library of Congress Cataloging in Publication Data

Schwartzman, Helen B
  Transformations.

  Bibliography: p.
  Includes index.
  1. Play. 2. Games, Primitive. 3. Ethnology — Methodology. I. Title.
GN454.7.S38   301.2'1   78-12577
ISBN 0-306-31128-3

© 1978 Plenum Press, New York
A Division of Plenum Publishing Corporation
227 West 17th Street, New York, N.Y. 10011

All rights reserved

Printed in the United States of America

For John

Preface

Writing a book about play leads to wondering. In writing this book, I wondered first if it would be taken seriously and then if it might be too serious. Eventually, I realized that these concerns were cast in terms of the major dichotomy that I wished to question, that is, the very pervasive and very inaccurate division that Western cultures make between play and seriousness (or play and work, fantasy and reality, and so forth). The study of play provides researchers with a special arena for re-thinking this opposition, and in this book an attempt is made to do this by reviewing and evaluating studies of children's transformations (their play) in relation to the history of anthropologists' transformations (their theories).

While studying play, I have wondered in the company of many individuals. I would first like to thank my husband, John Schwartzman, for acting as both my strongest supporter and, as an anthropological colleague, my severest critic. His sense of nonsense is always novel as well as instructive. I am also very grateful to Linda Barbera-Stein for her Sherlock Holmes style help in locating obscure references, checking and cross-checking information, and patience and persistence in the face of what at times appeared to be bibliographic chaos. I also owe special thanks to my teachers of anthropology—Paul J. Bohannan, Johannes Fabian, Edward T. Hall, and Roy Wagner—whose various orientations have directly and indirectly influenced the approach presented in this book.

I also wish to acknowledge the support of the Institute for Juvenile Research which has made the writing of this book possible, and I would particularly like to thank Merton S. Krause and Anne Seiden for their encouragement and support of my work on play. I would like to thank my friends and colleagues in The Association for the Anthropological

Study of Play for creating a context for the presentation and sharing of ideas about this topic. Brian Sutton-Smith and John M. Roberts in particular have been most generous in providing me with extremely valuable comments and critiques on various aspects of the book and, in general, offering their considerable wisdom on the subject of play.

I have been lucky to have had the help of Rose Lee Warren, Mary Dell Onley, Drue Cass and Leslie Bowman in the preparation of this manuscript. I would like to thank them especially for their accuracy and proficiency. I have also been fortunate to have the editorial guidance, assistance, and patience of Paulette Cohen, Harvey Graveline, Kirk Jensen, and Thomas Lanigan. I owe them a great deal of thanks.

Finally, I would like to acknowledge the influence of one very important individual. Over one hundred years ago, the Rev. Charles L. Dodgson, writing as Lewis Carroll, invented and then continued to transform an unusual form of child/adult fantasy literature. In the process, he produced both a commentary on and criticism of many of the philosophical and moral issues of concern in England during the Victorian era. Carroll's transformations are still relevant today as evidenced by the continued quotation of the Alice books in any number of manuscripts and textbooks, particularly the works of philosophers, logicians, mathematicians, and so forth. This is ironic because Alice was not always fond of lessons and I can only hope that she would approve of her appearance in a book about play and games, activities that she most definitely enjoyed.

HELEN B. SCHWARTZMAN

Acknowledgments

The author wishes to thank the following for permission to reprint copyrighted materials in this book.

From *Centuries of Childhood*, by Philippe Ariès, 1962, pp. 33, 129, and 132, New York: Vintage Books—Alfred A. Knopf. Reprinted by permission of the publisher and author.

From "The Message 'This is Play'," by Gregory Bateson, 1956, pp. 145–146, 148–149, Figure 20. In *Group Processes: Transactions of the Second Conference*, New York: Josiah Macy, Jr., Foundation. Reprinted by permission of the publisher and author.

From "A Theory of Play and Fantasy," by Gregory Bateson, 1955, pp. 40, 44, 50–51. In *Psychiatric Research Reports*, II, December, Washington, D.C.: American Psychiatric Association. Reprinted by permission of the publisher and author.

From *Balinese Character*, by Gregory Bateson and Margaret Mead, 1942, Plate 42 and caption notes, New York: New York Academy of Sciences, Special Publication, Volume II. Reprinted by permission of the publisher and Gregory Bateson.

From *Games and Pastimes of the Maori*, by Elsdon Best, 1925, Figure 51, Dominion Museum Bulletin, No. 8. Reprinted by permission of the National Museum of New Zealand.

From "A Tangu Game," by K.O.L. Burridge, 1957, pp. 88–89. In *Man*, 57: 88–89. Reprinted by permission of the Royal Anthropological Institute of Great Britain and Ireland and the author.

From *The Hopi Child*, by Wayne Dennis, 1940, Plate IV and pp. 141–142, New York: Appleton-Century-Crofts. Reprinted 1972 by Arno Press, New York. Reprinted by permission of Margaret W. Dennis.

From "Play and Inter-Ethnic Communication," by Claire R. Farrer,

1976, pp. 88–90. In *The Anthropological Study of Play: Problems and Prospects*, D. F. Lancy and B. Allan Tindall, eds., Cornwall, New York: Leisure Press. Reprinted by permission of The Association for the Anthropological Study of Play and author.

From "The New Englanders of Orchard Town, U.S.A.," by John and Ann Fischer, 1963, photo-p. 952c. In *Six Cultures: Studies of Child Rearing*, B. Whiting, ed., New York: John Wiley. Reprinted by permission of John L. Fischer and Beatrice Whiting.

From "Social and Psychological Aspects of Education in Taleland," by Meyer Fortes, 1938, Pp. 44–45, 49. In *Africa*, Supplement to Volume 11, Number 4. Reprinted by permission of the International African Institute and author.

From *Beyond the Pleasure Principle*, by Sigmund Freud, 1920, pp. 33–34, J. Strachey translation, New York: W. W. Norton, 1976 edition. Reprinted by permission of the publisher.

From "Deep Play: Notes on the Balinese Cockfight," by Clifford Geertz, 1972, pp. 23, 26 and 29. In *Daedalus*. Reprinted by permission of the American Academy of Arts and Sciences and author.

From *Child Studies Through Fantasy*, by Rosalind Gould, 1972, pp. 22–24, New York: Quandrangle/ The New York Times Book Co. Reprinted by permission of the publisher and author.

From *Doll Play of Pilagá Indian Children*, by Jules and Zunia Henry, 1944, pp. 55, 80. Research Monographs, Number 4, New York: American Orthopsychiatric Association. Republished 1974 by Vintage Books-Random House. Reprinted by permission of Random House, Inc., and Zunia Henry.

From "Australian 'Hoppy' Hopscotch," by Dorothy Howard, 1958, pp. 173–diagrams. In *Western Folklore, 17*: 163–175. Reprinted by permission of *Western Folklore*.

From *Speech Play*, Barbara Kirshenblatt-Gimblett, ed., 1976, pp. 21, 27, 29, 34, 92–93, 94, 95, 96, 103–104, 132, Philadelphia: University of Pennsylvania Press. Reprinted by permission of the publisher.

From *The Study of Culture*, by L. L. Langness, 1974, pp. 36–37, Chandler & Sharp Publishers, Inc., Corte Madera, California. Reprinted by permission of the publisher and author.

From *Late Gothic Engravings of Germany and the Netherlands*, by M. Lehrs, 1969, Plate 537, New York: Dover. Reprinted by permission of the publisher.

From "Taira: An Okinawan Village," by Thomas and Hatsumi Maretzki, 1963, photo. p. 456d. In *Six Cultures: Studies of Child Rearing*, B. Whiting, ed., New York: John Wiley. Reprinted by permission of Thomas Maretzki.

From *The !Kung of Nyae Nyae*, by Lorna Marshall, 1976, photo-p.

323, Cambridge, Mass.: Harvard University Press. Reprinted by permission of the author.

From "Tarong: An Ilocos Barrio in the Philippines," by William and Corinne Nydegger, 1963, photo-p. 792c. In *Six Cultures: Studies of Child Rearing*, B. Whiting, ed., New York: John Wiley. Reprinted by permission of William F. Nydegger.

From *The Lore and Language of Schoolchildren*, by Iona and Peter Opie, 1959, pp. 2, 10–11, 19, 88, 90, 361, 370, Oxford: Oxford University Press. Reprinted by permission of the publisher and authors.

From *Children's Games in Street and Playground*, by Iona and Peter Opie, 1969, photo by A. D. Webb (Plate VI), Oxford: Oxford University Press. Reprinted by permission of the publisher and authors.

From "The Mixtecans of Juxtlahuaca, Mexico," by Kimball and Romaine Romney, 1963, photo-p. 600d. In *Six Cultures: Studies of Child Rearing*, B. Whiting, ed., New York: John Wiley. Reprinted by permission of A. Kimball Romney.

From "The Gold Key" in *Transformations* by Anne Sexton. Copyright © 1971 by Anne Sexton. Reprinted by permission of Houghton Mifflin Company.

From "Game Cognition and Game Preference in the Yucatán," by Christine von Glascoe, 1977, Figure 1, Paper presented at the American Ethnological Society meetings, April, San Diego, California. Reprinted by permission of the author.

From *Six Cultures: Studies of Child Rearing*, Beatrice Whiting, ed., 1963, pp. 5 (diagram), 470, 683, 849–850, New York: John Wiley. Reprinted by permission of Beatrice Whiting.

From *The Relation of Man to Nature in Aboriginal America*, by Clark Wissler, 1926, figures-p. 16, New York: Oxford University Press. Reprinted by permission of Mary V. Wissler.

Contents

Chapter One

Anthropological Play 1

Play, Culture, and Anthropology 4
Play: Definitions, Classifications, and Reductions 7
Playing Anthropologist 7

Chapter Two

The Invention of Childhood 9

Conceiving Childhood: The First Invention 9
Reinventions of Childhood 13
The American Cultivation of Childhood: 1830–1945 14
The Cult of Childhood: 1945–1970 17
The Culture of Childhood and Anthropologists' Metaphors for Children 20
The Child as Primitive 21
The Child as Copycat 23
The Child as Personality Trainee 23
The Child as Monkey 24
The Child as Critic 25
The Great Pretenders 26

Chapter Three

Describing Play: Ethnographic Reports 27

Asia 30
Oceania 31

Central and South America 33
North America 35
Africa 37
Near East 38
Europe 38
Summary 39

Chapter Four

Staging Play: Evolutionary and Developmental Studies 41

Stages and Survivals 42
Recapitulation: G. Stanley Hall 46
On Morals and Marbles: Jean Piaget 50
The Ontogeny of Play 52
Staging Play: Comment and Critique 54
Summary 59

Chapter Five

Preserving Play: Diffusionism and Particularism 61

Game Diffusion and the *Patolli–Pachisi* Debate 62
Particularism: The Facts of Play 66
William Wells Newell: American Children's Games and Songs 67
Early Collections and Classifications 69
Walter Roth: Australian Aborigine Games 74
Elsdon Best: Maori Children's Games 77
Paul G. Brewster: Game Collections and Classifications 79
Brian Sutton-Smith: New Zealand and American Children's Games 82
Dorothy Howard: Australian Children's Games 85
Iona and Peter Opie: English Children's Games and Rhymes 87
Favorite Collectors' Items 91
Summary 92

Chapter Six

Socializing Play: Functional Analysis 98

A. R. Radcliffe-Brown and Bronisław Malinowski 98
Functionalists and Play 99
Socializing Play: The Kibbutz 106
Socializing Play: The Australian Aborigine 108
Socializing Play: The Kpelle 108
Play and Sex Roles 110
Games and Power Roles 115
Imitation, Imagination, and Culture 116

Play: Socialization, Satirization, or Innovation? 124
Summary 133

Chapter Seven

Projecting Play: Culture and Personality 135

Configurationists 136
Psychocultural Analysis 141
Freud on Play 145
Projecting Play: The Pilagá 150
Projecting Play: The Duau 153
New Methodologies: The Hopi and the Balinese 155
African Children's Play: The Luba, Sanga, and Yeke 166
Freudians on Play 174
Statistics and Culture: Freud and Learning Theory 179
Projecting Play in Six Cultures 184
Games and Culture 196
Summary 207

Chapter Eight

Saying Play: Communication Studies 210

The Difference That Makes a Difference: Gregory Bateson 211
Play and Paradox: The Message "This Is Play" 214
The Single Signal 220
Winking or Blinking? Text and Context 221
Saying Play: The Mescalero Apache Child 228
Saying Play: The American Preschool Child 228
  Children's Play in a Research Laboratory: Organizing Transformations 229
  Children's Play in a Day-Care Center: Sideways Transformations 232
Summary 245

Chapter Nine

Minding Play: Structural and Cognitive Studies 248

The Player's Perspective 252
The Researcher's Perspective 257
Minding Play: Piaget versus Sutton-Smith 268
Piaget's Assimilation of Play 269
Play and Learning 272
Rhymes and Reasons: Children's Verbal Play 283
  Play Languages 291
  Verbal Dueling 293
  Riddles 296

Vocabulary Games 297
Narratives 298
Summary 299

Chapter Ten

Defining Play: Ecology, Ethology, and Experiments 302

Environmental Definitions: Toys and Niches 303
Behavioral Definitions: Child Ethology 308
Play and Exploration.. 315
Behavioral Definitions: Experimental Studies 318
Play and Creativity 321
Summary 323

Chapter Eleven

Conclusion: New Metaphors for Old 325

Chapter Twelve

Selected References and Films 332

Films on Children's Play 334
Other Films of Interest to Play Researchers 339

References 344

Index 375

Transformations
The Anthropology of Children's Play

CHAPTER ONE

Anthropological Play

Anthropology is the study of man "as if" there were culture.
. . . It is a kind of game, if you will, a game of pretending that
the ideas and conventions of other peoples are the same (in one broadly
conceived way or another) as our own so that we can see what hap-
pens when we "play" our own concepts through the lives and actions
of others. As the anthropologist uses the notion of culture to control
his field experiences, those experiences will, in turn, come to control
his notion of culture. He invents "a culture" for people, and they
invent "culture" for him.
Roy Wagner, The Invention of Culture, 1975

Transform?
As if an enlarged paper clip could be a piece of sculpture.
(And it could.)
Anne Sexton, From "The Gold Key" in *Transformations*, 1971

Children transform sticks into houses, mud into food, and themselves into mothers and fathers; anthropologists transform houses into settlement patterns, food into subsistence economy, mothers and fathers into kinship systems, and people into cultures. Children's transformations are often described as frivolous play, as in "it's easy as child's play"; anthropologists' transformations are thought to be hard work, as in fieldwork. This book is about the anthropology of children's play; however, it is also about the play of anthropologists, as both children and ethnographers are continually constructing and transforming the contexts in which they exist in their efforts to make sense, and sometimes nonsense, out of the worlds in which they find themselves.

Transformations, then, are the subject of this book—children's and anthropologists'. The fact that young humans play in one way or

1

another, in all societies of the world, is illustrated by the numerous descriptions of this activity that appear in ethnographies. The fact that anthropologists play in one way or another, in all societies of the world, is less readily recognized. Therefore, in order to present an accurate anthropology of children's play, it is necessary to examine not only play in its various cultural contexts but also culture as it has been played (i.e., "metaphorized") in its various anthropological contexts. The first task is initially undertaken in Chapter Three, in which a brief overview of ethnographic descriptions of children's play is provided. The second task is more complicated, as it requires an examination not only of specific anthropological theories about and/or definitions of *play* but also an analysis of particular anthropologists' theories about and/or definitions of *culture*. This is necessary because anthropologists' views of culture and cultural activity have influenced both their theoretical analyses and ethnographic descriptions of play behavior. Therefore, in this book, anthropologists' reports on play will be evaluated in both their geographic and theoretical contexts. In this way this presentation of an anthropology of children's play is also a discussion of the history of anthropologists' ideas about culture as evidenced by their interpretations of children's play.[1]

In discussing this topic, however, it is important to remember that just as concepts of play have been transformed by both cultural contexts and concepts of culture, so too have children. Western notions of childhood have, as Ariès and other researchers continually remind us, changed several times over the course of Western history. And, anthropological monographs likewise document the variety of ways in which people interpret newborn *Homo sapiens* as "children." In this sense, then, a "child" is no more "natural" and no less "cultural" than his/her parents. Therefore, before embarking on a description of children's metaphors in play, a brief discussion of anthropologists' and others' metaphors for children is considered in Chapter Two.

The remaining chapters of this book are organized according to specific anthropological theories of culture that have influenced ethnographers' descriptions and interpretations of children's play behavior.

---

[1]Comprehensive discussions of the history of anthropology are conspicuously absent in the literature, which is ironic for a discipline that "began as the science of history" (M. Harris, 1968:1). For the preparation of this book I have found Langness's brief, but very informative, *The Study of Culture* (1974) to be useful when read in conjunction with the more detailed accounts of M. Harris (*The Rise of Anthropological Theory*, 1968) and Bidney (*Theoretical Anthropology*, 1967). Harris's analysis, however, is somewhat marred by his strident advocacy of "cultural materialism." More recent examinations of the development of anthropology are available by Voget (*A History of Ethnology*, 1975) and Honigmann (*The Development of Anthropological Ideas*, 1976).

The chapters are organized in a more or less chronological fashion in an attempt to reflect the development of theories both of culture and of play.

In Chapter Four, the approach of the early evolutionists in anthropology and the developmentalists in psychology is presented. The tie between these two disciplines is their interest in the stages of either cultural or individual development. It will come as no surprise, then, to find that these researchers concentrate on the *staging* of children's play activities.

The historical particularist and diffusionist tradition in anthropology was a reaction to the "armchair" stages of the early evolutionists. Particularists concentrated on the collection and preservation of culture traits, while diffusionists mapped the interactions between cultures. In Chapter Five the particularists' *preservations* and the diffusionists' use of play texts are examined.

Structure functionalists generated their own critique of the historical diffusionists by analyzing the mechanisms of cultural integration. Their interest was in the social maintenance of sameness, and faced with the deviant nature of play, they sought to *socialize* it. Functional studies of children's play are discussed in Chapter Six.

Culture and personality researchers, also in reaction to previous anthropological traditions, emphasized the importance of the individual in culture, while they also initiated studies of the impact of culture on individual personalities. These researchers viewed children's play and games as *projective tests,* capable of eliciting information on these topics. Culture and personality studies are reviewed in Chapter Seven.

The subtleties of human and nonhuman animal communication have attracted the attention of many researchers, and several anthropologists have proposed a view of culture as communication. Researchers adopting this perspective have often produced analyses of play because it is an activity that cannot be successfully initiated or maintained if the actors do not communicate, mark, or frame their actions as play. Communication studies that examine the *saying* of playing are discussed in Chapter Eight.

The relatively recent studies of ethnoscientists, structuralists, and also many cognitive psychologists are characterized by their search for either particular or universal structures of the mind. In their attempts to *mind* play, these researchers have conducted a variety of studies that include analyses of both player and researcher categorization systems, discussion of relationships between play and learning, and examination of children's verbal play. This diverse research tradition is considered in Chapter Nine.

In contrast to the "mentalist" approach of the ethnoscientists and structuralists, "materialist" analyses of culture emphasize the importance of ecological, economic, and behavioral variables. In adopting this approach for the study of play, investigators often advocate the use of experimental or quasi-experimental methodologies, and so a number of experimental studies of play conducted by psychologists are also considered in this discussion. Ecological, ethological, and experimental researchers, who search for "objective" (i.e., "materialist") *definitions* of play, are reviewed in Chapter Ten.

In Chapter Eleven a concluding evaluation of these research traditions and also suggestions for future research projects are offered as we continue to develop, to paraphrase Mead (1956), new metaphors for old in the study of children's play.

Finally, in Chapter Twelve, a brief summary of useful references and a survey of recent ethnographic films of children's play and games are presented.

In order to facilitate my specific assessment of this research, I use Sutton-Smith's (1974b) recent contrast between the *texts* (i.e., descriptions of the play or game itself) and *contexts* (i.e., the social, psychological or environmental correlates of the event) of play, assuming that those studies that provide information on both play texts and play contexts are most complete and most useful for future investigations.[2] In short, I am looking for studies, and cultural orientations, that assume that children's play is both "texted" and "contexted."

PLAY, CULTURE, AND ANTHROPOLOGY

Perceptions of play are intimately related to one's culture. In the West, our understanding of play has been most significantly influenced by shared attitudes about what play is *not*. Play is not *work*; play is not *real*; play is not *serious*; play is not *productive*; and so forth. These attitudes, which are related to that complex of beliefs that has come to be known as the Protestant Ethic, have made it very difficult for Westerners to see that work can be playful[3] while play can sometimes be experi-

---

[2]See Dundes (1964c) for an extended analysis of the importance of *text* (i.e., "a version of or a single telling of a tale, a recitation of a proverb, a singing of a folksong," p. 255), *context* (i.e., "the specific social situation in which [a] . . . particular item is actually employed," p. 255–256), *function* (i.e., "the analyst's statement of what [he thinks] the use or purpose of a given genre of folklore is," p. 256), and *texture* (i.e., "linguistic features" such as "rhyme and alliteration" or "stress, pitch, juncture, tone, and onomatopoeia," p. 254) in the study of folklore.

[3]Csikszentmihalyi (1975) has recently suggested that Weber, in *The Protestant Ethic and the Spirit of Capitalism* (1920), "never saw clearly that the ascetic withdrawal from all pleasures can in itself be enjoyable" although he did come "very close to seeing how arbitrary the

enced as work (particularly in the case of games); and, likewise, that players create worlds that are often more real, serious, and productive than so-called real life.

Anthropologists, of course, have often found that the separation of work and play (labor and leisure), which is characteristic of industrialized societies, is frequently absent in nonindustrialized cultures (see Bohannan, 1963:219; Norbeck, 1971:48; Turner, 1974b, 1977), where the more important contrasts may be between sacred and profane work (Turner, 1974b:63) or between play and ritual (Handelman, 1977a:185). It has also been suggested recently that the play–work distinction may not even be valid as applied to Western societies where play activities occur *at* work (e.g., Handelman, 1975, 1977b; Mergen, 1977) and *in* work (e.g., Csikszentmihalyi, 1975; Schwartzman, 1977a) and work occurs *at* play (e.g., Csikszentmihalyi, 1975; Manning, 1973).

Anthropologists, however, have often uncritically accepted the work–play distinction of Western societies. This is most obviously seen in the lack of attention that has been given to the study of play for the bulk of the discipline's history. It is true, however, that during the late 19th and early 20th centuries, a number of anthropologists and folklorists were very serious about the study of play and games. Inspired by the arguments of Tylor (e.g., 1879b) about the diffusion of games such as *pachisi* to the Americas, many researchers (e.g., Daniel, 1892; Dorsey, 1891; Hodge, 1890) contributed articles to the early issues of the *American Anthropologist*. It was also during this time that the extensive game collections of Newell (1883), Gomme (1894, 1898), and Culin (1895, 1907) were published. However, with the exception of Best's *Games and Pastimes of the Maori* (1925) and Lesser's *The Pawnee Ghost Dance Hand Game* (1933), the anthropological study of play did not advance much beyond the early investigations of Tylor and Culin until the late 1950s. In 1959, Roberts, Arth, and Bush (inspired again by Tylor) published an article entitled "Games in Culture," in which they attempted to develop a theoretical framework for the study of games that would explain both their geographical distribution and their sociocultural significance.

This article served effectively to re-open the field of play research for anthropologists; and, in a 1974 survey of anthropologists' views of play, Norbeck was able to suggest that the past history of neglect of this topic was currently (and *finally*) being challenged:

---

work-play distinction really is" (pp. 187–188). This is most clearly illustrated in Weber's concluding chapter. Here he suggests that, "In the field of its highest development, in the United States, the pursuit of wealth, stripped of its religious and ethical meaning, tends to become associated with purely mundane passions, which often actually give it the character of sport" (1920:182).

In view of the objectives of anthropology of learning the nature of man as a
living organism and the nature of his culture, the learned and socially transmitted ways of human life, the anthropological neglect of the study of play
seems astonishing. . . . the recent anthropological trend toward the study of
play may now be rephrased to state that a growing concensus sees human
play as strikingly conspicuous, common behavior of human beings
everywhere, a category of behavior so prominent that it must be studied and
interpreted in order to reach the objectives of anthropology. (1974a:267–268)

Norbeck went on to define human play as

characteristic behavior of mankind at all ages of life that arises from a geneti-
cally inherited stimulus or proclivity and is distinguished by the combination
of traits of being voluntary, somehow pleasurable, distinct temporally from
other behavior, and distinctive in having a make-believe or psychically tran-
scendental quality. (p. 270)

In another article (1974b), Norbeck outlined a "list of topics related to
play which appear profitable to study" (p. 5). These include: the study of
play as a mirror of the pervasive values and attitudes of a society; play as
a means of social control; play and social psychological problems in
Western society; play and linguistics, cognition, and symbolism; play
and religion; play and politics; play and law; play and aggression; the
didactic and socializing value of play among children and adults; play
and art; and play and creativity or cultural innovation (pp. 5–8).

In 1974, The Association for the Anthropological Study of Play
(TAASP) was formed in order to take up the challenge offered by researchers such as John Roberts and Edward Norbeck.[4] This book reports on
research conducted by several members of TAASP, and it will be seen
that these investigators have expanded, revised, and also critiqued Norbeck's definition of play and also his list of promising research topics.
This is a sign that the anthropological study of play is both a healthy and
a growing research field. In this book I have narrowed my coverage of
available studies to present a general overview, systematization, and
assessment of anthropological studies of children's play. However, because anthropologists have often used the studies of sociologists,
psychologists, and psychiatrists to inform their research in this regard,
relevant literature from these disciplines is also reviewed here. There are
also many recent studies of adult play and games and nonhuman primate play available in the literature, but these investigations are considered here only insofar as they have influenced studies of children's
play.

[4]Information in regard to TAASP membership, publications, etc., may be obtained by
writing to Elinor Nickerson, Box 297, Alamo, California 94507.

PLAY: DEFINITIONS, CLASSIFICATIONS, AND REDUCTIONS

In this book a variety of definitions, classifications, and reductions utilized by anthropologists and others in their studies of children's play will be considered. A word, however, must briefly be said about this "triple threat" to play. This is said not because I devalue attempts to define, classify, or reduce (by metaphorical transformation) phenomena in the research process, but because I am critical of the way definitions, classifications, and reductions of children's play have been formulated and used in the past. Definitions, for example, are often speculative attempts by investigators to arbitrarily define the nature of play, with little attempt made to collect information or data on the subject. Classifications, on the other hand, have frequently been formulated by researchers desperate to "make sense" out of the range of materials that they may have actually collected. Often such classifications are a useful first step, but all too frequently a classification scheme is formulated and that is all. Finally, in theorizing about play, a metaphorical transformation is often made (e.g., play is likened to a psychological projection, or play is viewed as a cognitive process). Unfortunately, this transformation is often disregarded and soon play *is* a psychological projection, or play *is* a function of cognitive processes, as the metaphor is now taken literally (Turbayne, 1968). When this happens, a reduction of play to some other phenomenon occurs. I would suggest that by forgetting the intrinsically playful, "as if" quality of theorizing, an injustice is done to all phenomena, but an injustice is done particularly to play.

PLAYING ANTHROPOLOGIST

Since I have suggested that anthropologists, as well as children, play, it may be of interest to see how a group of West African Yoruba children "play anthropologist." In so doing, these children reveal not only how anthropological contexts transform play texts but also how children's play texts transform, and comment on, anthropological contexts:

> During my work with their fathers these three children invented a new game—playing anthropologist. One sat in my chair or my cushion with paper and pencil in hand. The second sat in their father's chair, acting as "interpreter" while the third sat on a bench as the informant customarily did. The second child turned to the first and said, "You are my master," and then to the third child saying in Yoruba, "The white man wants you to tell about *Odua.*" The third child replied in Yoruba and the second turned to the first and "interpreted," making a series of meaningless sounds which were sup-

posed to sound like English. The first child scribbled on the paper and replied
with more nonsense syllables and the second child turned to the third with a
new question in Yoruba. (Bascom, 1969:58)

The implications of this quote will be discussed more thoroughly in
subsequent chapters. It is sufficient to say here that we learn as much
about anthropology from this event as we do about children's play. This
quote is important also because it illustrates the dual perspective of this
book, which has been written as if the study of anthropology could
transform the study of children's play (and it has), and as if the study of
play could transform the discipline of anthropology (and it could).

CHAPTER TWO

The Invention of Childhood

"What-is-this?" he said at last.
"This is a child!" Haigha replied eagerly, coming in front of
Alice to introduce her, and spreading out both his hands towards her
in an Anglo-Saxon attitude. "We only found it today. It's as large as
life, and twice as natural!"
Lewis Carroll, *Through the Looking Glass, and What Alice Found There*

Every culture develops its own view of children's nature, and with it a related set of beliefs about how best to "culture" this "nature." The formation of a distinctly American childhood ideology is closely related to the evolution of a childhood consciousness in Western Europe. Therefore, it is necessary to begin this study of the anthropology of children's play with a brief analysis of these historical inventions as they have affected ethnographic studies of both children and their play.

A child is not solely a biological creature who comes to be influenced by the present-day sociocultural circumstances of his birth. All children, because of the fact that they are born into a social environment, are affected by a construct that is peculiarly historical and, as such, has undergone many changes and reinterpretations in all societies. This construct is the concept of childhood that is used to interpret newborn *Homo sapiens* as *children* (with all the various social and biological characteristics that a society may ascribe to these persons) to the individuals responsible for their socialization.

CONCEIVING CHILDHOOD: THE FIRST INVENTION

Phillipe Ariès presented a documentation of the development of Western conceptions of childhood from medieval times to the 18th cen-

9

tury in his book *Centuries of Childhood* (1962).[1] In this study Ariès argued that the Western concept of childhood, as we know it today, has not existed from time immemorial. In fact, as Ariès stated his case, our present-day ideas about the essential nature and character of children and their childhood have come on the scene rather late in terms of Western European history. His evidence is drawn from a detailed analysis of Western European artwork (including paintings, frescoes, engravings, stained-glass windows, etc.) and literature from the 10th to the 18th centuries.

Anthropologists, of course, have known for a long time that American and Western concepts of children and childhood could not be universally applied to all cultures. And it would be easy to quote many ethnographic sources to support this idea (e.g., Dennis, 1940; Goodman, 1970; Leighton and Kluckhohn, 1947; Mead, 1928, 1930). However, Ariès's work is important to consider here because it shows us that many of our current ideas about children, childhood, and family structure have a history of their own within the development of Western culture. The notion that major orienting concepts, such as childhood, are relative to temporal or historical circumstances, as well as sociocultural context, is one that even anthropologists have not always been quick to recognize.[2]

Ariès began his analysis by suggesting that the idea of childhood, as we know it today, was nonexistent during medieval times. For example, he argued the following:

> Medieval art until about the twelfth century did not know childhood or did
> not attempt to portray it. It is hard to believe that this neglect was due to

---

[1] A growing interest in the study of the history of childhood is reflected by the recent creation of a journal specifically concerned with the topics of childhood and family history. This journal is edited by Lloyd de Mause and is called the *History of Childhood Quarterly: The Journal of Psychohistory.* De Mause, it should be noted, has also recently edited a book entitled *The History of Childhood* (1974), which includes articles on late Roman and early medieval childhood (Lyman); parent–child relationships from the 9th to the 13th centuries (McLaughlin); middle-class urban Italian children between the 14th and early 16th centuries (Ross); 15th-century English childhood (Tucker); 17th-century child-rearing patterns in France (Marvick) and England and America (Ilick); and 18th-century American childhood (Walzer). DeMause presented his views on childhood history in opposition to Ariès and stated his case most dramatically (and also ethnocentrically) in the introductory article of this book: "The history of childhood is a nightmare from which we have only recently begun to awaken. The further back in history one goes, the lower the level of child care, and the more likely children are to be killed, abandoned, beaten, terrorized, and sexually abused. It is our task here to see how much of this childhood history can be recaptured from the evidence that remains to us" (1974:1).

[2] See Goodman's *The Culture of Childhood* (1970) for an example of an important study in which various cultures' notions of childhood are discussed, but there is no mention of the historical development of this concept.

incompetence or incapacity; *it seems more probable that there was no place for childhood in the medieval world.* An Ottonian miniature of the twelfth century provides us with a striking example of the deformation which an artist at that time would inflict on children's bodies. The subject is the scene in the Gospel in which Jesus asks that little children be allowed to come to Him. . . . Yet the miniaturist has grouped around Jesus what are obviously eight men, without any of the characteristics of childhood; they have simply been depicted on a smaller scale. (1962:33; italics added)[3]

In other words, the only distinguishing feature of children that the medieval artist felt obliged to represent was their size; they are smaller than adults but in no way else is a special nature emphasized.

Ariès's arguments, however, were made not only in an attempt to suggest that at one time in Western European history individuals had no concept of childhood. His purpose was also to describe the development of concepts of childhood over many historical periods. According to this thesis, the evolution of our present-day ideas about childhood proceeded through several historical periods, which can be illustrated again by recourse to the art, and also the literature, of these times. For Ariès

[3]The miniature that Ariès used as an example in this quotation was taken from the Gospel Book of Otto III, Munich (see Ariès, 1962:420).

FIGURE 1A. Children's Play in the fourteenth century: Playing "La Crosse," fourteenth century French boy (from J. Jusserand, 1901:284).

FIGURE 1B. Children's Play in the fifteenth century: Two children playing, fifteenth century German engraving (from M. Lehrs, 1969:Plate 537).

the initial invention of childhood began in the 13th century, and its progress is particularly evident in the history of art in the 15th and 16th centuries (see Figure 1A & B). However, the documentation for its development is more numerous and significant from the latter part of the 16th and throughout the 17th centuries (p. 47). During this period, Ariès stated that

> A new concept of childhood had appeared in which the child, on account of his sweetness, simplicity and drollery, became a source of amusement and relaxation for the adult. (p. 129)

Ariès called this initial formulation of childhood consciousness the "coddling" attitude. He also pointed out that today we are more aware of this early "coddling" attitude toward children (as expressed in the latter 16th and 17th centuries) because of the critical responses made to it by individuals such as Montaigne. His point here is that we are more cognizant of the 17th century's *coddling attitude* toward children than we are aware of the *indifferent attitude* of the Middle Ages.

REINVENTIONS OF CHILDHOOD

In the 17th century, according to Ariès, a new feeling toward children was expressed.[4] Here the century's moralists and pedagogues shared Montaigne's dislike for the "coddling" attitude; however, these individuals were actually interested in children and their childhood. The authors of this period (Balthazar Gratien, Abbé Groussault) were not ignorant of the concept of childhood, nor were they totally overcome by the "sweetness and drollery" of children; rather, they were attempting to develop "a serious and realistic concept of childhood" (Ariès, 1962:132).[5] Ariès stated their purpose in these words:

> In order to correct the behavior of children, people must first of all understand it, and the texts of the late sixteenth century and the seventeenth century are full of comments on child psychology. The authors show a great solicitude for children, who are seen as witnesses to baptismal innocence, comparable to the angels, and close to Christ who loved them. But this interest calls for the development in them of a faculty of reasoning which is still fragile, a determined attempt to turn them into thinking men and good Christians. (p. 132)

Ariès suggested that the initial concept of childhood—coddling—was developed in an intrafamilial context; however, reactions to this concept, which finally developed into what he called "the second concept of childhood," developed in extrafamilial situations. In the 17th century, churchmen, moralists, and pedagogues began to formulate the concept of childhood discussed above, in which children were seen "as fragile creatures of God who needed to be both safeguarded and reformed" (p. 133). This idea in turn passed into family life.

Ariès reported that in the 18th century both of the above conceptions of children (i.e., the child as innocent creature of God and the child in need of moral teachings and reformation) existed in the familial context. However, at this time a new interest becomes apparent in the literature in the form of expressions of concern for children's hygiene and physical health. Ariès suggested that at this point everything related to children and family life was a matter of significance: "Not only the child's future but his presence and his very existence are of concern: the child has taken a central place in the family" (p. 133). Ariès terminated

---

[4]For an interesting combination of historical analysis in the fashion of Ariès (1962) and psychocultural analysis in the fashion of Erikson (1963), see David Hunt's (1970) description of children and families of 16th- and 17th-century France. Also see the articles in de Mause (1974) by Marvick and Ilick.

[5]The works that Ariès (1962:420, 426) noted here are Balthazar Gratien, *El Discreto*, Huesca, 1646, French translation of 1723 by Père de Courbeville, S.J.; Abbé Groussault, *Le portrait d'une honnête femme*, 1693.

his analysis in the 18th century, for he considered the above position of the child and the family to be the one that is representative not only of this era but also, in one form or another, of the 19th and the 20th centuries.

In order to illustrate his argument, Ariès described the development of schools and ideas about education, changes in the role of the family, the evolution of the idea of childhood innocence, and the history of children's dress and games and pastimes. In the case of games, he described how children, even in the early 17th century, played the same games as adults and, conversely, how adults played many games that are now considered to be strictly for children. Ariès documented this description by referring to a variety of paintings and engravings that depict young children playing card games and other games of chance for money, while adults are seen playing what are now thought to be "childish" games, for example, leapfrog, hot cockles, and blind man's bluff.

Ariès also described the important place of amusements, seasonal festivities, carnivals, and so forth in societies prior to the 18th century. These were times for "a society to draw its collective bonds closer, to feel united" (p. 73). In paintings and illustrations, children and adolescents are depicted as participating "on an equal footing" with adults in these celebrations. However, in the 18th century, the situation is quite different, as children and play are no longer integral parts of society. According to Ariès, it was at this time that adults of the upper classes appear to have abandoned many of their games and amusements to children and to the lower classes (p. 99). Now the idea of the separate status of children was symbolized by particular forms of dress and particular types of activities (e.g., play and games), and this separation of the generations was also associated, in Ariès's view, with the development of the idea of class and particularly the division between lower class and middle class.

THE AMERICAN CULTIVATION OF CHILDHOOD: 1830–1945

Bernard Wishy's study, *The Child and the Republic* (1968), documents the development of American notions of the nature and nurture of children from 1830 to 1900.[6] It was during this period that certain writers,

---

[6]For two descriptions of family life in America in the 17th century, see Demos (1970) and Morgan (1944); see also Ilick in de Mause (1974). An interesting (though not detailed) history of American child-rearing patterns, surveying the 17th to the 20th centuries, is also available by Cable (1975). A brief history of the status of play and of children in England and America is presented by Stone (1971).

whom he called "popularizers" (i.e., individuals who were not professional psychologists or philosophers), entered into the debate on the "nurture" of children. Wishy stated that this debate preceded the publication of Dewey's *School and Society* (1909) and Freud's *The Interpretation of Dreams* (1900) by several generations and, in fact, created a more sympathetic context for the presentation of both Freud's and Dewey's ideas. Writings of many of this era's "respectable moralists" (e.g., John Abott, Horace Bushnell, and Harriet Martineau) were used by Wishy to illustrate his point. Conduct books written for children and for parents about children (e.g., Peter Parley, 1833; Lydia H. Signorney, 1838) and magazines (e.g., *Mother's Assistant* and *Parents Magazine*) written to discuss the problems of parenthood were also analyzed by Wishy. And finally, Wishy examined a number of literary works written between 1830 and 1900 that are assumed to reveal the attitudes and conceptions of childhood in fashion at this time (e.g., Jacob Abbott, *Rollo in the Atlantic*; Louisa May Alcott, *Little Women*; Martha Finley, *Elsie Dinsmore*; Nathaniel Hawthorne, *The Scarlet Letter*; Henry James, *What Maisie Knew*; Anna Sewell, *Black Beauty*; Mark Twain, *Huckleberry Finn*).

All of these sources illustrate a change in the view of the child from 1830 to 1900. Wishy argued that between 1830 and 1860 children were thought to be in need of "redemption and protection." In terms of this view, the child was faced with two contradictory ideals. One stated that "human will" in the form of absolute self-determination and individualism could conquer every limit in life and offer protection against and also success within a "corrupt" society. In contradiction to this belief in individualism, the child was also told to bind himself to an absolute moral law that would ensure his redemption and also his protection against a corrupt society. In other words, moralists of the time were telling parents that it was their job to create new Americans who were "both fully powerful in will and perfectly pure in spirit" (Wishy, 1968:10).

After 1860, according to Wishy, the dominant American conception of the child changed from a view of "the child as redeemable" (pre-1860 beliefs) to a view of "the child as redeemer" (1860–1900). Here Wishy stated that

> The generation 1830–1860 had established ideas of the child as a redeemable creature. Now the child because of superior energy, purity or magic will become a redeemer of adult failures. . . . From this point on (circa 1870) the sentimental notion that somehow it is better to be a child than an adult, that the best standards of life are those of naive and innocent children becomes an increasingly powerful theme in American culture. (p. 85)

It should be noted, however, that Ariès also discussed the development of the idea of children's innocence, and he traced it as far back as the end of the 16th century in France and also England.

In Robert Sunley's (1955) examination, also of 19th-century American literature on child rearing, the themes that Wishy discussed are also outlined. In Sunley's analysis, which concentrates on the period 1820–1860, three main schools of thought concerning the nature and nurture of children are delineated. The Calvinist tendency held that the child was born a depraved creature. Parents, therefore, had to "vigilantly guard" children against their "depraved impulses," and only strict obedience to adult demands could ensure the child's "salvation" (p. 163). A second school of thought is described as the "hardening" theory, said to have been derived from the writings of Locke and Rousseau. According to this school's argument, "it was the external environment of civilization which was dangerous to children." Left to their own devices, children would be "strong, vigorous, unspoiled men like those in the early days of our country" (p. 161). In Wishy's terms, this is a reflection of the idea of the child as *redeemer*. Evil in this case did not spring from the child himself as in Calvinist thought, but from the "weakening effect of civilized society" (p. 163). A child's nature was therefore opposed to "civilized" culture. The third theory of child nature, which was to become much more popular beginning in the 1930s and 1940s, was what Sunley referred to as the "gentle treatment" school. Here the child was portrayed as "having certain needs and potentialities which the parents were not to frustrate or control, but rather were to help fulfill and encourage into full development" (p. 163).

According to Sunley, the "gentle treatment" school of thought prevails in the child-rearing literature of the mid-1950s. However, in tracing the development of what she called "fun morality," Martha Wolfenstein (1955) described a very significant change in American attitudes toward children between the years 1914 and 1945. Wolfenstein outlined this change by contrasting early (1914) and somewhat later reports (1941–1951) on infant and child care from the *Infant Care Bulletin* published during this period by the Children's Bureau of the U.S. Department of Labor. The most salient feature of this comparison is the evidence of a change in attitudes toward the *impulses of children* (Wolfenstein delineated most of these changes in reference to different ideas expressed about play in these reports). In the early bulletins, the impulses of infants were seen as "enjoyable" and, therefore, dangerous and probably erotic. Therefore, in terms of the reasoning exhibited in these bulletins, these impulses were harmful, wicked, and evil and must be curbed. In reference to these beliefs, the play of infants was also harmful and suspect because it most likely served to induce erotic excitement and behavior. For example, Wolfenstein noted that play things (e.g., rocking horses, swings, teeter boards) in the 1914 bulletin "are cited in connection with masturbation as a means by which 'this habit is learned' " (p. 172).

In more recent issues of the bulletin (1942, 1945, 1951), "play becomes associated with harmless and healthful motor and exploratory activities" (p. 172). However, *play* in these issues takes on another quality, that of *obligation* or *duty*. Here it is thought not only that the mother should perform necessary tasks for her young child but that she and the child *should also have fun and enjoy doing these tasks* (p. 173). Parenthood itself has now taken on a new dimension, for "parents are promised that having a child will keep them together, keep them young, and give them fun and happiness" (p. 173). In these cases, "fun has become not only permissible but required, and this requirement has a special quality different from the obligations of the older morality" (p. 174). Wolfenstein went on to make the point that if one does *not* have fun and enjoy oneself at an appropriate "fun time" activity, then one has failed, and this failure can become as "damning" as any that exists in the so-called work sphere of life.

The Cult of Childhood: 1945–1970

The years 1945–1970 have seen the rise in America of what can perhaps be called the *cult* of childhood.[7] To provide evidence for this suggestion, I return to Wolfenstein's analysis of the *Infant Care Bulletin* and begin where she terminated her analysis, in 1950. In this instance I have chosen to interpret material that, of course, was not available to Wolfenstein. This examination, of course, is hardly exhaustive of the great number of writings that one could turn to in order to explore these questions, but it does have one clear advantage: an analysis of one continuous work that ranges from 1914 to 1972 and presumably reflects changes in American conceptions of childhood during this period of time.

The 1963 bulletin appears in many ways to continue the trend set in the 1945 and 1951 bulletins, which Wolfenstein discussed. The most significant feature of this pamphlet is again its urging to parents to "enjoy! enjoy!" your child. According to this document, a parent's *enjoyment* of his/her child is perhaps *the* most influential factor in the child's later development. This is clearly stated in the bulletin's introduction:

[7]Even more recently a number of individuals and groups have begun to question this cult, as illustrated most obviously in the formation of the National Organization for Non-Parents (NON) and books such as Beth Whelen's *A Baby, Maybe?* (1976). These developments are, of course, also related to concern over the "population explosion."

> Now that your baby is here, the really important thing is to *enjoy* him. *Enjoying* the baby may seem much too simple a recipe when your mind is full of feedings, birth weight, or how to get some sleep. In the long run, though, your *pleasure* in him will be the most precious gift you can give. Through your *enjoyment* of him as an infant and child, he becomes an adult who gives *enjoyment* to others and experiences joy himself. (1963:1; italics added)

This urge to *enjoy your child* appears in many of the pages of this bulletin, and this injunction is also evident in many popular post-1945 books about infant care and child rearing (e.g., Gesell, 1948; Ginott, 1965; Spock, 1946). This theme is continued, although with somewhat less emphasis, in the 1972 *Bulletin* (now published by the Children's Bureau of the Office of Child Development, which is a part of the Department of Health, Education, and Welfare). The importance of "having fun" with a new baby is stressed in various chapters, and, in fact, the purpose of the bulletin is said to be to provide parents with basic facts and information about infant care so that they can "relax" and "have more fun" with their child:

> If you know a good and easy way to take care of most of your baby's needs, it should be much easier for you to relax and for you and your baby to have more fun with each other. (p. ii)

In the years since 1945, one factor that has had a tremendous impact on American conceptions of children must certainly be what is popularly referred to as the World War II baby boom. U.S. Bureau of the Census statistics show that in 1945, 2,888,000 live births were recorded, but five years later (in 1950), 3,632,000 live births were recorded (*Statistical Abstract of the United States*, 1972:50). In one sense, during the 1950s and for part of the 1960s, it could be said that people had to become more conscious of children because there were simply more of them around than there had ever been before. However, I do not believe that it is just this simple, because Americans bring specific expectations (some of which are distinctly Western and some of which are distinctly American) to their assumption of a parental role.

In most cultures, Western and non-Western, the bearing of children is seen as a crucial stage in the development of the individual. The birth of a child is almost always a significant event for the individual parents and for the society in general. In contrast to many cultures, however, in Western societies (and particularly in America) the importance of children does not derive simply from the fact that they will grow up to become functioning and contributing adults. Instead, children are important because they are naive and innocent. Set apart in a world of their own, their lives are "un-*adult*-erated," and because of this, it is believed that they instinctively know how to play and have fun.[8] Children are important because they *are* children, not because they will *become* adults. In comparing Chinese and American ways of life, Francis L. K. Hsu made a similar point:

> Worship of the young is obvious in American society wherever one looks, exactly as worship of the old is plain for all to see in the culture patterns of traditional China. In fact, no other country accords so much attention to infancy or so many privileges to childhood as does the United States. There are many expressions of this. Americans are very verbal about children's rights. There is not only state and federal legislation to protect the young ones, but there are also various juvenile protective associations to look after their welfare. . . . It is literally true that from the point of view of American children, parents have practically no rights. American parents not only wish to help their children according to their own experiences but they also must find out through elaborate research what the youngsters really want so they can satisfy the youngsters individual predilections. (1963:194–195)

The development of specific disciplines for the study of child psychology, child development, childhood socialization, and so forth are all expressions of this "glorification" (as is this particular book). It is therefore not mere chance that these specialized disciplines developed in the West, and particularly in American society. When parents talk to one another about "their children," or when (or if) they evaluate their child's development, these communications and judgments are affected by a series of explicit and also implicit assumptions made about a child's "nature" and his/her appropriate "nurture." This is also true, although it is generally not recognized, for "child researchers."

Margaret Mead illustrated this point nicely in her introduction to the book *Growth and Culture* (Mead and McGregor, 1951). Here she examined a number of American beliefs in reference to how they have affected the acceptance or rejection of particular research findings. She also asked the question, "To what extent is the research worker so bound by the premises of his own culture that he will ask only certain questions and make only certain observations?" (p. 8). In order to illustrate this argument, Mead discussed a number of specific research schools and traditions. For example, she suggested that the Watsonian ideas about conditioning, which were developed in the 1920s, were

> thoroughly congenial to Americans, who are accustomed to fix rather than cope, and are anxious to produce babies of superlative superiority. The baby was regarded as quite flexible. It was only necessary to arrange the scene and provide the right set of stimuli and a perfectly trained baby would emerge. (p. 10)

[8]A recent example of the use of the child as a model for "naturalness," "spontaneity," and "foolishness and fun" can be found in the psychotherapeutic literature on transactional analysis (TA) (e.g., Berne, 1964; T. Harris, 1968).

These ideas were quickly and often uncritically accepted, according to Mead, because of their *fit* with American beliefs about the manipulation of the external environment. Children could be *worked on* (by training, conditioning, nourishing, exercising, etc.), and adults could *work at* becoming successful parents (p. 10).

Mead also suggested that Freud's ideas were accepted by Americans because they emphasized "the susceptibility of the child to parental good and bad deeds" (p. 18). In contrast, Jung's ideas, which invoked the notion of "intractable constitution" and also a view of the "detrimental effects of nurture," were not popular. Finally, Mead discussed the transformation of Gesell's ideas about children's growth (the book *Growth and Culture* is an examination of Mead and Bateson's Balinese material in terms of Gesell's categories of growth) by American parents. Gesell's approach, according to Mead, was to champion the right of children to grow at their own pace. However, the Gesell norms, which were designed to help parents know what to expect in their child's development, became norms for the judgment of a parent's success at child rearing:

> Books that were designed as guides to help the mother know what to expect . . . are used instead as ways of comparing one's child with other children, simply to establish how well one is doing as a mother. (p. 20)

In order to understand what children *are*, it is necessary not only to empirically study children and their behavior from numerous theoretical standpoints but also to examine how a culture's general world view, and specific childhood ideology, may affect these theoretical standpoints. In turn, it must also be asked what effect the scientific studies of children, which have been carried on in America since the late 19th century, have had on Americans' metaphors for children and views of "normal" childhood development. This question is particularly important to ask because American children are probably the most widely studied group of individuals in the world, and investigations of their behavior and implicit assumptions made about their "nature and nurture" have surely influenced studies of non-American children.

THE CULTURE OF CHILDHOOD AND ANTHROPOLOGISTS' METAPHORS FOR CHILDREN

The study of child socialization has been a recognized subject of anthropological inquiry for some time. Early in this century, investigators such as Chamberlain (1901) began to pursue the study of "primitive" children, and since that time a number of significant investigations of children have appeared (e.g., Dennis, 1940; Leighton and Kluckhohn,

1947; Mead, 1928, 1930; B. Whiting, 1963; J. Whiting, 1941; J. Whiting and I. Child, 1953). More recently, in a series on education and culture edited by George and Louise Spindler, a variety of ethnographies of childhood have been published (e.g., Hostetler and Huntington, 1971; Leis, 1972; Williams, 1969).

The importance of metaphors in organizing scientific inquiry has recently been rediscovered by anthropologists (e.g., Fernandez, 1974; Lévi-Strauss, 1962; Turner, 1974b; Wagner, 1975), although as Fernandez (1974:119) suggested, its importance was recognized early in the discipline's history by such luminaries as Tylor, Frazer, and Boas. According to Black (in Turner, 1974a:30), metaphors "select, emphasize, suppress, and organize features of a principal subject" (e.g., culture) by "implying statements about it that normally apply to a subsidiary subject" (e.g., an organism, a text, or a drama).

The above studies of child socialization reflect the anthropologists' use of a variety of metaphors for children. Unfortunately, in many of these reports the theoretical pretense involved in the use of a particular metaphor has been forgotten, and the metaphor is taken literally as a depiction of the "innate" or "real" nature of the child.[9] It is therefore important to explore not only the different types of cultures in which children grow up but also the variety of cultural schools in which anthropologists have been socialized. For just as these various theories of culture affect interpretations of play, they also influence interpretations of children. As these different cultural schools will be discussed in detail in the following chapters, they are only briefly mentioned here in reference to the "root metaphor" (Turner, 1974a) utilized for descriptions of children's behavior in general and children's play in specific.

The Child as Primitive

Studies of children began in the late 19th century at a time when it was fashionable to collect and compile examples of the customs of various "primitive" peoples. Western children at this time were often equated with primitives (e.g., Appleton, 1910), and so their customs, often their games and rhymes, were likewise considered appropriate for collection and preservation. Evolutionary theories of biological and cultural development were in vogue during this era, and so when investigators chose to analyze material on children, they naturally relied on the evolutionary perspective. G. Stanley Hall's recapitulation theory of children's play is typical and is probably the most well known of these

---

[9]See Turbayne (1970) for a general discussion of the process of "using" and "being used by" metaphors.

studies.[10] Hall believed that "the best index and guide to the stated activities of adults in past ages is found in the instinctive, untaught and non-imitative plays of children" (1904:202). He assumed that the play "stages" of children recapitulated the entire biocultural history of mankind.

The impact of Hall's theories on both anthropological and psychological studies of children's play is discussed more thoroughly in Chapter Four; however, it is important to note here that he was the first theorist to incorporate the notion of "stages" into the study of childhood. The view that children, in the process of "growing up," must invariably pass through various stages, phases, or periods is a powerful model for conceptualizing childhood development, and it appears in both popular and scholarly reports. Today the most influential, as well as the most scientifically sophisticated, proponent of a stage theory of development (and the related view of the child as primitive) is Piaget (e.g., 1951). In early works by Mead (e.g., 1932), the evolutionary and ethnocentric assumptions of Piaget were questioned and criticized by material collected in New Guinea. For the most part, however, it has been left to the ethnographic psychologists (e.g., Cole *et al.*, 1971) to continue the critique of the use of the "child as primitive" and the "primitive as child" metaphors. Examples of these studies are discussed in Chapters Four, Five, and Nine.

The Primitive Child

Curiously, at the time that Western children were being described as "primitive," many non-Western, supposedly "primitive" children were being depicted as precocious, unusually bright, advanced, and so forth (e.g., N. Miller, 1928; Spencer, 1899). This precocity, however, was thought to be "arrested" at puberty because of such factors as sexual excess or alcoholism. Obviously, as Cole *et al.* (1971:14) have recently stated, these explanations are more accurate reflections of Western folklore than non-Western reality.

Another view, also current at this time, suggested that primitive children were basically dull and totally passive, and, most alarmingly to the Western observer, they were without the benefit of toys or schools. Baker, a British missionary, reflected this view in his book *Children of Rhodesia* (1913):

---

[10]Hall, of course, was a psychologist and not an anthropologist. He is generally regarded as the founder of developmental psychology and was in fact more heavily influenced by evolutionary theory and its potential for understanding children's behavior than most anthropologists at this time.

> The children of this land are nonentities. Nothing at all is done for them. They feed, sit about and sleep, and in this manner they grow until it comes time for them to get about for themselves, to do something in the gardens, or to seek work from the white man. They have no nurseries, no toys, no books, no treats, no tea-parties, and no instructions from their parents and friends. They are here and that is all. Their lives are one big nothing. (p. 20)

These views appear in anthropological monographs as well. For example, Ashton (1952) in a monograph on the Sotho now of Lesotho (which is located in southern Africa) described the children's lack of ingenuity and imagination in their play. He stated that their games "are aimless and desultory and consist chiefly of roaming about, playing hide and seek, digging in ash heaps, making slides" and so forth (p. 35). However, Ashton also described a system of secret languages, as well as a variety of riddles and "conundrums" developed by these children (p. 37). Apparently the ingenuity of this word play did not cause the ethnographer to question his description of these children's games as aimless and desultory.

The Child as Copycat

Children are frequently described as passive imitators of adult behavior in the ethnographic literature, and it is often suggested that this is the main form of education in "primitive" societies. This approach is particularly reflected in descriptions of children's play as imitation and/or preparation for adult roles and is most congruent with structural/functional theories of cultural behavior. This view of play and of learning was criticized as early as 1938 by Meyer Fortes and later by Otto Raum (1940). Nevertheless the idea has persisted and continues to influence anthropologists' and others' investigations of children and their play. There are, however, a number of recent critiques of this approach available, and views of both play as imitation and play as innovation are examined in Chapter Six.

The Child as Personality Trainee

Many of the earliest ethnographic studies of children were made by anthropologists influenced by Freud's psychoanalytic theory. The investigations of Malinowski (1922), Benedict (1934), Mead (1928, 1930), DuBois (1944), and many others on relationships between culture and personality were greatly influenced by this approach. This research led to an interest in the study of child socialization and/or enculturation (i.e., the study of how children grow up to become socially and culturally appropriate adults). More recently, the studies of J. Whiting (1941), J.

Whiting and I. Child (1953), B. Whiting (1963), and many others have wedded Freudian theory to Hullian learning theory or, in the case of LeVine (1973), evolutionary theory. This approach has produced a number of quantitative studies (e.g., testing the association between exclusive mother–infant sleeping arrangements and male initiation rites at puberty—Whiting, Kluckhohn, and Anthony, 1958) and also the well-known multidisciplinary ethnographic investigation known as the *Six Cultures* project (B. Whiting, 1963).

Implicit in both traditional culture and personality research and the more recent studies of psychological anthropologists is an assumption that children are "by nature" incompetent, immature, asocial, and acultural creatures.[11] In these works the task of adults as "trainers," "rearers," or "cultural transmission agents" is to turn their "trainees" (i.e., children) into competent, mature, social, and supremely cultural beings. In these investigations, children's play is treated as a type of projection-eliciting technique similar to a thematic apperception test (TAT) or a Rorschach test. Games, in particular, are viewed as expressions of the intrapsychic and interpersonal anxieties and hostilities engendered by the particular child-rearing or training practices of a culture. This view of children and their play is discussed in detail in Chapter Seven.

The Child as Monkey

The recent works of child ethologists (e.g., Blurton Jones 1967, 1972b) appear to offer anthropologists interested in the study of child behavior an approach that is at once both evolutionary and "objective" in orientation. Advocates (e.g., Barsamian and Clapp, 1974) of this method argue that it will produce more rigorous analyses of child behavior and also allow for more valid and reliable comparisons of human behavior with that of nonhuman primate activity. Adopting this approach, the child ethologist assumes that the behavior of children is directly equivalent to the behavior of monkeys, chimpanzees, gorillas, etc. This assumption of equivalence is reflected by the fact that behaviors that the investigator wishes to study are, whenever possible, defined in anatomical terms (e.g., smile—corner of mouth turned upward). These definitions are used in order to allow for interspecies behavioral comparisons. The advantages and disadvantages of a view of the child as

[11]See Mackay (1974) for a critique of these assumptions from an ethnomethodologist's viewpoint.

monkey as it affects interpretations of children's play are examined in Chapter Ten.

The Child as Critic

Children frequently act as interpreters, commentators, and even critics of their own as well as adults' activities. Sutton-Smith (1972b, 1974b) has recently undertaken a study of role reversals and inversions apparent within the structure of certain children's games, and implicit in this study is a view of the child as critic. Others who have attempted similar analyses of children's behavior are Chukovsky (1963), Goodman (1970), Mackay (1974), and H. B. Schwartzman (1973, 1974, 1976b).

Mackay (1974), in particular, has recently noted that the urge to view children as incompetent, asocial, and acultural often glosses over the actual competencies that children may display with their peers or with adults. For example, he suggested that adults often implicitly assume a high degree of sophistication and rational competency in children at the very moment when they are explicitly treating them as incompetent or even as children who will be unable ever to achieve a "normal" degree of competency. To illustrate this tendency, he reported on one research study with mentally retarded children (measured IQ between 50 and 75). In this investigation, the researcher administered a measure that consisted of a list of 22 personality traits, and each child was asked to rank him/herself for each trait on a five-point scale. The format for this rating was as follows:

> I am *happy* not at all, not very often, some of the time, etc.
> *clean*
> *lazy*, etc.   (p. 186)

Mackay commented on the absurdity of this test in relation to implicit and explicit assumptions made about the children's intellectual abilities:

> The researcher assumes that these children have interpretive competence if he assumes that they are able to reflect upon their personalities-as-traits, and then rate them on a five-point scale. After the measurement is completed it is assumed that the aggregated measure of self-concept is of persons unable to reason well—they are, *after all*, mentally retarded. (p. 186)

All of these studies are significant because they suggest that children's behavior (particularly play behavior) does not always serve as a socializing and social-ordering activity, as it may in fact be seen to challenge, reverse, and/or comment on and interpret the social order. Examples of this research, as it seeks to challenge functional interpretations of children's play behavior, are discussed in Chapters Six and Eight.

THE GREAT PRETENDERS

This exposition of anthropologists' metaphors for children is not offered in order to suggest that researchers abandon the use of all metaphors in their theoretical formulations. In my view, these metaphors are an intrinsic part of the process of theory building. However, anthropologists and other researchers must begin to recognize and acknowledge their utilization of theoretical metaphors and historical inventions in the study of play, in the study of children,[12] and in the study of culture. If this does not occur, ethnographers will continue to be mesmerized by their metaphors, thinking that they are "working" while they are also "playing."

[12]The fact that these metaphors also serve as a very effective form of symbolic domination for children as well as their adult caretakers (generally females) has yet to be realized by socialization researchers or by those interested in examining the nature and role of women in society (e.g., Rosaldo and Lamphere, 1974). The symbolic domination of women is achieved not only by viewing them as helpless and dependent but also by viewing their children as helpless, dependent, and incompetent.

CHAPTER THREE

Describing Play:
Ethnographic Reports

"What I was going to say," said the Dodo in an offended tone,
"was that the best thing to get us dry would be a Caucus-race."
What is a Caucus-race?" said Alice; . . .
"Why," said the Dodo, "the best way to explain it is to do
it. . . ."
First it marked out a race-course, in a sort of circle ("the exact
shape doesn't matter," it said), and then all the party were placed
along the course, here and there. There was no "One, two, three, and
away!" but they began running when they liked and left off when
they liked, so that it was not easy to know when the race was over.
However, when they had been running half-an-hour or so, and were
quite dry again, the Dodo suddenly called out, "The race is over!"
and they all crowded round it, panting and asking, "But who has
won?"

Lewis Carroll, *Alice's Adventures in Wonderland*

In Melanesia, Tangu children play a game called *taketak*. Kenelm O.
Burridge described how it is played:

The game . . . takes its name from the word for the hard spines of coconut
palm fronds. Before play the spines are stripped and stuck in the ground
about six inches apart. . . . Tops—hollow hemispheres about two inches in
diameter, made from a dried rind, the half of a wild jungle fruit, with a
spindle forced through the apex of the hemisphere—are also required. . . .

A player spins a top in the palms of his hands, and in one movement
throws it into the one lot of spines with the object of striking as many as
possible. . . . Those *taketak* which have been touched by the top are pulled
out and laid aside. When the first team have completed their play into one lot

of *taketak*, the second take up their tops and play into the other. Supposing the first team to have struck three *taketak*, and the second two, two *taketak* are replaced in the lot into which the first team is spinning. If, with their second turn, the first team hit one *taketak*, it is removed—leaving both teams with two *taketak* out of each lot. Both teams are now equivalent as to the number of *taketak* removed, but the second team owe their series of spins, their object is to throw their tops into the *taketak* without hitting one. Should they succeed in *not* hitting any *taketak*—and the top has to be thrown fairly into the middle of the lot—the game is over and both teams are equivalent. (1957:88–89)

Westerners, and Wonderland creatures, attempting to understand this game might well ask, "But who has won?" The answer, as Burridge's analysis of *taketak* reveals, is that the question, for the Tangu, is inappropriate:

One of the ideas dominating Tangu relationships and activities is equivalence: a notion of moral equality between persons which receives primary expression in the attempt to exchange equivalent amounts of foodstuffs. . . . (p. 88)

Taketak expresses this idea of equivalence in game form, and therefore there can be no "winning side" and no "losing side." The idea that games *must* produce a disequilibrial outcome is a Western belief; it is not a Tangu one.[1]

The transformation of Western competitive games into culturally appropriate games of equivalence or cooperation is a particularly interesting example of the culture-specific nature of the idea that games always produce winners and losers. For example, Nydegger and Nydegger (1963) reported that the children in the village of Tarong in the Philippines frequently "take turns winning" games (p. 485). K. E. Read (1959) reported that games played by the Gahuku-Gama of New Guinea are also guided by a principle of equivalence. For example, in football matches, which are themselves transformations of the earlier practice of intergroup feuding,

each "team" aims to equal the goals scored by the other and no team should win, that is establish its outright superiority. Games usually go on for days until the scores are considered equal. (p. 429)

Burridge's brief, but sensitive, interpretation of *taketak* is suggestive of what the anthropological study of children's play and games can achieve. Unfortunately, many ethnographic reports have been in-

---

[1]This is not to say that all non-Western societies exhibit the idea of equivalence in their game forms. There are many cultures in which complex forms of competitive games have been developed. However, Western societies (and particularly the United States) have developed the idea of disequilibrial outcome in games and sports activities to such an extent that it is almost impossible for individuals raised in these cultures to believe that it could be otherwise.

fluenced more by the anthropologists' ideas about play than by the reality of this phenomenon as constructed by members of the society under investigation. The result has been the utilization of four major metaphors for the description of this activity by ethnographers. In these reports, play is viewed (1) as structured games; (2) as imitation; (3) as a projective test; or (4) as irrelevant. These perspectives on play have been shaped as well by specific anthropological theories of culture and views of children. Therefore, those early anthropologists and folklorists who saw the child as a type of "primitive" exhibiting "exotic" customs in his/her games and rhymes were encouraged to collect and preserve examples of only structured and rule-regulated games. If investigators believed that all activities and institutions were functional for the perpetuation of the social order, then play's function was to provide children with an arena for learning about social roles and cultural institutions. Because it was thought that primitive children learned only by imitation, by being "copycats," play was also described as imitation.

On the other hand, if children were thought to be "personality trainees," the view of most culture and personality researchers, then play would be treated as if it were a projective test capable of revealing the anxieties and hostilities engendered by a culture's "training" (i.e., child-rearing) practices. Finally, if children were viewed as unimportant and irrelevant for anthropological analysis, then descriptions of their play would likewise be irrelevant and, accordingly, would not be noticed and/or not included in the ethnographer's monograph.[2]

Even though anthropologists have unnecessarily simplified their descriptions of children's play by frequently utilizing metaphors more reflective of their own culture's view of this behavior than of the society that they are studying, there are still significant discussions to be found in the literature. The range and type of material available for each major geographic/cultural area is briefly reviewed here. The most lengthy and elaborate descriptions have been made by ethnographers and folklorists interested in collecting examples of children's structured games. The most frequent, but least detailed, discussions have been made by researchers who have interpreted, and then dismissed, children's play as imitative of adult work activities. Variations on these themes will be noted in this review; however, detailed consideration of individual studies will be made in subsequent chapters.

[2]It is possible to speculate that anthropologists have frequently edited descriptions of play out of their published articles and monographs, even when they have actually collected material on the subject. For example, in Paul and Laura Bohannan's descriptions of the Tiv, the ethnographic reports (L. and P. Bohannan, 1953; P. Bohannan, 1965) do not discuss children's play; however, their published field notes do contain descriptions of this activity (P. and L. Bohannan, 1958:374–379).

ASIA

The classic anthropological study of the play and game activities of Asian civilizations is Culin's *Korean Games, with Notes on the Corresponding Games of China and Japan* (1895).[3] This detailed volume is based on an examination of museum collections of game artifacts as well as on an analysis of manuscripts and also interviews with Korean, Chinese, and Japanese immigrants and students (see Cheska, 1975:6). Therefore, emphasis is placed on descriptions of material implements involved in structured, and often extremely complicated, adult games. Children's games, particularly their unstructured play activities, are considered only insofar as toy implements (e.g., tops) were collected and described by ethnographers or where there are games that both adults and children play together.

Studies of children's play in Asian societies are actually quite scarce, partly because anthropological studies of child socialization in this area have been infrequently made (see Middleton, 1970). There are, however, a few significant accounts of children's play in India available. Brewster (1951) described four forms of the game of tag played by Indian children: (1) *uthali;* (2) *limbdi-pipali;* (3) *tadki chanyadi;* and (4) *langadi.* The style of play involved in these four games is compared to forms of tag in other countries, which Brewster stated are "far from India and among peoples widely different in language and cultural background" (p. 239). *Uthali,* for example, is said to be a type of squat tag found in America, Italy, Spain, Greece, Korea, England, etc. *Limbdi-pipali* is described as the equivalent of American "hang tag" and "tree toad" as played in Greece. This analysis is utilized to support the idea of the universality of particular types of children's games. Unfortunately, because Brewster focuses on the description of a particular type of game text (e.g., tag), a discussion of the social context of this play (e.g., who plays it, when, how frequently, etc.) is not offered. Instead, the implication is that all Indian children play these games, even though the reports come from only one area (Andheri). It may be that all (or many) Indian children do play such games, but we do not know this from the information presented by Brewster. A somewhat more contextual analysis of children's play is found in a later article by Brewster (1955), in which a number of games played by children in Bombay State are offered. Here descrip-

---

[3]In a recent survey of Culin's studies, Cheska (1975) reports that "only 550 copies of *Korean games* were printed and, with each book, Culin enclosed a letter of appreciation. . . . The first edition, which contained colored prints executed by a Korean artist, almost immediately became a collector's item" (p. 6). This book, published originally by the University of Pennsylvania, Philadelphia, has more recently been reprinted as *Games of the Orient* (1958).

tions of kite flying, top spinning, hide and seek, etc., are found, and their relation to games in other areas is discussed.

Mistry (1958, 1959, 1960) also presented an analysis of Indian children's play. In this series of articles, play behavior is discussed in terms of various childhood stages (e.g., infancy, babyhood, early childhood, later childhood, and adolescence). Unfortunately, the tendency to generalize about "The Indian Child and His Play" is also evident in these articles. However, Mistry does attempt to provide information about the prevalence of particular children's games within India.

A discussion of Indian children's play is also available in a monograph by Leigh Minturn and John Hitchcock, *The Rājpūts of Khalapur, India* (1963). This report was written as part of the "Six Cultures" project, and so the sociocultural context of Rājpūt children's play is presented in detail. A more detailed description of both play texts and contexts is available in Williams's (1969) discussion of Borneo childhood. Here a relatively lengthy discussion of children's play is provided, including descriptions of types of playthings, settings for play, and types of play engaged in at various ages.

For Thailand, Haas (1964) has written one of the very few anthropological studies of children's verbal play available in the literature. Here she reported on two language games, one played by younger (identical-initial-syllable game) and one by older children (rhyming-translation game). The purpose of these games is said to be to enlarge the children's vocabulary in Thai or in English (also see Palakornkul, 1971). An interesting examination of the play of Vietnamese refugee children in American (northern California) schools is also available by Robinson (1977).

OCEANIA

There are a number of significant reports on children's play available for Oceania. For Melanesia, there are two important early articles on New Guinea children's play. The first is by Barton (1908), a British colonial administrator, who described a number of Papuan children's song games in great detail and included photographs of certain of these games. A. C. Haddon (1908), the well-known British anthropologist, provided a supplement to Barton's report detailing the games of children at Saguane, Kiwai Island. Other reports available are Mead's (1930) classic study of New Guinea Manus children, which includes an interesting discussion of her view of the relation between imitation and play. More recent descriptions are found in Hogbin's (1946) discussion of Wogeo children's play; Aufenanger's (1958, 1961) detailed description and classification of Kumngo children's games and entertainments; and Rosenstiel's (1976) description of Motu children's traditional games. Reports on other Melanesian children's games are available in Róheim's (1941, 1943) interpretation of indigenous games and rhymes and nonindigenous doll play in Duau (Normanby Island) and in Watt's (1946) brief description of New Hebrides Tannese children's games. Finally, Lansley (1968) presented a classification of types of play engaged in by Melanesian children in four different societies and an analysis of the role of this play in maintaining the traditional culture of these groups.

Fijian children's play is described briefly in Hocart (1909) and in Stumpf and Cozens's (1949) reconstruction of traditional Fijian leisure and sports activities. Brief descriptions of other Polynesian children's play are available in Mead's (1928) work on Samoa; Dunlap's (1951) analysis of the functions of games, sports, and dancing in Samoan culture; Firth's (1930) study of dart matches in Tikopia; and Bolton's (1891) description of Hawaiian pastimes. More detailed discussions are available by Culin (1899) and Pukui (1943) on Hawaiian children's play and by Emerson (1924) on Hawaiian string figure games. Also available are two sociolinguistic analyses of Hawaiian children's stories (K. A. Watson, 1972; Watson-Gegeo and Boggs, 1977).

By far the greatest number of reports on Polynesian children's play are available for New Zealand children. In Best's (1925) study of Maori games, one entire chapter is devoted to a detailed description of children's games and toys, including photographic illustrations. Stumpf and Cozens (1947) also described the play of Maori children in their analysis of the role of games and sports in traditional Maori society. Sutton-Smith has produced the most extensive collection of New Zealand *Pakeha* (European) children's games. His studies report information based on a large-scale collection, classification, and analysis of these games (e.g., 1951b, 1952, 1953a,b,c, 1959b), including discussions of the fate of English traditional games in the New Zealand cultural environment (1952) and the effect of European culture on the unorganized games of Maori children (1951a).

For Australia, there are also a number of important studies to mention. An early report by Roth (1902) presents an extensive description and classification of games (30 different categories are presented) played by children and adults of various groups living in the North Queensland area. This study was briefly commented on by Haddon (1902), who also discussed similarities between Australian and Papuan children's games. Aboriginal children's games are also discussed in Berndt (1940), Harney (1952), and Salter (1967, 1974). More recently, a number of studies of Australian white schoolchildren's games have been made by Howard (1958a,b, 1959, 1960a,b).

FIGURE 2. A beetle-powered noisemaker, Tarong (W. Nydegger and C. Nydegger, 1963:792c).

There are specific studies and/or reports on Indonesian children's play available in Bateson and Mead (1942; including sequential photographs of certain play activities) and in Storey (1976) for the Balinese; in DuBois (1944) for the Alorese; in Royce (1972) for the Sundanese; and in Sherzer (1976) for the Javanese. For the Philippines, there are specific studies available by Beran (1973a,b), who presented a detailed analysis of play and its relation to social structure for Southern Filipino children, and there are brief descriptions of this activity in Culin (1900). William and Corinne Nydegger's monograph *Tarong: An Ilocos Barrio in the Philippines* (1963), written for the "Six Cultures" series, contains useful accounts of children's play activities (see Figure 2). Finally, Micronesian children's play is discussed in great detail by Thomas and Hatsumi Maretzki in their volume *Taira: An Okinawan Village* (1963), also in the "Six Cultures" series.

CENTRAL AND SOUTH AMERICA

Three useful review articles summarizing ethnographic reports of games (including children's games) are available for Central and South America. Edmonson (1967) reviewed material for Central American Indians, and Cooper (1949) and Schwartzman and Barbera (1976) performed a similar task for South American Indian groups. A specific study of South American Indian children's play is available in Jules and Zunia Henry's (1944) *Doll Play of Pilagá Indian Children*. In this report, however, the investigators concentrated on an analysis of the children's play behavior with introduced doll-play materials. Brief descriptions of children's indigenous play and toy objects may be found in Jackson (1964) for the Guarayu of central eastern Bolivia and in Shoemaker (1964) for the Chama (Tacanan) of northern Bolivia. A generalized study of Mexican children's play is found in Garcia (1929, 1932), while more specific analyses of children's play and its relation to specific social contexts are available by Maccoby, Modiano, and Lander (1964) and also Kimball and Romaine Romney in their "Six Cultures" ethnography, *The Mixtecans of Juxtlahuaca, Mexico* (1963) (see Figure 3). Modiano (1973) also presented a detailed discussion of children's play in various Indian communities in the Highlands of Chiapas, Mexico. She included lengthy descriptions of early childhood play activities; however, her informants were "older youths" or young adults. Von Glascoe (1975a,b, 1976; von Glascoe and Metzger, 1977) reported information on girls' game preferences in the Yucatán peninsula. Gossen (1976) discussed verbal dueling in Chamula, and Sherzer reported information on Cuna children's play languages (1970, 1976). The most extensive collection of Mexican chil-

FIGURE 3. Children's play, Juxtlahuaca (K. Romney and R. Romney, 1963:600d).

dren's play and game activities available has recently been published (in Spanish) by Scheffler (1976), who presented detailed descriptions for children living in the State of Tlaxcala.

For the Caribbean area, there are two volumes written by folklore collectors that report information on children's games: Beckwith (1922) on Jamaica and Elder (1965) on Trinidad and Tobago. Also there is information on children's play in Landy (1959) for Puerto Rican Vallecañese children and a description of Barbadian children's ring games and jingles by Elsie Clews Parsons (1930).

NORTH AMERICA

Culin (1907) has written the classic compilation and study of games of North American Indians. This report consists of a classified and illustrated list of virtually all of the North American Indian gaming implements held by American and European museums at the turn of this century. Culin also presented a thorough review of the literature available at this time on this topic. Culin noted in his preface that this work relates specifically to the study of games requiring the use of implements, and therefore various sorts of children's games that do not use implements (e.g., tag) are not considered. There are, however, brief descriptions of children's games that do require the use of implements (e.g., tops). Culin's report remains today the most exhaustive survey of games played by North American Indian adults. Specific consideration of North American Indian children's play is found in a number of reports. For southeastern groups there are reports by Rowell (1943) on the Pamunkey, Hassrick and Carpenter (1944) on the Rappahannock, and Speck (1944) on the Catawba. For groups in the north central and Plains region, there are specific descriptions available for the Chippewa (Hilger, 1951); Sioux (Daniel, 1892; Walker, 1906); Pawnee (Lesser, 1933); Arikara (Gilmore, 1926); and Potawatomi (Searcy, 1965). The most detailed description and classification available for all North American Indian groups is Dorsey's (1891) account of Teton Dakota children's play.

The play of children in southwestern Indian groups is reported in detail by Dennis (1940; for the Hopi), who encouraged children to play near his residence by building what he referred to as a play shelter. Dennis also recorded play material in a play diary, part of which is reproduced in this book. Less elaborate descriptions are available by: Hodge (1890) for the Zuni; Leighton and Kluckhohn (1947) for the Navaho; Mook (1935) for the Walapai; and Opler (1946) for the Jicarilla Apache. Finally, Farrer (1976) presented a comparison of the game of tag as played by Mescalero Apache and Anglo-American children.

Specifically, she illustrated how children's free play activities may be seen to replicate the communication system of their parents. Eskimo children's play is discussed by Ramson (1946), for the Aleut, and by Ager (1974, 1975, 1976), who described the games of the Tunanak children of Nelson Island and particularly the girls' game of "storyknifing." Oswalt (1964) has also described the practice of "storyknifing" for Yuk girls. Other reports of Eskimo children's games may be found in Lantis (1946), for the Nunivak.

Studies of American children's play have generally been undertaken by psychologists and psychiatrists, and this approach is reviewed in later chapters of this book. However, a number of accounts of this activity were made by folklorists and anthropologists writing at the close of the last century, including Newell's (1883) collection of American children's singing games; Babcock's (1888) description of children's games in Washington, D.C.; Culin's (1891) account of games of Brooklyn boys; Monroe's (1904) description of western Massachusetts children's counting-out rhymes; and Chase's (1905) collection of street games of children in New York City. Dorothy Mills (Howard) presented a detailed and more recent collection of Maryland children's rhymes and jingles (1944), and Brewster's *Children's Games and Rhymes* (1952) and *American Non-Singing Games* (1953) are both extensive and relatively recent compilations of American children's games. Party games and songs typical of various regional areas of the United States have been collected and described by a number of individuals (e.g., Wolford, 1916; Botkin, 1937; and J. Hall, 1941). Examples of studies of American children's speech play are found in Berkovits (1970), Abrams and Sutton-Smith (1977), Hirschberg (1913), Sanches and Kirshenblatt-Gimblett (1976), and Sutton-Smith (1974a, 1976a). Also within this genre of play are investigations of verbal dueling as practiced by both black and Anglo-American children and adolescents (Abrahams, 1962; Ayoub and Barnett, 1965; Labov, 1972, 1974).

American children's jump rope rhymes have also become a favorite collector's item (e.g., Browne, 1955, Southern California; Fife, 1946, North Carolina; Halpert, 1945, New Hampshire; Maloney, 1944, Idaho; Maryott, 1937, Nebraska; Mensing, 1943, Indiana; Pope, 1956, Texas; Randolph, 1953, Arkansas). The most thorough and recent compilation of these rhymes for English-speaking children (with an emphasis on American children) is found in Abrahams (1969). Sutton-Smith has also conducted a variety of studies of American children's play (e.g., Gump and Sutton-Smith, 1955a,b; Sutton-Smith and Rosenberg, 1961; Sutton-Smith, Rosenberg, and Morgan, 1963; Sutton-Smith, 1959c, 1966b). There are brief accounts of children's play available in ethnographies describing Amish children (Hostetler and Huntington, 1971) and more extensive reports for New England children (John and Ann Fischer, 1963). The Fischer study, entitled *The New Englanders of Orchard Town, U.S.A.*, is the fourth report of the "Six Cultures" project. Finally, an ethnography specifically devoted to the topic of children's sociodramatic play and its relation to the social context of a Chicago day-care center is available by the author (Beale [Schwartzman], 1973).

AFRICA

There are a number of significant reports available describing African children's play. The existence of these accounts is attributable to the fact that there are a number of important studies of childhood socialization for societies in this area. Schwartzman and Barbera (1976) presented a survey on children's play in Africa. Specific descriptions and/or studies of children's play for West African groups are found in Fortes's (1938) early and innovative analysis of children's play for the Tallensi of Ghana and more recently in Leis's (1972) account for the Ijaw of Nigeria; Olofson's (1976) description of how Nigerian Hausa children "play a kingdom"; and Lancy's (1974, 1975, 1976a,b) examination of the idea that play serves an enculturation function by analysis of material collected on the Kpelle of Liberia. Finally, Béart (1955) presented an extensive description of numerous West African societies' play activities, including children's play and game behavior. (This report is published in French.) For central Africa, Centner's (1962) study of Luba, Sanga, and Yeke children's play (published in French) is certainly the most detailed report available for all African groups, and possibly for all non-Western societies. Also, for this area, there are descriptions of play by Brewster (1944) for Makoa and Yao children; K. E. Read (1959) for Ngoni children; Leacock (1971) for urban Zambian children; and Turnbull (1961) for Mbuti Pygmy children. The most complete description of children's play for East African groups was presented by Raum for Chaga children in his important and classic study *Chaga Childhood* (1940). Other brief reports on children's play for this area may be found in Edel (1957) for Chiga children; in Harrison (1947) and Lambert (1959) for northern Kenyan children; and in Leakey's (1938) comparison of Kikuyu children's games with certain games of western Australian and New Guinea children. An early report on southern Sudanese children's games and songs is available by Tucker (1933).

South African children's games are discussed in detail by Kidd (1906) for the Kafir, by Van Zyl (1939) for Sotho peoples, and by Krige (1957) for South African Bantu groups in general. Lorna Marshall's recent monograph *The !Kung of Nyae Nyae* (1976) includes a detailed discussion of Bushmen children's games in the chapter "Play and Games" (pp. 313–362), which also includes numerous photographs.

The most common and widespread game in Africa, variously named *mancala, mueso, songo, nsoro*, etc., has frequently been described in the ethnographic literature (e.g., Culin, 1894; Anna, 1930; G. Martin, 1931; Powell-Cotton, 1931; Chaplan, 1956). Generally only descriptions of the adult version of this count-and-capture game are offered; however, Sanderson (1913) and Leacock (1971) are significant for their presentations of children's versions of this game in central Africa.

NEAR EAST

Archaeological reports of children's play objects are available for this area providing useful historical information on this subject (e.g., R. Martin, 1937; Tylor, 1879a). Studies of contemporary Near Eastern children's play are, however, not very prevalent. There are brief descriptions of Turkish and Iranian games available by Brewster (1960) and a detailed analysis of Turkish boys' dueling rhymes presented by Dundes, Leach, and Ozkök (1970). Arab children's play is discussed in some detail by Granqvist (1975) and also by Ammar (1954). Israeli kibbutzim children's play is discussed briefly in Spiro (1958), and Yakir (1973) described seven different play languages used by Israeli children. However, the most thorough investigations of children's play and games for this area are Eifermann's (1970, 1971a,b) collection, analysis, and comparison of a large sample of Israeli children's games and Smilansky's (1968) study of Israeli children's sociodramatic play.

EUROPE

European children's play has been the subject of several historical investigations and folklore collections. Ariès devoted a useful chapter in his book *Centuries of Childhood* (1962) to a description of the development of children's games in European societies. An early report on the history of hopscotch in European societies is available by Crombie (1886). Gomme's (1894, 1898) two-volume study of the games of Victorian England, Scotland, and Ireland includes extensive descriptions of "proper" children's play activities. Douglas's (1916) collection of London street games includes descriptions of many "improper" children's street games. The most recent and extensive collection of children's games and folklore available in English is found in Iona and Peter Opie's studies of

English schoolchildren's language and games (1959, 1969). Two recent studies of Danish children's play with a specific emphasis on the child's toy environment are available (Anderson and Mitchell, 1977; Mitchell and Anderson, 1977). The latter report presents a comparison of toys in Denmark and the United States. Also recent studies by Rich (1976, 1977) explore the relationship of Icelandic children's games to cultural values. Brewster has published numerous reports on his extensive collection of material on Eastern European games, including descriptions of children's games (e.g., 1948, Greece and Czechoslovakia; 1949a, Hungary; 1949b, Romania; 1959, Russia). Other specific descriptions of children's play are available by Milojkovic-Djuric (1960), who compared the Yugoslavian children's game "most" with certain Scandinavian children's games, and W. Watson (1953), who presented a discussion of urban Scottish children's play (also see Gullen, 1950). Pinon (1965) presented an extensive analysis of Belgian traditional games, and Sherzer (1976) described a series of play languages used by French adolescents. Finally, Chukovsky (1963) presented an interesting and unique discussion of Russian children's verbal play.

SUMMARY

On the basis of this brief overview of ethnographic studies of children's play, it appears that descriptions of this behavior are much more numerous than might previously have been suspected. However, the quality of these reports is extremely varied, and most, if not all, could be *much* better. In order to inspire anthropologists and others to observe and record games "in the field," Royce (1973) has recently formulated a detailed game questionnaire. This questionnaire is particularly valuable as a guideline for use by students of structured games, but it can also be adapted for studies of unstructured play activities or linguistic games. Fifty-four questions are suggested, including: name of game and references; people; observer; observation date and time; numerical composition of participant group; composition by age, sex; whether the game is played during a special time of year; whether the game is competitive; whether the game is mainly a form of "pretending"; whether game rules are flexible or rigid; how players learn the game; how players increase their skill; what value (if any) is attached to this game by the participants themselves; whether the game is "old" or "new," imported or evolved; and a description of the game, stating whether it was observed personally or gathered from informant(s).

Ethnographic descriptions of children's play are generally offered to illustrate a particular society's patterning of this behavior. Frequently, however, these accounts are also patterned by the anthropologist's culture, as well as by the particular theoretical approach that he/she adopts for the study of other cultures. These theoretical schools and their impact on the anthropological study of children's play are discussed and analyzed in the next seven chapters.

CHAPTER FOUR

Staging Play: Evolutionary and Developmental Studies

"I wish you wouldn't squeeze so," said the Dormouse, who was sitting next to her. "I can hardly breathe."

"I can't help it," said Alice very meekly: "I'm growing."

"You've no right to grow here*," said the Dormouse.*

"Don't talk nonsense," said Alice more boldly: "you know you're growing too."

"Yes, but I grow at a reasonable pace," said the Dormouse: "not in that ridiculous fashion."

Lewis Carroll, Alice in Wonderland

The establishment of anthropology as a separate discipline concerned with the "science of man" occurred during the late 19th century. It was also during this time that the ideas of biological (e.g., Darwin) and social (e.g., Spencer) evolution were formulated. The theory of social evolution was based on an analogy that viewed cultures "as if" they were biological organisms exhibiting similar processes of "growth" and "development." According to Nisbet (1969:7) this metaphor is one of the oldest and most powerful and encompassing metaphors in Western thought. The premises that underlie this view of cultural development are the following: change is seen as a process that is *natural* to both biological and social entities; social change is viewed as *immanent* (i.e., proceeding from forces within the entity); change is *continuous* and *directional*; and, therefore, it manifests itself in an orderly sequence of *stages,* which move cumulatively and linearly *from* one given point *to* another point; change is *necessary* because it is "natural"; change corresponds to *differentiation* and proceeds in a pattern from the homogeneous to the heterogeneous; and finally, change proceeds from *uniform* causes (Nisbet, 1969:212). Each of these premises was accepted as a "natural" fact by the early evolutionists in anthropology, and in the early 20th century, many of the ideas of the evolutionists passed into the disciplines of child psychology and child development.

Lewis Henry Morgan, an American lawyer turned ethnologist,[1] was one of the first anthropologists to propose a theory and schema of cultural evolution. Morgan was interested in the evolution of virtually all cultural institutions: subsistence, government, language, the family, religion, house life and architecture, property, and so forth. In his major work, entitled *Ancient Society* (1877) and subtitled *Researches in the Lines of Human Progress from Savagery through Barbarism to Civilization*, Morgan demonstrated his use of the metaphor of growth and in particular the idea of *cultural stages*. The first statement in this book reveals his approach:

> The latest investigations respecting the early condition of the human race, are tending to the conclusion that mankind commenced their career at the bottom of the scale and worked their way up from savagery to civilization through the slow accumulation of experimental knowledge. (1877:3)

STAGES AND SURVIVALS

According to Morgan, the three major stages of cultural evolution could be conceptualized hierarchically, with the *savagery* stage appearing first in time and, therefore, placed lowest on the scale, followed by the stage of *barbarism* and, finally, *civilization* (see Figure 4). Not surprisingly,

---

[1]It should be noted here that "playing Indians" is not a game to be solely associated with children. Anthropologists have also been known to engage in such sport. Morgan is reported by Langness (1974) to have formed, in 1843, "The Great Order of the Iroquois," "which was to be modeled on the customs of the Iroquois," where all lodge members "dressed in Iroquois costumes and even carried tomahawks to meetings" (p. 14). Today this same desire to "play native" may be observed at any large gathering of anthropologists (particularly the annual meeting of the American Anthropological Association). On these occasions, ethnographers as well as primatologists may be seen exhibiting the "customs" (i.e., clothes, accessories, languages, gestures, etc.) of their particular culture. And so Oceanists cluster together speaking "pidgin" to one another and trading stories while primatologists hoot and make threat gestures to one another across crowded rooms. Of course, these actions demonstrate all anthropologists' desire to participate in and become a part of the societies that they study. However, it also illustrates that the pretext of "play" is always mixed with the ethnographers' "work" in and out of the field.

RECAPITULATION	
Periods	*Conditions*
I. Older period of savagery	I. Lower status of savagery
II. Middle period of savagery	II. Middle status of savagery
III. Later period of savagery	III. Upper status of savagery
IV. Older period of barbarism	IV. Lower status of barbarism
V. Middle period of barbarism	V. Middle status of barbarism
VI. Later period of barbarism	VI. Upper status of barbarism
VII. Status of civilization	
I. Lower status of savagery	From the infancy of the human race to the commencement of the next period.
II. Middle status of savagery	From the acquisition of a fish subsistence and a knowledge of the use of fire to etc.
III. Upper status of savagery	From the invention of the bow and arrow to etc.
IV. Lower status of barbarism	From the invention of the art of pottery to etc.
V. Middle status of barbarism	From the domestication of animals on the eastern hemisphere, and in the western from the cultivation of maize and plants by irrigation, with the use of adobe-brick and stone to etc.
VI. Upper status of barbarism	From the invention of the process of smelting iron ore, with the use of iron tools to etc.
VII. Status of civilization	From the invention of a phonetic alphabet, with the use of writing, to the present time.

FIGURE 4. Morgan's cultural stages: recapitulation (adapted from L. H. Morgan, 1877:12).

European societies were thought to represent the "height" of civilization because they were the "most progressive."[2] The fact that present-day Europeans practiced customs that were thought to be characteristic of earlier cultural stages (e.g., nailing iron horseshoes on doors) was ac-

[2]The *comparative method* that was the system of classification used to divide cultures into the three stages of savagery, barbarism, and civilization was designed to "prove" the theory of social evolution, but it is actually a demonstration of circular reasoning as well as an example of "science" in the service of Western ideology (particularly the idea of progress). In this regard Nisbet (1969) suggests that "the Comparative Method . . . is hardly more than a shoring up of the idea of progressive development . . . and the belief that the recent history of the West could be taken as evidence of the direction in which mankind as a whole *would* and . . . *should* move. The . . . cultural qualities that seemed to . . . manifest the direction of Western history were adapted for comparative purposes to become the criteria of classification of the peoples and cultures of the world" (pp. 190–191).

counted for by the notion of *survivals* formulated originally by Edward Burnett Tylor.

Tylor, an English traveler and scholar, is often referred to as the father of anthropology. His studies (e.g., *Primitive Culture*, 1871) were also heavily influenced by the idea of evolutionary stages, and his concept of cultural survivals was employed as proof of the existence of such stages. He argued that the presence of a custom such as nailing horseshoes over doors in European societies was a survival of earlier beliefs in magic and witches (horseshoes were supposed to keep fairies away and make them powerless) (Langness, 1974:27). This survival, according to Tylor, indicated that European societies had passed through an earlier cultural stage that accepted witches and fairies as facts, not superstitions.

Tylor was also responsible for suggesting to anthropologists that games might be useful features of culture to study. He was mainly interested in the use of games as evidence for particular types of culture contact (to be discussed in detail in Chapter Five) and also as illustrations for his particular approach to the study of "the great world-game of evolution." This approach, which is much more in the tradition of multilineal schemas of evolution than his critics have suggested, is revealed in the following passage:

> It remains to call attention to a point which this research into the development of games brings strongly into view. In the study of civilization, as of so many other branches of natural history, a theory of gradual evolution proves itself a trustworthy guide. But it will not do to assume that culture must always come on by regular, unvarying progress. That, on the contrary, the lines of change may be extremely circuitous, the history of games affords instructive proofs. . . . If, comparing Greek draughts and English draughts, we were to jump to the conclusion that the one was simply a further development of the other, this would be wrong, for the real course appears to have been that some old draught-game rose into chess, and then again a lowered form of chess came down to become a new game of draughts. We may depend upon it that the great world-game of evolution is not played only by pawns moving straight on, one square before another, but that long-stretching moves of pieces in all directions bring on new situations, not readily foreseen by minds that find it hard to see six moves upon a chessboard. (1879a:76)

The study of children and children's play began during the time of the rise of evolutionary theory in the late 19th century. Two of the most famous collections of English-speaking children's play and games appeared during this period. The first, published in 1883 by William Wells Newell and entitled *Games and Songs of American Children*, illustrates the influence of the notion of survivals on interpretations of children's play. Although the whole of Newell's studies is more properly considered in the following chapter, his view of games as survivals, in childish form, of earlier societies' adult activities is briefly described here. Newell believed that the games of American children "preserved what the Old World has forgotten; and the amusements of children today picture to us the dances which delighted the court as well as the people of the Old England before the settlement of the New" (pp. 3–4). As an example of this idea, he suggested that the verses to be sung in the ring dances "Happy Is the Miller" or "Three Jolly Sisters" (collected "in the streets of Cincinnati and New York") are in fact transformations of adult dances and customs of earlier times:

> The children of the poorer class, therefore, who still keep up in the streets of our cities the present ring-dance [here "Three Jolly Sisters"], are only maintaining the customs which belonged to courtiers and noble ladies in the time of Shakespeare. (p. 124)

In versions of "London Bridges," Newell found allusions to "medieval religious conceptions" (p. 5), and over and over, he illustrated his view that "the social state and habits of half a thousand years ago unconsciously furnish the amusement of youth, when the faith and fashion of the ancient day is no longer intelligible to their elders" (p. 5).

Eleven years after the publication of Newell's study, Lady A. B. Gomme published a two-volume dictionary of *The Traditional Games of England, Scotland and Ireland* (1894, 1898). Included in this work are descriptions of many children's games and singing rhymes, with Volume 1 covering material from *A* to *N* and Volume 2 covering *O* to *Z*. Lady Gomme also utilized the notion of survivals in her studies. For example, she suggested that the game "Nuts in May" is a survival of an earlier society's practice of marriage by capture (1894:431). The text of the song that was sung in conjunction with the game is quoted here to illustrate the material on which Gomme based her interpretation:

> *Here we come gathering nuts in May*
> *Nuts in May, nuts in May,*
> *Here we come gathering nuts in May,*
> *On a fine summer morning.*
>
> *Whom will you have for nuts in May,*
> *Nuts in May, nuts in May?*
> *Whom will you have for nuts in May,*
> *On a fine summer morning?*
>
> *We'll have _____ for nuts in May,*
> *Nuts in May, nuts in May,*
> *We'll have _____ for nuts in May,*
> *On a fine summer morning.*
>
> *Who will you send to fetch her [or him] away,*
> *To fetch her away, to fetch her away?*

Who will you send to fetch her away,
On a fine summer morning?

We'll send _____ to fetch her away,
Fetch her away, fetch her away,
We'll send _____ to fetch her away,
On a fine summer morning.
(1894:424)

According to Gomme: "Through all the games I have seen played, this idea [of conquering or capturing] seems to run, and it exactly accords with the concept of marriage by capture" (1894:431).

RECAPITULATION: G. STANLEY HALL

Associated with the idea of unilineal stages of cultural evolution and the theory of survivals was the notion of recapitulation formulated originally as a "biogenetic law" (i.e., ontogeny recapitulates phylogeny) by Haeckel on the basis of his research in embryology. This recapitulation hypothesis came to be used by many early evolutionists to suggest that

> the aboriginal peoples that still survived represented arrested stages of cultural development that the more advanced races had passed through. Usually the backwardness of these savage peoples, implicitly, if not explicitly, was interpreted as an index of their limited mental capacities. Hence, the idea of different levels of mental development within the human race as a whole was supported by anthropology, despite the fact that there was no direct evidence that this was true. (Hallowell, 1955:15)

G. Stanley Hall inaugurated the "scientific" study of childhood development at the turn of this century, when the ideas of evolutionary stages, recapitulation, and survivals were still in fashion. Hall's *recapitulation theory* of children's play presents the clearest illustration of the impact of 19th-century evolutionism on studies of children. Hall believed that the play "stages" of children recapitulated the entire bio-cultural history of mankind:

> I regard play as the motor habits or spirit of the past of the race persisting in the present, as rudimentary functions sometimes of and always akin to rudimentary organs. The best index and guide to the stated activities of adults in past ages is found in the instinctive, untaught and non-imitative plays of children, which are the most spontaneous and exact expression of their motor needs. . . . In play every mood and movement is instinct with heredity. Thus we rehearse the activities of our ancestors, back we know not how far, and repeat their life work in summative and adumbrated ways. It is reminiscent, albeit unconsciously, of our line of descent; and each is the key to the other. The psycho-motive impulses that prompt it are the forms in

which our forbears have transmitted to us their habitual activities. Thus stage by stage we re-enact their lives once; in the phylon many of these activities were elaborated in the life and death struggle for existence. Now the elements and combination oldest in the muscle history of the race are represented earliest in the individual and those later follow in order. (Hall, 1904:202)

Expanding on the work of Hall, Mabel Reaney (1916) proposed that the various stages of childhood could be divided into "play periods" that corresponded with man's various evolutionary stages. For example, she suggested that the *animal stage* or period (birth to age 7) was reflected in swinging and climbing games; the *savage stage* (7–9) exhibited hunting and throwing games; the *nomad stage* (9–12) was reflected in skill and adventure games and "interest in keeping pets"; the *pastoral stage* and the *tribal stage* (12–17) were characterized by doll play, gardening, and finally team games (p. 12). Reaney's purpose in formulating this approach was to illustrate several propositions:

that the organized group game as the highest form of motor play represented the tribal stage of the race [and] therefore only appears in races which have reached a certain stage of development in which cooperation is combined with division of labour and loyalty to a leader—that the final development of the group game seems to have arisen as the accompaniment to civilization and has been evolved as a means of giving scope to those instinctive tendencies which are baulked by such civilization and that the evolution of this kind of game appears in the race which has inherited from its forbears the instincts of rivalry and pugnacity to a marked degree. (pp. 46–47)

Hall used his positions as president of Clark University and as founder and editor of *The Pedagogical Seminary* and *The American Journal of Psychology* to publicize his ideas on childhood development and the significance of children's play. And, by 1895, he had succeeded in

convincing a good portion of the educated public that the child developed sequentially, passing through definable stages of bio-psychic growth, and that its ontogenesis recapitulated, biologically and psychologically, the historical development of the "race." (Cavallo, 1976:376)

This approach was particularly appealing to certain reformers and "child savers" of the time concerned with the impact of American urban industrial society on the leisure time or play activities of youth, particularly children of immigrants living in urban slums. The playground movement began at this time as an attempt to organize the play and games of these children. Reformers such as Jane Addams, Lillian Wald, Jacob Riis, Henry Curtis, Joseph Lee, and Luther Gulick argued that "expertly supervised playgrounds" were needed in the nation's slums. This was so because they believed that

> if the child's recapitulatory development was observed carefully, and if the play impulses peculiar to each play form were filtered through specifically designed play forms, those instincts socially and morally adaptable to urban industrial civilization could be cultivated. (Cavallo, 1976:377)[3]

Many of these play advocates believed that urban adolescent peer groups were the "modern counterpart of the tribe"; however, it was their desire to replace interest in peer group *gangs* (which were thought to foster juvenile delinquency and sexual promiscuity) with interest in *athletic teams* (which would facilitate the development of a social and moral conscience).

The influence of Hall's recapitulation theory is also evident in the writings of Freud and Jung and their followers. In fact, in his capacity as president of Clark University, Hall was responsible for first inviting both Freud and Jung to the United States (Langness, 1974:35). The impact of evolutionism and the idea of recapitulation is evident in many of Freud's studies.[4] In *Totem and Taboo* (1918), which is subtitled *Resemblances between the Psychic Lives of Savages and Neurotics*, Freud suggested the following:

> totemism is a religio-social institution which is alien to our present feelings; it has long been abandoned and replaced by new forms. In the religions, morals, and customs of the civilized races of to-day, it has left only slight traces, and even among those races where it is still retained, it has had to undergo great changes. . . .
>
> In this book the attempt is ventured to find the original meaning of totemism through its infantile traces [e.g., animal phobias], that is, through the indications in which it reappears in the development of our own children. (p. xi)

These ideas were accepted and repeated by many of Freud's followers, such as Sandor Ferenczi, Marie Bonaparte, Melanie Klein, and Otto Fenichel. Fenichel, in particular, carried the idea of recapitulation to absurd lengths, asserting that "Animal crackers loved by children are significant remnants of early cannibalistic fantasies" (Fenichel, quoted in Langness, 1974:35–36).

Freud also believed that children passed through an innately determined sequence of libidinal stages that were associated with specific bodily zones. In the *pregenital period*, which begins at birth and lasts until age 5, the child is said to pass through the oral, anal, and phallic (or

---

[3]Recently, ideas reminiscent of this view have reemerged in the writings of a number of psychologists (e.g., Feitelson and Ross, 1973; Singer, 1973), who have developed a variety of "play intervention" techniques to improve the quantity and quality of children's imaginative play behavior. These studies will be examined in Chapter Six.

[4]See Hartmann and Kris (1945) for a critique of Freud's evolutionary assumptions formulated by two psychoanalysts associated with the "ego psychology" school.

Oedipal) stages. The next five to six years are characterized as "the quiet years" of the *latency period,* which are interrupted at puberty by the "resurgence of pregenital impulses." These are eventually displaced and sublimated by the ego as the person reaches the final stage of maturity, referred to as the *genital stage* (Hall and Lindzey, 1957:51–52). Freud also suggested that the wishes and conflicts of each of these libidinal stages (particularly those of the pregenital period) would be reflected in the child's play. For example, blowing bubbles would be interpreted as relating back to oral overindulgence, while sand and water play could be seen as acceptable substitutes for "soiling and wetting" (Millar, 1968:27–28).

Lili Peller (1954) has extended Freud's developmental theory of play by considering relationships between play, libidinal stages, and ego development. Adopting the view, as espoused by Freud and his followers (see particularly Waelder, 1933), that play alleviates anxiety, Peller described the various deprivations associated with each libidinal stage and then examined how play activities "assist the child in overcoming the blows and disappointments he suffers" during these stages (p. 181). Peller described four different "play groups" characterized by particular play themes or topics, anxieties, compensating fantasies, stylistic elements, social character, play materials, and "secondary play gains." For example, Group I is characterized by "themes" related to the body, which are in turn said to be associated with the anxiety "My body is no good; I'm helpless" (p. 184). The "compensating fantasy" of this play is expressed as "My body . . . is a perfect instrument for my wishes, my orders" (p. 181). Activity in this group is solitary, as opposed to social, and play material consists of extensions and variations of body functions and body parts. The "secondary play gains" are said to be increased body skills and mastery. Group II play activities involve "the child's relation to a pre-Oedipal mother" and the fear of losing a love object (p. 185). This play is characterized by endless repetitions (e.g., peek-a-boo games) that result in the compensating fantasy "I can do to *others* what she did to *me*" (p. 183). Group III play is associated with the Oedipal stage and relates to children's feelings that they cannot enjoy what adults do. In these play activities, children frequently pretend to be adults and act out the "family romance." Post-Oedipal play, or Group IV activities, begin at about age 6, according to Peller, and are associated with problems surrounding sibling relations and also fear of superego and superego figures (p. 183). These activities include team games and also card and board games.

The psychoanalyst Erik Erikson has also proposed a series of play stages in conjunction with his specific theory of psychosexual development. In *Childhood and Society* (1963), he suggested that "the child's play

is the infantile form of the human ability to deal with experience by
creating model situations and to master reality by experiment and planning" (p. 222). In Erikson's schema, play is said to develop first as
autocosmic play consisting of "exploration by repetition of sensual perceptions, of kinesthetic sensations, or vocalizations, etc." (p. 220). Play
in the *microsphere* occurs later, and it is often solitary as it relates to play
with "manageable toys," which is engaged in when the child "needs to
overhaul his ego" (p. 221). This play has its dangers, however, as it can
promote the expression of anxious themes and lead, therefore, to "play
disruption" (a phenomenon that Erikson has specifically investigated,
e.g., 1940). Generally, though, Erikson has suggested that play in the
microsphere will lead to pleasure in mastery of toys and mastery of
traumas projected on them. At nursery-school age, play occurs in the
macrosphere. This is "the world shared with others," and here others
"are treated as things, are inspected, run into, or forced to 'be horsie' "
(1963:221).

Predominant in the writings of many of these scholars is a view of
the child as "primitive" or "savage" and, by implication, the "primitive"
as child.[5] The clearest examples of this association are apparent in the
titles of books published at this time. For example, Chamberlain, who
was one of the first students of "primitive" children, entitled one of his
major works on this topic *The Child: A Study in the Evolution of Man*
(1901), and a specific study of children's play by Appleton is called *A
Comparative Study of the Play Activities of Adult Savages with Civilized Children* (1910). Frequently these associations are made in reference to an
assumed equivalence between the thought or reasoning process of children and "primitives." This usage is apparent in the work of most students of children and their play who were writing in the late 19th and
early 20th centuries: for example, Newell (1883), Gomme (1894, 1898),
Curtis (1915), Gulick (1920), and Freud (1920). The idea of unilineal
stages of development is also a theoretical "survival," which appears in
the writings of many psychoanalysts (e.g., Peller, 1954; Erikson, 1963)
and psychologists (e.g., Piaget, 1951) and has affected their interpretations of children's play behavior.

ON MORALS AND MARBLES: JEAN PIAGET

Jean Piaget began his career during the early part of the 20th century, when many of the evolutionary ideas discussed above were still in

[5]It is important to emphasize here that this view of the "primitive" as child clearly supported the practice of colonialism by providing colonial administrators with the belief that
it was their duty (i.e., 'noblesse oblige') to take care of their "primitive" (i.e., childish)
charges.

fashion. He has since become the preeminent student of child development in this century. Piaget has also been a student of children's play and is responsible for presenting the most widely used developmental schema for this activity.

In his early study of children's moral development (1932), Piaget investigated in detail how children learn the rules for playing the game of marbles. Most specifically, he analyzed (1) the *practices* of rules (i.e., how children of different ages effectively apply rules) and (2) the *consciousness* of rules (i.e., the ideas that children of different ages have of the character of game rules) (pp. 14–15). His findings suggested that there were various *stages* of game play and rule conceptualization. In this study, he detailed the differences between the *stage of motor or individual play*, when the child "handles the marbles at the dictation of his desires and motor habits"; the *egocentric stage* (2–5), when the child "receives from outside the example of codified rules" and may attempt to imitate this example but generally continues to play "on his own" without attempting to "unify the different ways of playing"; the *stage of incipient cooperation* (7–11), where "each player now tries to win, and all, therefore, begin to concern themselves with the question of mutual control and of unification of the rules"; and finally the *stage of codification of rules* (11–12 and above), where every detail of procedure in the game is fixed and "the actual code of rules to be observed is known to the whole society" (pp. 26–27).

Piaget also outlined three stages of rule conceptualization for children. In the first stage (1–3) rules are not coercive in character because they are "purely motor" or are received only as "interesting examples rather than as obligatory realities" (p. 28). During the second stage of *heteronomy* (4–8), children believe that game rules are absolute, immutable, and sacred. And during the third stage of *autonomy* (9–10 and above), children view rules as deriving from social consensus; however, they may be changed "on the condition of enlisting general opinion on your side" (p. 28).

Piaget stated that this study was not an attempt to provide a sociology of the game of marbles. However, this report stands as one of the most detailed descriptions of the game of marbles available in the literature. In particular, Piaget presented an extensive examination of variations in game rules in practice in Geneva and Neuchâtel at the time of his study. In this way, we learn about differences between the "square game" and the game of *courate*, as well as the game of *troyat* (hole) or *creux* (hollow) and many others. In this study, however, Piaget concentrated specifically on the "square game" and the various ways in which it is played. He also provided information on "ritual consecrations," which are expressions that players use to announce that they are going to perform a certain type of operation, and "ritual interdictions," which are expressions that an opponent may use, when he anticipates that a certain play will be made, to forbid this type of play.[6]

All of Piaget's studies are characterized by careful, sensitive, and detailed observations of, and conversations with, children. His study of "the rules of the game" illustrates this approach. Piaget's method of acquiring information on these rules was unique in psychological studies of children at this time, for he broke with tradition by assuming that the child was the expert and he was the student. His statement to each informant was the following:

> Here are some marbles. . . . You must show me how to play. When I was little I used to play a lot, but now I've forgotten how to. I'd like to play again. Let's play together. You'll teach me the rules and I'll play with you. (1932:24)

THE ONTOGENY OF PLAY

Piaget's most significant study of children's play appears in *Play, Dreams, and Imitation in Childhood* (1951). This work is based on observations of the play activities of his own three children: Lucienne, Laurent, and Jacqueline. In analyzing this material, relationships between play and intellectual functioning (Piaget's major interest) are clearly drawn. According to Piaget, there are two major aspects of cognition: accommodation and assimilation. *Accommodation* is that process whereby the child (or any organism) modifies his/her own mental set in response to external demands. In contrast, *assimilation* is that process whereby the child incorporates elements of the external world into his/her own schemata. Both processes are thought to be a part of all actions; however, at times, one may predominate over the other, while at other times they may be in balance or "equilibrium." Acts characterized by the "primacy of assimilation over accommodation" are described as play, whereas imitation is said to occur when accommodation predominates over assimilation (p. 87). Intelligent adaptation is said to occur when there is a stable equilibrium achieved between these two processes. The assumptions implicit in this model, as they influenced Piaget's specific theory of play as cognition, are discussed and critiqued in detail in Chapter Nine. In this chapter his specific developmental model of play behavior is examined.

For Piaget, the ontogeny of play must be viewed in relation to the development of intelligence in the child, and therefore each cognitive stage, which Piaget has outlined, exhibits a characteristic type of play activity. Play in the *sensorimotor* period is characterized by repeated per-

---

[6]Piaget questioned only males in this study.

formance of newly mastered motor abilities and evidence of pleasure in engaging in such activity. For example, Piaget described Lucienne's discovery that she could make objects hanging on top of her cot swing:

> At first, between 0;3(6) [zero years, 3 months, 6 days] and 0;3(16), she studied the phenomenon without smiling. . . . Subsequently, however, from about 0;4, she never indulged in this activity . . . without a show of great joy and power. (p. 92)

Symbolic play, where schemata generally applied to one object are used on a substitute, corresponds with the *representational* or *preoperational* phase of development. An early example of the appearance of a "true ludic symbol" is described for Jacqueline:

> [At 1;3(12)] . . . She saw a cloth whose fringed edges vaguely recalled those of her pillow; she seized it, held a fold of it in her right hand, sucked the thumb of the same hand and lay down on her side, laughing hard. (p. 96)

Make-believe or sociodramatic plays, where children pretend to be mothers, fathers, teachers, and so forth, are more advanced examples of "symbolic games" that characteristically, according to Piaget, *distort* the expressions or activities of adults. Corresponding with the *concrete operational* phase is the appearance of *games with rules.* Through the use and development of collective, as opposed to individualized, symbols (as this is promoted in games and other activities engaged in at this time), the child's reasoning becomes more "logical and objective." In Piaget's view, games correspond more closely to "reality," which helps to prepare children for the final cognitive stage of *formal operations.*

Each of these three types of play, as they are associated with a particular cognitive stage, may be further divided into substages or periods according to Piaget. For example, practice or exercise play may occur first as "mere practice" whereby skills are taken out of the useful context in which they are learned and repeated "for pleasure"; *fortuitous combinations* may be made by the chance patterning of acquired activities; *intentional combinations* will later occur as planned patterning of acquired activities; practice play may become constructive play; practice play may also occur in conjunction with symbolic play; and finally, practice play becomes "socialized" and rules are developed as play takes on the character of games with rules.

Symbolic play, on the other hand, occurs initially as brief isolated periods of "simple pretending and imitative play" (as in the example of Jacqueline cited above). Following this, *symbolic combinations* will be made involving the combination of pretending and imitative episodes into whole scenes, and then *ordered symbolic combinations* appear that are similar to symbolic combinations but have a greater degree of coherence and "realism." Finally, *symbolic constructions* occur that involve ordered symbolic combinations but with construction or "making of things" as part of or preparation for the dramatic play.

Games with rules are said to occur as either sensorimotor combinations or intellectual combinations. According to Piaget, either their source is "traditional" (i.e., they are handed down from one generation to another), or they are created and regulated by "spontaneous temporary agreement" among players.[7]

STAGING PLAY: COMMENT AND CRITIQUE

There are many questions to be asked of this developmental approach. For example, does assimilative play, in fact, become less frequent as one grows up? Is this schema applicable only to the Swiss upper-middle-class children of Piaget's studies? Does one note the same sequence of play in other Western children, and what about the ontogeny of play in non-Western children?

In relation to the first question, Piaget recognized that games with rules, characterized by assimilation, do occur among adults, and so, in this sense, play does not cease to exist in the formal-operational period. However, he also argued that over time, play becomes "more and more adequately adapted to reality" and characterized less by "the deformation and subordination of reality to the desires of the self," and so, in this sense, play does decrease with age (1966:339). Sutton-Smith suggested, in contrast, that play is "not displaced by reality or by greater rationality, nor does it cease to be a vital function with age" (1966a:339). The recent studies of Singer (1966) on daydreams and Klinger (1971) on fantasy would seem to indicate that, contrary to Piaget, adults (at least American adults) do engage in a variety of assimilative play activities.

A number of investigators have also recently commented on the fact that Piaget's play sequences do not appear in the same fashion in their own studies. For example, Singer (1973:3) noted his personal participation in make-believe football games in early adolescence. The Opies' (1969) work tends to confirm this observation, at least for British children, in that they reported a great deal of group fantasy behavior between the ages of 5 and 12. As reported by Singer, Smilansky suggested that play does not necessarily become more realistic during later childhood but rather that with a greater range of experience, it becomes possible "for children at older ages to engage in more bizarre and strange stories, albeit more organized from an adult standpoint"

---

[7]For a more complete breakdown and discussion of Piaget's play stages and substages, see Mouledoux (1976).

(1973:15). Smilansky (1968) also proposed that the symbolic, imaginative play said to be characteristic of early childhood by Piaget may be related more to cultural and socioeconomic factors than to developmental ones.[8] Research reports by El'Konin (1971) on the play of Russian nursery-school children indicate that their play consists of redundant and realistic, as opposed to imaginative, replications of the activities of adults and, in this way, appear to confirm Smilansky's studies. One of Margaret Mead's earliest studies (*Growing Up in New Guinea*, 1930; also see 1932), although not conducted to test Piaget's theory of play, indicates that Manus children engage only in active motor play (running and chasing games) and not at all in symbolic or imaginative play activities.

Rivka Eifermann's (1970, 1971a,b) recent research on children's play and games in Israel also reports negative findings for certain of Piaget's statements. Most specifically, she stated that Piaget's claim that "games with rules increase in number, both relatively and absolutely, with age" as they replace sensorimotor and symbolic play activities is generally disconfirmed by her findings (1971b:295). Instead, Eifermann found that an absolute decline in participation in games with rules appears around 11 years, but a relative decline in participation appears at a somewhat later age. In relation to this decline, she reported a corresponding rise in participation in unstructured play activities, particularly types of practice play (e.g., jump rope and running). Eifermann suggested that her information does, however, support Piaget's claim (although he did not specify this in terms of socioeconomic level) that symbolic play for "high" schools (upper-middle-class children) is already rare at ages 6–8, while in the "low" schools, children are found to engage actively in symbolic play in the first two grades (pp. 295–296).

There are many other discussions of developmental sequences for play available in the psychological literature. To name but a few, Gesell (1946), Hurlock (1934), and Lowenfeld (1935) have all presented descriptions of children's play stages. Also available are a series of papers on the topics of play and development presented by researchers such as Erikson, Piaget, and Lorenz (Piers, 1972).

Following the example of Piaget, these researchers all seem to assume, at least implicitly, that the play stages that they have delineated are *universal* and that all children can be expected to pass through them. This assumption points to what is perhaps one of the most glaring weaknesses of Piaget's developmental model: the neglect of the sociocultural context. Terrance Turner (1973), in a recent discussion of Piaget's "structuralism," has specifically commented on this problem:

[8]Eifermann, however, has challenged certain of Smilansky's findings. This particular dispute is discussed more thoroughly in Chapter Six.

As it stands, Piaget's model of psychogenesis is formulated in an artificial
sociological vacuum; he has never confronted the question of the sociocultural components of the mind at the level of the basic structure of the
psychogenetic process itself. (p. 364)

The fact that Piaget's model has been constructed in such a "sociological
vacuum" helps to explain the findings reported above by researchers
such as Mead, El'Konin, Eifermann, and Smilansky.

For the most part, anthropologists' studies of non-Western children's play have tended not to focus on developmental considerations.
In many instances, the various types of play discussed by Piaget and
others have been noted by those ethnographers who have chosen to
describe this activity. However, the age of children engaged in such
activities is often not reported in monographs, although this is less true
in more recent studies. Clearly, more detailed studies of the *sociocultural
contexts* of play must be conducted before the questions raised by
Piaget's developmental theory, as well as the recent studies of Eifermann, El'Konin, Smilansky, and others, can be answered.

More important questions must be raised about the idea of "stages"
of development or "stages" of play as used by developmental researchers such as Piaget. The view that development occurs in stages is
no longer a metaphorical "as if" image useful for theoretical conceptualization, as this metaphor is now an accepted, unquestioned, and
uncriticized psychological fact. In order to formulate a critique of this
concept, it must be remembered that Piaget developed his interest in
child development at a time when the evolutionary theories of Hall, as
well as of Freud and Jung, were still in fashion. However, because Piaget
has based his work on detailed and sensitive observations (as well as on
controlled experiments) of children, he has been able to transform a
unilineal (and acontextual) stage model, which contains within it a view
of the child as "primitive" and also the idea of recapitulation, into a
widely accepted theory of childhood development. For many researchers, and increasingly parents, teachers, and others, Piaget's ideas
are regarded no longer as theories but as *facts* of life.

Piaget's statements in both his early (see particularly 1928) and later
works (e.g., 1951, 1970a), however, reveal the extent to which he has
uncritically accepted many of the ideas of the early evolutionists, particularly the view that "ontogeny recapitulates phylogeny."[9] For exam-

---

[9]White (1976) has recently suggested that the idea that there is "a resemblance between the
cognitive development of the child and the movement of the history of science is itself an
idea with a very long history" (p. 654). He traced it through the writings of Vico, Hegel,
Spencer, Hall, Werner, and Piaget. The recent revival of interest in Vico's works (see
Volume 43, Numbers 3 and 4, of *Social Research,* in which White's article appears, which
are devoted to the topic "Vico and Contemporary Thought") suggests that this idea is still
attractive to many scholars. Mora (1976) presented a particularly interesting analysis of
parallels and differences in the studies of Vico and Piaget, also in this report.

ple, in a recent description of his conception of *genetic epistemology* (Piaget's term for his research approach), he suggested the following:

> The fundamental hypothesis of genetic epistemology is that there is a parallelism between the progress made in the logical and rational organization of knowledge and the corresponding formative psychological processes. Well, now, if that is our hypothesis, what will be our field of study? Of course the most fruitful, most obvious field of study would be reconstituting human history—the history of human thinking in prehistoric man. Unfortunately, we are not very well informed about the psychology of Neanderthal man. . . . Since this field of biogenesis is not available to us, we shall do as biologists do and turn to ontogenesis. Nothing could be more accessible to study than the ontogenesis of these notions. There are children all around us. (1970a:13)

Turner (1973) has recently argued that "the basic concepts of Piagetian theory are not intrinsically bound up with Piaget's evolutionist perspective" (p. 367). However, when one encounters statements such as the above repeatedly in Piaget's works, coupled with his model of unilineal stages of development, which proceed from "lower" to "higher" forms, it is hard to see how his specific theory of cognitive development is not "bound up" with his evolutionism.

Lévi-Strauss (1949) formulated an excellent critique of what he referred to as "the archiac illusion" and its affect on studies of "primitive" thought. Here he suggested that the "ontogeny recapitulates phylogeny" notion and the related view that children's thought corresponds with that of primitive adults *is* a recurring theme in many of Piaget's studies. In examining these views, Lévi-Strauss observed that the so-called parallels between the thought of "primitives" and Western children are apparent only because *all* societies designate strange activities and attitudes as "childish." Westerners compare the "strange" beliefs of primitives to those of their own children, and "primitives" reciprocate by comparing the "strange" behavior of Westerners to that of their children. Lévi-Strauss illustrated this by citing an example of how Navahos interpret the whites' habit of asking questions about *everything* (anthropologists are perhaps the most notorious in this regard):

> In the Navaho family, the art of weaving or jewelry-making is learnt from example. To the young native, to look is to learn. . . . Whence the complete absence of . . . the habit of asking questions such as "And that, why do that?" or "After that, what are you going to do?" It is this habit more than any other which has given natives their strange opinion of white men, for the Indian is convinced that the white man is a fool. (Reichard quoted in Lévi-Strauss, 1949:95)

Lévi-Strauss also noted that researchers who have conducted fieldwork frequently note that "primitive" children "are more mature and positive than a child in our own society" and that these children should therefore be compared to "civilized" adults (1949:92). This view is, in fact, supported by Margaret Mead's research with the Manus children of New Guinea. Mead began the anthropological critique of Piaget in 1932 with the publication of specific material on the thought of Manus children, which contradicted Piaget's claims regarding the development of animistic thought in children. Mead found that, contrary to Piaget's theories, Manus children's thought could be characterized as "naturalistic" and not "animistic." Manus adults, on the other hand, did exhibit animism in their thinking; however, Mead reported that Manus children frequently ignored or flatly rejected the animistic explanations or beliefs of their elders (see 1932:226, 229). This research is discussed in more detail in Chapter Seven. Currently, a number of fieldwork/experimental studies conducted by "ethnographic psychologists" such as Michael Cole and John Gay (e.g., Cole, Gay, Glick, and Sharp, 1971) are continuing the critique of Piaget (and also of other psychologists' theories) begun originally by Mead.

At present, Langness is one of the few anthropologists to have initiated a brief, but very useful, critique of the evolutionary assumptions implicit in Piaget's and other developmental psychologists' stage models. Because his remarks are particularly appropriate to matters discussed in this chapter, I quote at length:

> Thus, although it is true that Piaget does attempt to link mental development to actual studies of children and physical growth more precisely than do other theorists before him, he also incorporated the notion of "stages" and "levels" of development which are unfortunately often spoken of as "higher" and "lower." He also was interested "in relating the individual to the increase of knowledge in a society," a position he refers to as "genetic epistemology" (Ginsburg and Opper, 1969:210). Because of the great mass of his work, produced over such a long period of time, it would be difficult to assess just how much this "genetic epistemology" has influenced his theory of intelligence. But there is no doubt that it is closely identified with the recapitulation hypothesis.
>
> Thinking in terms of "higher" and "lower" stages of thought is characteristic of virtually all students of intelligence and development—even though it is perfectly obvious that such conceptualizations make sense as "higher" and "lower" only in accordance with some arbitrarily imposed standard of measurement. Thus we find ourselves speaking of "concrete" modes of thought which are "lower" than "abstract" modes of thought, prelogical as opposed to logical modes, animistic as opposed to scientific modes and the like. . . . Piaget and others have, it appears, established different styles of thought. No one, however, has devised an acceptable standard for rating styles as higher or lower. This is just as true for the thought of children (where a way of thinking is "higher" only because it in general appears later) as it is for cross-cultural differences in thought (where thinking is higher the closer it approximates our own). (1974:36–37)

SUMMARY

During the latter part of the 19th century, the idea that cultures evolved in a manner similar to biological organisms greatly influenced the study of social life. Ethnologists such as Lewis Henry Morgan and Edward Burnett Tylor became interested in the evolution of various aspects of culture (e.g., family and kinship systems and religion), arguing that their course of development could be traced through a series of stages from *savagery* to *civilization*. The study of children's play began during this era. Adopting the notions of unilineal stages, cultural survivals, and recapitulation, which were fashionable at this time, a number of researchers began to examine the play and games of Western children. These activities were interpreted as *survivals*, in childish form, of earlier societies' adult activities. And so, for example, the English children's game of "Nuts in May" was interpreted as a survival of an earlier society's practice of marriage by capture.

In the early 20th century, the search for universal stages of cultural evolution was sharply criticized as resulting from the speculations of "armchair" theorists who had had little, if any, actual fieldwork experience. Evolutionary theories soon fell into disfavor among anthropologists and have only recently made a reappearance in the discipline (e.g., Sahlins and Service, 1960). In psychology, however, the situation was different. It was during the late 19th century that the American psychologist G. Stanley Hall inaugurated the "scientific" study of children as the investigation of their sequential stages of biopsychic growth. And he specifically argued that the play stages of children recapitulated the entire biocultural history of mankind. These ideas, in turn, influenced the thinking of two of the most significant psychological theorists of this century: Sigmund Freud and Jean Piaget.

Jean Piaget is considered to be the preeminent student of *child development* in this century. He has spent a lifetime illustrating how children pass through various stages in their language learning, moral growth and, most specifically, cognitive development. Piaget has also been a student of children's play and, as such, has produced detailed descriptions of the marble games of Swiss children as well as the stages of development of play and games in Swiss children (in this case, his own children). In the words of Lewis Carroll's dormouse, Piaget has shown that *everything*, including the ridiculous, is "reasonably paced."

This research differs from the armchair speculations of many of the 19th-century evolutionists in that Piaget has based his theories on detailed and sensitive observations of (and also experiments with) children. Nevertheless, the stages that he has outlined are discussed as if they are present in *all* cultures, and some stages are described as if they are of a *higher* order than others. Piaget's ideas also perpetuate the belief that children engage in a more "primitive" (i.e., "lower") level of thinking (and playing) than do adults and, likewise, the notion that individuals in "primitive" or nonliterate societies exhibit a "lower" level of conceptual abilities than do individuals in Western cultures.

A number of researchers have indicated that Piaget's stages of play and game development do not occur in the same fashion in their research (e.g., Singer, Smilansky, and Eifermann). And Langness (1974:36–37) reminds us that the idea of "stages" is itself a cultural development. However, even though Mead challenged certain of Piaget's theories as early as 1932 and Lévi-Strauss presented an excellent analysis of the defects of "the archaic illusion" in 1949, the ethnographic critique of this view of cognitive development has just begun (e.g., Cole *et al.*, 1971), while a critical examination of Piaget's staging of children's play and game activities has yet to be formulated.

CHAPTER FIVE

Preserving Play: Diffusionism and Particularism

"What a useful thing a pocket map is!" I remarked.

"That's another thing we've learned from your Nation," said Mein Herr, "map-making. But we've carried it much further than you. What do you consider the largest map that would be really useful?"

"About six inches to the mile."

"Only six inches!" exclaimed Mein Herr. "We very soon got to six yards to the mile. Then we tried a hundred yards to the mile. And then came the grandest idea of all! We actually made a map of the country, on the scale of a mile to the mile!"

"Have you used it much?" I enquired.

"It has never been spread out, yet," said Mein Herr: "the farmers objected: they said it would cover the whole country and shut out the sunlight! So we now use the country itself, as its own map, and I assure you it does nearly as well."

Lewis Carroll, *Sylvie and Bruno Concluded*

Anthropology was, in part, formulated in response to an accumulation of 19th-century explorers', travelers', missionaries', and colonial administrators' reports about the "curious" customs of "primitive" peoples. Of course, ideas about the effect of customs or the influence of culture on the behavior of human beings can be traced back as far as the 14th century and perhaps even earlier (see Langness, 1974; also Harris, 1968). However, it was not until the publication of Tylor's *Primitive Culture* (1871) that the first English-language definition of culture was presented:

> Culture, or civilization, taken in its wide ethnographic sense, is that complex whole which includes knowledge, belief, art, morals, law, customs, and any other capabilities and habits acquired by man as a member of society. (p. 1)

61

Tylor, as was true of most scholars of his time, was heavily influenced by the idea of evolution as described in Chapter Four. For this reason, he developed a great interest in the study of the origin and evolution of particular "beliefs and customs" (e.g., religion). In these studies, Tylor also displayed an awareness that borrowing of one society's particular "traits" or "customs" by another society often took place. This borrowing process became known as *diffusion*, and it was used by anthropologists such as W. H. R. Rivers, Fritz Graebner, and Franz Boas to criticize what they considered to be the overly speculative arguments of the early evolutionists. The diffusionists' reaction, however, was also characterized by overly speculative theorizing, particularly as expressed in the work of G. E. Smith (1928) and Perry (1923), who suggested that "virtually everything on earth had originated in Egypt and had diffused outward from that point" (Langness, 1974:51).

GAME DIFFUSION AND THE PATOLLI–PACHISI DEBATE

While Tylor never accepted the extreme diffusionism of Smith and Perry, he did inaugurate the study of games in anthropology as the study of game diffusion, suggesting that these "trifling" customs were useful as evidence for particular theories of culture contact. His utilization of games in this manner is probably best illustrated in regard to the now famous patolli–pachisi question.

Tylor suggested in an article written in 1879 that the Aztec game of *patolli* shared many common features with the Hindu game of *pachisi* (e.g., the movement of counters as determined by a throw of lots, the crosslike shape of the mats or "board," and the type of scoring). Because of the similarities existing between these two games, Tylor argued that the American lot games must have come somehow from Asia prior to the time of Columbus:

> Lot-backgammon as represented by tab, *pachisi*, etc., ranges in the Old World from Egypt across Southern Asia to Burma. As the *patolli* of the Mexicans is a variety of lot-backgammon most nearly approaching the Hindu *pachisi*, and perhaps like it passing into the stage of dice-backgammon, its presence seems to prove that it made its way across from Asia. How it came is uncertain, though the drifting across of Asiatic vessels to California offers the readiest solution. At any rate, it may be reckoned among elements of Asiatic culture traceable in the old Mexican civilization, the high development of which in metal work, architecture, astronomy, political and religious institutions, etc., seems to be in large measure due to Asiatic influence. From Mexico, it appears that gambling by means of lots spread among the ruder north-west tribes, bearing the Aztec name of *patolli*, and being in fact the lot-casting part of that game but without the board and stone counters. (Tylor, 1879b:128)

In describing the purpose of his argument, Tylor illustrated his view of games and their value to the anthropologist:

> Now if any item of culture, even a matter so trifling as a game, can be distinctly made out to have passed over from Asia and established itself among the rude tribes of North America, this opens a way by which various other features of their culture may be fairly accounted for as due to Asiatic influence. (Tylor, 1879b:129)

Tylor elaborated the points made in this first paper in a later publication (1896). Here he attempted to provide more evidence for his original thesis by discussing the theory of probability[1]:

> The idea that the similarity between the American and Asian games resulted from independent invention has seemed probable to more than one anthropologist. . . . I have found it useful at any rate as a means of clearing ideas, to attempt a definite rule by analyzing such phenomena into constituent elements showing so little connection with one another that they may be treated as independent. The more numerous are such elements, the more improbable the recurrence of their combination. In the case of language recurrence may be treated as impossible. If the invention of the gun be divided into the blow-tube, the use of metal, the explosive, the lock, the percussion, etc., and classed as an invention of the 10th order, and the invention of chess with its six kinds of pieces with different moves indicated as perhaps of the 6th order, these figures would correspond to an immense improbability of recurrence. Such a game as *pachisi*, combining the invention of divining by lot, its application to the sportive wager, the combination of several lots with an appreciation of the laws of changes, the transfer of the result to a counting-board, the rules of moving and taking would place it in perhaps the 6th order, the recurrence of which might be less than that of chess, but according to common experience still far outside any probability on which reasonable men could count.
>
> If this argument be admitted, the relation of the *pachisi–patolli* groups of games in the Old and New World must be accounted for by intercourse before the Spanish conquest, other than that of the Northmen, which fails to answer the conditions. If the communication across the Atlantic fails, the alternative is communication across the Pacific from Eastern Asia, where the sportive material required could readily be furnished. (1896:92–93)

Tylor's resolution of the *patolli–pachisi* question was not shared by Stewart Culin from the University of Pennsylvania.[2] In one of his early studies of games, published in 1898, Culin suggested that the similarity of the games of Asia and America was due "to the identity of universal 'mythic' concepts which underlie them—such as the 'classification of all

---

[1]See Erasmus (1950) for a specific consideration of this argument and an extensive discussion of the *patolli–pachisi* debate.

[2]See Alyce Cheska's recent paper, "Stewart Culin: An Early Ethnologist of Games" (1975), for a brief biography of Culin and also an evaluation of his contribution to the study of games in culture. Also see Avedon and Sutton-Smith (1971:55–61) for a brief survey of Culin's major studies of games.

things according to the Four Directions' " (Erasmus, 1950:111). This view can be associated with the approach of many early evolutionists who argued for parallel (the idea that the development of similar traits in different places stems from a common cause and process) as opposed to convergent (similar traits in different places may develop for a variety of reasons) evolution on the basis of their belief in the "psychic unity of mankind" (see Langness, 1974:40, 49). However, in a later discussion, entitled "America the Cradle of Asia" (1903), Culin advanced the unorthodox notion that "identical customs originated in America and were disseminated thence over the world" (p. 495):

> Preoccupied with the notion that America is the new world, they [learned writers] have seemingly lost sight of the fact that these resemblances offer quite good proof of American intercourse with Asia as they do of an Asiatic invasion of our continent. (p. 493, quoted in Cheska, 1975:7)

In *Games of the North American Indians* (1907), Culin repeated his view that games were not "imported" into America, but now to validate this argument he presented an analysis that suggests that he was "inferring historical re-construction from space" (Erasmus, 1950:112):

> There is a well-marked affinity and relationship between the manifestations of the same game, even among the most widely separated tribes, the variations being more in the material of the implements, due to environments, than to the object or method of play. Precisely the same games are played by tribes belonging to unrelated linguistic stocks, and in general the variations do not follow the differences in language. At the same time there appears to be a progressive change from what seems to be the oldest form, from a center in Southwestern United States along lines radiating from the same center southward into Mexico. From such accounts of the Aztec games as have come down to us, they appear to be invariably higher developments of the games of the wilder tribes. Under no circumstances could they be regarded as the original forms. There is no evidence that any of the games described (this includes the lot games) were imported into America at any time, either before or after the conquest. On the other hand, they appear to be direct and natural outgrowths of aboriginal institutions in America. (Culin, 1907:31–32)

This new approach aligned Culin with the historicalist tradition of Franz Boas, Clark Wissler, Alfred L. Kroeber, and Robert Lowie. Boas began his studies in the latter part of the 19th and the early 20th century, traveling first to Baffinland in 1883 and, three years later, to the Pacific Northwest coast to work with the Kwakiutl. His approach to the study of culture was formulated as a reaction to what he considered to be the extreme generalizations of many "armchair" evolutionists. Boas argued that anthropology should be concerned with history and that its method should be inductive and not deductive. He also argued for convergent (as opposed to parallel) evolution, suggesting that similar cultural institutions could come about for different reasons and were not necessarily part of the same unilineal evolutionary process. Because he felt

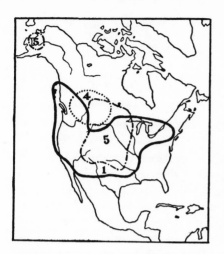 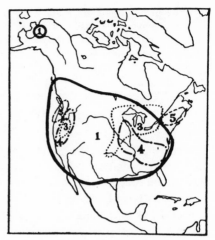

FIGURE 5. Distribution maps for American Indian games. Distribution for ring and wheel games; (1) the simple hoop; (4) the beaded ring; (5) the netted hoop. Distribution for ball and racket games: (1) shinny, also double ball; (3) side-ringed racket; (4) spoon-shaped racket; (5) side-meshed racket (C. Wissler, 1926:16).

strongly that "it was necessary to have detailed historical and ethnographic information on particular cases before any generalizations could be made," the school of anthropology that he formulated is often referred to by the label *historical particularism* (Langness, 1974:49).

Clark Wissler, one of Boas's early students, illustrated the historical particularists' adoption of a view of culture as trait in his analysis of the distribution of hoop and ball games among American Indian groups. Wissler was interested in the distribution of human traits, which he assumed were "segregated in patches over the earth" (1926:xiii).[3] These "patches" were referred to as *culture areas* characterized by the presence of particular culture traits that were thought to diffuse outward in all directions from a particular culture center. These distributions were best illustrated by maps tracing the spread of particular traits. In analyzing the distribution of games, Wissler believed that it was only necessary to describe different kinds of game objects:

> The children and the young of our Indian tribes were fond of games and the most universally distributed were those with hoops and balls. As a rule,

[3]This statement is reminiscent of Robert Lowie's "shreds and patches" analogy, which appears in the last paragraph of *Primitive Society* (1920) and is probably the most famous, and also controversial (see Harris, 1968:353–354, 520), description of culture made by an historical particularist: "To that planless hodgepodge, that thing of shreds and patches called civilization, its historian can no longer yield superstitious reverence. He will realize better than others the obstacles to infusing design into the amorphous product; but in thought at least he will not grovel before it in fatalistic acquiescence but dream of a rational scheme to supplant the chaotic jumble" (p. 441).

when the game differed, the wheel or ball differed also which simplifies our
problem and makes it objective. We need not, in fact, concern ourselves with
how the games were played, but merely take note of the different kinds of
balls and hoops that were used. (1926:16–17)

In Figure 5 Wissler's distribution maps for these games are presented.

PARTICULARISM: THE FACTS OF PLAY

A concern with the collection and compilation of ethnographic *facts*
with the expectation that some day (and in some way) these facts would
lead to theoretical generalizations was the characteristic feature of the
particularist tradition in anthropology. Similarly, a concern with the
collection of play facts or play texts (with little emphasis on theoretical
interpretations) was characteristic of the majority of anthropological and
folklore studies of children's play and games conducted in the late 19th
and early 20th centuries. Perhaps more than anyone else, Stewart Culin
in his "collecting expeditions" exemplifies this tradition. An excerpt
from the 1967 *Brooklyn Museum Handbook* (quoted in Cheska, 1975:8–9)
describes his approach:

> Stewart Culin was the ethnologist who practically filled up the Brooklyn
> Museum. Traveling to the Southwest, California, the Northwest, and
> Alaska, he shipped back the material in boxcar lots. . . . 4,703 specimens
> were installed to represent the Southwest alone. He went to India, China,
> Korea, and Japan and built Oriental collections that included a two-story Jain
> rest house embellished with a hundred carved musicians who actually
> clanged cymbals and blew into reeds upon the turning of a crank-operated
> bellows.

As has been illustrated, these play collections were often used by
ethnographers to argue for, or against, particular theories of cultural
evolution and/or cultural diffusion. Another factor motivating play and
game collectors was the prevailing view of the child as primitive. Here
the analogy that encouraged collections of the "quaint and curious customs" of "primitive" peoples, because these practices would soon become extinct, also suggested that the "curious" customs of children, in
the form of their games and rhymes, should be *collected* and preserved
because these practices were also expected to vanish.[4]

A view of the child as primitive and culture as custom or trait is
reflected in most particularist and diffusionist studies made at this time.

[4]Children's "customs" have, of course, survived and probably will continue to do so in the
future, although recently some researchers (e.g., J. and D. Singer, 1976) have suggested
that television and other devices emphasizing "sedantism" and passive involvement for
children may actually extinguish their more active and imaginative play activities. This,
however, remains to be seen.

This approach led researchers to view *play as the formalized, structured, and rule-regulated games* in which children participate, and therefore texts (or descriptions) of game activities were collected by researchers interested in preserving the most obvious *customs* (and, therefore, reflections of culture) of children.

WILLIAM WELLS NEWELL: AMERICAN CHILDREN'S GAMES AND SONGS

The preeminent student of children's play at this time was William Wells Newell. As discussed earlier, Newell was responsible for publishing the first large-scale systematic collection of English-speaking children's play *(Games and Songs of American Children,* 1883, expanded 1903). In this report, Newell was particularly interested in showing that

> the resemblance of children's songs (and games) in different countries, like the similarity of popular traditions in general, is owing to their perpetual diffusion from land to land; a diffusion which has been going on in all ages, in all directions, and with all degrees of rapidity. (p. 4)

In regard to his specific study of American children's games and songs, Newell believed that "these childish usages of play are almost entirely of old English origin" (pp. 1–2). Newell also suggested that in order to trace diffusion from one country to another, one should follow "the law that transmission usually proceeds from above to below" (p. xvi). In describing this law, Newell assumed that there were superior cultures that existed "above" inferior societies. This view, of course, is in keeping with the logic of the vertical metaphor as used most clearly by evolutionists, but it is also highly ethnocentric:

> When superior culture comes in contact with inferior, the former, itself but little affected, remodels the latter. Illustrations need hardly be offered, seeing that civilization itself is an example. With habits of play the principle holds; thus in America the African, even where in great majority, has abandoned his native custom to accept that of his white masters. In this manner negroes adopt old English rounds, which they repeat with every variation of accuracy, from perfect correctness to unintelligible confusion. (p. xvi)[5]

[5]Newell's argument is particularly questionable "with habits of play." An excellent example of a culture's adaptation of (not to) a Western game is available in a recent movie by Jerry Leach and Gary Kildea (see Chapter Twelve for details) entitled *Trobriand Cricket: An Ingenious Response to Colonialism* (1973). This movie illustrates the Trobrianders' transformation of the stuffy and staid British game of cricket (introduced at the turn of the century by missionaries) into an exuberant, sensual, and also political event. According to Weiner (1977), in her recent review of the movie, "When a group of elders describe the way villagers were determined to 'rubbish' (i.e., throw out) the British game and make cricket into a Trobriand contest, their words speak of cricket, but the camera beautifully com-

Newell also wished to collect texts of children's games because he was convinced that they were soon to become extinct. In fact, it was his belief that these games had already begun to "die off" or to be radically changed in England and were currently in a "purer" state of preservation in America. His duty, as he saw it, was "to pick and preserve" these traditions for all time:

> The vine of oral tradition, of popular poetry, which for a thousand years has twined and bloomed on English soil, in other days enriching with color and fragrance equally the castle and the cottage, is perishing at the roots; its prouder branches have long since been blasted, and children's song, its humble but longest flowering offshoot, will soon have shared their fate. (1883:1)[6]

Newell catalogued his collected game texts according to designated play themes: love games, histories, playing at work, humor and satire, guessing games, games of chase, and so forth.

Between the first publication of Newell's study (1883) and the issuance of an expanded edition in 1903, Lady A. B. Gomme had published her two-volume work on *The Traditional Games of England, Scotland, and Ireland* (1894, 1898). The similarity between the games that Newell had described in 1883 and that Gomme also described confirmed Newell's view that American children's games had diffused from England to America. Lady Gomme's research, however, caused Newell to alter his view that the games of England had been preserved more adequately in America.

Newell's studies were also conducted in order to make a very direct methodological point. It was his belief that "one fact is worth a thousand theories," and he continually argued that the study of folklore (including the study of play) could be done only by carefully collecting field material and by the use of authentic historical documents (Withers, 1963:xii). Newell advocated these methods because he wished once and for all to rebuke

> the armchair mythologists of his time who with few threads of facts were weaving elaborate fabrics of pseudo-theory regarding the "origin" of

---

municates to us the unique strength and resiliency of these people in the face of European dominating influences" (p. 506). Newell's depiction of "native Africans" as passive and/or confused imitators of their "white masters' " games and speech is also inaccurate. For example, Braithwaite (in R. and S. Price, 1976:38–39), in discussing the development of Creole society in Jamaica, suggested that "It was in language that the slave was perhaps most successfully imprisoned by his master, and it was in his (mis-)use of it that he perhaps most effectively rebelled."
[6]The idea that children's games preserved earlier societies' adult actions—the notion of games as survivals—has already been discussed in Chapter Four.

folktales and legends in early sun myths and their "survival" into the modern world from civilized man's "savage past." (Withers, 1963:xii)

If Newell's emphasis on induction sounds similar to the ideas of
Franz Boas, it is no accident. In 1888, five anthropologists and five literary scholars founded the American Folklore Society, and, among these
founders, were Boas and Newell. Newell edited the *Journal of American
Folklore* for twelve years (1888–1900) and acted as the executive secretary
of this society until his death in 1907 (Withers, 1963:xi). During these
years, Newell encouraged researchers to collect "accurate and responsible" folklore reports of "relics of Old English ballads, tales, songs, etc.,
in North America," "Negrolore in the South," the "lore of North
American Indian Tribes" and the "lore of French Canada, Mexico, etc."
(Withers, 1963:xi).

EARLY COLLECTIONS AND CLASSIFICATIONS

Along with Newell, Matilde Coxe Stevenson was an early student
of children's play and possibly the first female anthropologist to develop
an interest in this subject. She began her studies of the "habits, customs,
games and experiences" of Zuni children in 1879 while accompanying
her geologist husband on a survey of the American Southwest (Mergen,
1975:403). In 1883, she published a portion of her research on these
topics in the *Fifth Annual Report of the Bureau of American Ethnology* in a
section entitled "Religious Life of the Zuni Child." Along with producing some of the earliest ethnographic descriptions of children's activities, Stevenson is also significant for her interest in demonstrating
"that women had a special role to play in anthropology" (Mergen,
1975:403; also Lurie, 1971:373–374).

Tylor, who was the first anthropologist to study games, concentrated on the investigation of adult games. However, he was not opposed to utilizing children's games as evidence for particular theories of
diffusion when he thought this was appropriate:

An intelligent traveller among the Kalmuks, noticing that they play a kind of
chess resembling ours, would not for a moment entertain the idea of such an
invention having been made more than once, but would feel satisfied that we
and they and all chess-players must have had the game from the original
source. In this example lies the gist of the ethnological argument from artificial games, that when any such appears in two districts it must have travelled
from one to the other, or to both from a common centre. Of course, this
argument does not apply to all games. Some are so simple and natural that,
for all we can tell, they may often have sprung up of themselves, such as
tossing a ball or wrestling; while children everywhere imitate in play the
serious work of grown up life, from spearing an enemy down to moulding an

earthen pot. The distinctly artificial sports we are concerned with here are marked by some peculiar trick or combination not so likely to have been hit upon twice. Not only complex games like chess and tennis, but even many childish sports, seem well-defined formations, of which the spread may be traced on the map much as the botanist traces his plants from their geographical centres. (1879a:63)

Studies of some of these "childish sports" would illustrate, according to Tylor, how specific theories as to the origin of certain games fail:

Travellers, observing the likeness of certain children's games in Europe and Asia, have sometimes explained it on this wise: that the human mind being alike everywhere, the same games are naturally found in different lands, children taking to hockey, tops, stilts, kites, and so on, each at its proper season. But if so, why is it that in outlying barbarous countries one hardly finds a game without finding also that there is a civilized nation within reach from whom it may have been learnt? And what is more, how is it that European children knew nothing till a few centuries ago of some of their most popular sports? For instance, they had not battledoll and shuttlecock and never flew kites till these games came across from Asia, when they took root at once and became naturalized over Europe. The English boys kite appears thus an instance, not of spontaneous play-instinct, but of the migration of an artificial game from a distant centre. Nor is this all it proves in the history of civilization. Within a century, Europeans becoming acquainted with the South Sea Islanders found them down to New Zealand adepts at flying kites. . . . It looks as though the toy reached Polynesia through the Malay region, thus belonging to that drift of Asiatic culture which is evident in many other points of South Sea Island life. The geography of another of our childish diversions may be noticed as matching with this. Mr. Wallace[7] relates that being one wet day in a Dayak house in Borneo, he thought to amuse the lads by taking a piece of string to show them *cat's cradle,* but to his surprise he found that they knew more about it than he did, going off into figures that quite puzzled him. (1879a:63–64)

Influenced by the writings of Tylor, Newell, and Stevenson, a number of other scholars began to collect texts of children's play activities. Many of these studies were published in the early volumes of the *American Anthropologist*. One of the most significant of these investigations appears in the first volume (1888) of this journal, contributed by Henry Babcock, a patent lawyer. In "Games of Washington Children," Babcock began his article with a charming description of his methodology:

My method has been to wander through promising neighborhoods in the twilight of summer evenings—or lie in wait in my study and sally out when anything novel in the way of child music was borne in through the windows, hurried notes being taken . . . often under great difficulties. (p. 243)

---

[7]Tylor is referring here to Alfred R. Wallace, who proposed a theory of evolution based on his research in Indonesia that closely paralleled that of Charles Darwin. Today this theory is frequently referred to as the Darwin–Wallace theory of evolution.

Babcock's work is important because he limited his research to descriptions of play from one city and during one year. He devised a system of classification for the various games collected, dividing them into 15 different types, including ring games, archway games, games of chase, games of transposition, rigmaroles and jingles, and child-stealing games. He also attempted to compare examples of games collected by Newell with versions of these games as played by his particular informants. For example, he found a variant of Newell's "The Farmer in the Dell." His version went:

> *The man in the cell,*
> *The man in the cell,*
> *High O! Cherry O!*
> *The man in the cell.*
> (p. 254)

According to Babcock, this was sung by "colored children," and, to account for the textual variation, he suggested that these children were "perhaps more familiar with the phenomenon of station houses than with those of the hill country" (1888:254).

American anthropologists concentrated their early fieldwork efforts on the study of North American Indians. The study of games by these ethnographers was therefore almost solely the study of North American Indian games, as the research of Stevenson (1883) and Culin (1907) demonstrates. In many of the early issues of the *American Anthropologist*, reports on various North American Indian societies' game activities were offered by professional and amateur anthropologists (e.g., Daniel, 1892; Stevenson, 1903).

One of the most important early reports on North American Indian children's play is found in the fourth volume of this journal. Owen Dorsey's descriptions of "Games of Teton Dakota Children" (1891) were widely cited in Culin's (1907) compilation and remain today as one of the most complete accounts of this activity for North American Indian groups. Dorsey obtained his material from a collection of texts in the possession of the Washington Bureau of Ethnology written by George Bushotter, a Dakota Indian. Dorsey translated the relevant material on children's games into English and divided it into 10 different categories according to the sex of the players and also the season in which the game was played, when this information was available. In this way, he presented descriptions of a number of pretending games (e.g., "they make one another carry packs," girls and boys, spring and summer; "ghost game," girls and boys, no season reported; "trampling on the beaver," girls and boys, spring and summer; "taking captives from one another," boys, no season reported; "mystery game," girls and boys, no season reported; "grizzly bear game," girls and boys, no season reported;

"going to make a grass lodge," boys, spring; "they wound one another with a grass which has a long sharp beard," boys, fall; "sitting on wooden horses," boys, no season reported; "pretending to die," boys, no season reported; "playing with small things," girls, no season reported). Dorsey also included discussion of numerous other play activities (e.g., sledding; hide-and-seek; "jumping from a high object"; string figures; hoop games; egg hunting; "throwing chewed leaves into the eyes"; bow-and-arrow games; tops; tumbling and somersaults; and "how they are brought up," a type of "follow the leader").

Culin's studies (e.g., 1895, 1907) of games and gaming implements have already been briefly discussed. His major interest in these investigations was in the study of formalized games, and children's play activities (unless there were implements—toys—or structured rules to describe) were generally not considered in his works.[8] However, in his discussion of "minor amusements," Culin did present his views as to the nature of children's play, the availability of accounts of this activity, and the possible value of research on this topic:

> From the recorded accounts, meager as they are, it appears that the Indians of North America had the same kinds of minor amusements and children's plays as occur in other parts of the world and survive in our own civilization. . . . In accordance with the original plan I shall dismiss with this mere mention the games played without special implements. There is much, however, in them, as well as in the Indian toys and playthings, that would repay comparative study although our information is scanty. (1907:715–716)

Culin classified all reports of children's games as "games of dexterity," as opposed to "games of chance" (e.g., dice games and guessing games), his other major category. Thirteen different types or "heads" of dexterity games are described (e.g., shuttlecock, jackstraws, swing, stilts, tops, and cats' cradle), accompanied by illustrations of game implements (see Figure 6). These descriptions are followed by an enumeration of reports of those North American Indian groups in which the particular "amusement" was found (e.g., in the "Algonquin stock," reports of tops were available for the Arapaho, Blackfeet, Cheyenne, Cree, Grosventres, Norridgewock, Sauk, and Fox).

Even though Culin was not an active student of children's play, he did devote one of his earliest articles (1891) to a specific description of street games of Brooklyn boys. These games were described to him by "a lad of ten years, residing in the city of Brooklyn, N.Y." (p. 221). The

---

[8]It is interesting to note here that while these descriptions of games, implements, and rules are often quite detailed, they are also frequently quite confusing, so that after carefully reading the material, it is still quite difficult to understand exactly how the game is played (see Osgood's 1959 review of the 1958 republication of Culin's *Games of the Orient: Korea, China, Japan*).

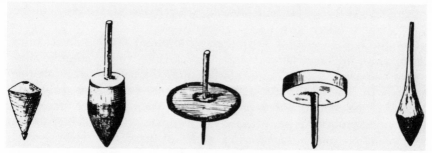

FIGURE 6. Eskimo tops (S. Culin, 1907:737). (A). Top; height, 2 inches; Labrador Eskimo, Ungava Bay; cat. no. 90281, U.S. National Museum. (B). Top; height, 4½ inches; Labrador Eskimo, Ungava Bay; cat. no. 90282. U.S. National Museum. (C). Top; height, 3¾ inches; Labrador Eskimo, Ungava Bay; cat. no. 90283, U.S. National Museum. (D). Top; height, 2½ inches; Labrador Eskimo, Ungava Bay; cat. no. 90284, U.S. National Museum. (E). Wooden top; height 4¾ inches; Western Eskimo, Bristol Bay, Alaska; cat. no. 56045, U.S. National Museum.

games are grouped into specific types and variations of types: (1) games of tag (e.g., wood tag, French tag, fence tag, squat tag, cross tag, last tag); (2) games of pursuit (e.g., hare and hounds, arrow chase, ring relievo, prisoners' base, blacktom, red rover, red lion, every man in his own den); (3) games of hiding (e.g., I spy or hide-and-seek, throw the stick, run a mile); (4) vaulting games (e.g., leapfrog, head and footer, par, Spanish fly, stunt master); (5) hopping games (e.g. hopscotch and variations—kick the stone out, pick the stone up); (6) baseball variations (e.g., kick the wicket; kick the can; kick the ball; hit the stick; one o'cat; one, two, three!; fungo; shinery; cat; roley poley); (7) miscellaneous games (e.g., handball and pictures). Also included in this article is a discussion of the "laws and customs" of boys' gangs, as well as a list of names of over 50 locations of Philadelphia boys' gangs (e.g., "Rats," Almond Street Wharf, and "Lancers," Twentieth and Fitzwater) and a description of "initiation" games for new gang members. For example:

> *Lame Soldier*—The new boy is made "doctor," while the rest are "lame soldiers" who have been to war, and been shot in the leg. The "lame soldiers" have covered the soles of their shoes with tar or mud; and, as they hobble past the "doctor," and he examines their wounds, he soon finds that his hands are much soiled, and discovers the object of the game. (p. 237)

Or:

> *Hide the Straw*—Bounds are agreed upon, and the new boy is made "it." All close their eyes while he hides the straw, and afterwards they searched for it, apparently with much diligence. At last they go to the boy and say: "I believe you have concealed it about you, let us search him." Then they ask him to open his mouth, and when he complies they stuff coal and dirt and other objects in it. (p. 237)

WALTER ROTH: AUSTRALIAN ABORIGINE GAMES

Walter E. Roth was the Australian government's "Chief Protector of Aboriginals" in Queensland (Harris, 1968:361). In this position he conducted a series of ethnographic studies of aboriginal groups located in this area. In "Games, Sports, and Amusements" (1902) Roth presented a detailed description and classification of these activities for North Queensland groups.[9] Also included in this report are 39 plates of drawings and photographs depicting examples of the games, with specific emphasis given to string figure illustrations.

Roth classified these games into seven different categories. *Imaginative games* are said to consist of "tales, legends and other fancies" (p. 7). Nine different tales or fables are presented, and they are said to be evaluated by speakers in terms of the cleverness and humor of presentation. Depending upon the specific area, men, women, or children may be the storytellers. *Realistic games* are "pleasures derivable from actual objects of nature, organic as well as inorganic" (p. 7). Examples are playing with "pets" (e.g., young rats, birds, frogs, dingos, wallabies); swinging on vines; making smoke signals; mud sliding; and bathing and "aquatic sports." *Imitative games* are said to include the largest number of games, and so they are subdivided into two types. The first variety consists of games where objects and phenomena of nature are imitated by attitudes, movements, gestures, and so forth and also games with string. Roth included illustrations of 74 different string-figures, ingeniously designed to represent animals, plants, manufactured objects, or human activities. For example, in Figure 7A & B, two of Roth's plates (III and V) are reproduced. The animal or action represented is indicated by a small drawing placed below or to the side of the string-figure drawing. In Figure 7A, the following are represented: (1) two boys carrying spears; (2) two women fighting with sticks; (3) four boys walking in a row holding hands; (4) two men walking down a valley; (5) a man climbing a tree; (6) a kangaroo; (7) a kangaroo pouch; (8) a wallaby pouch; and (9) a spear. In Figure 7B, string-figure representations of several birds are presented: (1) a cassowary; (2) an eagle hawk; (3) two cockatoos roosting side by side; (4) two white cranes; (5) a giant crane; (6) a duck in flight; and (7) a bird's nest in the bottom of a hollow stump. Also included in the category of imitative games are sand pictures of

[9]See Haddon's (1902) early review of Roth's investigation, in which he suggested that more attention should be paid to the study of the games of "primitive" peoples. In his brief discussion of this report, Haddon described similarities between the games enumerated by Roth and those that he had seen played by Papuan children. Haddon suggested that "this little memoir . . . opens up a new field to the student" (p. 381). Unfortunately most ethnographers at this time did not share Haddon's enthusiasm for this "new field."

animal and bird tracks, rock paintings, and the particularly hilarious (to
the aborigine) drawings of "a European bootprint . . . [made] about 10
or 12 inches in length" (p. 12). Finally, Roth described children's "imitative games," such as playing house, marriage, cooking, hunting,
searching for honey, and catching cockatoos (these are often hand
games that visually resemble the Maori children's game *upoko-titi* as
described by Best), and warfare imitations.

  Discriminative games include activities such as hide-and-seek and
guessing games, which both children and adults play. Roth classified
wrestling contests and a type of tug-of-war game as *disputative games*. In

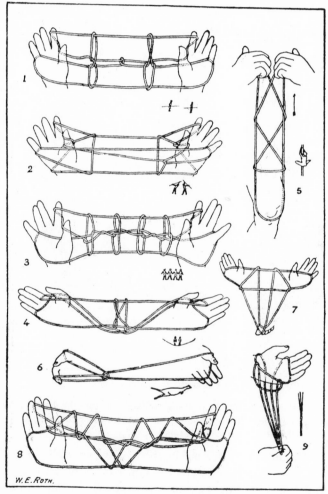

FIGURE 7A. Australian aborigine string figures (W. E. Roth, 1902:Plate III).

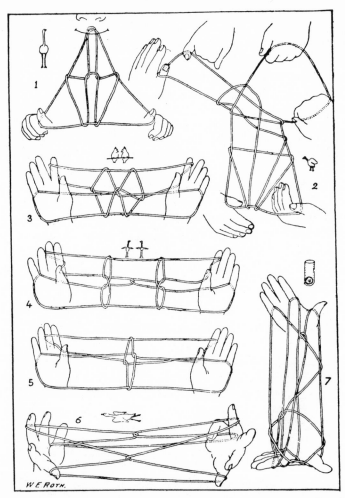

FIGURE 7B. Australian aborigine string figures (W. E. Roth, 1902:Plate V).

the latter, a pole instead of a rope is used and

> in place of pulling there is pushing. Indeed the fun consists mainly in balancing the pole *in statu quo* side against side for a few minutes, and then letting it fall with a deep grunt of relief. (p. 17)

Propulsive games are characterized by the use of a specially manufactured article ("toy"), where the enjoyment "consists in the particular form of motion which may be imparted to them" (p. 7). Examples of such toy objects and propulsive games are (1) balls (catchball, bowl ball, spin ball, etc.); (2) tops (spin tops, tee-to-tum); (3) sticks (shooting the grass blade, toy throwing-sticks); and (4) boomerangs (toy boomerangs). In describing the use of the boomerang as a toy, Roth suggested that the games played with these objects are the only partially competitive indigenous games that exist. And even here, Roth lamented, the "civilized" custom of prizes and awards is not found:

> The toy boomerang is thrown only by men and boys, and its throwing is the only indigenous North Queensland game wherein any real attempt is made to see who is the "best" man so to speak, but even then no so-called "prize" is awarded; indeed, it is apparently very difficult for these blacks to understand the more civilized custom of producing emulation by a system of awards. (p. 19)

The final category of games described is musical songs and instruments as well as dances and entertainments (designated by Europeans as "corrobborees"). These activities are referred to as *exultative games.* Roth concluded his report by listing several games introduced by missionaries, settlers, and others. These include "marbles, running races, high-jumping, throwing spears through a suspended hoop, [and] the use of skipping rope" (p. 24).

ELSDON BEST: MAORI CHILDREN'S GAMES

One of the most significant ethnographic studies of games published in the first quarter of the 20th century is Elsdon Best's *Games and Pastimes of the Maori* (1925).[10] This report was published by the Dominion Museum of New Zealand and is described as "an account of various exercises, games and pastimes of the Natives of New Zealand, as practiced in former times." The material was obtained from museum collections of artifacts, illustrations, photographs, and published accounts, as well as Best's own observations. In the monograph, he organized the game descriptions into eight different categories: military exercises and games viewed as useful training (e.g., wrestling, boxing, and foot racing); aquatic games and pastimes (e.g., swimming, surf riding, and canoe racing); games requiring agility or manual dexterity (e.g., jackstones, dart throwing, and cat's cradle); games and pastimes requiring calculation, mental alertness, or memorizing powers (e.g.,

---

[10]The collectors' tendency to accumulate file after file of handwritten field notes, leaving little time for transcription and analysis, was exemplified by Elsdon Best. He was, as described by Margaret Mead (1972:190), "that indefatigable chronicler of the Maori" filling cabinet after cabinet with field notes. Boas, as well, even with his many publications, never prepared his final summary on the Kwakiutl. Mead stated that "he would plan to do it, but by the third page of a new manuscript, he was entrapped in the description of some detailed technique on which he had notes that he had never had time to transcribe" (p. 190).

draughts, riddles, and word play); games and pastimes of children (e.g., kite flying, stilt walking, and swinging); introduced games; and Maori songs and Maori singing and musical instruments.

The chapter on children's games includes discussion of a number of play activities. Included here are descriptions and illustrations of Maori kite flying *(manu tukutuku)*; stilt walking *(pou toti)*; tobagganing *(horua)*; swinging *(tarere)*; skipping *(piu)*; top spinning *(ta potaka)*; hoops *(pirori)*; hide-and-seek *(taupunipuni)*; jumping jacks *(karetao)*; and numerous hand games (e.g., *upoko-titi*).

In order to play *upoko-titi*, according to Best (p. 98–99), one player holds out his/her right hand with his/her forefinger pointing downward. Players then begin to pile their hands one on top of the other, each with his/her forefinger pointing downward resting on the back of another player's hand. This procedure is then followed for the left hand at which point the player whose hand is on top (the leader) repeats a brief "jingle," and just as he says the last word, he lifts the hand next to his own and pushes it away. The player whose hand is pushed away holds it so that the index finger touches his chest. The jingle is repeated again and again until all players are holding their hands on their chests. At this point, the leader repeats a phrase, and all players throw their hands downward. This is followed by the question, "Who shall eat my face?"

FIGURE 8. Maori children playing *upoko-titi* (E. Best, 1925:96b).

followed by questions mentioning different parts of the body. After each question, the players throw their hands downward. Figure 8 illustrates the first portion of this game as exhibited by children in the Whanganui district. Best pointed out that the "players' fingers are not in the correct position" (p. 96).

Best's remarks concerning the game *upoko-titi* illustrate his view of children, their games, and also suggestions for how to proceed with childhood ethnography:

> *Upoko-Titi*—A childish pastime. It is played by three or more children, and represents simple pastimes practiced by young children in pre-European times. The writer has seen children joining in these simple pastimes, in the Tuhoe district as recently as the year 1900, and, by making friends with the children, was enabled to watch and describe their amusements. A small sum of money judiciously expended in the purchase of jews harps and sweets may often advance the science of ethnography. (1925:98)

PAUL G. BREWSTER: GAME COLLECTIONS AND CLASSIFICATIONS

More recent collections of play texts have been made by a number of investigators. One of the most productive in this regard is Paul G. Brewster, an American folklorist, who has compiled an impressive amount of material on the games of children and adults in various societies of the world. Brewster outlined a number of reasons for researchers to study games in his article "The Importance of the Collecting and Study of Games" (1956). His suggestions as to the importance of games for anthropologists illustrate his adoption of a diffusionist orientation:

> The benefits to be derived by the anthropologist or the ethnologist from a study, particularly a comparative study, of games are many. Perhaps one of the greatest of these is the evidence often found in games of direct borrowing or of adaptation of games materials of neighboring peoples. Sometimes these borrowings or adaptations are of fairly recent date. Sometimes the internal evidence points to a much earlier period. In either event, theories regarding culture contacts between peoples are often materially strengthened by the discovery of nonindigenous elements in the games played by a particular tribe or nationality. (1956:12–13)

Brewster also believes that anthropologists and folklorists should study children's games because:

> many of the games played by twentieth century children, even those of the most highly civilized societies, contain traces of very ancient and even primitive beliefs and practices. (p. 14)

Examples of these "beliefs and practices" as identified by Brewster are water worship, sacrifice, color symbolism, and witches. And so the survival theory of children's play may be seen to have survived itself in Brewster's theories.

Brewster's most detailed publication on children's play is his 1952 report on North Carolina children's games and rhymes. This study is based on the folklore collection of Frank C. Brown of Duke University made between the years 1912 and 1943. Most of the material in this report was collected from white informants living in the mountain districts of North Carolina. Brewster, in the tradition of the particularist, classified these game texts into 18 different types: ball games, hiding games, jumping and hopping games, practical jokes, battle games, dramatic games, guessing games, forfeit or penalty games, games of chase, games of dexterity, imitative games, courtship and marriage games, teasing games, tug-of-war games, games of smaller children, elimination games, dancing games, and miscellaneous games. Following a similar system for the rhymes, Brewster divided them into 16 different types: counting-out rhymes, game rhymes (exclusive of counting-out rhymes), rope-skipping rhymes, catches or sells, teasing rhymes, derisive rhymes, divination rhymes, charms, lullabies, finger rhymes, tickling rhymes, asseverations, recitations, "smart aleck" rhymes, friendship verses, and tongue twisters.

Brewster's style of presentation in this study is as follows. First, the major game category is given (e.g., hiding games), followed by the names of specific games included in this category (e.g., hide-and-seek). Before the actual description of the game, Brewster included "head notes," which give brief information on the game's age, history, and geographical distribution, as well as bibliographic references for other descriptions of the game available in the literature. For example, hide-and-seek is said to be an extremely popular game in America, and Brewster also stated that it appears to be a favorite in other cultures as well. Reports are cited of the game's existence among the Maori, Hawaiians, Kafir, Melanesians, Venda, English, Koreans, and ancient Greeks. Finally, variations in the game, as revealed by different collector's contributions from different counties in North Carolina, are offered.

Along with a number of articles written on the subject of children's play in various cultures (e.g., 1944; 1945a,b; 1948; 1949a,b; 1951; 1955; 1957; 1959; 1960), Brewster has also published a book entitled *American Non-Singing Games* (1953). Following the pattern of his previous study, Brewster acquired his material from various individuals (e.g., students, friends, and individual collectors). The style of presentation is similar to the 1952 work as he divided the games into 14 different types and then presented each game in its appropriate section, including mention of the state (e.g., Indiana, Missouri, Kentucky) in which the game was reported. Each game description is followed by brief comparative notes discussing various other cultures in which the game, or a variant of it, is played and references to the game available in the literature.

The games presented in this collection are

> only those in which singing is either not present at all or, if present, does not constitute an integral part of the game and hence could be omitted without injury to it. (1953:xv)

This approach was undertaken, according to Brewster, in order to correct for the overemphasis on the collection "of singing games to the virtual exclusion of those in which singing plays no part" (p. xv).[11] The types of games described in this volume are guessing games (e.g., odd versus even; stone, paper, scissor; thimble); forfeit games (e.g., poor pussy, poison, truth or consequences); hiding games (e.g., hide the belt, hide-and-seek, kick the can); chasing games (e.g., Molly Bright, prison base, squat tag); ball games (e.g., Indian ball, keep ball, Anthony over); elimination games (e.g., drop the handkerchief, pussy wants a corner, marching to Jerusalem); jumping and hopping games (e.g., leapfrog, hopscotch, Johnny on the pony); practical jokes (e.g., introducing the king and queen, just like me, mesmerizing); paper-and-pencil games (e.g., squares, ticktacktoe, ship, captain and crew); games of dexterity (e.g., jacks, mumblety-peg, lag marbles); courtship games (e.g., wink, post office, pillow); stick games (e.g., king stick, shinny, tippy); games of little girls (e.g., steps, wring the dishrag, statues); and miscellaneous games (e.g., crack the whip, follow the leader, red rover).

In the introduction to this collection, Brewster again emphasized his view that children's games preserve "vestiges of many ancient customs and beliefs," and so he finds in singing games such as "London Bridge" "traces of foundation worship"; in "Sally Waters," he sees "elements of water worship"; and in "Old Roger," "traces of tree worship" (p. xix). "Jenny Jones" is likewise said to exhibit a belief in the return of the dead in spirit form, while the practices of bride stealing and dowry payments are found in "Three Dukes," and ancient burial customs are represented in "Green Gravel." In nonsinging games, survivals of taboo are found in poison, of witchcraft in Molly Bright and chickamy, the belief in iron as a safeguard in iron tag, the practice of divination in guessing games, and traces of early judicial procedure in forfeit games. Finally, the right of sanctuary is said to be illustrated in escaping from a pursuer by crossing the fingers or by calling "King's X," and he also suggests that counting-out rhymes "may well be corrupted imitations of early incantations" (1953:xix–xx).

---

[11]This statement appears to be well-founded. For example, in Newell's 1883 study, over 75% of the games described are singing games.

In conjunction with Thomas Sebeok, Brewster (Sebeok and Brewster, 1958) has produced an extensive comparison of Cheremis (a Uralic culture) games with games in a variety of other cultures. Following the practice adopted in Brewster's earlier studies, the authors have classified the 97 collected game texts into seven different categories ("it" games, individual competition, team play, partners, rhythmic or dramatic games, practical jokes, and unclassified or unidentified). The Cheremis game (name and method of play translated into English) is first described and then examples of the game's appearance (or a variant of it) in other societies are presented. For example, an "it game" description:

> Blind ram—One covers his eyes with a kerchief. The other players, slapping him on the back, run away from him. He who is caught has his eyes covered and becomes the blind ram. (p. 7)

According to the authors, variations of this game (as reported in the literature) are played in the United States (known as "Watchdog"), Germany, England, Borneo, Morocco, Algeria, Turkey, Hungary, Russia, Finland, and Sweden.

BRIAN SUTTON-SMITH: NEW ZEALAND AND AMERICAN CHILDREN'S GAMES

One of the most prolific investigators of children's play activities writing today is Brian Sutton-Smith, who began his career as a collector of texts of New Zealand children's games. He has since demonstrated an almost unique flexibility in his studies, exhibiting his adoption of a variety of research orientations (e.g., folklore, anthropology, sociology, and psychology). In contrast to many past and present researchers, Sutton-Smith is also significant for his attempts to study changes in games over time or variations in games played from society to society, rather than emphasizing the universality and similarity of games in all historical periods or in all cultures.

Sutton-Smith was born in New Zealand, and he has suggested that his interest in the study of play might perhaps be related to "the somewhat monotonous post-Victorian social environment of New Zealand during the 1930's and 1940's" (1972a:xiii) in which he grew up. This environment most certainly affected the content of his first studies of play, leading him to match Best's early description of Maori children's games by producing the first detailed study of New Zealand *Pakeha* (European) children's play (*The Games of New Zealand Children*, 1959b). The material for this study was collected in a variety of ways: (1) manuscripts solicited by advertising in newspapers and requesting information on games; (2) interviews with adults; (3) questionnaires collected from university students; (4) teachers' reports; (5) written reports and visual demonstrations collected from schoolchildren; and, finally, (6) intensive observations made at one specific school playground during 1949 and 1950.

The games collected from this study are categorized according to structural (characteristic features of game texts) and developmental (characteristic age group or sex of players) criteria. References to comparative sources are included in the text only in certain instances. The games are divided into 10 major types: (1) singing games (e.g., ring-a-ring-a-roses, oka ball, Bobby Bingo); (2) dialogue games (e.g., ghost in the garden, Old Mother Gray, Harry Pots); (3) informal (or make-believe) games (e.g., dolls, Maoris, bushrangers); (4) leader games (e.g., may I?, statues, Queenie); (5) chasing games (e.g., hide-and-seek, prisoner's base, Tiki Tiki Touchwood); (6) rhythmic games (e.g., skipping, hand clapping, ball bouncing); (7) games of chance (e.g., pop 'em down gents, how many eggs in the bush?, hot cockles); (8) teasing activities (e.g., kick donkey kick, dummy parcels, teasing expressions); (9) parlor games (e.g., my Aunt Sally has gone to Paris, hide the thimble, queen of Sheba); and (10) games of skill (e.g., rounders, cricket, leapfrog). For each type of game described, an historical discussion is also offered of examples of games played between 1870 and 1920 and, then, 1920 and 1950. And finally, in a brief developmental synopsis, Sutton-Smith has presented an analysis of games in developmental terms. This necessitates dividing games into four different categories: (1) choral games, ages 6–9 (e.g., singing games); (2) central-person games, up to 11 years (e.g., dialogue games and leader games); (3) individual-skill games, beginning at age 11 (e.g., games of skill, marbles); and (4) team games, also beginning at age 11 or 12 (e.g., parlor games, games of skill, organized sports).

Sutton-Smith's first published study (1951a) was an attempt to examine the effects of European games on Maori children's unorganized games. Material was collected from correspondence and interviews with physical education teachers and other teachers in Maori schools and also former students of these schools. These reports indicated that a number of traditional Maori children's games were still being played. Examples of these games were hand games, knucklebones, stilts, whip tops, and string games. A number of more informal games had also persisted, such as vine swinging, hunting and fishing, sliding and sledging, throwing and skipping stones and pipi shells, slings, juggling, spears, skipping, sailing flax canoes, penny doctors, *putuputu*, *hotaka*, headstanding and acrobatics, swimming, mock fights, and racing. Sutton-Smith suggested that these game forms persisted because "the existence of the parallel games in European culture acted as a permissive factor on the same games in Maori culture" (p. 319). In conjunction with this idea, he also suggested that missionaries and other agents of culture change looked more leniently on "pastimes" that were seen as games of "civilized" as well as "heathen" children. To illustrate the fusion of the game traditions of both cultures, Sutton-Smith described the knucklebone game as played in the past by Maori children (relying here mainly on Best's 1925 account); the game as played by Europeans; and the game as it is now played by both Maori and Pakeha children.

A number of games introduced by Europeans were also played quite frequently by Maori children. These games were marbles, smoking, ball bouncing, stag knife, bow and arrows, shanghais, popguns, windmills and propellers, and ball hopscotch. Sutton-Smith also stated that the impact of European games on Maori games was not completely one-sided, for there were also reports of Pakeha children playing traditional Maori children's games (e.g., humming tops, team whip tops, building *raupo* huts, and sledging on cabbage tree leaves). In conclusion, Sutton-Smith suggested what might be seen as a revision of Newell's "diffusion law" by stating that

> in the meeting of these two cultures, there has been a tendency for the unique pastimes of the submerged culture to be cancelled out, and for the pastimes which both cultures shared to be strengthened. (p. 330)

However, he also found "a stronger tendency," which is that the influence of organized sport "has tended to cancel out all the minor games of both cultures irrespective of their nature" (p. 330).

In a more recent study with B. G. Rosenberg (1961), Sutton-Smith presented an analysis of patterns of change in the game preferences of American children. Here the authors compared the results of four large-scale studies of American children's play: (1) Crosswell (1898); (2) McGee (1900); (3) Terman (1926); and (4) Rosenberg and Sutton-Smith (1960). Each of these studies involved the use of questionnaires or checklists given to large numbers of school-aged children asking them about their game likes and dislikes. On the basis of this study, the authors reported a number of changes in game preferences over the 60-year time period covered by the investigation: (1) Games that are found to be less important to present-day children are singing games, dialogue games, team guessing and acting games, cooperative parlor games, couple and kissing games, all of which are generally girls' games and team games without role differentiation, which is a boys' game. (2) Games that were popular in the 1890s and are still popular today are imitative games, chasing games, and central-person games of low power. The authors also found that girls' responses had become more like boys' responses from 1896 to 1959. However, the findings indicated that boys' play roles were becoming increasingly circumscribed over this same time period so that it

> is much more deviant behavior for a modern boy to play at . . . dolls, hopscotch, jacks, horses, schools, cooking, jump rope, musical chairs, Simon Says and singing games than it was for a boy to play these things in the earlier historical periods. (Sutton-Smith and Rosenberg 1961:280)[12]

Finally, the authors suggested that the changes indicated by these studies "imply that the majority of children's formal games may themselves in due course become anachronistic" (p. 281). That is, children appear to be increasingly indicating preferences for informal, as opposed to formal, games. The authors suggested that this is so because formal games reflect "an earlier and more hierarchically arranged society," and the formalities that these games represent may have "become increasingly meaningless to new generations of children" (p. 281).

Other studies conducted by Sutton-Smith adopting an archival or text-collector approach are (1) a description of the New Zealand game "buck buck" (1951b); (2) a discussion of the fate of English traditional games in New Zealand (1952); (3) a brief description of the traditional games of New Zealand children (1953c); (4) a discussion of the game rhymes of New Zealand children (1953a); (5) a description of the "seasonal nature" of children's games, particularly marbles, in New Zealand (1953b); (6) a description of the kissing games of adolescents in Ohio (1959c); and (7) a discussion of the folk games of American children (1968). Many of these articles are reprinted in Sutton-Smith's *The Folk-Games of Children* (1972a).

DOROTHY HOWARD: AUSTRALIAN CHILDREN'S GAMES

Dorothy Mills Howard, an American folklorist and student of play, was sponsored by the University of Melbourne as a Fulbright Scholar at the age of 70 to collect examples of the games of Australian children. In this capacity, she produced a number of important descriptive articles reporting Australian white children's "hoppy" (or hopscotch) games (1958a), knucklebone games (1958b), ball-bouncing customs and rhymes (1959), the gambling device and game of toodlembuck (1960b), and marble games (1960a). Taken as a whole, her published studies represent one of the few explicit attempts available that record white Australian

---

[12]It would be extremely interesting to study American children's game preferences today, particularly to investigate whether boys' play roles and game preferences have become more or, with the effect of the women's movement, less circumscribed. See also Chapter Six for a discussion of play and sex roles.

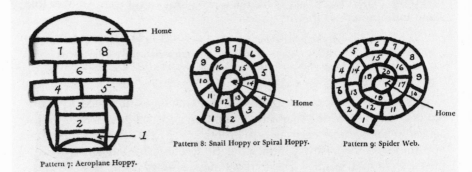

Pattern 7: Aeroplane Hoppy.

Pattern 8: Snail Hoppy or Spiral Hoppy.

Pattern 9: Spider Web.

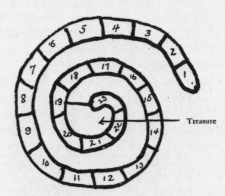

Pattern 10: Snake Hoppy—Version One.

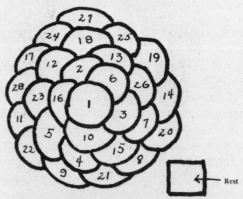

Pattern 11: Circle Hoppy or Circular Hoppy.

FIGURE 9. Australian "hoppy." (D. Howard, 1958a:173)

children's traditional games, to be compared with Roth's (1902) early description of aborigine games.

Howard collected her material in 1954–1955 in a number of ways: (1) observations of children playing (and also participation in games with them) on school and public playgrounds, streets, beaches, etc.; (2) written compositions from children; (3) written reports from schoolteachers, psychologists, etc.; (4) visits to toy shops; (5) library research; and (6) publicity in newspapers and magazines and on the radio. Her approach was as a collector of game texts, and her classification of these texts was by variation of patterns of play in particular types of games. For example, she described and illustrated by drawings approximately 26 different versions of the Australian children's game of "hoppy" (e.g., aeroplane hoppy, apple hoppy, base hoppy, circle hoppy, devil hoppy, horseshoe hoppy, river hoppy, ship hoppy, snake hoppy, square hoppy). Figure 9 depicts five of these illustrations. In describing each particular variation, she noted "individuals" who reported the game to her, where it was played, and the date of the collection.

IONA AND PETER OPIE: ENGLISH CHILDREN'S GAMES AND RHYMES

At present, the major collectors of English-speaking children's games are Iona and Peter Opie. Following in the tradition of Lady A. B. Gomme, the Opies have published two major collections of childlore. The first, *The Lore and Language of School Children* (1959), is a major compilation of English schoolchildren's speech play, including discussions of riddles, rhymes, chants, nicknames, and satire. The study is based on material collected from over 5,000 children attending 70 schools (in both rural and city areas) in different parts of England, Scotland, and Wales and also one school in Dublin. The authors' stated interest in their research is to provide information *not* on adult rhymes (e.g., nursery rhymes), which pass from mother to child, but on child lore and child rhymes, which circulate "from child to child, usually outside the home, and beyond the influence of the family circle" (p. 1). The view of the child as primitive is again apparent in the Opies' study. For example, they suggested that

> the folklorist and anthropologist can, without travelling a mile from his door, examine a thriving unselfconscious culture (the word "culture" is used here deliberately) which is as unnoticed by the sophisticated world, and quite as little affected by it, as is the culture of some dwindling aboriginal tribe living out its helpless existence in the hinterland of a native reserve. . . . No matter how uncouth schoolchildren may outwardly appear, they remain tradition's warmest friends. Like the savage, they are respecters, even venerators, of

custom; and in their selfcontained community their basic lore and language seems scarcely to alter from generation to generation. (p. 2)

In contrast to earlier researchers (e.g., Newell), the Opies have suggested that children's customs, unlike "primitive" societies' practices, are likely to remain in tact for a very long time. Emphasis is given in this report to the uniformity of children's lore as it is found in various regions and counties, "from country to city" and "from mining community to garden suburb" (p. 3). However, variations in traditional rhymes do exist, and these are traced both historically and geographically. One interesting example of the historical development of a playground rhyme is offered in the section entitled "Wear and Repair during Transmission." Twelve different versions of this rhyme are presented for the time period 1725–1954, showing how a play text adapts to the social context (pp. 10–11). Only two of these examples appear here:

1725

> Now he acts the Grenadier
> Calling for a Pot of Beer.
> Where's his Money? He's forgot.
> Get him gone, a Drunken Sot.
> 　　　Lines from Henry Carey's ballad "Namby Pamby"

1954

> I had a little beer shop.
> A man walked in,
> I asked him what he wanted.
> A bottle of gin.
> Where's your money?
> In my pocket.
> Where's your pocket?
> I forgot it.
> Please walk out.
> 　　　Used for skipping in York City (pp. 10–11)

Distinct differences are particularly found in the location and stability of "slangy lore" as opposed to "dialectal lore." The former consists of comic songs, jokes, catch phrases, fashionable adjectives, slick nicknames, and crazes that spread everywhere but enjoy only a brief existence. The latter comprises "language which children use to regulate their relationships with each other, such as their terms for claiming, securing precedence, and making a truce," or for "playing truant, giving warning, sneaking, swearing, snivelling, tormenting and fighting" (pp. 14–15). These terms are generally limited to very specific localities; however, in these areas, they have had a very prolonged existence.

The material in this study is classified according to specific features that characterize the particular rhymes or terms. There are chapters discussing satirical rhymes, nonsense rhymes, tangle talk, puns, tongue twisters, ghoulism, spookies, and Scout and Guide songs. Other chapters include descriptions of: street jeers; crooked answers; tricks; spitting jokes; bets; trick spelling and arithmetic; rhyming, punning, catch riddles, and conundrums; parodies of hymns and carols, nursery rhymes, and popular songs, etc.; topical rhymes (e.g., World War II victory songs, songs of legendary heroes, and Charlie Chaplin, Shirley Temple, Mickey Mouse, and Popeye rhymes); truthfulness tests; bargain making and legislation; secret keeping; nicknames and epithets (e.g., Fatties, Skinnies, Redheads, Spectacles, etc.); jeers and torments; omens and superstitions (e.g., lines on pavements, finding things, luck in exams or games); customs regarding the making and breaking of friends; songs and rhymes about authority figures (e.g., teachers, police); and pranks (e.g., door knocking, bell ringing, booby traps, window tapping).

The Opies' second major collection is entitled *Children's Games in Street and Playground* (1969). Material was collected for this volume in a similar manner to the 1959 study; however, as the title suggests, the play life of children living in cities is emphasized. In their preface, the authors noted the pioneering work of Strutt (1801), Gomme (1894, 1898), and Newell (1883, expanded 1903). The Opies suggested that one problem with these investigators is their desire to study games as "relics of antiquity" or "as if they were archaeological remains, rather than living organisms which are constantly evolving, adapting to new situations, and renewing themselves or being replaced" (p. vii). This work is an attempt by the authors to counter these tendencies by presenting a description of children's (ages 6–12) present-day games, which they "play of their own accord when out of doors, and generally out of sight" (p. v). Additionally, the Opies were motivated to conduct this research in order to dispel the presumption that present-day children

> have few diversions of their own, that they are incapable of self-organization,
> have become addicted to spectator amusements, and will languish if left to
> rely on their own resources. (p. v)

In organizing their material, the authors utilized the now-familiar classification by structural features of games. The "sporting" features of game preliminaries are outlined in detail (e.g., selection by chance, odd man out, dipping, Chinese counting, counting fists or feet) in the first chapter. The remaining chapters discuss (1) *chasing games*, where the similar feature is that "a player tries to touch others who are running freely in a prescribed area" (e.g., touch, bull, wacko, Tom Tiddler's ground, help chase, poison, cat and mouse, blind man's bluff); (2) *catching games*, "in which a player attempts to intercept other players who are obliged to move from one designated place to another . . . , and who if caught either take the catcher's place or, more often, assist him" (e.g., Chinese wall, stag, bar the door, British bulldog, prisoner's base); (3) *seeking games*, "in which a player tries to find others, who obtain safety by remaining out of sight or by getting back to the starting place" (e.g., hide-and-seek, one man plus, sardines, come to Coventry, whip relievo, gee); (4) *hunting games*, "in which there are no boundaries, in which both pursuers and pursued generally operate in teams, and in which the pursued generally have to give some assistance to their pursuer" (e.g., hare and hounds, tracking, paper chase); (5) *racing games*, which are "races, and chases over set courses, in which fleetness of foot is not necessarily the decisive factor" (e.g., may I?, aunts and uncles, letters, colors, black magic, time, drop handkerchief, puss in the corner); (6) *dueling games*, "in which two players place themselves in direct conflict with each other" (e.g., elbows, branch boy, piggyback fights, danger ride, knifie, knuckles, stinging, soldiers, lolly sticks, conkers); (7) *exerting games*, "in which the qualities of most account are physical strength and stamina" (e.g., tug-of-war, bull in the ring, red rover, statues, leapfrog, jumping games); (8) *daring games*, "in which players incite each other to show their mettle" (e.g., follow my leader, get the coward, chicken); (9) *guessing games*, "in which guessing is a necessary prelude or climax to physical action" (e.g., birds, beasts, fishes or flowers; three jolly workmen; Queenie; how far to London?); (10) *acting games*, "in which particular stories are enacted with set dialogue" (e.g., ghosties in the garret; Old Mother Grey; fox and chickens; Mother, the cake is burning); (11) *pretending games*, in which "children make-believe they are other people, or in other situations, and extemporize accordingly" (e.g., mothers and fathers, playing schools, road accidents, playing horses, war games, cops and robbers, fairies and witches).

In Figure 10 the game fox and chickens (also fox and geese, hen and chickens, wolf and sheep) is depicted. This game is classified by the Opies as an "acting game" because of the chants and questions that traditionally accompany the game, making it into a type of playlet or drama. The Opies indicated that "catching is an integral part of the game," and they also stated that "except in places where the words have been passed on by an adult, the drama is becoming a speechless shadow of its former self" (p. 310). As it is currently played, one child acts as "fox," and another as the "hen," while the rest of the players are the hen's brood. The chickens run in a line behind the hen, holding onto each other's waists or clothes, and the fox tries to catch the last chicken in line. The hen, with the chickens behind her, attempts to thwart the fox by swinging around to block him and holding out her hands ("wings") to prevent him from catching the last chicken. When the fox

FIGURE 10. English children playing fox and chickens (Photo by A. D. Webb, from *Children's Games in Street and Playground,* 1969, by I. and P. Opie, published by Oxford University Press).

does touch the last person in line, that person becomes the fox. In the photograph, the "fox" has dodged past the "mother hen" and is moving toward the last "chicken."

FAVORITE COLLECTORS' ITEMS

Researchers in the archival tradition have often concentrated on the collection of specific types of children's games or rhymes. One of the most recent studies of this sort is Abrahams's (1969) collection of English-speaking (particularly American) children's jump rope rhymes. This particular game has undergone an interesting sex change, as reported by Abrahams, for until relatively recently, it was exclusively a boys' activity and did not have rhymed games associated with it (p. xv). Now, however, jump rope is a girls' game with an elaboration of rhymes and jumping techniques. Jump rope is also reported to be an urban phenomenon for the most part. In this study, Abrahams presented a brief review of the literature available on jump rope rhymes with a specific discussion of various attempts to categorize this activity (e.g., classification by style of jumping; position, action, or number of ropes; pattern or purpose of accompanying verse). Abrahams, however, chose to present his information in dictionary form (similar to Gomme's) noting literature sources and geographic locations below each rhyme. Examples of other studies and/or descriptions of jump rope rhymes are available by Babcock (1888), Douglas (1916), Hall (1941), Britt and Balcom (1941), Sonnenberg (1955), Browne (1955), Goldings (1974), I. and P. Opie (1959), Pinon (1965), Hawthorne (1966), and Buckley (1966).

There are several examples of other games and rhymes that have become favorite "collectors' items." Many early diffusionists and particularists considered string figures to be useful culture "traits" for description and examination. According to Haddon (in Jayne, 1906:xi), Boas (1888) published the first description of string figures employed by a "primitive" group (in this case, the Eskimos of Baffinland and Hudson Bay). The most extensive comparative analysis of string-figure games is Caroline F. Jayne's *String Figures: A Study of Cat's Cradle in Many Lands* (1906). There are many other descriptions of this play form in the literature (e.g., Roth, 1902; A. C. Haddon, 1903; K. Haddon, 1917–1918; Emerson, 1927; Brewster, 1953; Maude, 1958). Counting-out rhymes for games (e.g., "eeny, meeny, miney, mo") have also been singled out for special collections and analyses (e.g., Bolton, 1888; Monroe, 1904; Goldstein, 1971). Other games receiving attention are hopscotch, said to be a representation of the progress of the soul from earth to heaven (e.g., Crombie, 1886; Brewster, 1945b; Howard, 1958a); marbles (Piaget, 1932; Howard, 1960a; Sutton-Smith, 1953b); play party games and songs (e.g., Payne, 1916; Randolf, 1929; Brewster, 1939; Hall, 1941; Wolford, 1916); and, of course, song games in general (e.g., Newell, 1883/1903, 1906; Ford, 1904; Gomme and Scarp, 1909; Cox, 1942). Significant collections and descriptions of children's play organized according to geographic/culture areas are presented in detail in Chapter Three.

SUMMARY

Responding in part to the armchair-based theories of the evolutionists, students of children's play in the late 19th and early 20th centuries began to emphasize the need for careful, detailed, and sensitive collections of game texts (e.g., Newell). These studies were also motivated by the desire of researchers to preserve these childhood "customs," which many thought were soon to vanish. Therefore, compilations were produced that treated games as if they were "ancient relics" or "archaeological remains" requiring pickling and preservation. If analysis of these texts was undertaken at all, it generally consisted of interpretations of games as survivals (e.g., Gomme, Brewster), reinforced by a view of the child as primitive, or as illustrations of particular patterns of diffusion (e.g., Tylor, Newell, Brewster). These latter interpretations were often made in order to illustrate the notion that games were universal features of all cultures due either to constant and criss-crossing diffusion or the psychic unity of mankind and the conservatism of all children.

The approach of the particularists and diffusionists encouraged investigators to view the study of children's play as the study solely of children's formalized and structured games and/or rhymes. This orientation was also promoted by the tendency, at this time, for ethnographers to concentrate on descriptions of spectacular, conspicuous, and ritualized events. Games were seen as the most obvious form of play, and so anthropologists and others began to search for ways to learn about the "pure" (i.e., nonacculturated) games of a society's past. This tendency affected the study of children's play by encouraging researchers to use adults, as opposed to children, as informants, urging them to reminisce about (or "re-collect") the games of their past (e.g., Dorsey, 1891; Pukui, 1943; Stearns, 1890). Unfortunately, in utilizing this approach, researchers often ignored the present-day activities of children, which were likely to include variations on traditional, or possibly innovative, games created in response to new physical and/or social environments. These games could have been viewed as comments on both traditional and Western culture.

Finally, game collectors faced with the diversity and quantity of their "data" (i.e., texts) generally sought to categorize this material in some fashion. For the most part, researchers imposed their own classification schemata on these texts, categorizing them on the basis of selected structural criteria focusing on one or another feature of the game (e.g., chasing games versus hiding games; ball games versus string figures). Table 1 may be consulted for a summary presentation of significant collectors' works in regard to geographic area of research, type of informants utilized, and classification schema employed.

Particularist and diffusionist studies of children's play are characterized by their focus on the *preservation of game texts*. Attention to the *contextual* character of play (e.g., how frequently it is played, who does and does not play it, age and sex of players, why it is played, what the players think about the game, how it relates to the cultural context) is seldom evident except for brief notes occasionally describing the region in which the game was reported and perhaps the date of the collection.

TABLE 1

Collections and Classifications, 1880–1970

Author	Date	Geographic culture area	Source	Classification system
Newell	1883, expanded 1903	United States—general	Teachers' reports; children's reports; historical texts.	Structural features of game texts (e.g., love games, humor and satire).
Babcock	1888	United States—Washington, D.C.	Observations of children.	Structural features of game texts (e.g., ring games, archway games).
Dorsey	1891	North American Indians—Teton Dakota	Dakota Indian informant.	Division according to sex of player and season in which game was played (e.g., "little girls'" game—summer).
Culin	1891	United States—Brooklyn, N.Y.	Ten-year-old Brooklyn male informant.	Structural features of game texts (e.g., games of tag, games of pursuit).
Gomme	1894, 1898	England, Scotland, Ireland	Teachers' reports; individual game collectors' reports.	Alphabetical.
Roth	1902	Australia—north Queensland aborigine	Adult and children's reports and observations of children and published accounts.	Structural features of game texts (e.g., imaginative games, imitative games).
Culin	1907	North American Indians	Museum collections; published accounts.	All children's games classified as one type: "games of dexterity," listing by culture area.

Author	Date	Location/Group	Sources	Focus
Best	1925	New Zealand—Maori	Museum collections; published accounts; observations of children.	Structural features of game texts (e.g., aquatic games, games requiring agility or manual dexterity).
Mills (Howard)	1944	United States—Maryland	Teachers' reports; individual game collectors' reports; children's reports; observations of children.	Structural features of game texts (e.g., ball games, hiding games).
Brewster	1952	United States—rural North Carolina	Frank C. Brown game collection, including teachers', children's, and individual game collectors' reports.	Structural features of game texts (e.g., jumping games, battle games).
Brewster	1953	United States—general	Reports from university students, friends; individual game collectors' reports; published accounts.	Only nonsinging games and, within this category, structural features of game texts (e.g., guessing games, forfeit games).
Sebeok and Brewster	1958	Uralic-Cheremis	Reports from a university student informant and game collector's reports; published accounts.	Structural features of game texts (e.g., "it" games, team play).
Howard	1958,a,b 1959 1960,a,b	Australian white children	Interviews with adults; university students', teachers', and children's reports; observations of children; published accounts.	Structural features of game texts (e.g., marble games, hopscotch games).
Sutton-Smith	1959	New Zealand—*Pakeha* children	Interviews with adults; university students, education teachers' reports; children's written reports; observations of children.	Structural features of game texts and developmental criteria (e.g., age and sex of players).

TABLE 1 (*continued*)

Author	Date	Geographic culture area	Source	Classification system
I. and P. Opie	1959	England, Scotland, Wales, Dublin	Teachers', children's reports; individual game collectors' reports; observation of children.	Structural features of game texts (e.g., riddles, parody, jeers).
I. and P. Opie	1969	England, Scotland, Wales, Dublin	Teachers', children's reports; individual game collectors' reports; observation of children; historical analysis of books on children's games written for children.	Structural features of game texts (e.g., chasing games, catching games).
Abrahams	1969	United States—general	University students' reports; individual collectors' reports; published accounts.	Alphabetical.

Nevertheless, these studies are important in the general history of research on children's play and, specifically, in the history of anthropological studies of this activity. This is particularly true because these investigators persevered and often excelled in their preservations during an era when most researchers would have nothing to do with a topic so obviously inconsequential as that of children's play.

CHAPTER SIX

Socializing Play: Functional Analysis

"Kitty, dear, let's pretend ————." And here I wish I could tell you half the things Alice used to say, beginning with her favourite phrase "Let's pretend." She had had quite a long argument with her sister only the day before—all because Alice had begun with "Let's pretend we're kings and queens"; and her sister, who liked being very exact, had argued that they couldn't because there were only two of them, and Alice had been reduced to say "Well, you can be one of them, then, and I'll be all the rest."

Lewis Carroll, *Through the Looking Glass, and What Alice Found There*

Beginning in the early 1920s a number of anthropologists began to indicate their disenchantment with the atheoretical approach of the historical particularists and diffusionists. Two of the most prominent critics in this regard were A. R. Radcliffe-Brown, a British anthropologist trained at Cambridge, and Bronisław Malinowski, a Pole who studied anthropology at the London School of Economics. Together these two men were responsible for formulating what was to become known as the functional approach in anthropology.

A. R. RADCLIFFE-BROWN AND BRONISŁAW MALINOWSKI

In reacting to what they considered to be the overly inductive approach of many of their predecessors, Radcliffe-Brown and Malinowski argued "that anthropology should be a science, that it should not be history," and that, to be a science, it must be deductive and begin to search for generalizations or laws of social behavior (Langness, 1974:74, 82). In arguing against the trait-list approach of the historical particularists, they presented the idea that cultures or social systems must be studied as wholes, not as separate and disconnected traits or parts. Society, in their view, could be conceptualized as a biological organism; however, Radcliffe-Brown and Malinowski were attracted to this analogy for very different reasons than the early evolutionists, who used it to formulate stages of cultural growth. In contrast, functionalists (see particularly Radcliffe-Brown, 1952:188–204) used the organismic metaphor as a way to describe the stability and consistency, as opposed to change and development, of social systems as cultures. In this way Radcliffe-Brown and Malinowski suggested that the parts or *structures* of any whole (e.g., an organism or a culture) had to *function* for the "maintenance," "unity," "harmony," "consistency," or "solidarity" of the whole. The goal of functional analysis was, therefore, to explain how it is that structural systems maintain *sameness*.

In formulating and accepting the basic premises of functionalism, Radcliffe-Brown and Malinowski presented two quite different orientations to the actual practice of functional analysis. Radcliffe-Brown's approach is generally referred to as *structural-functionalism* and is characterized by the study of social structures as sets of relationships that can be discovered "between acts of diverse individuals" and *not* within the "mind" or in the "acts of behavior of one and the same individual" (Radcliffe-Brown, 1957:45–46). Radcliffe-Brown believed that this latter focus was the province of the psychologist, not the anthropologist.

The approach of Malinowski, however, was quite the opposite of his contemporary's, particularly in regard to his emphasis on the combined study of psychological, biological, and social needs. Malinowski emphasized, in his "pure functionalism" (now sometimes called *psychological functionalism*), that culture was the instrument through which man's needs were met. According to Malinowski, individuals had seven "basic needs": reproduction, bodily comforts, safety, relaxation, movement, growth, and health (1944:91). These needs were satisfied by various cultural responses (e.g., marriage and family systems were direct responses to the reproductive need). Malinowski differed most strongly with Radcliffe-Brown in his insistence that these were individual, not group, needs, therefore bringing in the taboo topic of individual psychology.

FUNCTIONALISTS AND PLAY

Faced with the spontaneous, seemingly useless, and often deviant nature of play, functionalists might well despair. However, one of the earliest interpretations of play is Groos's (1898, 1901) *practice theory,* which in essence is a functional explanation of this activity. It was Groos's suggestion that play allowed "animals" and "man" to practice or rehearse the daily activities of their present (not past) life. This view of play as practice or rehearsal for adult activities has since become one of the most commonly accepted explanations available in the literature (Loizos, 1967:236).

An early application of functional analysis to the topic of children's play is available in George Herbert Mead's classic study *Mind, Self and Society* (1932). In this work, Mead paid particular attention to the development of language, play, and games in children. Play and game activities are clearly differentiated here as they are thought to have distinct functions in relation to the development of the child's sense of self. According to Mead, "ordinary play" (e.g., playing Indians) allows the child to imagine himself in various social roles and, by so doing, to "build up" his own character. In order to play games, however, the child must be able "to take the attitude of everyone else involved" and to see that "these different roles must have a definite relationship to each other" (p. 151). For example, in the game of baseball, the child must know his own role in the game (e.g., as a catcher) and must also be able to take the role of others (e.g., the pitcher) by being willing to risk his own identity for the sake of the "generalized other" (e.g., the team). In Mead's view, once the child is able to take the attitude of the other, he/she is on the way to "becoming an organic member of society" (p. 159).

The most common expression of this approach in the anthropological literature appears in descriptions of play as imitative or preparatory activity and, therefore, functional as an enculturative mechanism. Malinowski illustrated this perspective by contending that play should be studied in terms of its educational value and in relation to its "function as preparation for economic skills" (1944:107). He also suggested that peer play groups perform a socializing function in meeting the "growth needs" of individuals:

> The foundations of all synthetic knowledge, the first elements, that is, of the scientific outlook, the appreciation of custom, authority, and ethics, are received within the family. Later on, the growing child enters the group of his playmates, where, once more, he is dulled towards conformity, obedience to custom and etiquette. (1944:107–108)

Adopting this perspective, the seemingly nonpurposeful actions of children's play, particularly their make-believe or sociodramatic play, are transformed into activities functional for the maintenance (i.e., "unity," "harmony," "consistency," and "solidarity") and perpetuation of the social order.

Radcliffe-Brown paid little attention to the play of children in his studies, and there are almost no reports of this activity in his ethnographies. As he was adamant about the fact that the study of individual psychological processes was not an appropriate topic for anthropological analysis, this neglect is perhaps understandable. Radcliffe-Brown (1952) did, however, develop an interest in at least one adult play form: the joking relationship. He believed that this activity functioned to channel, ritualize, and, therefore, neutralize hostile feelings in social systems. And this is now a standard explanation for the function of adult "expressive" behavior in culture.[1]

Functional explanations of children's play most commonly employ the play-as-imitation/preparation metaphor. Malinowski used this perspective in both his theoretical and his ethnographic works, but he was certainly not unique in this regard. The assumption that children's play is always based on imitation of adult activities and, therefore, either implicitly or explicitly functional as a socializing activity is far and away the most common anthropological interpretation of this behavior (see Schwartzman and Barbera, 1976). Turnbull's description of the play of Mbuti Pygmy children is quite typical:

> Like children everywhere, Pygmy children love to imitate their adult idols. . . . at an early age boys and girls are "playing house" or "playing hunting." . . . And one day they find that the games they have been playing are not games any longer, but the real thing for they have become adults. (1961:129)

Edel's (1957) description of children's play for the Chiga of western Uganda also expresses this theme:

> Playing with a small gourd, a child learns to balance it on his head, and is applauded when he goes to the watering place with the other children and brings it back with little water in it. As he learns, he carries an increasing load, and gradually the play activity turns into a general contribution to the household water supply. (pp. 176–177)

And Kenyatta illustrated this emphasis on imitation and preparation in his discussion of Kikuyu children's play. He stated that

> children do most things in imitation of their elders and illustrate in a striking way the theory that play is anticipatory of adult life. Their games are, in fact, nothing more or less than a rehearsal prior to the performance of the activities which are the serious business of all members of the Gikuyu tribe. (1939:101)

[1]The idea that children's play serves an expressive and cathartic function for individuals and society was developed much more thoroughly by psychoanalytic and psychological researchers. The effect of this view on anthropological studies is discussed in Chapter Seven.

These descriptions portray the major themes evident in functional discussions. Children's play is simple imitation, therefore, because it is "simple" and because it is "mere imitation," it can be quickly dismissed with a few short descriptions. Play "works" because it serves an obvious socialization function for society. The possibility that these activities were not as simple nor as imitative as they appeared to be was, for the most part, not considered by these researchers.

Functionalism reigned between the 1930s and the 1950s in anthropology, and during these years, the study of children's play advanced little beyond statements such as those appearing in the above quotations. It is probably true that Radcliffe-Brown's antipsychological stance contributed to this neglect, along with the fact that most young anthropology students at this time were attracted to the structural functionalism of Radcliffe-Brown and not to the psychological functionalism of Malinowski (see Langness, 1974:79). Functionalists examined only "serious" social structures (e.g., kinship and political systems) and, for the most part, neglected the study of play and games. Even with the recent resurgence of interest in the "psychological" topic of socialization evidenced by British social anthropologists (e.g., Mayer, 1970), there is little indication that the study of play is considered an important research field by these authors. In Mayer's (1970) collection of papers, there is only brief mention of play and games in the article written by P. and I. Mayer (pp. 159–189), discussing the youth organization of the Red Xhosa, and a specific consideration by Loudan (pp. 203–332) of teasing and ridicule as socialization techniques utilized on the island of Tristan da Cunha.

One important exception to this history of neglect is presented by one of Radcliffe-Brown's most famous students: Meyer Fortes. Fortes's study of "Social and Psychological Aspects of Education in Taleland" (1938) includes one of the most significant and insightful investigations of children's play available in the ethnographic literature. This article also includes one of the few early critiques of the play-as-imitation metaphor utilized by most ethnographers at this time. Play, according to Fortes, "is the paramount educational exercise of Tale children" (p. 44). *It is never, however, simple and mechanical reproduction of adult activities:*

> In his play the child rehearses his interests, skills, and obligations, and makes experiments in social living without having to pay the penalty for mistakes. Hence there is already a phase of play in the evolution of any schema preceding its full emergence into practical life. Play, therefore, is often mimetic in content and expresses the child's identifications. But the Tale child's play mimesis is never simple and mechanical reproduction; it is always imaginative construction based on the themes of adult life and of the life of older children. He or she adapts natural objects and other materials, often with great ingenuity, which never occur in the adult activities copied, and rear-

ranges adult functions to fit the specific logical and affective configuration of play. (pp. 58–59)

In this paper, Fortes also specifically recognized the need for anthropologists and others to rethink their view of imitative learning:

> Writers on primitive education have often attributed an almost mystical significance to "imitation" as the principle method by which a child learns. The Tallensi themselves declare that children learn by "looking and doing," but neither "imitation" nor the formula used by the Tallensi help us to understand the actually observable process. Tale children do not automatically copy the actions of older children or adults with whom they happen to be without rhyme or reason and merely for the sake of "imitation." (p. 54)

In describing a typical play situation (pp. 59–61) for the Tallensi children of Ghana, Fortes illustrated the complex nature of this activity and the way that "recreational and imaginative play are interwoven with practical activities," as well as the moment-to-moment changes in a child's interests in specific types of play. The episode that he described lasted for 30 minutes and involved four children: Gɔmna (male, 7 years), his half-sister Zɔŋ (female, 6 years), his friend Zoo (male, 7 years), and Tɔŋ (male, 10 years). The event began with the first three children scaring birds from their parents' grain fields. Soon Gɔmna located three locusts and described them to Zɔŋ and Zoo by saying, "These are our cows, let's build a yard for them." Immediately the children began to build a yard out of pieces of decayed bark, with Gɔmna giving orders while all three maintained a running verbal commentary about their activities. Tɔŋ helped Gɔmna build and roof the yard, and then Gɔmna pushed the "cows" in and declared, "We must build a gateway." Two large pebbles were found and set up as gateposts, and then an argument ensued about how they should stand. At this point, the structure collapsed, and Tɔŋ began to build it again. Meanwhile Zɔŋ found a pair of stones and a potsherd and began "grinding grain." Suddenly Gɔmna and Zoo ran after birds to scare them and then returned to the "cattle yard" discussing wrestling. Tɔŋ was called away, and Zɔŋ finished her "grinding" and brought "flour" to the two boys, saying, "Let's sacrifice to our shrine." Gɔmna said, "Let Zoo do it," but Zoo said that Gɔmna was senior to him, and they then began to argue about who, in fact, was senior. Eventually Gɔmna declared, "I'm the senior." Zɔŋ put down her "flour" and forgot about it, and then Zoo challenged Gɔmna's assertion. However, Gɔmna reacted by saying that he had to be senior because he could throw Zoo in wrestling, which Zoo denied. Soon the two boys were wrestling with one another, and Gɔmna managed to throw Zoo, but they both stood up and were still friends. At this point, Gɔmna climbed up on a baobab branch, followed by Zoo, who said, "Let's swing." They swung for a few minutes, and then Gɔmna remembered the "cows." He accused Zɔŋ of having taken them, but she denied this, at which point he challenged her to "swear" to this. She agreed to do so, and he took a pinch of sand in his left hand and put his right thumb on it. Zɔŋ licked her thumb and pressed down with it on Gɔmna's thumbnail. He stood still for a minute and then quickly withdrew his thumb. (Fortes stated that this is a children's play ordeal.) Gɔmna examined Zɔŋ's thumb and found sand adhering, and he said, "There you are"; and he then rapped her on the head with a crooked finger. The "cows" were forgotten again, and they began to ask Fortes questions. After this, Gɔmna, who had been looking at Fortes's shoes, said, "Let's make shoes"; and he took a few pieces of bark (formerly used for the cattle yard) and proceeded to make shoes. He and Zɔŋ found some grass and string and tried to tie the pieces of bark onto the soles of their feet. Gɔmna now noticed his "cows" and began to move them about. He said, "I'm going to let them copulate," and he tried to put one locust on top of the other. Suddenly he looked up and noticed birds in the field and cried to Zɔŋ, "Scare the birds!" All three children ran after the birds into the grain field and spent the next five minutes shouting at the birds and throwing handfuls of gravel at them.

Along with presenting this unique and lengthy description of Tallensi children's play, Fortes also offered a detailed discussion of the developmental phases of these children's play behavior. Here he described the play of boys and girls at various ages, concurrent with a discussion of the children's expected economic duties and activities (a chart that summarizes these play phases appears at the conclusion of this article). For example, Tallensi boys between the ages of 3 and 6 initially have no economic duties to perform; however, as they get older (e.g., 5–6), they begin to assist in pegging-out goats and in scaring birds from newly sown fields and from crops (as Gɔmna, Zɔŋ, Zoo, and Tɔŋ did). The play of boys of this age consists at first of "motor and exploratory play"; later they use "mimetic toys" (e.g., bows and drums) in "egocentric" play; and then they begin to engage in social and imaginative play at "cattle" and "house-building" activities, often playing with older children of either sex (p. 72).

Another relatively early critique of the simple imitation view of play appears in Otto Raum's well-known study of *Chaga Childhood* (1940). Raum, whose father spent 40 years working with the Chaga as a missionary, was born and raised in Tanzania and developed an intimate knowledge of this group, which he reported both skillfully and sensitively as an educator and a scholar. In *Chaga Childhood*, Raum presented an extensive account of this group's socialization patterns and included a lengthy discussion and description of children's games, in which the "representative" (as opposed to strictly "imitative") quality of these activities is stressed. In this regard, Raum suggested the following:

> The essential feature of "imitative" play is . . . make-believe, the tendency of the child to construct an imaginary adult society from the scraps he is allowed to know about it. . . . In the majority of cases, the themes of "imitative" play are not immediately suggested by events in adult life at all. Rather, the choice of subject and its development are a result of the child's independent and spontaneous action. (p. 256)

Furthermore, Raum argued that so-called childish imitativeness is directed not so much "to making the copy exact, but towards caricaturing the pattern" (p. 257). This interest in caricature is revealed, Raum suggested, when one looks closely at the selection process used by children in their presumably "imitative" representations. In these events, the process "tends more and more to stress aspects which make adults appear to be ridiculous" (p. 257).

This view of play as caricature or as satire is discussed in more detail in a later section of this chapter; however, Raum presented an amusing series of examples of Chaga children "imitating" (but actually caricaturing) "the white man" and his institutions, which are described briefly here. A popular play theme for Chaga children is said to be "school and teacher," where the teacher's obsession (to the Chaga) with time is symbolized by placing "a great clock of sand in front of the make-believe school" (p. 258). Likewise, the emphasis on memorization and recitation of literature is parodied by children reading from "books" of vegetable leaves in the monotonous tone of the teacher. The sermons of missionaries are also satirized by exaggerating the linquistic mistakes and mannerisms of the minister, which are said to cause "uproarious applause" from the "congregation." Baptism ceremonies are also favorite events for caricature, as the "minister" is able to sprinkle

> his converts with water according to their deserts, while in the choice of names he selects characteristic ones, such as "Lover-of-Food," "Stupid," "Dwarf," and "Bully." (p. 258)

Raum delineated three different types of play activities: the playful exercise of sensory and motor activities (see pp. 140–146); representative play (see pp. 250–264); and competitive games (see pp. 264–272). Raum also discussed the "culture" or social system of play groups, emphasizing how these groups develop leaders (pp. 273–274, 277–278); allocate resources (pp. 275–277); expel "cheaters" (see his discussion of children's ordeals, pp. 278–279); create secret languages ("speech perversions," pp. 280–282); and invent new games and/or "toy" objects (pp. 283–284). Raum specifically emphasized the ingenious nature of many of these inventions. He cited examples of Chaga children's inventions of "bicycles," "carts," "cars," and a particularly creative "machine gun." This was produced by making 12 shallow cuts into the midrib of a banana leaf. These "tongues" would be cocked, "and when the hand passed over them they fell back, each producing a report" (pp. 284 ff.).

Recent attempts to explore the idea that play functions both to socialize and to enculturate children have been made by Langsley (1967), Eifermann (1970), Salter (1974), and Lancy (1974, 1975, 1976 a,b).[2]

SOCIALIZING PLAY: THE KIBBUTZ

Rivka Eifermann (1970) used information collected in her large-scale quantitative study of Israeli children's play to investigate whether the life of the kibbutzim, with its stress on cooperation, the achievement of common aims, and egalitarianism, is expressed in kibbutz children's games. In formulating this study, she devised a classification scheme of collected games based on guidelines related to (1) competitiveness; (2) grouping in the game; and (3) symmetrical or nonsymmetrical relationship of players. On the basis of this classification, eight categories of games are considered in the study: (1) single-party games (e.g., "feet canon," in which "two players who face each other skip in different styles, but in rhythm, aiming to reach in harmony a predetermined number of skips"); (2) symmetrical single-party games (e.g., "head ball," in which "a ball is kept from falling to the ground by the cooperative efforts of all players who bounce it off their heads for as long as they can"); (3) singletons (e.g., "Dutch rope," in which "two players stretch an elastic band between their legs, while others jump within it; failure of a jumper leads to an exchange of places with one of the holders"); (4) singletons, with (roughly) interchangeable roles (e.g., variants of hopscotch, chess); (5) singletons versus many (two or more) singletons (e.g., simple tag, hide-and-seek); (6) singletons with overprivileged and/or underprivileged singleton(s) (e.g., jump rope "with a leader who calls out the jumping rhymes and participates in the jumping herself"); (7) two groups (e.g., soccer, basketball); and (8) two intrasymmetrical groups (e.g., cops and robbers, tug-of-war) (pp. 580–581).

Eifermann formulated two major hypotheses utilizing this classifica-

[2]The terms *socialization* and *enculturation* have been variously defined. For example, Margaret Mead defined *socialization* "as the set of species wide requirements and exactions made on human beings by human societies" and *enculturation* as "the process of learning a culture in all its uniqueness and particularity" (1963:187). It is, however, extremely difficult to consider these two processes separately in discussing a topic such as play, and so I have chosen to use the term *socialization* to refer to both processes.

tion scheme for this study: (1) "Since kibbutz children are raised in the spirit of cooperation with the other members of the kibbutz, their games tend to be of less competitive types"; and (2) "Since kibbutz children are raised in the spirit of egalitarianism—one child, one vote in their societies—their games tend to be of the more symmetrical types" (p. 581). On the basis of the first hypothesis, it was expected that more kibbutz than nonkibbutz players would participate in (1) single-party games and (2) two-group games. Furthermore, it was expected that fewer kibbutz than nonkibbutz players would participate in singleton games. On the basis of the second hypothesis, it was expected that more kibbutz than nonkibbutz players would participate in (1) symmetrical single-party games; (2) singleton games with interchangeable roles; and (3) games of two intrasymmetrical groups. And it was also expected that fewer kibbutz than nonkibbutz players would participate in (1) singleton games with overprivileged and/or underprivileged singleton and (2) one singleton versus many (two or more) singletons.

For this study, Eifermann selected four different schools from her larger sample: two moshav and two kibbutz. She pointed out that the moshav is a family-based cooperative settlement "in which economic equality is maintained only to a degree," whereas complete equality is maintained in the kibbutz. Also, in the kibbutz, the family is neither an economic nor the central educational unit (p. 582). All schools were located in rural areas.

On the basis of her comparative analysis of material on these four schools, it was found that five of the eight predictions from Hypotheses 1 and 2 were confirmed, and two predictions (those regarding single-party games) were disconfirmed. Most significantly, it was discovered that single-party games were scarcely played by kibbutz children. However, group games, which call for cooperation toward the achievement of a common aim within a competitive framework, were found to be more popular among kibbutz children than among moshav children. She related this finding to Spiro's (1958) observation that while kibbutz grammar-school pupils are opposed to personal competition, they are indeed competitive about group activities and also the fact that some practices in the kibbutz educational policy encourage "cooperation within competition" (p. 585). It was also found that kibbutz children insist, more readily than moshav children, that in singleton games there should be as few overprivileged or underprivileged participants as possible (p. 386). She argued that this is a way to preserve egalitarianism.

Eifermann suggested that the results of this research appear to support theories of play that view it as a preparatory or practical activity (as kibbutz children prefer games that are cooperative and egalitarian). In contrast, she stated that this study does not support the idea that children's games are "expressive of a hidden revolt against adult values, or as measures taken to reduce conflicts created by adults' attempts to impose their values on them" (p. 586).

SOCIALIZING PLAY: THE AUSTRALIAN ABORIGINE

Michael Salter (1974) has also recently explored the idea "that play serves as a major vehicle of enculturation" (p. 3). In this study, he examined the games played by a number of central Queensland aboriginal groups, and he specifically described how these indigenous play forms both *reflect* and *reinforce* cultural subsystems such as *the economic system* (e.g., tree climbing, underwater endurance, play with miniature canoes); *the normative order* (e.g., mock marriage, pretend families, play with dolls); *the political system* (e.g., mud-ball fights, stick dueling, hide-and-seek); and *the world view* (e.g., evil "spirits," string figures, singing).[3] He also discussed a category of games that do not seem to be directly related to the maintenance of the traditional culture (e.g., top spinning, mud sliding, skipping). Salter pointed out that play was *a* (if not *the*) form of learning for the aboriginal child, and he suggested that given the cooperative, egalitarian nature of these societies, it would be expected that their play forms would be of a cooperative and not a competitive nature (p. 18). This expectation is confirmed, Salter reported, by the fact that most games in these societies "are group, as opposed to team oriented, play forms"; and there is also a general lack of emphasis on victory (p. 18). This study, therefore, coincides with Eifermann's investigation of kibbutz children's games.

SOCIALIZING PLAY: THE KPELLE

David Lancy (1975) has recently noted that the idea that play functions to enculturate and/or socialize children is frequently expressed in the ethnographic literature but has rarely been tested. In order to explore its validity, he has used a variety of techniques (e.g., participant observation, interviews, and experiments) in studies of African (Liberia–Kpelle) and, more recently, American children (1973, 1974, 1975, 1976a,b).

In his studies of Kpelle children's play (1973, 1974, 1975, 1976a,b),

---

[3]Cheska (1977) has recently presented a similar analysis of North American Indian games as "strategies of social maintenance." Here the relationship of games to the social processes of sex role differentiation, group identity, decision-making models, and symbolic identification is examined.

two strategies were used. First, information was collected on linguistic distinctions made in this society between work *(tii)* and play *(pele)* activities. On the basis of these data, an attempt was made to move *backwards* "from adult work to children's play, interviewing informants and speculating on possible play antecedents of adult skills" (1975:4). In conjunction with this effort, Lancy also started from play and moved *forwards*, analyzing play forms for evidence of skills, etc., to be used later in adult life. Lancy presented a great deal of information on all types of children's and adults' play activities in Kpelle society (see particularly 1974), and, taken as a whole, these accounts represent one of the few detailed collections and analyses of children's play behavior in a non-Western society available in the literature. One of the few comparable studies is Centner's (1963) description of Luba, Sanga, and Yeke children's play, which is discussed in Chapter Seven.

Lancy's study, however, is most significant for his attempt to examine explicitly whether or not play serves a socialization function in Kpelle society and to relate play behavior to work activities in this culture. He specificially made these associations in his discussions of "make-believe" blacksmith play, hunting play, the *bambé* game (a model of the adult secret society), warrior play, and new occupations incorporated into children's play (e.g., driver, soldier, and rubber tapper).

The most important description of relations between play and work and play as socialization is Lancy's discussion of "talking matter." "Talking matter" is a type of "court appearance" that virtually all Kpelle adults, and many adolescents, engage in at some time as defendant, plaintiff, witness, elder, or judge. However, this legal process is loosely structured and does not depend on a codified set of laws:

> This means that the degree of success that an individual achieves in his/her "court appearance" is heavily dependent on their verbal fluency, memory of past events, and ability to use one or several of the "speech events" (self-evident, staged-anger, penitent, and expository). One's wealth, prestige in the community, marriage and family relations, even one's place of residence may hinge on how well an actor can "perform" in the public drama of the court. (1975:17)

Lancy illustrated how a variety of children's play activities serve to develop the verbal and acting skills necessary to engage successfully in "talking matter." For example, in telling *mini-pele* stories, boys are frequently challenged in jest about the meaning and validity of what they are saying, causing frequent interruptions in the teller's narrative. Similar interruptions are reported to occur frequently in "talking matter," and the speaker (just as the player) must develop the ability of "verbal agility in the face of a hostile audience" (p. 18). *Pole-yee* stories (telling long stories, of which the content is generally known by the audience) require that the narrator hold an audience's attention for a long time. In order to do this, events are dramatized in a variety of ways through gestures, changes of speech tone, facial expressions, and so on. All of these skills are useful to the participant in "talking matter" because it is to his benefit to hold the attention of the court. *Sia-polo* (riddles) are also appropriate play models for "talking matter," where evidence is presented and cannot be referred to again and also where one's rationale for his/her position must be defended (p. 19). Finally, the *kolong* game (a verbal memory game involving the memorization of proverbs) also provides practice for serving as "elder" in "talking matter." Elders use jokes and proverbs either to lower the esteem of a speaker in the eyes of the audience in the "court appearance" or, in the specific case of proverbs, to justify an action (similar to the manner in which legal precedents are cited in the West). Lancy suggested that

> children learn the syntax of proverbs and jokes in their play, but learning the
> semantics and meaning of jokes and proverbs comes only through exposure
> to, and participation in, adult-play and "talking matter." (p. 19)

A number of other associations between children's play behavior and adult work activities are presented (including a variety of field experiments conducted by the investigator). In concluding his 1975 paper, Lancy summarized the examples presented in his study of how play "trains" children for four major cultural subsystems: (1) social relations (e.g., sex-role behavior, patterns of deference); (2) language (e.g., vocabulary, speech-making skills); (3) technology (e.g., tool use and practice); and (4) ideology (e.g., reticence, ambition, cleverness). The results of this study indicate, according to Lancy, that

> the evidence for the learning of adult roles, patterns of thought, and values in
> play, while not impressive, is at least encouraging to a theory of play in
> enculturation. (p. 13)

PLAY AND SEX ROLES

A current interest of anthropologists, sociologists, and psychologists is the study of sex roles. Anthropologists are particularly concerned with examining how cultures transform the obvious biological differences between men and women into social systems that are almost universally characterized by some degree of male dominance and, therefore, sex-role asymmetry (see Rosaldo and Lamphere, 1974:3). Accumulating evidence collected in a number of different societies suggests that there are sex differences in the behavior of children (e.g., Barry, Bacon, and Child, 1957; Ember, 1973; Whiting and Edwards, 1973). Boys are reported to behave in a more aggressive, assertive, and self-reliant fashion than girls, while girls are said to be more nurturant, obedient, and sensitive to others than boys (but see Mead, 1935). The existence and possible universality of these differences does not, however, mean that these are innate, biologically determined characteristics. A number of researchers have suggested that there are features present in *all* cultures that are responsible for the production of these differences (e.g., the sexual division of labor and differential sex-role socialization [Maccoby, 1959] and, more specifically, differential task assignment for boys and girls [Whiting and Edwards, 1973; Ember, 1973][4]; the universal symbolic association of women with "nature," an association that all cultures devalue [Ortner, 1974]).

Children's play has been investigated as both an indicator of children's gender identity and also as a vehicle for the learning and practicing of culturally appropriate sex roles. Psychologists have concentrated on investigations of the former topic, using a variety of "toy preference" or "doll-play" tests that presumably indicate the child's sexual identification (e.g., boys choose "masculine" objects such as soldiers or trucks, while girls choose "feminine" toys such as dolls—see Garvey's 1977 discussion of these investigations).

Studies of sex differences exhibited in children's "play configurations" have also been made (e.g., Erikson, 1941, 1951). In this investigation, a group of 11-year-old children were asked to construct a scene for a "movie" using a variety of toys (e.g., dolls, cars, animals, blocks) and a small stage that was set up on a table. After the child had constructed his/her scene, the investigator asked for an explanation of what it was about. These scenes were interpreted in a variety of ways in conjunction with Erikson's psychosexual theory of development, which has been discussed in Chapter Four. The most interesting sex-typed features of these constructions relate to the children's differential preference, use, and arrangement of toys in the "movie" scene. Here boys were found consistently to "erect structures, buildings and towers, or to build streets," while girls viewed the play table as "the interior of a house" and proceeded to arrange furniture and place people inside the "house" (p. 136). Boys concentrated on height of structure and the downfall or

---

[4]Whiting and Edwards (1973) reported that in societies where boys are required to take care of infants and perform other domestic chores, there are fewer sex differences between boys and girls. Ember's (1973) study of the effect of feminine task assignment on the social behavior of Luo (a Nilotic people living in southwestern Kenya) boys supports this finding. However, Draper (1975) reported that sex differences observed in the behavior of !Kung Bushmen children "are not attributable, at least not in any obvious way, to differential socialization" (p. 605).

"ruins" of these structures, with a related emphasis on motion and its arrest.

The "high–low" concern of boys is interpreted, not surprisingly, as "a doubt in, or a fear for, one's masculinity" (p. 137). The "enclosure" or "open–closed" configurations of girls are viewed as a reflection of concern over the feminine role, or as "over sensitiveness and selfcenteredness" (p. 137). Both types of configurations are explained as unconscious reflections of biological sex differences because they are said to parallel the morphology of the sex organs (e.g., the *"external* organs of the male,"* which are "erectible and intrusive," and the *"internal* organs of the female with vestibular *access* leading to *statically expectant* ova," pp. 139, 142).

The psychologists' preoccupation with "toy tests" probably reflects the object orientation of Western adults as much as it does the sex-role identification of their children. Observational studies of what children *actually do* in free play and game activities are more likely to provide investigators with useful information on sex differences. Fortunately, there are a number of interesting studies of this type focusing on children's sociodramatic or role play and games. These studies also tend to view play as both a shaper and an indicator of sex differences. Sutton-Smith and Savasta (1972) have recently reviewed a number of these studies covering the age period of 5–12, and they suggested that these investigations indicate the following:

> for males games may be an exercise in power tactics but . . . for females they generally are not. . . . The games preferred by boys show a greater emphasis on bodily strength and bodily contact, the use of larger spaces, for success achieved through active interference in the other play activities, for well-defined outcomes in which winners and losers are clearly labelled, for games permitting personal initiative, for a continuous flow of activity, for motor activity involving the whole body, for players acting simultaneously or in concert. Any type of sport could be taken to exemplify these dimensions. Girls for their part show a greater interest in games where turns are taken in ordered sequence, where there is choral activity, song and rhyme, verbalism, where rhythm is involved, where the stages in play are multiple but well-defined, where competition is indirect, where there is a multiplicity of rules dictating every move, where only parts of the body are involved and where there is much solitary practice, where there is competition between individuals rather than groups. The games of hopscotch, jump rope and jackstones are good examples. (pp. 2–3)

A recent investigation of sex differences in children's games has been reported by Lever (1974, 1975). In this research, a group of American, white, middle-class, fifth-grade children was investigated (using observations and also reported game preferences) to determine: (1) if there are any sex differences in their game patterns and preference, and (2) if involvement in particular games affects the performance of adult roles. Most specifically, an attempt was made to test whether boys' games are more "complex" (in the way that complexity is defined in formal organizations) than girls' games. It is argued that, if this is so, then it can be proposed that boys' games better prepare them "for successful performance in a wide range of work settings in modern complex societies" (1975:3). The dimensions of game complexity outlined and analyzed here are role differentiation, interdependence between players, size of play group, degree of competition and explicitness of goals, number and specificity of rules, and degree of team formation. On the basis of her research, Lever reported that there are indeed sex differences displayed in the games played by children and that, with respect to each of the six dimensions described above, "boys' activities were often more complex" (1975:12).

In another study of sex-typed behavior exhibited in children's spontaneous play on school playgrounds in Austin, Texas, Robinson (1978) reported specifically on "self-structured chase games." Differences in boys' and girls' (7- and 8-year-olds) styles of play in these games reflect again the differences that have been generally noted regarding the behavior of boys and girls; that is, the boys' chase style is aggressive and physical, while the girls' style is passive and teasing. Robinson also discussed the "chaotic and disorderly" style of chase games that involve both boys and girls (these games are frequently initiated by girls). She suggested that these games allow the girls to abandon the restrictive conventions of traditionally "nice" and appropriately "feminine" games, such as hopscotch and jump rope, and to experiment with a form of aggression (although performed in a "feminine" style). Robinson proposed that these games may also allow girls "to experiment with disorder and the challenges of a changing society," which is particularly appropriate in a cultural context where women's roles are currently in flux (p. 17).

In order to investigate whether sex differences are exhibited in the play of younger (3- to 4-year-olds) American children, Sutton-Smith and Savasta (1972) initiated a videotape study of a group of 17 children attending a university nursery school. It was expected that because of the professional nature of the parent group, there would be a reduction in marked sex differences in the children's play activities. This was indeed found to be true. However, for the observational category "social testing" (i.e., the child asserts something about him/herself), it was found that boys engaged in significantly more episodes of this type of play than girls. By breaking this category into four subcategories, each with three modes (physical, verbal, or strategic techniques)—(1) supplication, (2) inclusion-exclusion, (3) attacks, and (4) authority or dominance—it was found that the difference between boys' and girls' engagement in "social testing" was produced by the boys' larger amounts of attack. However, this difference was not just isolated to physical attack; it was also evidenced in verbal and strategic attacks. Therefore the boys did not just engage in more frequent physical and aggressive attacks but also in more frequent verbal and strategic attacks and concern with defining their place within a group. It is suggested that what is evidenced here is perhaps an early stage in the exploration of power phenomena, such as dominance hierarchies. The girls in this study engaged more frequently in inclusion–exclusion "social testing" (e.g., controlling others by promising inclusion; threatening exclusion; physically through smiling, giving gifts, etc.). The authors suggested that these inclusion–exclusion tactics, because they are generally applied to smaller groups than boys, may be "power tactics relevant to the nuclear or intimate group, whereas boys' tactics are more relevant to the larger gang type group" (p. 11). Finally, it is suggested that, if, indeed, there are sex differences in the learning of power or testing tactics at this age, the next step for researchers is to discover how it is that sexes learn these differences from their mothers and fathers at such an early age.

These findings are also supported by a recent study by Grief (1976), similarly conducted with American, white, middle-class, preschool-aged children. Children in this study were reported to engage frequently in sex-role play in free play situations, with older ($4\frac{1}{2}$–$5\frac{1}{2}$) children exhibiting more use of sex roles than younger ($3\frac{1}{2}$–$4\frac{1}{2}$) ones. Grief also reported instances of role reversals, where a dominant girl attempted to adopt a male role, much to the distress and protest of the defined male "mother." This is interpreted as evidence of the general view that male roles have more status (p. 390).

In attempting to sort out the problem of early sex-role learning, a topic of great importance as suggested by Sutton-Smith and Savasta, an interesting study of sex differences exhibited in the play of infants is useful to consider. Goldberg and Lewis (1969) have investigated the play behavior of a sample of American infants (13 months) with their mothers in a standardized free play situation. In these settings, "striking" sex differences were observed (e.g., girls were extremely reluctant to leave their mother's lap; in response to a barrier placed between infant and mother, girls stood still and cried or motioned for help, whereas boys attempted to get around the barrier; girls sat quietly and played with toys, while boys responded more actively, standing up and banging the toys around). On the basis of earlier observations of these mothers' interactions with their infants at 6 months, it was found that mothers behaved very differently toward girls and boys, which, the authors suggested, reinforced sex-typed behavior at a very early age.

In all of these studies, and also in most ethnographies that contain information on children, it is reported that children engage in culturally defined sex-appropriate behavior and sex-appropriate roles in their play activities. This is not surprising because the first activities and roles that children encounter are always culturally defined caretaker roles and activities, and these are generally sex-typed. It is important to emphasize here, however, that most investigators have *not* studied children's play *with* sex roles but rather how sex roles *play* children. This follows from the play-as-imitation/preparation/socialization perspective adopted by most functional analysts, who seek to examine how children are "dulled towards conformity" (in the words of Malinowski, 1944:107–108) by the socialization pressure of play. A view of play as caricature (see Raum, 1940) or satire would lead researchers to investigate the various ways in which children's behavior exaggerates and parodies the behavior of adults, and, particularly, of mothers and fathers. These would truly be studies of play *with* sex roles. This point will be returned to in a later section of this chapter.

GAMES AND POWER ROLES

Power roles and sex roles are frequently inseparable; however, there are a number of studies available in which types of role and status positions within specific games are investigated and then relationships between these roles and the larger social context are drawn. In one study, by Gump and Sutton-Smith (1955b), an attempt is made to classify rule games on the basis of the kinds of status positions that they contain (e.g., leader–follower, attacker–defender, taunter–taunted) and the controls over the allocation of such positions (e.g., leader chosen by popularity, leader chosen by chance, leader chosen by defeat or triumph). After classifying a variety of games in this way, the authors proceeded to analyze the status positions and allocation of power in "it" games (e.g., tag, king of the mountain) with the idea that such roles offer players the opportunity to gain experience and/or practice in handling such positions. In other related studies, Sutton-Smith (Sutton-Smith, Roberts, and Rosenberg, 1966; Sutton-Smith, 1966b) examined associations between sibling relationships and role involvement in play. In one study (1966b), a role-reversal phenomenon is noted in which it is found that firstborn children who occupy a dominant/leader role in sibling relations within the family often act in nondominant/follower roles in peer play situations.

More general studies of games as models of power are available in Roberts, Arth, and Bush (1959); Roberts and Sutton-Smith (e.g., 1962, 1966); Roberts, Sutton-Smith, and Kendon (1963); and Sutton-Smith and Roberts (e.g., 1964, 1967, 1970). As these studies are discussed in more detail in Chapter Seven, they are only briefly described here. The basic argument of the investigators in this research is that three different types of games found in various societies of the world (i.e., games of physical skill, games of chance, and games of strategy) are systematically related to both psychogenic (child training) and sociogenic (economics, politics, etc.) cultural variables. Examples of these relationships are illustrated by the fact that games of physical skill are found in cultures where physical abilities are essential to survival; games of chance appear most frequently in cultures where divinatory procedures are important in decision making; and games of strategy exist in cultures where class stratification and warfare are institutionalized. In cultures where all three types of games appear, there tends to be more emphasis on achievement. These findings led the investigators

> to view these competitive games as models of the larger cultural processes and, in a sense, as a preparation for the use of the type of power relevant to life in the larger culture. (Sutton-Smith and Savasta, 1972:1)

In looking at variations in these types of games in American society, it was found that males more frequently played physical skill games, whereas females were more likely to play strategic and chance games. And it was also found that strategy games were more often preferred by individuals of higher social status, whereas chance games were preferred by persons of lower social status.

IMITATION, IMAGINATION, AND CULTURE

A recent interest of students of children's play is the study of relationships between play behavior and culture. In these investigations, it is assumed that play serves a socializing function for society and that certain types of cultures encourage the development and elaboration of certain types of play forms. The studies of Roberts, Arth, and Bush (1959) and Roberts and Sutton-Smith (1962) described above illustrate this approach, particularly in relation to the association of particular types of competitive games with particular types of cultures.

More recently, studies of the relationship between children's imaginative play and culture have been made. Smilansky's (1968) investigation of children's sociodramatic play in Israel is probably the most well known. In this work, Smilansky's adoption of the play-as-imitation/socialization perspective is evidenced in her view that make-believe play *aids* imitation as it is "a technique by which the child's limitations can be overcome and by which a richer reproduction of adult life is made possible" (p. 7). Sociodramatic play is said to be characterized by six play elements: (1) imitative role play; (2) make-believe in regard to objects; (3)

make-believe in regard to actions and situations; (4) persistence; (5) interaction (two or more players); and (6) verbal communication (Smilansky, 1971:41–42). On the basis of this research, Smilansky suggested that certain groups of children have less facility for imaginative role play than others. In her study, children of North African and Middle Eastern parents (referred to here as "disadvantaged preschool children") are said to engage in this type of play with much less frequency and with less ability than children of European parents.[5] (Children of Kurdish Jews who have recently immigrated to Israel are also reported to exhibit a paucity of imaginative play; see Feitelson, 1954, 1959.)

Smilansky suggested that this research and also more recent studies of the play of "culturally disadvantaged" children in Ohio and Chicago indicate that "without some degree of positive intervention by parents and/or teachers, these children will lack the requirements essential to develop sociodramatic play" (1971:39; also see 1968). If this type of play does not develop, children may be retarded in the development of skills and behavior patterns that are "necessary for successful integration into the school situation or full cooperation in the 'school game' " (p. 42). Sociodramatic play is said to develop three aspects of children that are essential to this "school game": (1) creativity; (2) intellectual growth (and particularly the "power" of abstraction); and (3) social skills. Therefore, because of the importance of sociodramatic play to children's development, Smilansky believes that adults, as parents and teachers, must actively intervene in order to improve or "raise significantly" the "low performance in play" that certain children exhibit (p. 45). A variety of intervention techniques are described (e.g., adult modeling of sociodramatic play techniques), and Smilansky reported that in both the Israeli (1968) and the American (1971) studies, these interventions improved the children's ability to engage in this form of play behavior.

In a study of Russian nursery-school children, El'Konin (1971) reported that these children engage *only* in imitative play activities. It is suggested here that what look like imaginative, spontaneous play productions on the part of children are often, in fact, direct copies of adult behavior. According to El'Konin, it is possible to discover the adult source of a child's pretense if the investigator knows the history of these transformations. For example, he cited an instance in one school in which a stick was called a "thermometer" by a child in a play situation simply because a teacher had suggested this transformation to the child some time earlier.

Sutton-Smith used Smilansky's and El'Konin's research, as well as

[5]Samples of play texts for both the so-called disadvantaged and advantaged children are presented in an appendix to the 1968 report.

the earlier study of Roberts, Arth, and Bush, to argue for the existence of "The Two Cultures of Games" (1972c; also see Herron and Sutton-Smith, 1971:218–219). In "ascriptive game cultures," children are said to engage in imitative and nonimaginative play activities that are hierarchically organized, where one child bosses all the others and is often quite aggressive. Central-person games and, later, games of physical skill are most commonly played in these cultures. The types of societies associated with "ascriptive" games, however, are not clearly described except insofar as they are said to be characterized by (1) extended families; (2) leaders' domination by the use of arbitrary power; and (3) the lack of a clear separation of children and adults (p. 299). Children in "achievement games cultures" are said to play imaginatively and in a more egalitarian style. Likewise, there is less physical aggression and less emphasis on ritualized and formalistic games (e.g., singing games). Western (i.e., Western middle-class) societies are said to be typical of "achievement game cultures." In these cultures children are segregated from the rest of society, and nuclear families predominate (pp. 303–309).

More recent experimental studies (e.g., Feitelson, 1972; Feitelson and Ross, 1973; Freyberg, 1973; see also Singer, 1973; J. and D. Singer, 1976) report both cultural and class differences in the quantity and quality of children's imaginative play behavior. For example, Freyberg (1973) stated that a group of 80 "urban disadvantaged" American kindergarten children, who were the subjects of her study, exhibited very little imaginative play (using a rating scale described in Singer, 1973) in free play settings prior to the introduction of a training program. Before this intervention occurred, "there was very little role-playing or elaboration of themes; seldom was a pretend situation concerned with themes not in the child's direct experience" (p. 151). However, following a series of training sessions,

> there was more and qualitatively different imaginative play. There was much
> more organization in the pretend situations, which often involved themes
> not part of the daily life of the child. (p. 151)

Feitelson and Ross (1973) also reported similar results in a study of white, lower-middle-class kindergarten children living in the Boston area. These children were found to exhibit "surprisingly low levels of thematic play" prior to participation in a series of play-tutoring sessions (which stressed adult modeling of thematic play), which led to a "significant increase" in their thematic play (p. 218). Feitelson and Ross argued that this research (in conjunction with the studies of Smilansky and Feitelson in Israel and El'Konin in the Soviet Union) indicates that thematic play must be learned by some form of modeling, and that, if this does not occur, then this play does not develop naturally or spontaneously in all children. The investigators appear to assume, however, that "high levels" of imaginative or thematic play are found among middle- and upper-middle-class children (where presumably such modeling occurs). Unfortunately, we do not know that this is the case from their study because the investigators did not use their assessment techniques to rate a group of middle- or upper-middle-class children (comparisons of this sort were made by Smilansky, and Freyberg's study is somewhat comparable to Pulaski's 1973 investigation of American upper-middle-class children's imaginative use of toys, because similar rating scales were used).

Feitelson and Ross also cited "accumulating ethnographic evidence" in support of the view that children in "rural communities" do not engage in thematic play because this activity is not modeled for them by adults or because sufficient "play props" and play spaces are not available (pp. 204–206). Aside from Feitelson's research on the children of Kurdish Jews who have recently immigrated to Israel (1954, 1959), the authors also cited the studies of Ammar (1954) on Egyptian village children and LeVine and LeVine (1963) on Gusii children in Kenya. In this regard, it is interesting to note that Ammar devoted one entire chapter (pp. 144–160) to a description of Silwa children's play and games. Although he reported that these children (particularly boys) play mostly competitive games, engaging only infrequently in constructive or imaginative play (which he considered transformations of *objects*), he stated that a popular play situation for girls is the representation of adult female occupations and ceremonies. As he described this play, it would certainly seem to fit most investigators' definitions of sociodramatic or thematic play. According to Ammar, this play involves

> making straw figures, bedecked in bits of cloth as men and women and children, and with the help of stones, building a house. All the details of an event or ritual are played out in a make-believe way. Thus marriage, circumcision, cooking, and social meetings are all imitated. (p. 154)

The LeVines' study is discussed in more detail in Chapter Seven; however, one variable contributing to these children's reported lack of thematic play appears to be the geographic distance between households, which makes it difficult for groups of children to form. In this case, instead of a scarcity of space, there appears to be too much space.

The most important thing to emphasize here, however, is that "accumulating ethnographic evidence" does *not* support the idea that rural or non-Western children do not engage in thematic play activities. Considering the fact that most ethnographers have not systematically studied this behavior (Ammar stated that he made "no detailed observations of play situations," 1954:159), the reports of children's ingenuity in constructing thematic play events that do appear in the literature (e.g.,

Roth, 1902; Fortes, 1938; Raum, 1940; DuBois, 1944; Centner, 1962; Maretzki and Maretzki, 1963; Nydegger and Nydegger, 1963; Lancy, 1975) suggest that this is, in fact, a well-developed play form in many non-Western cultures.

As Sutton-Smith particularly used the work of Smilansky to support his "two cultures" view (and Freyberg, Feitelson and Ross, and Singer also utilized her research to support their arguments), it is important to consider again Eifermann's recent studies of children's play in Israel (1971a,b). In this study, she challenged Smilansky's findings by suggesting that the form of play (i.e., sociodramatic/imaginative) that Smilansky reported to be lacking in her sample of "disadvantaged" children appeared at a later age (i.e., at age 6–8 rather than 3–6) for a comparable group of children in Eifermann's own study. And she stated that her analysis indicates that at this later age, "culturally deprived" children not only develop the ability to engage in symbolic/thematic play but also "engage in such play at a significantly higher rate than do their 'advantaged' peers" (1971b:290).

There are other problems as well with these research studies that propose that children from certain cultures or classes are "imaginatively disadvantaged." In many of these investigations, associations between imaginative (or thematic or sociodramatic) play and particular cognitive and social skills are made. These associations are reflected in hypotheses that suggest that children who receive training in imaginative play (1) will also improve their scores on standard creativity tests (e.g., CATB tests for exploratory and innovative behavior; the Torrence "Thinking Creatively with Pictures" test) (Feitelson and Ross, 1973; also see Lieberman, 1977); (2) display a "higher degree of concentration," "more positive affect," and also "more tolerance and consideration" than children who do not receive training (Freyberg, 1973; Smilansky, 1968, 1971); (3) exhibit more verbal communication (i.e., longer and more complete sentences) after training sessions (Smilansky, 1968); (4) exhibit increased attention span and also improved "waiting behavior" (Singer, 1973; Singer and Singer, 1976); or (6) improve problem-solving abilities, specifically the ability to think abstractly (e.g., Smilansky, 1968).

These associations may be very valid, but they encourage researchers to neglect the investigation of alternate expressions of imagination or creativity, which lower-class children may display. Instead, these children are found to be *deficient* in the style of play associated with middle- and upper-middle-class children, which is then taken to indicate (or at least suggest) deficiency in the cognitive, verbal, and social skills said to be associated with this form of play and these children. In order to correct this deficit (which may actually be an artifact of the investigators' theories and/or the testing context), researchers then proceed to train children to play in a "middle-class" manner, which is then said to produce improved scores in the display of cognitive, verbal, and social skills.

Since middle-class children are, on the whole, more successful at playing the "school game" (in Smilansky's terms) than lower-class children, it may be that teaching them to engage in a middle-class form of play will improve their performance in school. Unfortunately, however, this view leads investigators not only to assume that lower-class children are deficient in the style of play in which middle-class children excel, but also to assume that these children are generally deficient in imaginative abilities and related cognitive, verbal, and social skills.

This is both an inaccurate and a dangerous assumption for researchers to make. For example, studies (e.g., Reissman, 1964; Labov, 1972) of lower-class children's expressive and imaginative use of language in role play and other situations *outside* of the school or the experimental context indicate that in these situations these children are highly creative, are more verbal, and display a variety of social and survival skills. This research also points to the importance of considering situational factors in the analysis and rating of children's play behavior (e.g., the "disadvantaged" children in Smilansky's study may have been fearful of the new and strange school that they were attending; neither Smilansky, Feitelson and Ross, nor Freyberg conducted observations of play outside of the school context; and, in the case of Feitelson and Ross, observations were not even conducted in the child's school, but instead in a strange and possibly frightening "Mobile Laboratory," where children were observed "one at a time" instead of in an "interaction" situation with other players, which Smilansky defined as an essential component of sociodramatic play). Freyberg has recognized these problems by suggesting the following:

> Lower-class children should perhaps be observed away from school, in which authority figures may be inhibitory. Use of para-professionals from the community may be essential in determining whether differences in verbal and cognitive style mask abilities among lower-class children when observed by middle-class persons. (1973:136)

These studies, however, are also problematic in a way that I believe most investigators have not realized. These problems are best expressed in Labov's (1972) excellent critique of the verbal and cultural deprivation theories of Bernstein (1966) and Deutch (1967) and the pragmatic programs formulated by individuals such as Bereiter and Engelmann (e.g., 1966) to correct such deprivations. In his analysis of the Black English Vernacular (BEV), Labov suggested that the view that black children in ghetto areas receive little verbal stimulation, hear very few well-formed sentences, cannot speak complete sentences, do not know the names of common objects, cannot form concepts or think logically, and are generally improverished in their means of verbal expression "has no basis in social reality" (p. 201). Instead, his study demonstrates that, in fact, these children do receive a great deal of verbal stimulation, hear more well-formed sentences than middle-class children, have the same basic vocabulary, possess the same capacity for conceptual learning, and use the same logic as anyone who learns to speak and understand English (p. 201). Labov also demonstrated how the situational factors of schoolrooms and testing contexts influence the verbal productions of urban black children (see pp. 205–213; also see Dickie and Bagur, 1972).

Labov presented a particularly interesting analysis of what he believes to be the faulty reasoning of the verbal-deprivation theorists. The six statements, or logical steps, that Labov outlined are strikingly similar to the reasoning of what may be called the play-deprivation or play-training researchers. Therefore, following each step described by Labov (1972:229–230), I will present my view of these researchers' use of this logic:

1. "The lower-class child's verbal response to a formal and threatening situation is used to demonstrate his lack of verbal capacity or verbal deficit." (The lower-class child's play response to a formal and threatening situation is used to demonstrate his lack of imaginative capacities or his play deficit.)
2. "This verbal deficit is declared to be a major cause of the lower-class child's poor performance in school." (It is suggested that this play deficit is a cause of the lower-class child's poor performance in school.)
3. "Since middle-class children do better in school, middle-class speech habits are seen to be necessary for learning." (Since middle-class children do better in school, middle-class play habits are seen to be necessary for learning.)
4. "Class and ethnic differences in grammatical form are equated with differences in the capacity for logical analysis." (Class and ethnic differences in expressions of imagination are equated with differences in the capacity for logical analysis, verbal communication, and social skills.)
5. "Teaching the child to mimic certain formal speech patterns used by middle-class teachers is seen as teaching him to think logically." (Teaching the child to mimic certain play patterns displayed by middle-class children, and adult play tutors, is seen as helping him to develop imaginative skills and to improve his cognitive, verbal, and social functioning.)
6. "Children who learn these formal speech patterns are then said to be thinking logically and it is predicted that they will do much better in

reading and arithmetic in the years to follow." (Children who learn these play patterns are then said to have improved their imaginative, cognitive, verbal, and social skills, and it is suggested that they will do better in school in the years to follow.)

Even if this logic can be shown to be faulty, is it necessarily harmful to teach children new ways to play? Labov asked a similar question in his study in regard to the effect of verbal training programs on children, and he suggested that on the surface, such programs are not harmful. However, he argued that these programs may actually prove to be very damaging to children in the long run because of the problem of *labeling* (e.g., teachers who hear children speaking BEV will constantly label them as illogical or nonconceptual thinkers) and also because when these programs fail to improve scholastic performance (which he feels is inevitable), they will be used to support the belief in the genetic inferiority of blacks (as an example, he cited Jensen's use of these studies in his controversial 1969 paper in the *Harvard Educational Review*).

It does not necessarily follow that the play-deprivation or play-training research discussed above will be used in the same manner. However, as this is a new field, it is not too soon to ask questions about the implications of this research, particularly when there appear to be striking correspondences between the arguments of these investigators and those of the verbal- or cultural-deprivation school. In both instances, the deficiencies of children are thought to be related to personal deficiencies residing *in* the child or *in* his home or neighborhood environment. Adopting this view, programs (such as Head Start or play-tutoring sessions) are designed in Labov's terms, "to repair the child, rather than the school," and to the extent that they are based on this "inverted logic," they are "bound to fail" (1972:232). Feitelson and Ross illustrated this view of the child's personal inadequacy in the following statement:

> Our study showed that some present day preschool pupils are unequipped to show initiative in the use of equipment, and in engaging on their own in those kinds of behavior deemed especially conducive to their future development. . . .
> Marion Blank, the Deutsches, Bereiter and Engelmann and others have demonstrated succinctly that improved performance can only be achieved by way of well planned tutoring sequences which rely on active participation by the child. (1973:221)

Instead of assuming that some form of play deprivation exists and then proceeding to formulate training or facilitation programs, it would be much more valuable at this time for researchers to move out of the school or laboratory context to investigate whether or not they may have created (by the use of inappropriate theories and/or methods) the idea of play deprivation. In formulating these studies, researchers may discover that children are often critical observers of the adult world who have as much to say about adult behavior as adults who are researchers have to say about theirs.

PLAY: SOCIALIZATION, SATIRIZATION, OR INNOVATION?

Anthropologists have frequently commented on specific forms of symbolic inversion found in various societies of the world. The Cheyenne *massaum*, or contrary, ceremony; the *incwala*, or kingship, ceremony of the Swazi; and the Ndembu twin ritual, *wubwang'u*, are all rites of reversal and examples of play in religious dress (Norbeck, 1971:51–52). These institutionalized play forms sanction insults and derision of authority figures, social status inversions, parody, satire, lampooning, and clowning (see Norbeck, 1971; also Turner, 1974b).

Sutton-Smith has recently undertaken the study of symbolic reversals and inversions apparent within the structure of certain plays and games of children (1972b, 1974b). He called these the "games of order and disorder" and suggested that examples may be found in both Western and non-Western societies. Examples of such games for Western children are: ring-around-the-rosy, poor pussy, and Queen of Sheba. In the Trobriand Islands, similar games are played by children. For example, Malinowski described a game where all the players hold hands like a long string and wind around each other until they are a tight ball, and then they run out until it breaks, at which point everyone falls down or apart (Sutton-Smith, 1972b:24).

Sutton-Smith stated that these types of games are significant because they suggest that play and games are not always socializing or social-ordering activities, as they may, in fact, seek to challenge and reverse the social order. This is so because these games often model the social system "only to destroy it" (e.g., everyone acts in concert and then collapses) (1974b:12). These games also often mock conventional power roles and frequently provide unconventional access to such roles (e.g., everyone gets a turn).

Four different types of order–disorder games were described by Sutton-Smith, and these categories were arranged to reflect "a series of structures of succeeding complexity" (1972b:10). The first level (presumably the least complex) is made up of games in which "everyone acts at the same time either diffusely or more or less in parallel, and the outcome may occur to one or all. The outcome is usually a motor collapse" (e.g., ring-around-the-rosy or the Trobriand game mentioned above) (p. 10). The second level consists of games in which "there is role differentiation to the extent that one or more players have a central role in bringing about the collapse" (e.g., I see a ghost) (p. 11).[6] In games of the third level, "actions are coordinated in turns through a cumulating series of actions and there is a common outcome" (e.g., consequences) (p. 12). Finally, fourth-level games are said to be those in which "the actions of the players are coordinated as in a dramatic plot toward the downfall of some central person" (e.g., Queen of Sheba) (p. 13). Younger children are said to engage in play at the first two levels, while older children play at levels 3 and 4.

In analyzing these games, Sutton-Smith was particularly concerned with examining the innovative quality of these activities. A view of play as an integrative mechanism or socializing force for society is a perspective focusing on only one aspect of the character of play and games. The novelty that these forms give rise to may ultimately be their most significant "function." Sutton-Smith suggested this in the following quote:

> If play is the learning of variability, a position for which we now have increasing experimental evidence, then we can perhaps say also that all these forms of inversion involve experimentation with variable repertoires. All involve the development of flexible competencies in role taking and the development of variable repertoires with respect to these roles. . . . In this view the anti-structural phenomena [the games of order and disorder] not only make the system tolerable as it exists, they keep its members in a more flexible state with respect to that system, and, therefore, with respect to possible change. Each system has different structural and anti-structural functions. The normative structure represents the working equilibrium, the anti-structure represents the latent system of potential alternatives from which novelty will arise when contingencies in the normative system require it.[7] We might more correctly call this second system the *proto-structural* system because it is the precursor of innovative normative forms. It is the source of new culture. (1972b:20)

However, the innovative quality of play texts is also dependent on the ideology of the larger culture or context in which such activities exist.

---

[6]An equivalent from Mota Banks Island, Melanesia, was cited by Sutton-Smith (p. 11) from Lansley's (1969) studies. The game is played in the following manner. Two lines face each other and chant about a magic wand. In order to get the wand, a player must make faces and twist his body or distort his voice. If he makes the rest of the group laugh, he becomes the possessor of the wand and someone else must try to get it.

[7]In these remarks, Sutton-Smith invoked and expanded on the notions of structure and antistructure articulated by Victor Turner in *The Ritual Process* (1969). Turner has recently expanded on these ideas in an essay attempting to delineate differences between liminal phenomena ("ergic-ludic" rituals characteristic of tribal and early agrarian societies) and liminoid phenomena ("anergic-ludic" games and actions and literature characteristic of societies shaped by the Industrial Revolution) entitled "Liminal to Liminoid in Play, Flow, and Ritual: An Essay in Comparative Symbology" (1974b).

Therefore,

> in a closed work ethic society there is no scope for the novelty and facetious-
> ness to which play gives rise. In an open society this novelty is a source of
> potential adaptation, albeit an over-productive source being no guarantee of
> preparation, as Groos thought, but at least of the promise of being ready.
> In this interpretation . . . play, games and sports both mirror and pro-
> vide potential novelty for the larger society. In this interpretation also, social
> scientists, including anthropologists, have been mainly concerned with what
> I would like to consider the *integrative* functions of play in society. They have
> been concerned . . . with normative socializing. The more static, the more
> relevant, the type of play theorizing is. What an increasingly open society
> like ours needs, however, is to consider the innovative functions of playing
> and to try to account for ways in which novelties introduced into the text
> ultimately transfer back to the society at large. (1974b:15)

While play may encourage "experimentation with variable reper-
toires" and can be a "source of new culture," it is also frequently an
arena for comment and criticism on the "old" culture, the status quo.
Satire and parody, caricature and burlesque are all examples of play
forms that *invert* and may also seek to *subvert* (see Turner, 1974b:72) the
existing social system. Sutton-Smith has recognized (but does not emphasize) the fact that certain children's play and games may mock, make
fun of, and, in a sense, challenge the status quo. For children, the social
order is most obviously symbolized by adult figures, who represent the
existing power and authority structure of society (i.e., the "older" culture) as parents, teachers, police, and so forth.

A number of researchers have remarked on the antiauthoritarian
themes evident in many children's games. For example, Abrahams reported that, in the content of English-speaking children's jump-rope
rhymes, "a strong antitaboo and antiauthoritarian tone is assumed"
(1969:xxiv). He went on to suggest that this theme is

> evident in the numerous taunts and parodies throughout this volume and in
> the attachment to clown figures . . . that is, to adult figures that children can
> at the same time both identify with and make fun of. Parents, when they
> appear, are portrayed more often than not as ridiculous, more to be laughed
> at than feared, and the same could be said of other authority figures such as
> policemen, doctors, judges, even movie stars. (p. xxiv)

Iona and Peter Opie also noted similar forms of parody and satire of
adults—as well as adult-taught hymns, carols, and nursery rhymes—in
their collection of the language and lore of English schoolchildren (1959).
They suggested that these sorts of satirical rhymes are often created and
recited "just for the fun of versification, and perhaps because, in the
crude images evoked, adults are made to look undignified" (pp. 18–19).

As already mentioned, the butt of many of these jokes and parodies is the adult *as parent:*

> Mother made a seedy cake.
> Gave us all the belly ache;
> Father bought a pint of beer,
> Gave us all the diarrhoea.
>
> I. and P. Opie (1959:19)

> You're mad, you're barmy,
> Your mother's in the army,
> She wears black britches,
> With pink and white stitches.
>
> Sutton-Smith (1959b:133)

As teacher:

> God made the bees,
> The bees make honey;
> We do the work,
> The teacher gets the money.
>
> I. and P. Opie (1959:361)

As law official:

> No wonder, no wonder, the coppers are so fat,
> They go around the market and eat up all the fat,
> And what they can't eat they put in their 'at.
> No wonder, no wonder, the coppers are so fat.
>
> I. and P. Opie (1959:370)

> Order in the court,
> The judge is eating beans.
> His wife is in the bathtub,
> Counting submarines.
>
> Evans (1955:16)

And as political figure:

> Roosevelt in the White House,
> Waiting to be elected;
> Dewey in the garbage can,
> Waiting to be collected.
>
> Withers (1947:218)

Adult-taught prayers, hymns, and rhymes are also the subject of satire and parody, as well as historical commentary. For example, *the Christmas carol:*

> No ale, no beer, no stout, sold out,
> Born is the king with his shirt hanging out.
>
> I. and P. Opie (1959:88)

> *Hark the herald angels sing,*
> *Mrs. Simpson's pinched our king.*
>
> I. and P. Opie (1959:6)

Or the nursery rhyme:

> *Mary had a little lamb,*
> *She also had a bear;*
> *I've often seen her little lamb,*
> *But I've never seen her* bear.
>
> I. and P. Opie (1959:90)

In these examples, satire, parody, and implied criticism are found in the content of the rhyme or song. However, ridicule and challenge may also be evident (as Sutton-Smith, 1972b, 1974b, has suggested) in the structure of the game itself. In the example of ring-around-the-rosy, the harmony of the social order is modeled and then mocked as everyone falls down and collapses. Similarly, conventional power roles, which are generally asymmetrical with unequal provision for access to leadership, are reversed as everyone (no matter who he/she is) gets a turn.

Satire may also be apparent in games in which the content looks imitative—and therefore functional for socialization—while the enactment of the game (i.e., the way it is played) is mocking and farcical. The following interpretation of the game "Mother, May I?" appears in Dolhinow and Bishop's (1970) recent article, which stresses the importance of play in the development of motor skills and social relationships in primates (particularly nonhuman primates). In their interpretation of this game, the use of a play-as-socialization perspective is clearly illustrated:

> Just as the nonhuman primates learn and practice the appropriate "rules" of adult behavior in the play group, so does the human child. He is actively discouraged from developing a second set of standards for conduct. The American game, Mother, May I, is an example of this principle, in which we find a sequence of a mother–child interaction.
> MOTHER: Susie, you may take two baby steps.
> SUSIE: Mother, May I?
> MOTHER: Yes, you may, or, no you may not. You may take three umbrella steps.
> SUSIE: Mother, May I?
> There is no element of strategy or chance in this game; the "mother" is in strict control, and a "child" is penalized for a breach of etiquette (i.e., not asking, "Mother, May I?"). (pp. 188–189)

However, if American children are watched actually playing this game, the socialization perspective, as articulated above, may not be so immediately apparent. Sutton-Smith (personal communication) states that the enactment of such a game may suggest not rigid control and perfect socialization but a burlesque of social etiquette and rules, as when the "child" inches forward while "mother" is not looking and everyone conceals this transgression while laughing and giggling. In short, when the game is played, we cannot necessarily assume that "mother" is always in control of her "children," as they may sometimes (or often) act to make her look foolish and ridiculous.

The children of the !Kung Bushmen of Southwest Africa also play a number of caricature games. Lorna Marshall presented a detailed description of play and games in Bushmen society in her most recent account (*The !Kung of Nyae Nyae,* 1976) of this now vanished way of life. In chapters entitled "Play and Games" (pp. 313–362) and "Music for Pleasure" (pp. 363–381), Marshall surveyed the various forms of recreation engaged in by both adults and children. Here she described the play of very young children (e.g., "imitation" plays, vocabulary and counting games), boys' play (e.g., tree climbing, sand patterns, cartwheels, somersaults and hopping, string figures, and toy inventions) and games (e.g., war games, tug-of-war, stick throwing), and girls' play (e.g., sand patterns, hopping, riding games, string figures, dolls) and games (e.g., ball games that involve singing, dancing, and clapping—see Figure 11; jump-rope; a type of London Bridge; dances). Marshall also discussed the !Kung children's ingenuity in manufacturing foreign objects (e.g., a

FIGURE 11. !Kung Bushmen girls' ball game (L. Marshall, 1976:323).

toy gun made out of a reed; "autos" made from tubers and bulbs modeled after the Marshalls' jeeps and accompanied by motor sounds imitated by the boys, who specialized "in the roar of low gear pulling out of heavy sand," p. 342). A number of short movies of Bushmen play and games are available that depict tug-of-war, playing with toy assagais, baobab (a large tree) play, the lion game, playing with scorpions, and song games. These films are discussed in more detail in Chapter Twelve.

Marshall stated that !Kung children play "all their waking hours," either free play or structured games and that adults also engage in a variety of play and game activities (p. 313).[8] However, the !Kung do not play competitive team games (except tug-of-war),[9] and the idea of winners and losers is not emphasized as this is a culture that stresses the importance of group and not individual performance. On the other hand, conflict, satire, and mimicry (of animals, other !Kung, and also the practices of other societies[10]) are evidenced in a variety of Bushmen play activities. Marshall described a series of "dramatic games" (pp. 356–362) that can be viewed as expressions of conflict in the form of playful satires of three of the "basic polarities" of !Kung life: parents–children, herders–hunters, and humans–animals.

One of these games is called "frogs," and it can best be described as a reverse "Mother, May I?" because, instead of stressing obedience (although in conjunction with covert transgressions), the game emphasizes disobedience to the parental figure, which results in chaos and pandemonium (perhaps this is the game's "moral"). The game is played by girls and boys (between the ages of 8 and 12) and sometimes women. All players begin by sitting in a circle, and one player is chosen to be "mother of all" while the others become her "children." First, "mother" taps each of her children on the ankle with a stick, and they lay back, pretending to fall asleep. The mother then pulls some hairs from her head and places them on an imaginary fire in the center of the circle. These hairs represent "frogs," which the mother has gathered for food. After the frogs have "cooked" on the fire, the mother calls to the children, and they all stand up in the circle. She goes to each child and taps him/her on the chest with a twig and asks him/her to fetch her mortar and pestle so that she can finish the preparation of the frogs. Each child

[8]In fact, according to Draper (1975), the "nomadic !Kung are a remarkably leisured society. Men and women work on the average only about three days per week in the food quest" (p. 609). This finding challenges the conventional assumption that significant amounts of leisure time are only found in industrialized societies.

[9]An ancient tale of the !Kung describes how the fate of the Bushmen was decided by a tug-of-war (see Marshall 1976:336–337).

[10]The movie *The Lion Game* shows the !Kung's clever satire of Bantu hunting practices. The !Kung do not hunt lions.

turns away, refusing to perform this task while mother feigns annoyance and finally leaves to retrieve her mortar and pestle.

While mother is away, the children steal the frogs and run off to various hiding places. When she returns, she pretends to be very angry and starts looking for her disobedient children. When she finds one, she strikes him/her on the head with her forefinger. This action "breaks the head" so that the child's "brains run out," and she then pretends to drink the "brains." The final part of the game frequently ends in chaos and pandemonium as the children try to dart away from mother's grasp. Soon everyone is chasing everyone else, shrieking and laughing and whacking each other on the head. The other "dramatic games" described by Marshall are "ostrich," "cattle," and "python."

Children may also act as critics and satirists of adult speech. For example, Mary Ellen Goodman, in her book *The Culture of Childhood* (1970), provided a brief example of two American 4-year-old boys caricaturing the greeting behavior and intonation patterns of two adult women. The burlesque is evident as the boys, in repeating the set phrases and exaggerating the word intonation, are reported to be laughing and "convulsed by their own wit":

> Jack: It's *lovely* to see you!
> Danny: I'm *so* happy to see you!
> Jack: How *are* you? How have you been?
> Danny: Sorry I have to go so quick. (p. 138)

Kornei Chukovsky, the Russian children's poet, presented an analysis of the thought processes and imagination of children as reflected in their language in his book *From Two to Five* (1963). Although this study is not intended to be a scientific investigation of Russian children's verbal play, it is one of the few detailed descriptions of this activity available for any group of children (other examples will be discussed in Chapter Nine). Chukovsky attempted to illustrate the "linguistic genius" of a young child in his/her word inventions, which are created "in accordance with the norms made known to him through adult speech," as when a bald man is described "as having a barefoot head" or a mint candy is said to "make a draft in one's mouth" (pp. 2, 9).

Chukovsky believes that "the basis for all linguistic aptitude attributed to the child . . . is imitation. . . . However, he does not copy adults as simply (and docilely) as it seems to the casual observer" (p. 9). In a special section entitled "Children as 'Critics' of Adult Speech," Chukovsky presented evidence designed "to show that in the process of assimilating his native spoken language the child, from the early age of two, introduces a critical evaluation, analysis, and control" (p. 9). As examples, he cited a number of instances of the child's sometimes mocking and often "strict and even disparaging criticism of the way adults use certain words and expressions" (p. 11).

> "I'm dying to hear that concert!"
> "Then why don't you die?" a child would ask sarcastically. (p. 11)

> After a long separation, a mother said to her little girl: "How thin you've become, Nadiusha. All that's left of you is one little nose."
> "Well Mommie, did I have more than one nose before you left?" (p. 12)

> An exasperated mother said to her son: "Some day you'll lose your head, so help me God!"
> "I'll never lose *my* head," was the reassuring reply, "I'll find it and pick it up. (p. 13)

> A visitor asked about five-year-old Seriozha's baby sister, "Does your little Irishka go to sleep with the roosters?"
> "No, she doesn't go to bed with the roosters. They scratch! She sleeps in her cradle." (p. 13)

It is possible that implicit in the imitation/socialization interpretations of children's play, which consistently disregard the critical and satirical qualities of these activities, is the child-centered view of many Western and also non-Western adults. That is, if adults as parents are expected to direct a large portion of their time and energy toward children (i.e., to raise or rear them), then perhaps it is necessary to believe that children reciprocate by directing all of their time in play toward adults (i.e., by imitating them). At least, at one level, it may be that interpretations of play as imitation are actually manifestations of, and rationalizations for, these common-sense (i.e., adult) beliefs (see Mackay, 1974).

In searching for ways to understand and evaluate social roles, and particularly sex roles, it may be useful to consider the role and structural inversions and satirical content characteristic of many children's games. Perhaps in certain of their play and game activities children have been questioning and/or mocking culturally stereotyped sex roles all along, and as adults we thought (or hoped) they were just being socialized.[11]

In searching for ways to understand and evaluate the role of anthropologists in the societies that they study, it may be useful to turn back to the description of Yoruba children "playing anthropologist," which appears in Chapter One. Is this an example of children "merely imitating" in play the anthropologist at work, or is there possibly an element of playful satire and parody apparent? If this play incident is viewed from the latter perspective, it is possible to learn something new

---

[11]Another way to explain (and again "adulterate") these games would be to say that they provide children with the opportunity to practice "role distance," in Goffman's (1961) terms.

not only about the child at play but also about the anthropologist at work.

SUMMARY

In the 1920s and 1930s a new approach to the study of culture was advocated by anthropologists who had grown tired of the overly inductive methods and atheoretical approach of the diffusionists and particularists. A. R. Radcliffe-Brown and Bronislaw Malinowski were the two major spokesmen for this new movement, which came to be known as *functionalism*. Although they differed greatly in regard to their particular orientation to functional analysis, they agreed on one basic premise: "that the parts of any whole, whether a social system or a culture, had to function for the maintenance of that whole" (Langness, 1974:82).

During the reign of functionalism, anthropologists pursued the study of the "serious" social systems of kinship, religion, politics, and economics. Because of the popularity of Radcliffe-Brown's structural-functionalism and his deemphasis on psychological studies, the study of childhood socialization, and in particular children's play behavior, was neglected. Except for analyses of adult joking relationships in various societies (e.g., Radcliffe-Brown, 1952) and Fortes's (1938) excellent discussion of Tallensi children's play behavior, detailed considerations of play phenomena were generally avoided by the functionalist.

Investigations of children's play that were conducted by researchers at this time—whether they were anthropologists, sociologists, or psychologists—gave emphasis to the imitative character of this activity. In these instances, children were depicted as imitating the activities (generally economic) of adults in their play behavior. The function of this imitative/mimetic play was to provide children with an opportunity to learn and practice culturally appropriate adult roles. These studies are important because, by stressing play's value as a socialization mechanism, they were able to challenge traditional views of play as a frivolous and useless activity. In this way, play itself became socialized and legitimated as proper and respectable behavior.[12] Unfortunately, in describing children's play as imitation of and/or preparation for adult activities, investigators examined only the social *contexts* (i.e., social functions) of play, to the exclusion of analyses of specific play *texts*.

Over the years, a number of researchers have indicated their dis-

[12]For an expanded critique of the play-as-socialization perspective, see Sutton-Smith's new book, *The Dialectics of Play* (1976b; also see 1977).

satisfaction with a view of play that emphasizes only its imitative character and socializing function (e.g., Fortes, Raum, Chukovsky, Sutton-Smith, Schwartzman). Recently, studies of children's play and games that stress the innovative and satirical qualities of game and play structure, content, and enactment have been made (e.g., Sutton-Smith, 1972b, 1974b). This research concentrates on studies of Western children's play, but it is also necessary to investigate the extent and kind of "games of order and disorder" in non-Western societies. These investigations are also important to initiate in order to question the validity of the "two cultures of games" notion. At present, because detailed material on this topic is scarce, cultural and class differences in children's play behavior are often interpreted as evidence of deficiency rather than variation in play styles. As anthropologists know from their studies of other topics, such views generally last only as long as there is a deficiency of rich ethnographic material.

All of these recent studies challenge and criticize the prevailing theoretical order of the times (which is still functional analysis for play researchers), just as they claim that certain children's games challenge and parody the existing sociocultural order of adult society. This research also reflects current critiques of the structural–functional approach in anthropology (see Jarvie, 1969) and emphasize this theory's inability to deal with social change, deviance, or novelty in a cultural system and its implicit and explicit acceptance and perpetuation of the status quo.

Projecting Play: Culture and Personality

And once she had really frightened her old nurse by shouting suddenly in her ear, "Nurse! Do let's pretend that I'm a hungry hyaena and you're a bone!"
Lewis Carroll, *Through the Looking Glass, and What Alice Found There*

While British ethnographers were busy reacting to the exaggerated induction of the historical particularists, new developments were taking place in America. During the 1920s and 1930s, a number of researchers, inspired by the linguist Edward Sapir, became interested in investigating relationships between the individual and culture. Although this concern differentiated this school from the British social anthropology of Radcliffe-Brown (although not from the psychological functionalism of Malinowski), there were several points of similarity between them. According to Langness (1974:85), both structural-functionalism and culture and personality studies "attempted to be scientific and nomothetic as opposed to historical and idiographic. They also attempted to consider wholes rather than merely parts. And they were avowedly theoretical." Along with Sapir, a number of anthropologists, psychiatrists, and psychologists have come to be associated with the culture and personality approach, including Ruth Benedict, Margaret Mead, Abram Kardiner, Ralph Linton, Cora DuBois, Géza Róheim, Erik H. Erikson, Clyde Kluckhohn, Francis L. K. Hsu, John W. M. and Beatrice Whiting, Melford Spiro, Anthony F. C. Wallace, and Robert LeVine.

CONFIGURATIONISTS

In 1925, when Margaret Mead sailed to the island of Samoa, she initiated the first of her several field studies designed to investigate the malleability of human "nature." According to Mead, the early culture and personality investigations of the 1920s were attempting to demonstrate

> over and over the fact that human nature is not rigid and unyielding . . . that cultural rhythms are stronger and more compelling than the physiological rhythms which they overlay. (1939:x)

Three of her earliest works repeatedly seek to demonstrate this thesis while centering on the investigation of different ethnographic "problems": (1) the cultural variability of adolescent behavior *(Coming of Age in Samoa,* 1928)[1]; (2) child-rearing practices in a "primitive" society and the thought of "primitive" children *(Growing Up in New Guinea,* 1930); and (3) the cultural patterning of male and female personalities *(Sex and Temperament in Three Primitive Societies,* 1932).

In these works, Mead illustrated the approach of what has come to be called the *configurationist school* of culture and personality research. Adopting the perspective of her teacher, Ruth Benedict, Mead sought to demonstrate two points: (1) that cultures have a basic "rhythm" or "pattern" to them; and (2) that it is only in relation to this pattern that an individual's or an entire society's actions can be judged. This latter view is generally referred to as *cultural relativism.* Finally, in relation to the above two points, Mead was interested in illustrating how culture influenced the personality of individuals, and it was this latter emphasis that was to become the major orientation of culture and personality studies.

Mead's view of the importance of studying primitive children, expressed in an article written in 1933 for the *Handbook of Child Psychology,* reiterates the major themes of the configurationists' approach:

> The primitive child is of interest to science chiefly as an excellent subject for experiments in social psychology. . . . Assuming . . . that the primitive child starts life with the same innate capacities as the child of civilized parents, the startling differences in habit, emotional development and mental

[1]It is interesting to note that this particular problem was chosen for her by Boas, who, according to Mead, was beginning to see the necessity of investigating the problem of the individual and culture. In *Blackberry Winter* (1972), she described Boas's shift and his formulation of "her" problem: "Now he wanted me to work on adolescence, on the adolescent girl, to test out, on the one hand, the extent to which the troubles of adolescence . . . depended upon the attitudes of a particular culture and, on the other hand, the extent to which they were inherent in the adolescent stage of psychological development with all its discrepancies, uneven growth, and new impulses" (p. 137).

outlook between primitive and civilized man must be laid at the door of a difference in social environment. Investigations will therefore be fruitful in direct proportion as they seek to study those aspects of human nature which are most subject to social influences. . . . Primitive children should be regarded primarily as subjects in an already constructed control culture. The investigator is spared the almost impossible task of creating control conditions, but is presented with such conditions ready made. Every primitive society thus presents a laboratory to the social psychologist, where he may test out whether certain aspects of human behavior are or are not socially determined. (pp. 909–910)

In concluding this article, Mead again suggested what she believes to be the major advantage of studies of primitive children:

> If we avail ourselves of this opportunity, we shall go far towards constructing a realistic psychology, corrected and informed by a detailed knowledge of the power of the social environment, a psychology which transcends the narrow bounds of Indo-European culture. (p. 925)

Mead's interest in the study of primitive children was therefore directly related to her desire to demonstrate the effect of culture on human nature. This concern influenced her suggestions for appropriate topics to be investigated by students of culture and personality. In the above-mentioned article, Mead outlined a number of prospective research topics, including studies of breast feeding patterns; weaning habits; sleeping habits; attitudes toward personal hygiene; development of typical gestures and postures; types of affection shown children; self-reliance expected of children; studies of whether or not children are stimulated through play; testing of various developmental theories; studies of variations in formal educational methods; investigations of how, and with whom, children develop friendships; studies of fear responses and stylization of anger and jealousy; investigations of children's thinking patterns and methods of reasoning; studies of language learning; studies of children's curiosity; and investigations of children's dreams. In formulating these suggestions, Mead was attempting to address topics that were part of current Western theories of child training, personality development, and character formation. She specifically included these topics because she wanted to put these theories to the ethnographic test. As will be noticed, the specific study of children's play was not emphasized in her listing of research problems. This lack of emphasis, however, is not surprising, given the fact that most child development theorists of the time viewed play as expressive (but not generative) of a child's personality. Adopting this same view, Mead chose to use the play and games of "primitive" children to investigate other topics. And this practice of *using* play for the study of other phenomena was to become the dominant approach taken to play by culture and personality researchers.

In *Coming of Age in Samoa* (1928), Mead described the play and games of Samoan children and adolescents only incidentally. For example, we hear that certain children "frolic and play together" (p. 29), while others do not, or that, after working all day, a child may slip away "to play games on the green" (p. 66). Unfortunately, we never hear in any great detail what types of play and games these children are actually participating in. Nevertheless, Mead did present an excellent discussion contrasting Samoan and American attitudes toward work. According to Mead, in American society there exists a false division between work, play, and schools that is taught to children, who then believe that

> work [is] for adults, play for children's pleasure, and schools [are] . . . an inexplicable nuisance with some compensations. These false distinctions are likely to produce all sorts of strong attitudes, an apathetic treatment of a school which bears no known relation to life, a false dichotomy between work and play, which may result either in a dread of work as implying irksome responsibility or in a later contempt for play as childish. (1928:228)

However, the fact that this "contempt" for play may actually have influenced anthropologists' observations of children's behavior was not considered.

Mead's second monograph documents the child-rearing practices of the Manus in New Guinea (*Growing Up in New Guinea*, 1930). In this book, more thorough discussions of children's play are presented. Mead's original research problem for this study was to investigate the thought of primitive children. She examined this problem in her monograph and also in an article written in 1932. Most specifically, she asked the question:

> was the thought of primitive children characterized by the type of animistic premise, anthropomorphic interpretation and faulty logic, which had been recorded for civilized children, or was this type of thought a product of special social environment? (1932:215)

Mead used the play and games of Manus children to study the problem of animistic thought that she had set for herself. In order to investigate this problem in her fieldwork context, Mead utilized several different techniques: (1) observations; (2) collection of spontaneous drawings; (3) interpretation of ink blots; and (4) answers to questions designed to provoke animistic responses.

In her attempt to discern what type of child behavior was characteristic of Manus children, as well as whether or not they exhibited animistic thought patterns in their daily activities, Mead spent a good deal of time observing the children's play and games. She reported that because the Manus child is trained to operate relatively independently of adults, he/she grows up largely in a world of peers or age-mates. In this world, Mead stated that they spend most of their time in "energetic," nonimaginative play activities.[2] For example, she stated that she observed "no instance of a child's personalizing a dog or a fish or a bird, of his personalizing the sun, the moon, the wind or the stars" (p. 225). Adults do not encourage the development of spontaneous animistic thought by telling stories or legends or by formally teaching children their religious concepts (which are animistic according to Mead). Likewise the Manus language is said to be "a bare simple language" without figures of speech or rich imagery and, therefore, providing little stimulation for the development of spontaneous animistic thought (pp. 234–235). Another example of the children's nonanimistic thinking patterns is their "naturalistic" responses to Mead's attempt to attribute malicious intent to a canoe that had drifted away. In these instances, she asked the question, "That canoe is bad, isn't it? It has drifted away" (p. 231). She received a variety of answers from the children (ages 3–6), but they were all very "matter-of-fact." For instance, "No, Popoli didn't fasten it"; "No, it wasn't fastened right"; "No, the punt (used to fasten canoes with) slipped" (p. 231).

Growing up in this context, the Manus child develops a naturalistic and not an animistic view of the universe *as a child*. This view changes, however, when children become adults, for Manus adults frequently display animistic thinking, according to Mead. Of course, these findings contradict the evidence, as marshaled by Piaget (see 1926, 1928, 1929, 1930) and others, that spontaneous animistic thought is a function of the child's developmental stage and his/her intellectual immaturity. In this instance, Mead has tested, in her "ethnographic laboratory," at least one aspect of the theory of universal stages of children's intellectual development, and, in her view, the theory failed. Accordingly, she stated:

> When such a reversal is found in two contrasting societies, the explanation must obviously be sought in terms of the culture; a purely psychological explanation is inadequate. (1932:233)[3]

[2]In *New Lives for Old* (1956), Mead discussed changes in Manus society between 1928 and 1953. Included here are descriptions of changes in Manus children's play during this time period. Mead particularly contrasted the "non-imaginative" play life of the children observed in 1928 with their "more imaginative" play activities seen in 1953 (pp. 339–343). This discussion is important because it is one of the few descriptions of changes in non-Western children's play behavior that has been observed, rather than inferred, by the ethnographer.

[3]Wayne Dennis (e.g., 1943) has disputed Mead's contention that animism is absent among Manus children because he believes that her methods for determining this were inadequate. He noted that she did not utilize Piaget's methods for eliciting animistic con-

The implications of this research for studies of children's play are, however, more germane to the concerns of this particular book. On the basis of these findings, Mead concluded that for children to engage in imaginative play activities, they must be encouraged to do so by adults:

> If the children's imaginations are to flourish, they must be given food. Although the exceptional may create something of his own, the great majority of children will not even imagine bears under the bed unless the adult provides the bear. (1930:257–258)

These statements are strikingly similar to those of El'Konin (1971) (discussed in Chapter Six), commenting on research conducted with Russian preschool-aged children. However, relationships between imitation, imagination, and sociocultural context were certainly imperfectly understood in 1930, when Mead made her remarks, and, as I have already argued, they are still today. Nevertheless, Mead drew the conclusion that progressive education would produce no effect unless it became more "content based" and in particular provided "children with something upon which to exercise their imagination" (1930:256). In her opinion, the Manus material illustrated the fact that children "do not produce rich and beautiful results spontaneously, but only as a response to material provided them by the adult world" (p. 256).

Mead believes that her third study, *Sex and Temperament in Three Primitive Societies* (1935), is her most misunderstood book. This misunderstanding relates primarily to some critics' belief that Mead was suggesting that her research proved that there was no such thing as sex differences. However, she was not suggesting this but, rather, continuing her critique of biological determinism by describing how three different New Guinea groups (the Arapesh, the Mundugumor, and the Tchambuli[4]) created contrasting expectations for appropriate male and female behavior. Once again culture was found to triumph over nature:

---

[4]*Tchambuli* is now spelled *Chambri*.

---

cepts from children, which involve specific questioning of the child by the researcher. The fact that Mead found that Manus children did not "spontaneously construct" animistic explanations in play or other situations is not enough for Dennis. He does not believe these observations of children's behavior because, in his view, "children's explanations are seldom stated clearly or fully unless they are brought to light by the questioning of the investigator" (p. 34). In other words, children's behavior in natural situations is to be distrusted, and only when they are confronted with an unfamiliar task, placed in an unfamiliar setting (e.g., a laboratory), and/or asked unfamiliar questions will their *real* beliefs (i.e., those that coincide with the investigator's) be discovered. For his part, Dennis suggested that his research (e.g., Dennis, 1942, 1943; Dennis and Russell, 1940) indicated that "The early childhood notions of the sort described by Piaget probably are world-wide. It is likely that they develop out of universal experiences, such as the experiences of self-movement, of visual movement, of frustration and success, of sleeping and waking—experiences which are common to all societies" (1943:33).

> We are forced to conclude that human nature is almost unbelieveably malleable. . . . The differences between individuals who are members of different cultures, like the differences between individuals within a culture, are almost entirely to be laid to differences in conditioning, especially during early childhood, and the form of this conditioning is culturally determined. Standardized personality differences between the sexes are . . . cultural creations to which each generation, male and female, is trained to conform. (1935:280)

The part that play and games have to "play" in this training process is only briefly mentioned by Mead. Arapesh culture is characterized by cooperation and unity, and both men and women are reported to act in a mild, maternal, and cooperative manner, in much the way that Americans expect women to behave. In this context, it is not surprising to find that Arapesh children are reported to play very few games and none that encourages aggressiveness or competition (i.e., no races or games with two sides, etc.). If a quarrel should develop during play, Mead reported, an adult immediately breaks up the game. The child who is angry is allowed to kick, scream, and carry on in any way he/she desires as long as another child or adult is not harmed.

In contrast to the cooperative Arapesh, the formerly cannabalistic Mundugumor are described as distrustful, hostile, competitive, and aggressive. In this group, Mead reported, both men and women are fierce and aggressive—behaving as American men are supposed to. Mundugumor children both reflect and learn these characteristics in their play activities, and so older boys "are continually pinching, pushing, threatening, bullying smaller children" (1935:198). Younger children are said to play

> endless little games with their hands, with pieces of stick, or with their toes, the emphasis always being on the skill with which the trick is performed, one child attempting to emulate and outdo another. (p. 198)

In this work, Mead appears to have described play in terms of its socialization function; however, for the most part, she described this activity in only a cursory manner, concentrating on a discussion of other factors to account for the differences in sex and temperament exhibited by Arapesh, Mundugamor, and Tchambuli society.

PSYCHOCULTURAL ANALYSIS

Milton Singer has suggested that the rise of culture and personality studies in the 1920s and 30s was brought about by the encounter of anthropology with psychoanalysis (1961:10). Whether anthropologists were reacting negatively to certain aspects of Freudian theory (e.g., Kroeber, 1920; Malinowski, 1927, 1929) or attempting to vehemently defend it (Róheim, 1943), there can be no doubt of its influence on anthropology in general and on culture and personality studies in specific.

In the late 1930s, Abram Kardiner, a neo-Freudian psychiatrist, together with Ralph Linton, an anthropologist, began to hold a joint seminar at Columbia University that was to have a great impact on future culture and personality studies. During these seminars, it became the practice for an ethnographer to describe a particular culture. Following this presentation, Kardiner would offer an analytic interpretation, which would then be discussed by the group. A number of researchers participated in this seminar, including Cora DuBois, Carl Withers, James West, Ruth Benedict, and Ruth Bunzel.

Kardiner believed that Freud's *The Future of an Illusion* (1928) contained a most important suggestion for adapting psychoanalytic theory to cultural analysis. In this work, Freud argued that there is a direct correspondence between a culture's religious beliefs and its early childhood practices (e.g., the Judeo-Christian God was said to be a "projected image" of Western man's stern patriarchical father) (Harris, 1968:436). Kardiner particularly stressed the importance of Freud's concept of a projective system:

> For the first time, Freud describes here the origin of what may be called a *projective system,* that is to say, a system for structuring the outer world and one's relation to it in accordance with a pattern laid down in an earlier experience during ontogenesis. This is a powerful idea and one with many uses. (Kardiner and Preble, 1961:236)

In their studies (e.g., 1939, 1946), Kardiner and Linton attempted to move beyond attempts to document the malleability of human nature, so characteristic of configurationists, by outlining a "psychocultural" theory synthesizing a neo-Freudian orientation with the contextual perspective of anthropology. In developing this theory, Kardiner postulated the existence of a "basic personality structure," which was said to be typical of the members of a particular society. This structure was thought to be formed by the "primary institutions" of a society. Primary institutions consisted, for the most part, of institutions and practices concerned with the rearing of young children. Research on these institutions was, therefore, to focus on the study of

> family organization, in-group formation, basic disciplines, feeding, weaning, institutionalized care or neglect of children, anal training, sexual taboo, subsistence techniques, etc. (Kardiner, 1939:471)

Secondary institutions existed, according to Kardiner, to "satisfy the needs and tensions created by the primary or fixed ones" (p. 471). These secondary institutions were described as projective systems and included such things as rituals, religion, taboo systems, folktales, and techniques of thinking. A number of ethnographic research studies were influenced by this approach. Two of the most well known are Cora DuBois's *The People of Alor* (1944) and Thomas Gladwin and Seymour B. Sarason's *Truk: Man in Paradise* (1953).

Cora DuBois's monograph represents a study of the village of Atimelang located on the island of Alor in Indonesia. Included in this study is the presentation of a general ethnography of the Alorese, as well as an analysis of eight lengthy biographies collected by DuBois during the 18 months of her fieldwork stay. In addition to this material, DuBois also included discussion and analysis of several psychological tests (e.g., Rorschach, word association test, Porteus maze test, and children's drawings) that she administered to Alorese informants.

The unique feature of this monograph is that DuBois submitted the results of her testing, as well as the life history material, to three different psychiatrists for independent analysis and interpretation. Abram Kardiner interpreted the life history material, while Emil Oberholzer, a Rorschach expert, prepared a "blind" analysis of these tests. In this case, Oberholzer knew nothing of Kardiner's conclusions, and Kardiner knew nothing about Oberholzer's analysis. Likewise, the children's drawings were submitted to Trude Schmidl-Waehner for "blind" analysis. In each case, there was a striking correspondence between the analysts' conclusions as to general tendencies in Alorese personality (Barnouw, 1973:155).

In brief, the child-rearing practices of the Alorese are as follows.[5] Women in this society are the primary producers and collectors of vegetable foods, while men spend the bulk of their time negotiating financial exchanges involving pigs, gongs, and kettledrums. This division of labor is crucial to the analysts' interpretations of Alorese personality. Following the birth of a child, the mother frequently returns to her agricultural work within two weeks. She does not take the baby to the fields with her, leaving it in the care of its father, brother, sister, or grandparent. Other women may or may not nurse the child, which, according to DuBois, leads to oral deprivation. Toilet training is not harsh in this society, and, likewise, the child is not encouraged to walk or talk during infancy. However, walking is reported to begin at a time similar to its occurrence in the West (12–18 months). Weaning does not occur before this time.

Between the ages of 1½ and 5 or 6 years, the child experiences a considerable amount of stress, according to DuBois. Oral frustration is continued because the mother leaves the child between the hours of 8

[5] I am following Victor Barnouw's (1973:154–162) summary of *The People of Alor* in this description.

A.M. and 5 or 6 P.M., and it can expect to be fed only irregularly during these hours. Therefore it is presumably hungry much of the time. Weaning and toilet training generally occur by age 3. Last-born children may sleep with their mother until they are 7 or 8. Sexual training is reported to be quite lenient. Sibling rivalry may be stimulated by a mother's teasing of her child, attempting to make him/her jealous of a new baby.

One of the most striking aspects of Alorese childhood is the frequent temper tantrums engaged in by children, usually at the time the mother is leaving for the fields. After the age of 6, however, these tantrums diminish in frequency and intensity as children begin to associate with same-sex peers. Boys are reported to be the most mobile in this activity, often running in groups searching for food, running errands for young men, or beginning to work in the fields, pulling weeds, etc. Girls remain nearer to their mothers during this period, learning household chores as well as agricultural duties. Also, both boys and girls may be given responsibility for the care of a younger child during this time.

All of these practices result, according to DuBois and the other analysts, in the existence of much tension and ambivalence in male–female relationships. Men are said to be constantly searching for a nurturing mother as wife. According to Kardiner, the childhood experiences of the Alorese create a situation where parental figures are not idealized and superego formation is weak. In conjunction with this, he also found a lack of artistic creation and interest in the outer world, both of which he also attributed to the effects of the child's maternal frustrations. Oberholzer found evidence of suspicion, distrust, passiveness, and indifference as well as little development of a "conscience and its dynamic expression" in the Rorschach responses. Schmidl-Waehner also found evidence of poverty-stricken relationships and absence of creativity in the children's drawings.

It is interesting to compare DuBois's descriptions of Alorese children's play with the suggestions made by these analysts regarding the lack of creativity and imagination displayed by children and adults. For example, DuBois reported the following:

> Children play a great deal. Girls emphasize food-gathering activities and cooking; boys emphasize hunting. It is noteworthy that the children have many games and toys, *some of which are very ingenious*—for example, a pressure squirt gun that is fashioned of bamboo. (1944:59, emphasis added)

DuBois went on to discuss a variety of games played by children, and she stated that this is in contrast to the behavior of the adults, who play no games. Adult recreation consists of dancing, ceremonial gatherings, and, for males, gong beating (p. 59). Children, on the other hand, exhibit a rich play life, which includes tops (boys), cat's cradle (girls), marbles, jacks, swinging, hunting, hide-and-seek, hide-the-grass, and mimicry and mockery games (see pp. 59–61, 70–73, 256–257, 444–445).

DuBois's analysis of Alorese personality and its determinants has been subjected to a number of critiques. DuBois herself stated that the prevalence of dysentery, respiratory infections, malaria, and yaws, experienced in early childhood, may heavily influence the child's personality. Powdermaker (1945) believes that too much emphasis has been placed on negative prohibitory features (particularly in Kardiner's analysis), ignoring the existence of positive, permissive, and restitutive practices also included in the monograph. Also, the size of the test sample on which the analysis was based was small in comparison to the population size (approximately 600) of the Alorese at the time of the study. DuBois's study is, however, representative of the type of psychocultural analysis that Kardiner, Linton, and others were perfecting for investigators interested in culture and personality research issues.

FREUD ON PLAY

The anthropological studies of children's play conducted in the 1930s and 1940s must be understood in the context of the Kardiner/Linton/DuBois school of culture and personality research. However, because of the impact of Freudian theory on this school, it seems important to backtrack briefly here to survey the various explanations and interpretations that Freud himself offered on this subject.

Psychoanalytic theories of play as developed initially by Freud (e.g., 1905, 1909, 1920) fall into the larger category of cathartic theories, of which Aristotle's ideas as expressed in the *Poetics* are perhaps the earliest example (Gilmore, 1969:320). Freud's explanations for this behavior are varied; however, two recurring themes appear in most of his interpretations: (1) the notion that, in play, children act out and repeat problematic life situations in order to *master* them; and (2) the idea that, in achieving mastery in play, the child *projects* his own anxious or hostile feelings onto other individuals or objects (e.g., the mother doll is roasted in the stove) (see Millar, 1968:27).

Two brief examples of Freud's interpretation of children's play are presented here. The first, and most commonly cited, example appears in *Beyond the Pleasure Principle* (1920). Here Freud described the behavior of his 18-month-old grandson, who had developed the habit of throwing all available objects into a corner of his room or under his bed at those times (which were apparently quite frequent) when his mother left him.

As Freud happened to be staying in the family's home at this time, he had the opportunity to observe the child's activities over a period of several weeks:

> This good little boy . . . had an occasional disturbing habit of taking any small objects he could get hold of and throwing them away from him into a corner, under the bed, and so on, so that hunting for his toys and picking them up was often quite a business. . . . I eventually realized that [this] was a game and that the only use he made of any of his toys was to play "gone" with them. One day I made an observation which confirmed my view. The child had a wooden reel with a piece of string tied around it. . . . What he did was to hold the reel by the string and very skillfully throw it over the edge of his curtained cot, so that it disappeared into it. . . . He then pulled the reel out of the cot again by the string and hailed its reappearance. . . . This, then, was the complete game—disappearance and return. As a rule one only witnessed its first act, which was repeated untiringly as a game in itself, though there is no doubt that the greater pleasure was attached to the second act. (pp. 33–34)

Freud suggested that this game represented the child's "great cultural achievement":

> the instinctual renunciation . . . which he made in allowing his mother to go away without protesting. He compensated himself for this . . . by himself staging the disappearance and return of the objects within his reach. (p. 34)

Freud's indirect, but by now very famous, treatment of "Little Hans" (1909) also includes information on his diagnostic use of play. This study is well known because Freud conducted his analysis through correspondence with the child's father, a Viennese physician who was also an adherent of Freudian theory.[6] Freud encouraged his friends and students to report to him anything of interest regarding the development of sexuality in their children. Hans's father frequently wrote letters to Freud about this subject. In *Analysis of a Phobia in a Five-Year-Old Boy* (1909), Freud quoted at length from many of these letters and so made available in a more explicit form than in any of his other studies, the actual "data" on which he based his interpretations.

Hans was born in Vienna in 1903, and in 1906 his sister (Hanna) was born. In 1908, when he was 5 and his sister was 2, he suddenly developed attacks of anxiety and then a phobia of horses and horse carts. Most specifically, he was afraid that a horse would bite him in the street, and so he was afraid to go out of the house. (Later he reported that he was also fearful that a horse would fall down, and he was particularly afraid of horses with "black around their mouth" and ones that wore

---

[6]Freud actually saw "Little Hans" on only one occasion. However, he had treated his mother, who had "fallen ill with a neurosis as a result of a conflict during her childhood," and this was, in fact, the beginning of his connection with Hans's parents (p. 142).

blinders.) Hans's father, in great distress, wrote immediately to Freud and was advised to talk to the child and carefully observe his behavior in order to discover the cause of the phobia. There followed a lengthy correspondence, a part of which is reproduced in this case history.

Even though Hans was greatly afraid of horses, he enjoyed pretending that a new maid in the house was *his* horse, and he would occasionally ride around on her back crying, "Gee-up." He also pretended at times that he was a horse, and he would trot around, fall down, kick about, and neigh. He reported that he used to play horses with his friends in Gmunden (where the family had spent the summer prior to Hanna's birth) and in particular with a little girl named Berta and a boy named Fritzl. Hans's father reported in his letters many dreams, fantasies, conversations, and other activities of this type in which Hans engaged.

Hans's phobia was interpreted by Freud as symptomatic of problems and anxieties with which the boy was trying to cope revolving around his feelings toward his father, his mother, and his new sister, Hanna. Most specifically, Freud believed that Hans was struggling with the Oedipus complex as well as feelings of sibling rivalry and also an interest in learning about conception. Accordingly, Hans harbored both hostile and affectionate feelings toward his father, who kept him from his mother and also refused to tell him the "facts of life"; and he also expressed hostile feelings toward Hanna. Horses and horse play, which previously had brought him pleasurable experiences, began to take on a new and fearful meaning when they became associated, through a somewhat convoluted process in Freud's interpretation, with his father. This process was reconstructed by Freud on the basis of Hans's father's reports:

> Behind the fear to which Hans first gave expression, the fear of a horse biting him, we had discovered a more deeply seated fear, the fear of horses falling down; and both kinds of horses, the biting horse and the falling horse, had been shown to represent his father, who was going to punish him for the evil wishes he was nourishing against him. . . .
>
> . . . It is especially interesting, however, to observe the way in which the transformation of Hans' libido into anxiety was projected on to the principal object of his phobia, on to horses. Horses interested him the most of all the large animals; playing with horses was his favorite game with other children. I had a suspicion—and this was confirmed by Hans' father when I asked him—that the first person who had served Hans as a horse must have been his father; and it was this that had enabled him to regard Fritzl as a substitute for his father when the accident [Fritzl fell down while playing horses] happened at Gmunden. When repression had set in and brought a revulsion of feeling along with it, horses, which had till then been associated with so much pleasure were necessarily turned into objects of fear. (1909:126–127)

Horses, however, could also be objects of recovery. On the one visit that Hans made to Freud's office, it became clear that Hans was afraid of horses with "black around their mouth" and "blinders on their eyes." Freud suggested that the first represented a moustache and the second eyeglasses, and his father had a moustache and also wore eyeglasses:

> Finally I asked him whether, by "the black around the mouth" he meant a moustache; and I then disclosed to him that he was afraid of his father, precisely because he was so fond of his mother. It must be, I told him, that he thought his father was angry with him on that account; but this was not so, his father was fond of him in spite of it, and he might admit everything to him without fear. (p. 42)

Some time later Hans's father reported that Hans was very interested in playing with horses; "he trots about, falls down, kicks about with his feet, and neighs. . . . He has repeatedly run up to me and bitten me" (p. 52). Freud interpreted this behavior as the beginning of the child's identification with his father:

> In this way he was accepting the last intepretations more decidedly than he could in words, but naturally with a change of parts, for the game was played in obedience to a wishful phantasy. Thus he was the horse, and bit his father, and in this way was identifying with his father. (p. 52)

In fact, Freud believed that one step on the road to resolution of the Oedipus complex was the child's identification with the same-sex parent. This identification would be exhibited by the child's imitation of his parent's activities in play. In relation to this idea, Freud believed that all children wished to be "grown up," and so their imitative play allowed them to make possible what was at present impossible and, thereby, once again to master a frustrating (although not necessarily psychically painful) situation. In *Jokes and Their Relation to the Unconscious* (1905), he suggested that

> mimicry is the child's best art and the driving motive of most of his games. A child's ambition aims far less at excelling among his equals than at mimicking the grown-ups. (p. 227)

Erik H. Erikson is one of the most well-known neo-Freudian analysts to have revised and expanded on Freud's theory of play. In his studies, Erikson stresses the growth-enhancing, as opposed to anxiety-reducing, qualities of play. In *Childhood and Society* (1963), he suggested that "the child's play is the infantile form of the human ability to deal with experience by creating model situations and to master reality by experiment and planning" (p. 222). Erikson has produced numerous studies of children's personalities and their relation to social context, including accounts of Oglala Sioux (1963) and Yurok (1943, 1963) childhood. These two reports contain discussions of children's play. He has also focused on the development of play behavior in children (e.g., autocosmic, microspheric, and macrospheric play) (see Chapter Four), and, as will be seen, this schema greatly influenced Bateson and Mead's (1942) interpretations of Balinese childhood development. Finally, Erikson has investigated the phenomenon of "play disruption" (1949) and the reflection of sex differences in children's play configurations and constructions (1941, 1951).

The most obvious use and expansion of Freud's ideas are apparent in the widespread utilization of children's play for diagnostic and therapeutic purposes. Melanie Klein (1954) was one of the most significant developers of the play therapy field, and she has repeatedly stressed the importance of symbolic play for child analysis. Klein believed that this behavior is, in fact, an appropriate substitute for the verbal free associations traditionally used in adult analysis.[7] In order to encourage and facilitate projective play of this type, Klein developed the use of miniature toys (generally dolls representing family figures) in her analytic sessions with children.

The doll play and play therapy approach, adopting, as it does, a view of play as a projective eliciting device similar to a TAT or Rorschach test, has now become widely used for clinical purposes. The approach of Virginia Axline (1947), Clark Moustakas (1953), and others continues, with certain variations, the Kleinian tradition of *using play* for the therapeutic treatment of children.

In the 1940s, the use of the doll play technique in personality research became quite common. Levin and Wardwell (1971) presented a comprehensive review of this research, which covers the time period 1940–1960. The value of the doll play approach for researchers, according to the authors, is that "it is possible to study a great variety of human problems 'in miniature' " (p. 156). Examples of the various types of problems investigated by the use of this technique are (1) aggression and its relation to age, sex, and child-rearing factors (e.g., Sears *et al.*, 1946); (2) stereotypy (e.g., Bach, 1946); (3) parental identification (e.g., R. B. Ammons and H. S. Ammons, 1949); (4) the effect of a child's separation from its parents (e.g., Bach, 1946; Sears *et al.*, 1946); and (5) racial and religious identifications and biases (e.g., R. B. Ammons, 1950). In all these studies, play was used as a context (i.e., a testing ground) for the study of other aspects of children's behavior. Rarely, if ever, was play made the subject of the investigator's test.

---

[7]Anna Freud is well known for her disagreement with Klein over this particular issue. In *The Psychoanalytical Treatment of Children* (1935), Anna Freud suggested that symbolic play is not an appropriate substitute for verbal free association and that "instead of being invested with symbolic meaning it may sometimes admit a harmless explanation" (p. 35).

The approach of the doll play researchers, as influenced by Klein and particularly Freud, significantly affected the anthropological study of children's play. Culture and personality researchers beginning in the late 1930s and the 1940s became increasingly interested in administering psychological tests such as Rorschachs and TATs to informants in various fieldwork contexts. This interest has already been illustrated in the discussion of DuBois's *The People of Alor* (1944), which includes a brief report on her use of the doll play technique (see pp. 70–72). It was during this period, and extending into the 1950s, that a variety of anthropologists began to use doll play techniques to elicit projective material from non-Western children in order to investigate a number of topics.

PROJECTING PLAY: THE PILAGÁ

The most well known and extensive of these doll play studies is Jules and Zunia Henry's *Doll Play of Pilagá Indian Children: An Experimental and Field Analysis of the Behavior of the Pilagá Indian Children* (1944). Intrigued by the work of David Levy (1937), who utilized doll play techniques to study sibling rivalry among American children, the Henrys adopted this approach for use in investigating the patterning of this behavior among the Pilagá Indians living in the Argentine Gran Chaco. The dolls consisted of a father, a mother, and several child dolls, and, as they were presented to the children, each doll was named after an appropriate family member.[8] The children also had available for use a mechanical turtle, a ball of plasticene, and scissors. They often made breasts and genitalia with this material, and, if they did not, the examiner (Z. Henry) would suggest that they do so.

In attempting to investigate whether or not the syndrome of sibling rivalry, as reported by Levy, was evident in Pilagá culture, the Henrys used information collected from field observations and the more standardized setting of the doll experiments. However, standardization for these experiments was difficult to obtain because the Pilagá did not value isolation and privacy, and children and adults were always

[8]Pilagá girls are reported also to play with dolls that their mothers make out of baked clay (female dolls) and bird bones wrapped in colored thread or cloth (male dolls). They do not specifically name their dolls, and the Henrys stated that these indigenous dolls are "made to go through all the formal cultural patterns in an utterly impersonal way" (p. 32). This is in contrast to their play with the Henrys's dolls, where the "play became intensely personal and hostility was vividly acted out" (p. 32). The Henrys suggested that the naming of the dolls after specific family members was a strong factor in producing these personal reactions.

around. The children's constant presence enabled the Henrys to spend a great deal of time recording and observing their behavior, but it also made the collection and interpretation of the doll play material somewhat problematic. Frequently two or more children were manipulating the dolls at the same time, hence stimulating one another in their activities and making the recording of their interactions with each other and with the dolls almost unbelievably difficult. It is a testament to the Henrys' patience, tolerance, sensitivity, and humanity (not to mention their anthropological training) that they did not quickly adopt the experimentalists' solution and force the children to play with the dolls individually, creating an artificial context for play with what was already foreign material. The Henrys illustrated their approach (and it is one that any anthropologist who chooses to work with children should heed) by stating that their doll play experiment "was set up not only in reference to the needs of a specific problem, but also in response to the children's spontaneous demands on the material" (1944:57).

There remains some degree of controversy over the findings of this study. For their part, the Henrys suggested that the material shows that patterns of sibling rivalry in Pilagá society "follow with little difference those found among children in our own society" (p. 80). However, there are some important differences:

> The most important difference between sibling rivalry patterns in our own society and those found among the Pilagá is that among the Pilagá remorse and self-punishment do not occur as consequences of hostility. Inasmuch, however, as remorse and self-punishment, while outstanding as general cultural sanctions in our own culture, do not occur as sanctions in Pilagá culture at all, it must be concluded that the difference in the sibling rivalry pattern between the two cultures is culturally determined. Remorse and self-punishment are not, therefore, fundamental to the sibling rivalry syndrome. (p. 80)

David Levy, the psychiatrist whose works originally stimulated the Henrys, makes much more grandiose claims for this research. He believes that this study indicates that this is a biologically based behavior. In his terms, the sibling rivalry syndrome

> represents a universal experience whenever a mother has more than one child in her own care. It is part and parcel, therefore, of the biology of maternal function . . . we are dealing, for all practical purposes, with a universal situation among people regardless of their various cultural forms, arising directly out of biologic behavior. (pp. xvii–xviii)

In contrast, Stanley Diamond, in the introduction to the recent 1974 reissue of this study, suggested that the Henrys were much too modest in their claims as to its significance. Diamond argued that instead of substantiating the American concept of sibling rivalry, the Henrys had, in fact, "exploded" the idea that the Western syndrome of sibling rivalry was a cultural universal:

> What they revealed, in no uncertain terms, was that among the Pilagá there was no guilt as we would define it, no chronic corrosion of self-esteem, no compulsive efforts at restitution . . . and in contrast with Dr. Levy's material, little or no evidence of destruction of property or effort to deface the image of the other. (p. xiii)

This debate should by now sound familiar, for it is a reflection of what was *the* classic argument in culture and personality research: Is it nature, or is it culture? In the meantime, however, what has happened to the study of play? Because the Henrys had adopted a view of play as projection for the purposes of their study, they did not provide extensive detail on the everyday play and games of Pilagá children. Instead, as has been found to be the case in other culture and personality studies, play was *used* as a context for the study of the cultural patterning of other aspects of children's behavior (in this case, sibling rivalry).

Even though they did not concentrate on the specific study of Pilagá children's play, there are interesting descriptions of this activity available in the monograph. Most noteworthy is the Henrys' realization that previous anthropological descriptions "list only the formalized games of children and ignore all the spontaneous and unstructured play" (p. 5). This unstructured play, however, is not unpatterned behavior. According to the researchers, "unstructured play is patterned by culturally determined psychic processes that compel the same repetitions of play form day after day" (p. 5).

In Pilagá society, where discussions of sexual matters are very open and where sexuality and violence seem fixed in the eyes of both children and adults, it is not surprising to find that the Henrys report that the children spend many hours each day engaged in "violent sexual" unstructured play activities.[9] This behavior would certainly startle and probably shock most American parents, but it was routine for the Pilagá child:

> Kapíetn [male, age 3½] fights with Yatákana [female, age 5] and thrusts his hand against her vulva and says: "It stinks." . . . Tapáñi [female, age 8–9] and Yatákana box. When Yatákana turns toward ZH [Zunia Henry], Tapáñi pounds her on the back. Tapáñi separates Yorodaikolík's [male, age 4] buttocks and drags him off the dirt pile. Yatákana snatches at Kapíetn's penis from behind. Then she pounds him on the back. . . . Yorodaikolík, Darotoyí [male, age 4], and Denikí [male, 15 months] are masturbating. Darotoyí has exposed his glans by pulling back the foreskin. Yorodaikolík shoves his foot against it and pushes him down. (p. 55)

[9]In fact, reports of various types of sex play are often the only mention of this activity made by culture and personality researchers.

PROJECTING PLAY: THE DUAU

One of the most controversial figures of the culture and personality school was Hungarian-born Géza Róheim. Róheim conducted fieldwork on Normanby Island with the Duau, a Melanesian people (living in what was then British New Guinea) related to the Massim and the Trobriand Islanders. The Duau live in matrilinear village groups in monogamous families. Róheim chose his fieldwork site carefully, for he was also a lay analyst and a firm believer in Freudian theory.

In studying the Duau, Róheim planned to dispute Bronisław Malinowski's criticism of what was central to classical Freudian theory: the universality of the Oedipus complex. The Trobriand Islanders, whom Malinowski had lived with for two years (1914–1916), were also a matrilinear society, where residence was patrilocal or virilocal after marriage (i.e., the bride goes to live in her husband's community). On the basis of information gathered in this context, Malinowski *(Sex and Repression in Savage Society,* 1927) examined and criticized Freud's concept of the Oedipus complex. Most specifically, he asked whether or not this was a universal or a culture-specific phenomenon. In other words, was the Oedipus complex, as described by Freud, to be found in a society with distinctly different family patterns, such as the Trobriand Islanders (Barnouw, 1973:114)?

In Trobriand society, males do not inherit property from their fathers but from their mothers' brothers. Likewise, the principal food provider for a family is the mother's brother, and he is also the disciplinarian for his sister's children. In contrast, the children's father is permissive and indulgent with his offspring, and it is suggested that he spends much more time playing with them than most Western fathers. Trobriand children are also allowed a great deal of premarital sexual freedom and experimentation; however, there is a strong taboo on brother–sister incest.

For these reasons and many more, which will not be elaborated here, it is the mother's brother, and not the father, who is seen as the principal family authority. Because of the position of the mother's brother in Trobriand society, Malinowski argued that a boy's antagonism and hostility were directed toward this figure and not toward his father. Furthermore, Malinowski suggested that the Trobrianders exhibited a repressed desire to marry their sisters and not their mothers, as argued by Freud:

> Applying to each society a terse, though somewhat crude formula, we might say that in the Oedipus complex there is the repressed desire to kill the father and marry the mother, while in the matrilineal society of the Trobrianders, the wish is to marry the sister and to kill the maternal uncle. (1927:80)

Malinowski's statements were challenged by many adherents of Freudian theory. The criticisms of Ernest Jones (1925) are probably the most famous and seem, according to Barnouw (1973:65), to have caused even Malinowski to rethink his original stand.[10] Géza Róheim also criticized Malinowski's arguments. However, Róheim went further than Jones and suggested that if researchers could not discover the Oedipus complex *just as Freud had described it,* then they must themselves be suffering from unresolved Oedipus complexes:

> But the point we are now making is that the impression of complete diversity of various human groups is largely created by the Oedipus complex, that is to say, the Oedipus complex of the anthropologist or psychologist. He does not know what to do with his own Oedipus complex—he therefore *scotomizes* clear evidence for the Oedipus complex, even where his training ought to enable him to see it. (1950:362)

Róheim also argued that the Trobriand child would, in fact, experience the Oedipus complex because the mother's brother does not begin to play an important role in the family until the child is 7 or 8. It is at this time that the boy goes to work in his uncle's village; however, the child has spent his early years (1–6) in the company of his father, his mother, and his siblings. It is during this early period that the crucial events related to the formation and resolution of the Oedipus complex are said to occur. Therefore, according to Róheim, the Oedipus complex is a universal, and not a culture-specific, phenomenon.

Just in case his audience was not convinced, however, Róheim sought to demonstrate the existence of the Oedipus complex and other Freudian notions in a matrilinear society. Róheim used his material on the Duau to illustrate these ideas, and this is most obvious in his analysis of the doll play behavior of these children (1941). Once again, we have an example of an anthropologist using children's play as a context for the examination of other topics.

During his work with the Duau, Róheim encouraged the younger children to play near his house by providing them with a variety of toys (particularly dolls). The play materials consisted of two large male and female dolls, two small male and female dolls, two smaller Indian dolls, a dog, a rabbit, a snake, a red and yellow bird, and a hollow elephant with lollipops stuffed into it. Often Róheim would give the toys names (e.g., this is your "child," this is your "mother") in order "to get the game started," and he told the children that the elephant represented himself (p. 524).

In interpreting this material, Róheim found evidence for, among other things, the universality of the Oedipus complex, the use of the

---

[10]Jones argued, for example, that the father was really hated by the Trobrianders but that this hostility was deflected toward the maternal uncle.

snake as a phallic symbol, and reactions to the primal scene. If the children were not themselves quickly led to act out these themes in play, Róheim was quick to encourage them to do so by engaging in the well-known practice of "leading the witness." In fact, he appears to have greatly enjoyed the results of his "interventions":

> Now they start a real *Lojawe* (lovemaking) game. The big doll and the little one (father and son) go to the same girl together; they climb up the house (represented by Deororo's leg) and now he rubs the dolls, in great excitement on Deororo's shirt. They both have intercourse with the same girl. Now the big and small doll are rubbed against each other as if one of them were female. "Why standing?" I ask. "All right, they will do it lying," he says. "But she must take her shirt off," I say. Both little girls are terribly shocked at this and protest at such a break of etiquette.
>
> Now they get terribly excited. "Your husband cohabits with you," Illaisa says, and throws the father doll at the girls. "Your wife cohabits with you" . . . the girls say, throwing the female doll at them. . . . The three children are in a frenzy of excitement and they press and rub the dolls at each other's feet. . . . Now the big male doll is cohabiting with the big female doll; I put the small doll beside them and say, "Here is the child." The result is unexpected; suddenly they all get gloomy, depressed. This was too much like the primal scene for them. However, the next time they came, they enjoyed the primal scene game. (pp. 525–526)[11]

NEW METHODOLOGIES: THE HOPI AND THE BALINESE

During the 1940s and 1950s, a number of ethnographic studies of child-rearing practices were conducted. Researchers continued to use the doll play technique to acquire projective material from children (see particularly Jane Ritchie's study of Maori children, *Childhood in Rakau: The First Five Years*, 1957), while others began to question its interpretive validity. For example, David Landy used this technique to investigate personality patterns of lower-class Puerto Rican cane workers (1960) and found that he could not determine when he was eliciting projective material from his child subjects and when the play reflected everyday life situations. Therefore, he suggested that this was not a viable approach for use in cross-cultural studies.

Other researchers continued to explore relationships between individual development and cultural context by collecting written autobiog-

---

[11]It is unfortunate that Róheim did not offer an interpretation of the children's play with the elephant toy (which was said to represent the ethnographer). For example, "Illaisa played with the elephant. It has been passive in a *coitus per anum* and the guts have been pulled out! Illaisa shouts triumphantly" (p. 527). Clearly the Duau children had interesting things to say to the ethnographer here, although he chose not to comment on them.

raphies, in-depth interviews, and results from intelligence tests (e.g., Arthur Point Performance Scale, Goodenough Draw-a-Man test), and projective tests (e.g., free drawings, Murray's Thematic Apperception Test, Rorschach test). One of the most well-known examinations of this sort, initiated in 1941 and published in 1947, is Dorothea Leighton and Clyde Kluckhohn's study of Navaho child development, *Children of the People*. This monograph does not contain an extensive description or analysis of children's play. However, the authors did indicate that the work–play dichotomy of other Americans is not shared by the Navaho because, in this society, play is always part of work and vice versa. This is briefly illustrated in the report that

> while the little shepherd works by taking the sheep out in the morning, he spends considerable periods of the time . . . in playing with them or the dog or his fellow shepherd or the sticks and rocks around. (p. 169)

Unfortunately, detailed descriptions of this play at work are not offered.

In the early 1940s, two studies appeared that reported information on the play of Hopi and Balinese children. These monographs did not suggest new theoretical approaches; however, they did present new methodological innovations for the study of children's play. *The Hopi Child*, published in 1940 by the psychologist Wayne Dennis, outlines both the child-rearing practices of Hopi adults and the typical behavior of Hopi children. Dennis spent two summers (1937, 1938) collecting information on this topic for this group of Pueblo Indians. During this time he lived, together with his wife and his daughter, Mary (age 8), in a native house in the village of New Oraibi.

In order to observe more easily the behavior of children (and in particular their play activities), Dennis constructed a "play shelter" next to his residence. This shelter was built over a sandy area to provide protection from the hot summer sun, and it was patterned after the type of constructions that were frequently built in the fields. The shelter was located next to a window of the Dennis residence, and so, when they were at home, they were always able to observe the activities of the children.

Dennis noted that whenever he or his wife were in the house, they attempted to observe, at least once per hour, the play activities that were in progress in the shelter. In these instances, they would observe the children for about 10 minutes, then write a summary of what they had seen, then observe for another 10 minutes, and so on. Their daughter was frequently an active participant in many of these play sequences. These notes are presented in their entirety in this monograph in the form of a *play diary*. Accompanying this diary is a list of play participants, which includes the name, age, sex, and siblings of those children who most often played in this shelter area. Because Hopi children ordinarily play in sex-differentiated groups, Dennis's daughter developed friendships with a group of village girls, and they often played together in the shelter. Therefore, the play notes that Dennis recorded are more detailed with respect to the play activities of girls.

This play diary contains daily reports covering the time period June 27–August 8, 1938. The type of play activities described are quite varied, including house play and house building (generally girls); playing with a log seesaw and numerous variations; swinging on a rope tied to the supports of the shelter; rolling auto tires (boys); tag; riding stick-horses; fireworks (boys); mock fights and teasing between boys and girls; racing; bone dolls (girls); rabbit hunts improvised by throwing sticks at tin cans (boys); circle games; tug-of-war; and rolling hoops made from the hubs of old wagon wheels (boys).

The play notes also report the time of day in which the activity occurred. As might be expected in this northern Arizona desert environment, the children were most active after sunset during the summer months. An example of the type of material that appears in this diary is reported below, describing the events of the evening of July 11:

8:00 PM. Vie [female, age 10], Fran [female, age 8], Min [female, age 10], Mary [female, age 8—Dennis's daughter] were in the shelter pulling each other in a circle and often causing each other to fall. Har [male, age 10], a small boy who was in the swing, was accidentally hit in the eye by one of the girls. He cried slightly but went home with dignity. The girls continued their former play. Note that it is much cooler tonight.

Min suggested that they play "I spy" but the suggestion did not take.

Pam [male, age 12], Pete [male, age 6], and Frank [male, age 9] came by rolling tires, and stopped to play on the seesaw. Pam with two tires balanced the two smaller boys. Pam made the log stand as nearly vertical as was possible, almost spilling the two smaller boys. The boys shrieked, yelled and laughed most hilariously. The seesaw play stopped after ten minutes and the boys watched the girls' game for awhile. After this, the boys picked up their tires as if starting away and then ran them at the girls.

The girls began a game of tag, and the boys, to our surprise, joined the girls. The rules which evolved after a few minutes of play were as follows: One person is "it" until he tags someone else. A player is safe if he is touching a post or a rafter of the shelter, but only one person may touch each piece. When a second person touches a piece of timber, the first person is forced off. He may, of course, go to another timber and force someone else off.

This made a very active game and it was played vigorously and noisily for half an hour, when it became desultory and broke up. The rules were always adhered to.

In the course of the game, Ann [female, age 2] came down the lane and stood in the shelter in the midst of the seven scrambling older children. She did not attempt to play, but merely stood and watched. The girls moved her outside the shelter several times because she was in danger of being knocked over, but she returned each time. When the game ended, she started toward the main road. We brought her back to the shelter and her mother came for her. (pp. 141–142)

In another section of this book, Dennis provided a description of the play and game activities of children living in the more conservative and traditional Hopi village of Hotavila. Because he did not live in this village, many of these reports were collected from interviews with older informants. However, the ethnographer did have the opportunity to observe children actually playing many of these games in New Oraibi and occasionally in Hotavila. Organized and unorganized games are described in considerable detail (pp. 48–69).

The method by which Hotavila girls build play houses is quite ingenious. First, house walls are modeled from wet mud and then they are filled with dry sand while a wet earthen roof is applied to the top of the structure. After the adobe roof has dried, the sand is removed through the windows and doors and a miniature Hopi house has been created. These houses are furnished with all manner of items that the girls scavenge from the village. A small piece of mirror is used as a dressing mirror, a piece of linoleum is the rug, and a small can becomes the stove, while an empty spool of thread stands in for the sewing machine. Sticks with clothing tied onto them become the Hopi child's dolls and also the inhabitants of these villages. Another traditional doll form is created by making the different parts of the forefoot of a sheep or calf impersonate various family members (see Figure 12). Gardens, cornfields, and fruit orchards are often built around these houses by sticking twigs and leaves into the ground. Houses of this type are generally built and fur-

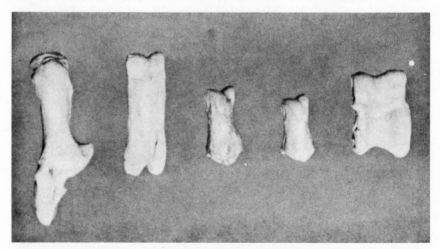

FIGURE 12. Hopi children's bone dolls. From left to right, the bones represent a father, mother, two children, and a grandmother (W. Dennis, 1940:Plate IV).

nished jointly by a group of young girls under the age of 12. Interspersed with this play, the girls perform the task of baby-sitting, as they are responsible for the care of their younger siblings between the ages of 1 and 3.

The young boys do not build play houses, but they do construct small corrals using peach seeds as sheep, and they also construct small fields. Boys also play at riding horses by using sticks or themselves, in which case they may hold tin cans in their hands as hoofs and run around on all fours. Rabbit hunting is also dramatized by using a tin can for the rabbit and throwing sticks at it.

Many of the play activities described for the children of New Oraibi are also played at Hotavila. Children from both areas use logs as seesaws and also make swings out of ropes. One of the most popular activities of boys is to roll and race old automobile tires or hoops down hills. Boys and girls also keep (and also torment) pets: dogs for boys and cats for girls. Young birds, rabbits, and prairie dogs, when they can be caught during the summer, also become pets. These small animals are often treated as inanimate objects or toys and, accordingly, are played with quite roughly, dragged and pushed around as a small toy bear might be by a Western child.

A variety of organized games are also played by Hotavila and New Oraibi children. Many of these games occur only during certain seasons. For example, boys are given shinny balls and clubs at the bean dance, traditionally held in February. Goals are marked at either end of a field, and the ball is placed in a hole in the middle and covered with dirt. The teams take turns striking at the ball until it comes out, and each time a goal is made, the teams exchange sides. There is no agreed-upon stopping time, and Dennis reported that the games sometimes go on by moonlight. Generally there are no forfeits and no prizes, although occasionally a losing side may give up its ball. Girls sometimes play this game (although never with the boys), but they are not given shinny equipment.

Tops are played only during March because they "sound like the wind" and might bring wind, which would damage the crops. Therefore, tops are only allowable in the spring before the crops are planted. Tops are played by children between the ages of 4 and 8, and they are generally whittled from wood by a father or an older brother. Tops are spun by winding a string around their top and then pulling the string. Sometimes a game of top "tag" is played by older boys, who form into teams. The boys whip their tops and try to make them jump suddenly to touch a player from the opposite side. A player who is touched is "out," or he may have to join the side of the player whose top has "tagged" him.

Another game played by boys, and less frequently by girls, is the "snake game," which occurs during the late summer and early fall. A leader starts the game by forming a line, and other players then line up behind him according to their size by grasping the boy in front by the waist or the belt. The leader guides the line along a crooked course, like a snake, and they sing a song that is used only in this game. (Dennis did not provide the words for this song.) Once the snake line has been created, the players are privileged to go anywhere they wish in the village. They frequently wind through homes singing for gifts of food, and, when they receive melons, fruits, etc., they sing a song of thanks. When they have collected a large quantity of food, they go outside the village and have a small feast.

Many other seasonal games and sports are described, including archery, rabbit hunting, stick throwing, dart throwing, and parchesi (*totolospi*). A number of nonseasonal games are also discussed, such as war games (boys); breaking the *piki* stone (a combination sand painting/guessing game played by girls); *alalatami* (a circle game initiated by older girls as an entertainment for the younger children); pursuit game (a variation of tag played by girls); playing witch (an older boys' game played at night); practical jokes, which boys and their "grandfathers" (father's sisters' husbands) play on one another; and stories told for children.

The presentation of this play diary, as well as these detailed discussions of both organized and unorganized play activities, is a unique methodological and descriptive contribution to the anthropological study of children's play. Dennis's interest in combining observations of children's behavior with the collection of information from adult informants on child-rearing practices led him to pay particular attention to children's play. This is one of the first ethnographic studies to emphasize the importance of acquiring information on play from actual observations of children. The fact that Dennis's daughter accompanied him on these field trips may also have encouraged him to focus on careful and detailed observations of children, for, in the process of watching out for Mary, he began to watch her and her various friends at play.

Gregory Bateson and Margaret Mead were married in Singapore in 1936, and soon afterwards, they were sailing to Bali to begin a new two-year fieldwork project. Bateson was 31 and Mead was 34 at the time, and both had previously worked in other cultures. They had met in New Guinea while Bateson was studying the Iatmul and Mead the Arapesh, Mundugumor, and Tchambuli with her former husband, Rio Fortune. Breaking with anthropological "custom," they planned to write a book that would *not* be about Balinese custom

but about the Balinese—about the way in which they, as living persons,
moving, standing, eating, sleeping, dancing, and going into trance embody
that abstraction which (after we have abstracted it) we technically call culture.
(1942:xii)

They also wanted to develop a new methodology that would combine
Bateson's training in biology and interest in the subtleties and nuances
of culture with Mead's experience in investigating the ways that cultures
influence the development of individuals (Mead, 1972:244–246).

For their fieldwork site, they chose to study the mountain village of
Bajoeng Gede, which expressed a simpler and less elaborate version of
the "high" culture of the Balinese lowlands. They worked here at a
feverish pace for nearly two years, attempting to discover and capture
on movie film and in stills and field notes the themes of Balinese culture
as illustrated by the day-to-day actions of these villagers:

> Gradually we developed a style of recording in which I kept track of the main
> events while Gregory took both moving pictures and stills . . . and our
> youthful Balinese secretary Made Kaler kept a record in Balinese, . . . which
> provided us with vocabulary and a cross-check on my observations. We soon
> realized that notes made against time provided the only means by which the
> work of three people could be fitted together and which would enable us,
> later, to match the photographic records of a scene with the notes. (Mead,
> 1972:253)

In the end they took 25,000 stills and 22,000 feet of 16mm film and
produced one joint monograph, *Balinese Character* (1942). This book is
both a unique record of Balinese culture, as revealed by the behavior of
the inhabitants of Bajoeng Gede, and a model of what it is possible to do
with film and still photographs in the study of social systems. Langness
has recently noted that this experiment in anthropological communication (which was itself an elucidation of the process of cultural communication) has never been replicated (1974:107). And this is so even with the
recent development of more sophisticated and more durable photographic and recording equipment.

Probably because of their interest in the study of how culture is
communicated from parent to child in subtle and seemingly inconsequential ways, coupled with the fact that Balinese culture is animated by
play in the arts, in music, and in drama, much more so than most
societies, Bateson and Mead produced a number of photographic/note
sequences on the play activities of both children and adults.[12]

Balinese children (particularly boys) learn very early to make what

[12]Balinese culture has been extensively studied by a number of researchers, and particular
emphasis has been given to drama and plays, arts and music, ceremonies and trance.
See, for example, Jane Belo (1937, 1953, 1960); Miguel Covarrubias (1938); Clifford Geertz
(1972, 1973); and Beryl de Zorte and Walter Spies (1937).

could be regarded as the ultimate transformation, for they learn to turn their own bodies into toys.[13] As infants they are treated as toys and playthings by their mothers, sisters, and also fathers; and for the Balinese, who avoid overresponsiveness of any sort in their personal interactions, "a baby is *the* most responsive of human beings" (1942:23). The young child's first experience with living creatures is with baby birds, puppies, beetles, grasshoppers, and so forth. In playing with these animals, the child concentrates on how his/her actions affect the behavior of the "toy"; how the bird flutters or the puppy yelps when they are pushed, poked, or pulled on a string (see Figure 13). Most importantly, it is suggested that in these play activities, children are "learning to experiment with their own bodies" and, in particular, "the sense of a body-part symbol which is attached, but by a thread, and which has a life and willfullness of its own, becomes strongly developed" (p. 25). The idea that body parts (particularly the phallus) are only loosely attached and are independently animated is particularly true for boys.

This idea is acted out, although in somewhat different ways, for both males and females as they grow up and acquire new "playthings." Little girls are expected to take care of their younger brothers and sisters, and so, in this way, they have new "toys" to play with; and Bateson and Mead reported that girls rarely invent substitute dolls. Later they become mothers and have their own babies to fondle and take care of. Little boys soon develop an interest in the playthings of men—fighting cocks—which are constantly fussed over, bathed, fluffed, and ruffled. Cocks, however, are handled as if they are extensions of the man's body, while babies are treated as something separate and apart from the woman's body. Nevertheless, both boys and girls develop a heightened sense of body consciousness. This is exhibited most obviously in a Balinese audience's reaction to the dancers in a theatrical performance:

> A Balinese audience at any performance is a group of people who are technically interested; they are uncaught by the plight of the princess lost in the forest, blown away on her silken cobwebs, but they are deeply concerned with the twist of her little finger. (p. 28)

Bateson and Mead used Erik H. Erikson's classification of play to interpret this behavior of the Balinese. As discussed in Chapter Four, Erikson (1963) stated that *autocosmic* play occurs as "exploration by repetition of sensual perceptions, of kinesthetic sensations, of vocaliza-

---

[13]For another examination of the development of Balinese children based on the Bateson and Mead data, see Margaret Mead and Francis C. Macgregor (1951). Also see Jane Belo (1937) for an analysis of Balinese children's drawings and Colin McPhee (1938) for a discussion of children and music in Bali.

tions"; it is play centered on the body (p. 220). Play in the *microsphere* exists as play with manageable toys and manipulation of these toys (p. 221). Play in the *macrosphere* occurs in the "world shared with others," and these others become part of the play situation (p. 221). Erikson proposed these categories as a developmental scheme, with autocosmic play occurring first with the infant, while macrospheric play was said to be typical of the activities of nursery-school-aged children. In many cultures (certainly in America), toys and adult play with children may encourage play activities to unfold in the fashion proposed by this schema, so that a child's attention is slowly drawn away from his/her body and into the outside world and the world of others. In contrast, in Bali,

> everything combines to refocus the child's attention back upon himself. His whole body . . . is like a toy . . . upon which those about him play; they make toys which tell the same tale, and it is not surprising that he develops a bodily consciousness very different from our own. (p. 26)

Seven plates of photographs (Numbers 38–44) with accompanying contextual notes were presented by Bateson and Mead to document and illustrate the autocosmic play and symbols of the Balinese in this monograph (see Figure 13).

Balinese children do, however, engage in a variety of group play and game activities. Boys, particularly because they do not have childcare and ceremonial responsibilities, as do girls, join "ragamuffin" gangs and engage in a variety of seemingly rowdy and boisterous games. However, the aggression and rowdiness are frequently feigned, for no one actually gets kicked, hit, or hurt. Boys also spend a great deal of time away from the village, as each one takes care of a particular ox, which must be tethered in the fields during the day to graze and brought home at night, leaving the rest of the day for roaming, exploring, and playing. Even with their greater responsibilities, the girls also engage in roughhouse play, crack-the-whip games, sand drawings, and group play. A sequence of play activities of small girls is reproduced on Plates 76–78, and the play of young boys is illustrated on Plate 83 in *Balinese Character* (1942).

Children growing up in this culture gradually learn to withdraw into themselves, "thrown back on their own bodies for gratification" (p. 26). This occurs in a number of ways and in a number of contexts. First, the child will begin to avoid the incessant teasing and toying of his/her parents and elders by going out of his/her way to avoid groups of adults. In other instances, after a particularly active work or play experience, a child or parent, student or teacher will suddenly look vacant and become totally unresponsive. At this moment—and it can occur when the individual is alone or in a group—the person is closed to the outside

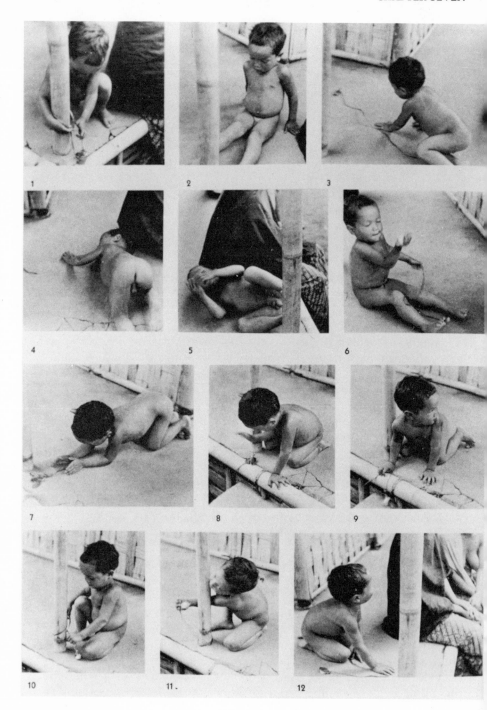

FIGURE 13. A bird on a string, Bali. Photographic sequence and contextual notes (G. Bateson and M. Mead, 1942:139, Plate 42).

This sequence illustrates the variety of behavioral patterns which a single child exhibits in playing with an autocosmic genital symbol. The whole sequence, as recorded in M. M.'s notes, lasted about 15 minutes, but of this period only about 7 minutes was recorded with the camera. At this point the film in the still camera finished, and the remainder of the sequence was recorded with the motion-picture camera.

Extracts from M. M.'s notes:

"Suddenly, while looking at carvings (brought by a seller), I noticed that I Karsa had a tiny bird on a bark string, which he was dragging about—dropping the end of the string so that it fluttered away—dragging it about again. Karsa took the bird over to his father, asked some questions about it and tried to hide it in his father's blanket (cf. Pl. 64, fig. 2).

"Karsa drops the string. Watches the bird flutter.

"He falls on it—feet locked together. Mutters over it with his mouth right over it. Curls over it.

"He crawls with it in his fingers toward mother. Drops it. Says 'It's dead.' He climbs up on his mother's back, rollicks, kicks his heels up, on his mother's back.

"Another woman asks him some question about the bird. Karsa says 'I'll tie it up.' Comes over to the corner post (of our veranda) and fastens the bird with two twists round the post (fig 1). (At this point, Karsa sat back away from the bird and looked at it, while extending his legs on each side of the post. This behavior is shown in fig. 2, but was not recorded in the verbal account.)

"Karsa loosens string, and the bird, freed, flutters across the floor. Karsa hurts his finger as he goes after it (figs. 3 and 4).

"Karsa cries—rolls over, crying (fig. 5).

"I say 'Where's the bird?' Made Kaler (our secretary) says 'Is the bird lost?' Karsa goes and gets the bird again.

"He holds it up loose in his upraised hand and lets it flutter down (fig. 6).

"Repeats this. The bird cries.

"Karsa holds the bird over the step" (figs. 7, 8, and 9).

During this episode M. M. could not see what Karsa was doing. In fig. 7, he has the bird on the floor and holds his hands in an open V. In fig. 8, he has the bird on the edge of the veranda and is slowly patting at it with his right hand (cf., Pl. 41, fig. 7). In fig. 9, he has let the bird fall down over the edge, where it hangs while he looks back at his mother.

"Karsa ties the bird to another post (figs. 10 and 11). (Apparently he first tied it by twisting the free end of the string around the post in fig. 10, and then varied this by carrying the bird itself round the post in fig. 11.)

"Karsa feints at pouncing on the bird with both hands cupped.

"He says 'Oh! It's dead' and holds it out to his mother. He beats at his mother with his hand. She says 'No. It's alive' " (fig. 12).

In the second half of the sequence, he again ties the bird to a post; and again plays with the notion that his mother is responsible for the bird's "death." In addition to these repeats, he starts a new type of play by putting the bird between his legs, leaving it for a moment behind his back pretending to have forgotten it (cf. Pl. 41, fig. 3). Then he suddenly turned and "found" it, as if surprised. After this play with the bird between his legs, he held the bird in the opening of his mouth, letting it flutter against his lips.

I Karsa.

Bajoeng Gede. March 4, 1937. 5 G 2, 5, 7, 8, 9, 11, 13, 14, 15, 16, 18, 20.

world and to the rigors of interpersonal relations; they are *away*, as Bateson and Mead termed this behavior.

Balinese adults learn as children to make themselves into toys, to turn into themselves and their bodies, or to attend to the stimulus of others' bodies or body parts. Balinese culture places a high value on spatial togetherness and formalized and stylized social interaction. In groups or crowds *(rame)*, individuals will pack together to enjoy a theatrical performance or an orchestra. However, in a strange and paradoxical way, at the same moment that individuals are together, they may also be *away*, or they may fall into a trance, moving as one with the bodies of the performers. Awayness describes the state of inwardness, disassociation, and distance from social formalities exhibited most obviously in trance, but it is the flip side of Balinese togetherness, and it reveals their world as a "play world" of a very special sort. Bateson and Mead examined this world in their monograph by using methods (film, stills, and simultaneous field notes) that were as exacting as they were innovative. It is strange that they have yet to be imitated, let alone surpassed, even with the sophisticated equipment at the disposal of researchers in the 1970s. The study of children's play would be vastly advanced by the formulation of such a project. But, most importantly, *Balinese Character* is a model of an exceptional fieldwork study. Mead said it best:

> I think it is a good thing to have had such a model, once, of what anthropological field work can be like, even if the model includes the kind of extra intensity in which a lifetime is condensed into a few short years. (1972:264)

AFRICAN CHILDREN'S PLAY:
THE LUBA, SANGA, AND YEKE[14]

In the mid-1950s, based on the inspiration of Ralph Linton's studies, a remarkable investigation of African child development and play was initiated by H. Centner. This study was finally published in 1962 after much difficulty, and, therefore, the context and evolution of this project are briefly traced before the actual material is presented.

The Belgian Congo became independent in 1960, and immediately a series of violent disturbances occurred throughout the country. The fighting and upheaval were probably greatest in the southern province of Katanga (now Shaba), which seceded from the newly formed Congo

---

[14]In keeping with the standard practice of dropping the Bantu prefixes in ethnic names, the terms *Luba, Sanga,* and *Yeke* are used in this discussion instead of *Maluba,* etc. (singular), and *Baluba,* etc. (plural).

Republic (now known as Zaire). These disturbances forced Mademoiselle H. Centner, a missionary working in the town of Luena since 1955, to take refuge in Elisabethville (now Lubumbashi), the capital city of Katanga. And here she was invited by the Center for the Study of Indigeneous Social Problems (CEPSI) to write a book about the children of Katanga based on her observations and experience and her specific research on the subject of play.

This situation seems a most unlikely context for a study of children's play. However, it was Centner's desire to document the processes of acculturation and their effect on children's personalities and particularly on their play behavior. Acculturation occurs both gradually and rapidly in a turbulent situation such as that which existed in Katanga in 1960. In order to understand these processes, Centner chose initially to document the position of children and play in a traditional village setting, after which she felt it would be possible to describe the transformation of these activities in an urban context. This was necessary because she believed that only by "illuminating the point of departure would the point of arrival make sense" (1962:17).[15] *L'Enfant Africain et Ses Jeux* (1962) is Centner's description of children and their play in a traditional village setting. This account is based on her observations and research among the Luba, the Sanga, and the Yeke, Bantu groups living in or near the town of Luena in Katanga. Unfortunately, the companion volume, which was to present information on play in an urban setting, has not, to my knowledge, been published.

In attempting to investigate relationships between culture and individual personality, Centner was influenced by the work of Ralph Linton, particularly *The Cultural Background of Personality* (1945). Linton, as was true of most culture and personality researchers, was interested in how the interaction of individuals with their culture determined their particular personalities and patterns of conduct. Centner adopted this viewpoint, giving special emphasis to play in the development of personality, as well as in the formation of particular cultural patterns. For Centner, these interactions could be depicted very simply and systemically (p. 17):

While it is true that Centner could have more thoroughly developed her particular theoretical perspective, there is no lack of descriptive de-

---

[15]This study is published in French. All translations are my own.

tail in this study. Centner herself stated that this report is "purely de-scriptive," as conclusions would be made following the publication of the second account. In fact, *L'Enfant Africain et Ses Jeux* is *the* most exten-sive account of children's play available for all of Africa and at present for all non-Western societies.[16]

Because she was concerned with the individual's development within a cultural context, Centner began her study with a discussion of the importance and place of children in the traditional cultures of the Luba, the Sanga, and the Yeke. She also included a description of the various stages of childhood development as marked by celebrations or rituals in these societies. As is true in many cultures, children are highly valued by these groups, for they are a "blessing" to both the parents and the general society. All women, once they are married, hope and expect to become pregnant.[17] Pregnancy (particularly if it is the first) is an-nounced and celebrated by particular ceremonies held by the wife's family. (These societies have a matrilineal descent system.) A number of dietary precautions are followed at this time that may forbid or encour-age the mother to eat certain foods. Close to the time of birth, a special name ("inner name") taken from one of the child's maternal ancestors is chosen. Immediately after the child is born, he/she is washed and rubbed with red earth from a termite mound. Other ceremonies are held marking the first time the child sits up by him/herself, the appearance of the first teeth, the first steps, and the appearance of the complete set of baby teeth. Infants are weaned by the age of 2, and so begins the process of separation from the mother, as now other persons begin to enter the child's life as caretakers (e.g., the maternal grandmother and, later, older siblings).

As the children grow up they are taught that, first and foremost, they are responsible to their family and to their clan. They learn the hierarchy of relationships and their particular place in this system, and emphasis is placed on group, not individual, achievements. However, they are also allowed a considerable amount of freedom in their activities (particularly the boys) and, by the age of 5 or 6, they have developed

---

[16]See Béart's *Jeux et Jouets de l'Ouest Africain* (1955) for an extensive description of play in West African societies. This report, however, includes less detailed information on chil-dren's play for each society discussed than is available in Centner's account. This is also true of Griaule's studies, *Jeux et Divertissements Abyssins* (1935) and *Jeux Dogons* (1938). For a discussion of childhood socialization practices among central African groups published in English, see particularly Margaret Read's *Children of Their Fathers: Growing Up among the Ngoni of Malawi* (1960), which includes a description of Ngoni children's play activities (pp. 41–45).

[17]In some societies (e.g., the Fulani of northern Nigeria), a woman is not officially con-sidered to be married until she has given birth to a child.

friendships and engage in a variety of group play activities. When they are 8 or 9, they stop sleeping in their parents' home and begin to sleep in separate huts for boys and girls. At puberty, elaborate initiation rites are held for boys and girls. Boys are circumcised during this time, and both males and females are formally instructed in various aspects of the culture. Most importantly, the ceremonies emphasize the idea that "the child is dead, and the adult is born" (p. 28).

Work and play are intermixed in these cultures, but they are often related to seasonal constraints. The dry season (May to September), after the last harvest of crops (maize and manioc), is *the* time of play for the whole society. Adults do devote themselves to the special tasks of hunting and fishing, but this is the preeminent time for festivals and rituals celebrating the land and commemorating the dead, as well as the initiation camps. For children, this is also a time of play because they have few economic duties to perform.

In these societies, however, children engage in play of various sorts during *all* seasons, and Centner devoted the bulk (approximately 300 pages) of her account to documenting and illustrating these activities. All in all, 23 chapters are presented that provide information on numerous types of play and games. The activities discussed are traditional dolls; children's villages *(masansa)*; play re-creating family life; play re-creating village life; hunting; fishing; play with the body; practical jokes, teasing, and hazing; games of skill; hiding games; games of chance; sculptures and molding; drawings, weaving, and braiding; memory games, songs, dances; musical instruments; verbal play; stories; theater and puppets; and, finally, juggling, string figures, and children's versions of the popular African game of *mancala (kisolo)*.

This is an extensive report and a major monograph for students of play. Each chapter includes detailed discussions and generally illustrations or photographs depicting the children at play. The most interesting and unique chapters are those in which information is presented on traditional dolls, the *masansa* or children's villages, and the various forms of children's verbal play found in these societies.

Dolls are quite popular as playthings for these children. They are generally modeled out of clay with special emphasis given to hairstyle and tattoo markings. They may also be made out of bananas on which faces and ornamentation are drawn or an ear of corn, in which case a hairdressing made out of braided rope is added (see Figure 14). Generally, young girls play with these dolls and spend many hours feeding, nursing, bathing, and caring for them. They may also build small huts for the dolls out of sand and twigs. Young boys do not play with dolls, but they may help the girls gather the materials needed to create them. Boys do, however, have their own special playthings, which they con-

FIGURE 14. Luba girl's corn dolls with braided hairdressings (H. Centner, 1962:Figures 5 and 6).

struct from twigs, boards, rope, clay, and so on. Many of their most inventive items are constructed in an effort to replicate "modern" objects and life, such as cars and trucks (see Figure 15) and, more recently, military personnel, weapons, and vehicles.

The *masansa* or children's villages have been infrequently described in the ethnographic literature for this area. *Masansa* are built during the dry season, when the weather is good and food is not in short supply and children have few economic duties to perform. Younger and older children participate in this activity, each with a role to play as they set about to re-create elaborately the life of the village. Small huts are constructed near the village, where the children engage in this play during the day—but not at night because of fear of witches and evil spirits. The *masansa* generally last one week, as the huts apparently cannot take the wear and tear they receive for much longer than this period.

The children group themselves into families, with a "husband," a "wife" (or "wives," as polygyny is valued but does not occur fre-

FIGURE 15. Luba boy's car (H. Centner, 1962: Figure 96).

quently), and "children" (played by young children), and then into clans. The husbands perform male tasks by building the huts and hunting and fishing. The wives prepare meals and take care of the children. They cook in pots that they have made, sometimes using sand as a substitute for cassava. Or they may prepare and eat food that their mothers have given them or that their "husbands" have caught on a hunting expedition (e.g., a small bird or other game or a fish).

There are other roles that certain children play in the *masansa*. A *chief* is chosen from among the older boys to take care of and coordinate village activities, and he may appoint subchiefs as assistants. A *crier* is also chosen to "awaken" everyone and also to announce when it is "nighttime," at which time everyone retires to his/her hut to go to "sleep." The crier's house is located apart from the *masansa*. As every play must have a villain, the children choose *l'hyène* to act the part of the ogre who lives away from the village and comes in periodically to try to steal the children.[18] Recently the role of *policeman* has been added as someone who keeps order and puts those who do not pay their taxes in prison. In the *masansa*, the children may also re-create the tribunal or law court, dances and religious rituals, the process of divining, and the activities of circumcision camps (as the children believe them to be).

According to Centner, missionaries in this region have discouraged the *masansa* practice because they believe that it encourages children to

---

[18]Centner reported that no one likes to be chosen to play the roles of crier or *l'hyène* because they live away from the village and because the children think that it will bring them bad luck in later life. Nevertheless, someone must play the roles, and she reported that generally the smallest and/or weakest or most unpopular are chosen for these parts.

engage in sex play. However, she reported that such behavior occurs only infrequently and is discouraged and punished by parents. In any case, missionaries and the general process of modernization and urbanization do not seem to have caused the disappearance of the *masansa*, as Centner reported seeing one miniature village built near the center of Elisabethville (Lubumbashi).

Luba, Sanga, and Yeke children play a number of language games, which have rarely been described in monographs. In fact, the study of verbal play is itself an impoverished subject in anthropology because one must be very fluent in the native language before the nuances and subtleties of verbal humor can be recognized. Centner discussed eight different types of language games, stressing that these are only a sample of what is actually a very diverse and rich play form for these children (as well as for adults).

Some of the most popular games played by younger children are hand/finger and rhyme games, which are played either individually or in groups. Children play this game using the fingers of either the left or the right hand. For example, a Luba version:

Kaka kamindwamindwa	This is the little finger.
Yeu tutwa kamindwa	This is the big brother of the little finger
Yeu munwe mulampe	This is the long finger, and so on. (p. 327)

Another game which seems to facilitate the learning and expansion of vocabulary is played by younger and somewhat older children in group situations.[19] Someone starts by asking the group to enumerate names of persons, animals, birds, fish, trees, rivers, or mountains. The group must respond, without hesitation and without error, by naming between 5 and 10 of the items requested.

Children growing up in the context of the village develop an extensive knowledge of their environment at a very early age. (This is true for non-Western children in general.) They know what is and is not edible, what is and is not dangerous, how to recognize a bird by its distinctive song or call or a tree by its leaves or an animal by its tracks and sounds. They also practice and perfect imitations and parodies of specific animal habits and characteristics. Centner reported that Luba, Sanga, and Yeke children have developed a number of bird calls that imitate the tone of the actual call with amazing perfection. Examples of calls and also

[19]Unfortunately, Centner was not specific as to the age of the children. The designation "younger" appears most generally to refer to children under the age of 7, and "older" to children above this age.

rhymes that accompany them are described for species of turtledoves, pigeons, owls, sparrow hawks, and others.

Centner also discussed a number of rhymes, alliterations, riddles, puzzles, and jokes that children make up and pass on from generation to generation, or that they transform from adult sayings, proverbs, myths, riddles, and so forth. She stated that much of this word play is impossible to translate because it is dependent on subtle tone changes and shifts of sound and meaning and/or repetition of nonsense words. However, she did present several examples of children's riddles and jokes that illustrate the ingenuity and imaginativeness of these players:

> I am a child born among thorns.
> Who am I? A pineapple.
>
> I am a child who always wears a hat.
> Who am I? A mushroom.
>
> This house does not have a door.
> What is it? An egg. (p. 347)

Finally, these children have invented their own secret languages, which are similar to the American child's "pig Latin." This appears to be a very common occurrence among children in all societies; however, once again, it is rarely reported in the ethnographic literature. Sanga boys use the technique of inverting the syllables of each word to create their particular "code" words. For example:

> *Obe Mukwetu* (You, my friend) becomes *Beo tukwemu*.
> *Iya kuno* (Come here!) becomes *Yai noku*. (p. 347)

Girls, on the other hand, have developed a system that requires more patience to produce a series of not very deceptive transformations. In this case, each syllable of each word is duplicated, producing phrases such as the following:

> *Mukwetu twaya ku madimi* (My friend, let's go to the fields) becomes *Mumu na kwekwe na tutu natwatwa na yaya na kuku na mama na didi na mimi*. (p. 348)

For Centner, children's play is an activity that is both free and spontaneous and yet also very serious and very important from the child's point of view. It is not, however, a simple diversion, mere relaxation, or pure abandonment, because it is necessary and even crucial for the assimilation of experience. Play is significant because it serves a dual purpose; it both *forms* and *affirms* a child's personality. A person exists, of course, in a sociocultural context, and this environment influences and is influenced by individuals and the play forms that they create and "re-create." These relationships are proposed and tentatively explored in this, the most detailed descriptive report of non-Western children's play activities.

FREUDIANS ON PLAY

Freud's interpretations of play influenced many anthropological researchers. This has already been illustrated by the doll play studies of Jules and Zunia Henry with the Pilagá Indians of Argentina and Géza Róheim's analysis of Melanesian Duau children's play. Likewise, the psychosexual theories of Erik Erikson greatly influenced Gregory Bateson and Margaret Mead's interpretations of Balinese behavior, and the works of Ralph Linton inspired the extensive collection of Luba, Sanga, and Yeke children's play made by H. Centner. Over the years, the psychoanalytic theory of play has been revised, expanded, and critiqued by many psychologists and psychiatrists. Some of the most interesting of these examinations attempt to broaden and extend Freud's original ideas on play (e.g., Alexander, 1958; Bühler, 1930, 1935; Gould, 1972; Lowenfeld, 1935; Peller, 1954; Waelder, 1933; Winnicott, 1971).

D. W. Winnicott, a British psychoanalyst, presented one of the most recent psychoanalytic examinations of this phenomenon in his study *Playing and Reality* (1971). Winnicott believes that a theoretical statement on play is lacking in the psychoanalytic literature because child analysts have been "concerned almost entirely with the use of play" (p. 39). In his opinion, "in the total theory of personality the psychoanalyst has been too busy using play content to look at the playing child, and to write about playing as a thing in itself" (p. 40). Winnicott argued that play should be viewed as a universal, natural and healthy activity (which both children and adults engage in), not as something supplementary to physical excitement or as a compensatory activity and, therefore, useful mainly as a means for therapy or for understanding pathology. In fact, according to Winnicott, psychotherapy is itself animated by play, for it "takes place in the overlap of two areas of playing, that of the patient and that of the therapist" (p. 38).[20]

In presenting his specific theory of play, Winnicott drew on his clinical experience to examine the role of "transitional objects" and "transitional phenomena" in the development of individuals. According to Winnicott, play begins with an infant's first "not-me" possessions and the first "playground" is the "potential space between the mother and the baby or joining mother and baby" (p. 47). The sequence of

---

[20]Winnicott was here advancing, although he did not seem to know it, a notion earlier discussed by Bateson (1955). This idea is explored more thoroughly in Chapter Eight.

events in these play experiences occurs first with the infant's "fist-in-mouth" activities, and then an external object, such as a sheet or a blanket, may be taken into the mouth along with the fingers. These are *transitional phenomena* in Winnicott's terms, and they become very important to the infant for going to sleep, in anxious situations, and so on. At some point, one object may become extremely important to the infant (e.g., a teddy bear, a doll, a soft or hard toy), who constantly carries it around, cuddling and sometimes mutilating it. These objects are said to stand for the breast or for the objects of the infant's first relationship, and they must never be changed; however, eventually they lose meaning. This happens because

> the transitional phenomena have become diffused, have become spread out over the whole intermediate territory between "inner psychic reality" and the external world as perceived by two persons in common, that is to say, over the whole cultural field.
>
> At this point my subject widens out into that of play, and of artistic creativity and appreciation, and of religious feeling, and of dreaming. (p. 5)

Several characteristics of play were discussed by Winnicott (see pp. 51–52). Most importantly, he suggested that play is a *creative experience* that occurs in the "space–time continuum." It is *precarious* because it "belongs to the interplay in the child's mind of that which is subjective (near-hallucination) and that which is objectively perceived (actual, or shared, reality)" (p. 52). In play, the child takes objects or phenomena from the external world and invests them with meaning from his "inner" or "personal" reality. Playing also involves *preoccupation*, a "near-withdrawal state" that does not easily allow intrusions. Playing involves *trust* because it relates to the space that was first existent between a baby and a mother figure. And play involves the *body* because objects are manipulated and because "certain types of intense interest are associated with certain types of bodily excitement" (p. 52). However, this "instinctual excitement" always threatens play because it may eliminate the child's sense of autonomous action. Play is pleasurable as long as instinctual arousal is not excessive. Play is also *inherently exciting* and *essentially satisfying*. Finally, Winnicott suggested that there is a "direct development from transitional phenomena to playing, and from playing to shared playing, and from this to cultural experiences" (p. 51).

An even more recent psychoanalytically oriented study of children's play is available in Rosalind Gould's *Child Studies through Fantasy* (1972). Gould is a psychologist trained also as a Freudian analyst. In this book, she presented an examination of children's spontaneous play fantasy productions collected for her by teachers in an American middle-class nursery school. In interpreting these texts, she drew on the studies of both Freud and Piaget in an attempt to relate these events to the cognitive and affective developmental level of individual children. In this way, she expanded on the earlier synthetic work of Susan Isaacs (*Intellectual Growth in Young Children*, 1930; *Social Development in Young Children*, 1933).

As is revealed by the book's title, Gould adopted the traditional psychoanalytic orientation toward play by describing her research as a study of children *through* (i.e., *by using*) fantasy:

> Hence one may find in young children's fantasy expressions . . . reflections of ways affects and cognitions may evolve and entwine in interdependent patterns, that advance or handicap learning and personality development. (p. 3)

Most specifically, she views these fantasy productions as *expressions* or *reflections* of children's cognitive and affective patterns and capacities. For the most part, these productions are not viewed as significant in the *generation* of these patterns (see particularly p. 26).

Gould used her "fantasy records" to reveal individual differences in cognition and affect and to derive constructs that clarify relationships between "experiences" and "the developmental progression" of individual patterns (p. 5). These constructs focus on three significant features.

1. Patterns of individuation and identification, of which three major types are outlined: (a) *identification with the provider and/or protector;* (b) *identification with the victim;* and (c) *identification with the aggressor.*
2. Modes of defense, of which two types are discussed: (a) *oscillation* and *fluctuating certainty*, which relate to the inability to distinguish between a pretend or a real danger; and (b) *direct and distance modes of defense and self-identification*, which describe the variation in identifiable familiarity or irreality in fantasy characters, targets, or symbolic activities.
3. The foundations of morality are discussed as these are expressed in four different ways: (a) *limited* or *global self-condemnation;* (b) *internalization of conflicts* and *differences in self-alignment;* (c) *superego constancy;* and, (d) *sense of entitlement* and *wish-to-please* as mediating influences in superego formation (see pp. 6–9).

These constructs are presented "as they are interrelated in form and function with both aspects of cognitive development in the early years and the child's relative balance of aggressive/libidinal experiences (internal and external)" (p. 5).

The unique feature of this book is found in the presentation of the actual fantasy texts or records. Gould analyzed 24 "records" using the above somewhat complicated schema. Included with these records are descriptions of the spatial context and time of the collection, as well as occasional information on the familial background of the child and, less frequently, discussion of the social context of the nursery school (e.g., the child's relation with other children, with teachers, and so on).

"Digging for a Princess," a fantasy record produced in May, 1964, by a group of "fours," illustrates the type of material available in this book, and it is reprinted here in its entirety. This is a charming text, which seems ready-made for psychoanalytic (as well as many other) types of interpretations:

Record 1

Digging for a Princess

Fours   Yard Time, May, 1964

Chris: I hate women!

Teacher: Why do you say that, Chris?

Chris: Because when ya' marry them ya' hafta' get your blood tested.

Teacher: What else do you think about women, Chris?

Chris: I think they're kookie! I think I'm gonna marry a princess . . . because they're better—they're prettier.

Jim: Yeah, because they have jewels and gold—and they have crowns!

Olivia (comes over to the boys): What are you doing?

Jim and Chris: We're digging and looking for princesses.

Olivia: Well, I have a bride dress at home.

Chris: Aw, who cares about that.

Jim: Yeah, ya' need a princess suit. (To teacher): Don't tell her we're gonna marry a princess.

Chris: Princesses have to wear their princess suits all the time or else they'll be stripped of their beauty.

Olivia (to teacher): What means "stripped of their beauty"?

Chris: Aw, go away! We hafta keep diggin'.

Jim: Yeah, ya' don't find them in New York. We're digging our way to find one.

Chris: Well, ya' just don't marry one like the regular way. Ya' hafta save one first. Princesses fall in love with princes. Did ya' ever eat a princess?

Jim: NO! (They dig for awhile silently.) I dream about army things.

Chris: Well, I dream about that I'm a lieutenant with a lovely princess.

Olivia: Boys! Boys! I just found a real live earring from a princess. (She hands them a piece of crumpled paper.)

Jim and Chris: Get out of here! (They chase her away.)

Chris (running around the hole he has dug): Romance! (Running full circle again.) Princesses! (Running full circle a third time.) Jewels! Let's get digging for those princesses!

Jim: No, we don't really want them. We hafta wait till we're grown up for that.

Chris: Yeah, till we're twenty-one!

Jim: Yeah.

Chris: And then we can buy a real drill and shovel and a pick.

Jim: And a whole car—and one of those things that go rrr-rrr-rrr.

Teacher: You mean a pneumatic drill?

Jim: Yeah.

Chris: But I wanna dig for princesses.
Jim: No!
Chris: Oh shucks. Josh, do you wanna' marry a princess?
Josh: Sure I do.
Olivia: Do you know where you could get a real princess? In Ireland or England or something.
Chris: Yeah, then we could find one and . . . we could see the Beatles while we're there!
Jim: I love the Beatles. Yeah! Yeah! Yeah!
Chris (running back from the group of girls in another part of the yard): I just went up to the princess' house and guess what—they scared me away. (pp. 22–24)

Doctrinaire Freudians have often produced analyses of behavior that exaggerate to the point of parody the psychoanalytic perspective. It is perhaps fitting, then, to find that this tendency appears in certain interpretations of children's play activities. For example, Róheim went to elaborate lengths to find and/or produce Freudian themes in Duau children's play, and in Chapter Four, we saw how Fenichel absurdly interpreted Freud's ideas on recapitulation. In a more recent article by Marion Sonnenberg, "Girls Jumping Rope" (1955), an equally incredible analysis of the symbolic significance of rope skipping is presented. She suggested that

the girl in jumping rope acts out the to and fro movement of the man during sex intercourse. Her own body takes the part of the active man, while the swinging rope imitates her own body in *adjusting* to the movement of the man's. Thus, in this game the girl acts both the role of the man and of the woman. (pp. 59–60)

It is, however, unnecessary to go to such extremes to find Freudian themes in the play and game activities of Western children. In a recent article by Herbert Golding (1974), also concerned with jump rope, the tendency to Freudian excess appears again in many interpretations, but who could deny the feelings of sibling rivalry as expressed in the following popular rhymes, which he quotes:

I had a little brother
His name was Tiny Tim
I put him in the washtub
To teach him how to swim.
He drank up all the water
Ate up all the soap
He died last night
With a bubble in his throat.
(p. 438)

Fudge, Fudge call the judge
Mamma's got a newborn baby
Ain't no girl; ain't no boy

Just a plain old baby
Wrap it up in toilet paper
Put it in the elevator
First floor—miss
Second floor—miss
Third floor—miss
Fourth floor—kick it out the door.
(p. 439)

STATISTICS AND CULTURE: FREUD AND LEARNING THEORY

It will be recalled that Kardiner's psychocultural theory postulated the following causal chain: primary institutions → basic personality → secondary institutions. However, in this system, there is no explanation provided for the existence of "primary institutions." Langness has suggested that "without such an explanation the schema does no more than attempt to explain one aspect of culture and/or personality by another in a strangely circular manner" (1974:95). In the late 1940s and early 1950s a group of researchers at Yale, particularly George P. Murdock and John W. M. Whiting, began the development of a theory and a methodology that they felt would overcome certain of the basic deficiencies of the Kardiner approach.

Two specific developments must be considered here. First, the launching of the Cross-Cultural Survey File (later to be known as the Human Relations Area Files—HRAF) by Murdock made possible the classification of a large quantity of ethnological data into an easily accessible, if not always comprehensible, file system. This system was created in order to facilitate the search for comparative ethnographic information and to make possible the formulation of statistical cross-cultural investigations. These studies would set forth specific hypotheses, which would then either "stand or fall on the basis of statistical evaluation" of data obtained from the Cross-Cultural Survey File (Barnouw, 1973: 167).

John Whiting and his co-workers were responsible for formulating the theoretical approach that would generate many of the hypotheses to be tested in the above fashion. This theory is an amalgam of several different traditions in both psychology and anthropology:

In this group several lines of development converge, foremost among which are the neo-Freudian, as transmitted through Kardiner; learning theory through the influence of Hull[21]; and the statistical versions of the compara-

[21]Clark L. Hull taught learning theory at Yale, where he influenced a number of psychologists (e.g., O. H. Mowrer, John Dollard, Neal Miller, Robert R. Sears) and anthropologists (e.g., George Murdock, John Whiting) (see Barnouw, 1973:168). And it was during the 1930s and 1940s, at the Institute for Human Relations at Yale, that an integrated behavioral-science approach was developed by many of these researchers.

tive method as outlined by Tylor and further perfected through the development of the Human Relations Area Files under George Murdock. (Harris, 1968:450)

Modifying the arguments of Kardiner, Whiting added a new "system" to the proposed causal chain. This approach was first presented in the book *Child Training and Personality*, published originally in 1953 by Whiting and Irvin L. Child. As it appears here, the new argument is: Maintenance Systems → Child Training Practices → Personality Variables → Projective Systems (p. 310). The most significant feature of this chain is the separation of "maintenance systems," defined as "the economic, political and social organizations of a society—the basic customs surrounding the nourishment, sheltering and protection of its members," from "child-training practices" (p. 310). In Kardiner's schema, property, economy, and child-rearing patterns had been combined together as "primary institutions." Whiting and Child's "maintenance systems," however, are seen as primary to and, in fact, generative of certain types of "child-training practices," "personality variables," and "projective systems."

In this theory, a "system of behavior" is defined as "a set of habits or customs motivated by a common drive and leading to common satisfactions" (Whiting and Child, p. 45). The five significant behavioral systems of child-training practices are outlined as oral (nursing and weaning); anal (toilet training); sexual (masturbation, parental treatment of sex play, modesty); dependence (parental reaction to crying and asking help); and aggressive (parental treatment of fighting and insults) systems (J. Whiting *et al.*, 1966:vi). It was assumed that these systems would occur and "be subject to socialization" in all societies (Whiting and Child, 1953:45). In fact, this assumption of universality had to be made in order to make comparison between societies a possibility. This view harkens back to the early evolutionists' belief in "the psychic unity of mankind" (Barnouw, 1973:168). And, likewise, this theory also reinvokes a view of culture as separable "customs," although here the researchers chose to define customs as behaviors and *not* artifacts (which Tylor, for example, had included in his famous culture as custom definition). It was equally essential to believe that these "systems of behavior" or "customs" could be taken out of their original cultural contexts for comparative purposes. This view, of course, conflicts with the functionalists' perspective as well as with the cultural relativism of Ruth Benedict.

A number of investigations have been influenced by the Whiting and Child approach: for example, Beatrice Whiting's *Paiute Sorcery* (1950) and, more recently, Margaret Bacon, Herbert Barry, and Irvin L. Child's "A Cross-Cultural Study of Drinking: II" (1965); John Whiting, Richard

Kluckhohn, and Albert Anthony's "The Function of Male Initiation Ceremonies at Puberty" (1958); William Stephen's *The Oedipus Complex: Cross-Cultural Evidence* (1962); John Whiting's "Effects of Climate on Certain Cultural Practices" (1964); and Thomas K. Landauer and John Whiting's "Infantile Stimulation and Adult Stature of Human Males" (1964).

This approach has been criticized by a number of researchers. Its adherents, however, claim that by adopting the "operationalism" of experimental psychology (particularly the neobehaviorist learning theory of Hull), culture and personality studies can at last be lifted from the fuzzy humanism of earlier investigations and become "paragons of methodological purity" (see Harris, 1968:449). This remains to be seen, and at any rate, some would ask if anthropologists should, or even can, adopt the methods of psychologists, who have themselves copied the procedures of the physical sciences in a somewhat questionable manner (see Sigmund Koch, 1971). Putting aside these larger epistemological and methodological issues, however, there are specific questions to be asked about the value of correlational studies as a research method. For example, Morris Cohen suggested in the early 1940s, before the Whiting and Child studies had ever been proposed, that:

> correlations are often mere coincidences that do not indicate any signifi-
> cant connection, or any reason for expecting such correlation to continue.
> I have on several occasions referred to the high correlation of 87% for 13
> years between the death-rate in the State of Hyderabad and the member-
> ship in the International (American) Machinists Union. If there are not many
> instances of this sort, it is because we do not, as a rule, look for them.
> (1942:16)

More recently, Victor Barnouw (1973) has suggested that the process of classifying and coding the HRAF data, developing measurement indices, and so on is a terribly involved procedure and, in certain instances (e.g., indirect indices of traits), often unconvincing. In fact, he suggested that "the complexity of the Whiting and Child demonstration sometimes takes on the dimensions of a Rube Goldberg machine" (p. 187), although Marvin Harris argued that "it is precisely this complexity which carries the approach beyond ordinary culturological perspectives" (1968:452). Some of the most telling criticisms of this orientation have been formulated by the investigators themselves. For example, Beatrice Whiting stated:

> The causal relationships implied in this schema are open to discussion, and
> such discussions with present available knowledge, ultimately end with a
> problem similar to that of the priority of the chicken or the egg. (1963:5)

In the early 1950s, a number of conferences were held involving psychological and anthropological researchers from Cornell, Harvard, and Yale. These seminars were planned in order to discuss the formulation of an "extensive and intensive study of child-rearing in a few different societies" (Barnouw, 1973:195). These investigations would be conducted to make up for the lack of detailed and comparable ethnographic material available on this subject and also to increase the validity and reliability of statistical cross-cultural studies. The *Field Guide for a Study of Socialization in Five Societies,* originally a mimeographed publication and now available as Volume 1 in the *Six Cultures Series* (Whiting *et al.,* 1966), was one result of these planning conferences. The most important result of these conferences, however, was the initiation of what was to become known as the *Six Cultures Project.*

In the fall of 1954, five research teams established field sites in order to pursue this cross-cultural study of socialization in communities ranging between 50 and 100 families. Each team was to concentrate on the study of 24 mothers who had children between the ages of 3 and 10. The mothers were interviewed, and their interaction with their children was carefully and systematically observed, all according to guidelines laid out in the original field guide publication. In the interviews and observations, nine "behavioral systems" (an expansion of the original Whiting and Child 1953 formulation) were given special attention. The systems were succorance, nurturance, self-reliance, achievement, responsibility, obedience, dominance, sociability, and aggression (see B. Whiting, 1963:7).

The locations chosen for the first five field sites were varied (see B. Whiting, 1963:3). Thomas and Hatsumi Maretzki began work in the village of Taira on the northeast coast of Okinawa. Leigh Minturn chose a group of families of the Rājpūt caste in the town of Khalapur in Utter Pradesh in northern India and collaborated with John Hitchcock, who was at the time the director of Morris Opler's Cornell field station in Khalapur. William and Corinne Nydegger began a study of a group of Ilocano-speaking families living in northern Luzon in the Philippines. A. Kimball and Romaine Romney worked with a group of families in the Mixtecan barrio of Santo Domingo in the town of Juxtlahuaca in Oaxaca, Mexico. John and Ann Fischer stayed home and set up residence in a neighborhood in Orchard Town, New England. And in 1955, Robert and Barbara LeVine began work with the Gusii in the Kisii Highlands of the South Nyanza District of Kenya. With the addition of this team, the research project now had six fieldwork sites.

The results of the *Six Cultures Project* were published first in one large volume edited by Beatrice Whiting *(Six Cultures: Studies of Child Rearing,* 1963). Later, the reports were published in a series of seven separate volumes (1966) (the previously mentioned field guide is Volume 1 of this series). Other studies using this material are Leigh Minturn and William Lambert's *Mothers of Six Cultures: Antecedents of Child Rearing* (1964) and Beatrice Whiting and John Whiting's *Children of Six Cultures: A Psycho-Cultural Analysis* (1975).

In the 1963 publication, a new element, ecology, was added to the original Whiting and Child schema (see Figure 16). And in the 1966 publication, a further feature, "Biological Needs, Drive, Capacities," was added to the causal chain. These "needs," etc., are said to be affected by the "child-training practices" and, in turn, to influence "child and adult personality."

The status of play in the Whiting and Child approach is clearly revealed in the 1963 diagram. Here these activities fall into the category of projective systems and are manifest in child behavior as "games" and in the cultural products of "fantasy" and "recreation." In adult behavior, play is described as "leisure time activity." Following in the tradition of earlier culture and personality studies, play is accorded an expressive, but hardly formative, status. Another thing to be noticed is the fact that formalized children's games are singled out for special attention, while unorganized, spontaneous play behavior is not emphasized. This approach is also illustrated in the field guide volume, where the category "Recreation" is discussed (Whiting *et al.*, 1966). Here it is stated that "Information on recreation is important as a source of projective data" (p. 36). And a list of important things to notice is offered, including hobbies (e.g., individual pastimes, collecting, woodworking); games (e.g., types of games; participants—children and/or

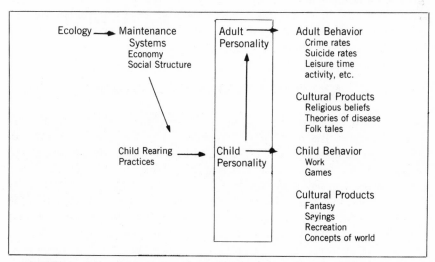

FIGURE 16. The Whiting culture–personality–behavior chart (B. Whiting, 1963:5).

adults; equipment—toys, cards, etc.); athletic sports (e.g., types of sports, participants, equipment); rest days and holidays; entertainment (e.g., state performances, occasions, actors, musical performances, orational performances); and also aesthetic expressions (e.g., graphic art, representation art, music, dancing and drama, literature and literary texts) (pp. 36–37).

Clues as to the view of play adopted by the Whiting and Child school are also evident in other studies. In John Whiting's first fieldwork study, *Becoming a Kwoma* (1941), an investigation of the effect of child-rearing practices on the personality development of these Melanesians is offered. However, in this study, there are no detailed reports of children's play behavior. In studies by other investigators who influenced the Whiting and Child approach, and so the *Six Cultures Project,* there is scant attention paid to play except insofar as it may be used to provide projective material about other "more important" topics. For example, the psychologist Robert Sears (who worked with Whiting at the Institute for Human Relations at Yale and who also assisted in the planning of the *Six Cultures Project*) has studied the effects of father separation (1946), frustration and anxiety (1951), and interpersonal aggression (1950) on American children as evidenced in their doll play or fantasy expressions. However, for the most part, Sears "gives little attention to play" according to an analysis of his particular theory of child development by Henry Maier (1965:152).

It will come as no surprise, then, to find that, while the *Six Cultures Project* is a landmark in the collection and presentation of comparative ethnographic material on child-training patterns, it is a disappointment for students of children's play. Nevertheless, there are interesting differences to be noted in the types and amount of play behavior recorded by the six research teams.

PROJECTING PLAY IN SIX CULTURES

In comparing the material on children's play collected by the six research teams, the most obvious difference in frequency and type of play observed appears for the Gusii children living in the community of Nyansongo in Kenya (R. and B. LeVine, 1963:19–202). The LeVine's reported that fantasy play is almost nonexistent for these children. They observed two instances of such play in a boys' herding group. One time "a six-year-old fashioned a plow out of wood and hitched his younger brother to it"; and once the 10-year-old leader of the group "built a 'house' out of reeds" (p. 173). In between moving the cows and watching that they do not trample a neighbor's garden, the boys climb trees, shoot birds with slingshots, watch buses and cars, and fight and tease one another. One girls' group gathers together from time to time to cuddle and play with the smaller infants (who are being taken care of by some of the girls); they also whisper and giggle and watch activities on the road. At other times, they may engage in somewhat more animated joking, teasing, pushing, and shoving, but this is the extent of their play repertoire.

Why should these children have such a sparce play life? The LeVines suggested that the physical isolation of the Nyansongo homestead makes it difficult for larger children's groups (except groups of siblings) to gather together. Also, in this community, women are the main agricultural workers (planting and harvesting maize and beans). Men may plough the fields and build fences, but for the most part, their main activities are politicking and court litigations, or else they may take a wage-earning job away from the community. Previously men were herdsmen, but population growth and land scarcity, which limit the size of the herds, have made it difficult for them to continue their traditional occupation. Because of the mother's heavy workload, "she trains the children to share it with her as soon as they are able" (R. and B. LeVine, 1963:162). The oldest uncircumcised boy is expected to take charge of herding, and the oldest uncircumcised girl is in charge of all the younger children. She is also responsible for protecting the house from theft. This means that she must stay in or near the homestead with her younger charges.

These responsibilities curtail both the child's spatial mobility and his/her ability to develop contacts with peers, although such contacts occasionally do occur when a pasture is shared by various families and herding groups develop. The effect of the isolation of the homestead on children's interaction is illustrated perhaps most clearly in the ethnographers' description of problems that they had in making the systematic child observations required for the project:

> Each extended family homestead is located on its own land, as much as several hundred yards from its neighbors, and the terrain is hilly. A great deal of time was thus spent in search of the child in the sample. . . . This proved to be extremely time-consuming . . . especially since finding the child was no guarantee that he was in an interactive situation that could be observed. (R. and B. LeVine in J. Whiting *et al.*, 1966:113)

It is not surprising, then, to find that the LeVines reported that there are no organized children's groups in Nyansongo. They also stated that the children's behavior often seems listless, while their verbal interaction is "slow and sparse" (p. 114).

Sutton-Smith (1974b) suggested that the Gusii material shows that, in cultures where children play an active role in the economy, there is little time available for actual play:

> This does not mean that all relatively simple cultures do not play, because the records of play amongst Australian Aboriginal groups are very extensive. What seems to be critical is whether or not the adults have a direct economic need to train the children in highly normalized means of survival. In such cultures the "work ethic" makes real sense. The adults know what must be done to survive and they cannot afford the wasted time of child play. (p. 6)

This suggestion needs to be examined by more thorough research on the play activities of non-Western children and also by a reexamination of the *Six Cultures* material. In almost all of the six cultures (except Orchard Town, U.S.A.), children have economic or child-care duties to perform, particularly in later childhood (after age 6). However, in many of these cultures a considerable amount of play activity is reported, as well as variation in types of games. Frequently the children develop ways to combine their work with their play (see particularly the children living in the communities of Taira in Okinawa and Tarong in the Philippines). Also, in Nyansongo, the situation is not quite the economic grind that Sutton-Smith suggested (at least not for males). Children are put to work at an early age by their mothers, who have the major economic and child-care responsibilities and cannot or, at least, do not expect their husbands to share their load. However, if it is true that the Gusii "cannot afford the wasted time of child play," it is also true that they *can afford,* using the same measures, the "wasted time" of the men's politicking.

A more likely explanation for the lack of play reported for the children of Nyansongo is the physical isolation of the homesteads and the effect of this isolation on the formation of peer groups and, hence, play groups. It is also worth noting that children's play is vaguely mentioned in various sections of the monograph; for example:

> the yard in front of the main entrance (to the house) is the scene of many daytime activities: the grinding and winnowing of grain, the play of children. (R. and B. LeVine, 1963:26)

However, little more is said about such activities, suggesting that perhaps the ethnographers did not consider this behavior of much importance.[22]

In contrast to the Gusii, the children living in the Okinawan village of Taira, studied by the Maretzkis (1963:363–539), appear to have an extraordinarily active play life. Sutton-Smith (1974b) stated that play

---

[22]In this regard it is also interesting to note that in Robert LeVine's recent book, *Culture, Behavior and Personality* (1973), which is his formulation of an approach for culture and personality studies, there is virtually *no* mention made of children's play or games.

reports are most numerous for this group. In Taira, the staple is wet rice, and men and women both work in the fields. Houses are built very close together and are easily accessible from the street, and the village as a whole is compact, with streets laid out in a rectangular grid. Few places in the village are forbidden or inaccessible to children, and so aside from playing in or near their homes, their are several favorite village play areas: a large banyan tree near the village office is a popular gathering area (and the meeting place for the "kindergarten" children—ages 2½–6—and their teacher), vacant lots, and former house sites where some walls may still be standing. Anywhere there is water and mud is also a favorite spot for children's play: on side roads, near water tanks, in beach areas, at swimming holes, and in river areas.

Young boys and girls (e.g., "kindergarten" children) are said to engage in various sorts of play activities all day long. In the kindergarten, which is described as a "mass baby sitting session," the children play tag, play marbles, jump rope, sing, count, race, do sand drawing, dance and so on. In the afternoon, the younger children accompany their mothers to the fields and play near them at this location.

Older children (6 or 7 years old) begin going to school, and so their play life is somewhat curtailed, although here they play organized and unorganized games at recess or during recreation periods. After school, the girls play "house," "marketing," "shops," or other games while they may also be taking care of their younger siblings, who are strapped on their backs (see Figure 17). The behavior of their young charges rarely interferes with their involvement in a play or game event, as this description illustrates:

> H. (an 8 year old girl) carrying her baby sister on her back is playing on the beach. She straightens up suddenly with a wry expression of her face. "She urinated, wet," she exclaims, standing up and spreading her dress at the back which is completely soaked. The baby is bare-bottomed and crowing happily at the older children playing around her. The older sister waves her dress briefly in the wind, then squats to continue her play. When asked if she was not going home to change, she exclaims that she would dry soon enough, and, as for the baby, she was dry. The day is warm and windy and the dress dries off rapidly. (p. 470)

As the children grow up, other tasks aside from baby-sitting will be expected of them, such as fetching water, cutting grass for the horse or goats, caring for the pigs and chickens. However, they continue to engage in a variety of play and game activities, although there is little play equipment available and few toys. In fact, the Maretzkis reported that the children of Taira meet the "minimum of equipment" with a "maximum of inventiveness and enthusiasm" (p. 536): stones, peas, or seeds may be used as marbles; empty cartons are trucks and boats;

FIGURE 17. Playing house, Taira (T. Maretzki and H. Maretzki, 1963:456d).

cabbage leaves become helmets; and bamboo pieces are daggers. Innumerable games are reported as well, including jacks, stick ball, a version of prisoner's base, kick the can, hopscotch, and rubber-band games (which are quasi-gambling games). Boys, in particular, practice various sports activities, such as wrestling, high jump, broad jump, and relay running. All of these play groups are said to display a great ability to manage themselves: "Fights occur, and disagreements crop up frequently, but almost without exception these matters are settled within the group and without dramatic scenes in which adults become involved" (p. 536).

The New England community of Orchard Town (J. and A. Fischer, 1963:873–1010) represents the only nonagricultural culture in this study. The fathers are wage earners, and the mothers generally do not have jobs. Each family lives in its own house, which has many rooms and also a large yard. Because of the cold climate during the winter months, as well as the dispersed placement of houses, women and children spend much of their time indoors during the winter. In fact, the Orchard Town mother is unique in comparison to all other societies in that she spends most of her day with her children, isolated from other adults. She also has the least help with child care and other tasks, and parents do not generally demand help from their children in either household or child-care tasks. In warmer weather, children may play in their own or a neighbor's yard, and, as they grow older, they are allowed to play further from home. For example, they may go to a friend's house in another neighborhood.

All children from ages 5 to 17 are required to attend school, and many, if not most, friendships are established in this context. The children spend approximately seven hours a day in school, and many play and game activities occur during recess or gym time. It is also interesting to note that teachers in Orchard Town "make a conscious effort to make school enjoyable for their pupils" (p. 987). According to the Fischers, these attempts are related to the teacher's belief that this is the desire of parents:

> There seemed to be an assumption that, if a parent or other adult came to visit a class, he or she would want to see, most of all, evidence that the children were having a good time. (p. 987)

At recess, the younger children engage in somewhat "disor-ganized" play activities. The boys form gangs and run around, playfully scaring other children. Jump rope is a favorite game of the girls. Older children are said to engage more frequently in organized, formal games during this time, although a detailed discussion of these activities is not offered. Children also participate in organized after-school activities, such as Boy Scouts and Girl Scouts, the church junior choir, baseball teams, and swimming and dancing classes. Of course, television is also a popular activity for younger and older children.

As might be expected, Orchard Town children have more ready-made toys available for play than any of the other children in this pro-ject. Preschool children, in particular, would be thought to be deprived if they did not have blocks, stuffed animals, miniature trucks and cars, and tricycles available. Also, girls have dolls and their accessories, while boys have toy guns and soldiers. Board games are popular for older children, particularly for use during cold weather. Children are encour-aged to play outside if the weather permits. Young children play in their own or a neighbor's yard—riding tricycles or scooters or playing in their sandbox, making roads and bridges or houses and "cupcakes." Children are generally presented with two-wheeled bikes when they are of school age, and they may use these to travel to school or to a friend's house.

William and Corinne Nydegger (1963:697–867) studied an Ilocos barrio called Tarong in the Philippines. As is the case in Taira, the staple for the community of Tarong is wet rice, and both men and women work in the fields. Here houses face a shared yard that from two to six related families use as a common space. Several of these yard groups form a *sitio,* and several *sitios,* connected to one another by foot paths, form a barrio. These yard areas are often the site for young children's play activities.

Sutton-Smith suggested that the play life of the children of Tarong is not terribly varied, and yet a number of play and game activities are mentioned. Peek-a-boo is reported to be a favorite game of young children, and, as they grow older, they are allowed to play with their same-age cousins in the central yard of the *sitio.* Solitary play is not encouraged. Here they re-create adult activities by building twig houses and pretending to cook, cut cane, string tobacco, and so forth. The ethnographers reported that the children are very ingenious in "finding substitutes for adult implements when they cannot be borrowed" (p. 836). One first-grade boy was reported to have "developed a wonderfully realistic stethoscope from pieces of inner tubing and a jar cover" (p. 836).

Older children, who may have hip babies to take care of after school, are said to organize "junior" versions of school games in these yards, which are "fantastic games labeled basketball or baseball but bearing little resemblance to the originals" (p. 834). They may also play versions of hide-and-seek, tag, drop the handkerchief, and stick tossing and rock hitting games with their younger relatives. School-aged children play structured games such as volleyball, and girls, in particular, like jacks and hopscotch, while boys prefer tops, marbles, pitching pennies, bolo tossing, tag, and wrestling (p. 854).

Child care is the major responsibility of school-aged children, and, as is the case in other cultures, the child frequently puts his/her young charge "on his hip and runs off to play" (p. 851). In fact, the Nydeggers suggested that

> in many training situations it is peers and older siblings or cousins who step
> in to solve problems, parents contenting themselves with occasional verbal
> instructions. Although the children see themselves as helping, they are in
> fact doing most of the training. (p. 852)

Children also work in the fields harvesting rice or helping to prepare pig food or the family meal. Seven-year-old boys may be given a goat to care for and raise.

The Rājpūts, living in the community of Khalapur in India studied by Leigh Minturn and John T. Hitchcock (1963:207–361), are also farmers (although formerly they represented the warrior caste) who grow wheat and other grains. Because all married women are in purdah, they spend almost all of their child-bearing years in enclosed courtyards, where they live in large, extended families. Rājpūt women do not work in the fields. Young children are confined to these courtyards along with their mothers, and here they engage in play with their same-age cousins, or they may play with their older siblings. Their only "imaginative play" activities are said to be "play farming for boys" and "play cooking" for girls (p. 331). Other play activities are described as "random" climbing, chasing, teasing, or seesaw games on a wagon wheel (p. 333). There are few ready-made toys available. Young children are not expected to perform any chores or tasks.

Older children (5–7 years old) play outside the crowded courtyard in the streets, on the men's platform, by a pond, or in the fields. Here they may play various versions of tag (e.g., tree tag), field hockey, a version of red rover, jacks played with pebbles, and hopscotch. Children of this age also go to school, and they are also expected to perform some tasks. Girls, for example, may wash dishes, sweep, baby-sit, pick water-chestnuts, and so forth. Boys may run errands for men or for their mothers, who are confined in the courtyard; they may also water and pasture the cattle and help with the field work. However, the Rājpūts believe that they should never require a child to work if an adult can (and is available to) perform the task, and this holds for both younger and older children (p. 355).

Descriptions of play activities for these children are not vivid or detailed. Often all that is said is "the children go to the streets to play" (p. 244), or they "run out to play" (p. 245). Extensive descriptions covering the what and the how of this play are not offered.

The Mixtecan Indians living in the barrio of Santo Domingo in the *ladino* (Spanish-speaking) town of Juxtlahuaca in Mexico were described by Kimball and Romaine Romney (1963:545–691). The Mixtecans live in closely spaced houses, each with a partially enclosed courtyard. Men work in the fields (growing maize and beans), which are located on mountain slopes beyond the town. Women do not work in the fields. The school that the children attend is located in the *ladino* section of town, and here the Mixtecan children are generally treated as an inferior minority.

As in the Rājpūt study, detailed reports of children's play activities are not provided. However, this can also be related to the fact that it is said that young children do not engage frequently in animated, organized, or interactive play activities. Play generally occurs in the courtyard area and is almost always with close relatives (e.g., siblings or cousins). Imitative house play and sex play occur during this time, and a few examples are offered of actual play events (see pp. 659–660).

Older children engage in more organized games and some sports activities at school. The Romneys also suggested that in some of these games (e.g., one called "carry the word"), the Mixtecan children learn techniques for interacting with *ladino* children, such as aggression, telling lies, accepting subordinate positions, and so forth, which are different from those used with barrio children (see pp. 676–678).

After the age of 6, children are expected to perform an increasing number of tasks and chores. Most specifically, girls begin to care for their younger siblings, carry water, run errands, care for small animals such as turkeys and chickens, sweep, and so forth. Boys begin to gather produce or fodder in the fields to bring home, care for goats and burros, and also run errands.

In comparing all six ethnographies, a number of things stand out. First, in contrast to Sutton-Smith's suggestion that play does not occur when children must contribute to the economy, in almost all of the societies (except Orchard Town and, to a lesser extent, Khalapur), children, at least by age 5 or 6, are expected to perform some household or economic tasks. In some of the societies (e.g., Tarong), they may become the primary socializing agents, and yet they frequently devise ways to combine their work with their play.

Sutton-Smith suggested that the variables of "complexity," "play groups," "privacy," "father stimulation," and "lack of chores" may all be important for producing different types and frequencies of play activities (1974b:1). Discussions of complex versus simple societies are, of course, always relative to the criteria utilized to make these distinctions. In this paper, Sutton-Smith was using Murdock's (1967) ratings (see also Roberts, Arth, and Bush, 1959), and on this basis, he stated that the "more complex groups" are Orchard Town, Khalapur, and Taira and that the "least complex" groups are Mexico, Tarong, and Nyansongo. In this division, the Rājpūts represent a "complex group," and they also require few tasks from their children; however, their play activities are reported to be much sparser, more "disorganized," and less "imaginative" than those of the "less complex" (in Sutton-Smith's terms) village of Tarong. The variable of "lack of chores" has already been discussed. In regard to "privacy," it is unclear exactly what is meant, but certainly the Orchard Town children have the most privacy and are the most isolated in their houses. All of the other groups live in situations that encourage interaction, at least with other relatives (e.g., cousins), although in this case, the children in Nyansongo are quite isolated in their play and work activities, given the nature of the environment and the location of homesteads. Rājpūt children are also isolated to a certain degree, given the nature of their residences and the practice of purdah. However, here the children, unlike their mothers, are allowed to move outside the courtyard as they grow older. The children of Taira in Okinawa have the most spatial mobility and the most opportunity to develop peer groups and, significantly, the most reported play activities. Next, in terms of spatial mobility, are the children of Tarong and then the Mixtecan children in Mexico, who may move freely within the barrio but find social interaction more difficult and more uncomfortable outside it.

Spatial and social mobility, coupled with the various effects of schools, appear to influence the types of "play groups" that children form. In all of the societies, some type of school exists. In Kenya, the school has the least effect, as many children do not attend. In contrast, in Orchard Town the school has the most powerful impact on children's lives, as all children *must* attend.

The variable of "father stimulation" is also not clearly defined. Sutton-Smith suggested that the active play of Taira children is affected by this factor, whereas the Gusii children have "little interaction with their father" and are "very much under the mother's control and dominance," where they must perform many chores (1974b:7). It is not clear why fathers should necessarily be characterized as "stimulating" and mothers as "dominating." And in any case, it appears that *peer* stimulation is one of the most important factors contributing to the active and varied play life of the children of Taira and Tarong.

One variable that Sutton-Smith did not discuss, but that may be important for producing certain types of play activities, is the presence or absence of ready-made toys. In all of the societies except Orchard Town, there are few toys available for children. In Taira and Tarong, the children respond to their lack of toys by making ingenious inventions and creations with the materials available. In contrast, the Orchard Town child plays with incredibly realistic toys that duplicate (sometimes in minute detail) the activities of their parents but do not necessarily encourage the production of imaginative "re-creations" (see Figure 18).[23]

Another variable on which children's games may be compared is the degree of competition exhibited in the actual enactment of the game. In Orchard Town, games, and children's social interaction in general, are often competitive. This is amusingly revealed in a brief description offered by the Fischers of their 4-year-old daughter's first meeting with another child (age 6). They begin by relating their recent achievements:

Daughter: I can climb a ladder. (There is a ladder resting on a fence.)
Girl: I can climb a ladder—*that* ladder.
Daughter: I can climb *any* ladder.
Girl: So can I. Can you dance?
Daughter: No

[23]The reverse of this argument has recently been presented by Frank and Teresa Caplan (1973), who made the obviously ethnocentric and also inaccurate statement that cultures without toys produce unimaginative children and adults. For example, "If more Indian children were exposed to active free play with sturdy playthings, it is our belief that India may be able to put itself into the twenty-first century" (p. 253). After reading statements such as these, it is not surprising to learn that the authors used to own the company "Creative Playthings," and so they appear to be advocating what might be called "toy colonization."

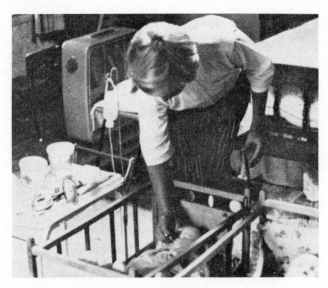

FIGURE 18. Playing hospital, Orchard Town (Photo by Louis J. Chiaramonte, from J. Fischer and A. Fischer, 1963:952c).

> Girl: *I* can dance.
> Daughter: I can dance around in a circle.
> Girl: Oh, I can do *that;* I can *really* dance—ballet dance.
> Daughter: I can do Farmer-in-the-Dell.
> Girl: Oh anybody can do *that.* . . . (1963:991)

The competitiveness of American children's sports activities, such as Little League, are also obvious examples of this orientation.

In contrast, the children in all of the other cultures approach their play and game activities with a much less competitive attitude. For example, for the children of Tarong, winning is said to be only incidental for a game to be enjoyed. The Nydeggers reported that "the players often take turns winning, distorting the games completely from our point of view" (1963:834). In Taira, the Maretzkis stated, there are "few expressions of achievement motivation and competitive spirit" (1963:485). And for the Rājpūt school-aged child, it is said that "no one seems to take winning too seriously" (Minturn and Hitchcock, 1963:352).

Even though the *Six Cultures Project* investigators often reported play in a very vague and undetailed manner, there are a few interesting actual play events presented. In Taira, for example, older children are said to devise "instructive" games, which may transform their work into a younger child's play, proving that Tom Sawyer is alive and well in Okinawa. In this instance, one 10-year-old boy devised a game for his two male cousins who are 3 and 4 years old:

> They were hunting for a type of milkweed . . . to be fed to the chickens. The older boy would walk on a way . . . stop when he spotted some milkweed, and call to the younger ones, "There are some near the spot on which I am standing!" The two little boys would rush over. . . . With a shout one of them would drop to the ground, uproot the plant, and bear it triumphantly to his older cousin. (T. and H. Maretzki, 1963:513–514)

In Tarong the *sitio* friendship group is very strong and can often close itself on outsiders. However, such rebuffs must be indirect, "for the sake of politeness," as the following example shows:

> We observed two girls (third and fourth graders) who were *sitio* mates playing jacks on the porch of the main school building after classes had been dismissed for the day. The girls were lackadaisically but happily playing when a fourth-grade girl from another *barrio* came over and sat down with them, saying, "I will join you?" as if conferring a favor. One of the players, Anita, said "Hynh. You are very good," with considerable annoyance; the other reluctantly handed over the ball to let the newcomer begin a game. The girl played for about four minutes without error. During this time the original players spoke exactly two words. . . .
>
> At length the ball hit a crack in the cement and rolled out of reach. The newcomer got up to retrieve it and stopped to talk to some friends, at which point Anita jumped up and got the ball. She and her friend . . . returned to their game, this time enjoying the play noisily. [Then] . . . the girl who had joined them returned followed by a first grader, Nelly.
>
> The newcomer said loudly, "Ah, I'll join you also." Anita glowered, then loudly proclaimed: "Yes, la! Nelly will join us also. Let's have teams. Nelly will be my companion!" This pointed preference for a young first grader rather than for the fourth grader was received, as it was intended, as a vicious insult, and the newcomer glared at Anita but did not leave. Most Tarongans would have left after the initial silent treatment, but this girl was of sterner stuff. Another girl joined the game, and Anita, with evident distaste, left the group and was soon followed by her friend. (W. and C. Nydegger, 1963:849–850)

A more overt expression of the effect of friendship and social groups on patterns of play is described for the Mixtecan children of Mexico. As discussed above, these children are treated as inferiors and sometimes as nonentities by the children from the town whom they encounter at school and on their way to and from school. A particularly poignant characterization of these relationships is presented in the following description of one barrio child's (Jubenal) reaction to a street baseball game being played by a group of town children. In this instance, Jubenal is walking home from school with a friend, also from the barrio:

> The two boys walk alongside one another in silence. In the middle of the street ahead of them, there are some central children playing a form of baseball. As they approach the group, Jubenal and the other child stop to look. Jubenal smiles at the children and makes motions as if he were going after the ball. . . . The boy with whom Jubenal was walking continues to

walk while Jubenal stops. . . . Jubenal begins to shout, "No play. . . ."
. . . The other child who was walking with Jubenal is now beyond the group
and quite a distance from Jubenal. Jubenal looks at him and goes on walking
very slowly and walking backward, still watching the game. The other boy
stops, and when Jubenal catches up with him, he says to him, "Shall we
play?" The other boy stands leaning on his hoe. Jubenal continues looking at
the players, and smiling. The other children from the center of town continue
playing, but they do not recognize his presence nor do they invite him to join
them. . . . When one of the childrn passes close to him, he smiles at him, but
the central child does not pay any attention to him.

Jubenal, looking serious, scrapes his teeth with a finger. When another
central child comes close to him, Jubenal cries out to him encouragingly,
"How you play, eh?" The central child ignores him as if he didn't see him.
Jubenal seems more serious. He puts his hands in his pockets and continues
looking. The other barrio child puts his hoe on his shoulder and touches
Jubenal's shoulder without talking, gesturing that they leave. Jubenal turns
around, the two go down the street, walking slowly. (K. and R. Romney,
1963:683)

GAMES AND CULTURE

There was one person interested in the topic of play who attended
the seminars held during the early 1950s to discuss the cross-cultural
study of child-rearing practices. John M. Roberts attended these conferences, and in 1959, he reintroduced anthropologists to the study of
games in his article "Games in Culture," written with Malcolm J. Arth
and Robert R. Bush. Inspired by both the methodological possibilities of
the Cross-Cultural Survey Files (HRAF) and the original studies of Tylor
on game diffusion, Roberts and his co-workers attempted to develop a
theoretical framework for the study of games that would explain both
their geographical distribution and their sociocultural significance.

In this article, an important distinction is drawn between "amusements" and "games." Surprisingly, this is one of the earliest attempts by
an anthropologist to construct a definition of play or games.[24] Previously
ethnographers appear to have assumed that play and/or games were
social givens and that everyone knew and understood what was meant
by the terms. In recent years, researchers have become more and more
concerned with formulating *the* definition of play, and there are both
advantages and disadvantages to this trend, which will be specifically
discussed in Chapter 10. In "Games in Culture," Roberts *et al.* defined a
game as a recreational activity that is characterized by "(1) organized

---

[24]In the early 1950s, Gregory Bateson presented what can be regarded as the first detailed
theoretical and definitional examination of play by an anthropologist. However, this
analysis originally appeared in the psychiatric literature and has only recently begun to
make an impact on anthropology. Bateson's approach is discussed in Chapter Eight.

play, (2) competition, (3) two or more sides, (4) criteria for determining a winner, and (5) agreed-upon-rules" (p. 597). In contrast, *amusements* are said to be "other recreational activities which do not satisfy this definition, such as non-competitive swimming, top-spinning, and string-figure making" (p. 597).

Right away, of course, there are problems to be noted in these distinctions. For example, why is competition and the production of a disequilibrial outcome (e.g., winners and losers) a necessary component of games? We have already seen examples of "games" (e.g., *taketak*) where these criteria are not relevant. And, likewise, we have also discussed examples of "amusements" that may be, at least partially, competitive (e.g., "top tag" as played by Hopi children). Finally, the investigators did not define what they meant by "recreational activity," assuming apparently that we know what this overarching terms means. It should be remembered, however, that definitions are always subject to such questions and qualifications. For the purposes of their study, Roberts, Arth, and Bush believed that it was necessary to narrow the broader category of play, and they were quite clear about the criteria that they used to do this.

The category of competitive games was further delimited by the researchers by classifying games on the basis of how an outcome is determined. Three types of games are enumerated in this fashion: (1) *games of physical skill* (e.g., marathon races, hockey); (2) *games of strategy* (e.g., chess); and (3) *games of chance* (e.g., dice, high card wins). The investigators used material from the ethnographic literature as well as the Cross-Cultural Survey Files (HRAF), and in this way, they collected information of varying degrees of reliability on the geographic distribution of these game types in approximately 100 tribes. Ultimately 50 groups were said to be "well covered" or "apparently well covered" with respect to descriptions of games (p. 598).

It is suggested that games are expressive cultural activities similar to music and folktales. Games are also said to be models of various cultural activities (e.g., "games of physical skill simulate combat or hunting, as in boxing and competitive trap shooting"; "games of strategy may simulate chase, hunt, or war activities, as in backgammon, fox and geese, or chess"; and games of chance and the practice of divining, which is often a religious activity, are said to be related; p. 599). Because games are models of cultural activities, they may be viewed as exercises in cultural mastery. Therefore, the authors suggested that games of physical skill may be related to mastery of specific environmental conditions; games of strategy are related to mastery of social interaction and may be related to the complexity of the social system; and finally, games of chance are related to mastery of the supernatural.

One of the most significant features of this article relates to the investigators' discussion of associations found between "complexity" of cultures and the presence or absence of certain types of games. Complexity of cultures is here defined on the basis of Murdock's (1957) ratings of 565 tribes on levels of "political integration" and levels of "social stratification." Societies said to have "low political integration" were those rated in Murdock's terms as "no political integration" and "autonomous local communities"; those classed as having "high political integration" were "minimal states," "little states," and "states" (p. 601). The ratings "absent," "formal age groups," and "wealth distinctions" were described as societies with "social stratifications absent"; and "hereditary aristocracy" and "complex stratification" were classed as societies with "social stratification present" (p. 601). On the basis of these distinctions, it was hypothesized that

> since games of strategy simulate social systems, those systems should be complex enough to generate such needs for expression. Simple societies should not possess games of strategy and should resist borrowing them. (p. 600)

Statistical analysis of material from 43 groups rated in the above fashion confirmed the proposed relationship between the presence or absence of games of strategy and "social complexity." (The relationship, however, did not hold for games of chance or games of skill.) For example, 12 groups (BaVenda, Chagga, Dahomey, Jukun, Korea, Lakher, Lamba, Mbundu, Siwa, Tanala, Vietnam, Yap) classed as "high political integration" with "social classes present" were found to have games of strategy. Only 3 of these groups (Kababish, Rwala, Bedouin) did not have games of strategy (p. 600).

Even though this article relates most specifically to the study of adult games, it is crucial to an understanding of the direction taken in the 1960s in the cross-cultural study of children's games. In 1962, building on the work of Roberts, Arth, and Bush (1959) and Whiting and Child (1953), John Roberts and Brian Sutton-Smith proposed a *conflict–enculturation hypothesis* in their article "Child Training and Game Involvement." This hypothesis was developed to explain relationships existing between types of games, child-training variables, and cultural variables. Briefly stated, the hypothesis holds that conflict engendered by the specific child-training procedures of a culture leads to an interest and involvement in specific types of game activities that model this conflict in the role reversals sanctioned by the game rules. Furthermore, it is suggested that involvement over time in these activities leads to mastery of appropriate behaviors that have functional and culturally useful value. The hypothesis was tested in a manner similar to the Roberts *et al.* 1959 study and found to hold cross-culturally. Relationships were found to exist between games of strategy and training for obedience, games of chance and training for responsibility, and games of physical skill and training for achievement.

In this research study, an attempt at "subsystem validation" was also made whereby the cross-cultural findings were used to predict intracultural variation. In this case it was suggested that "If a universal association exists between child-training variables and ludic preferences and expressions, it would be possible to predict the game preferences of American boys and girls" (p. 176). Accordingly, it was predicted that (1) girls with higher obedience training should prefer games of strategy more than boys; (2) girls with higher responsibility training should prefer games of chance more than boys; (3) boys with higher training in achievement should prefer games of physical skill more than other boys; and (4) differences between boys' and girls' preferences should be less in regard to games of physical skill than in the case of games of physical skill and strategy because the former are less related to achievement anxiety.[25] These hypotheses were tested using the responses of 1,900 school-aged children to a list of games. The results of this test were all in the direction predicted.

The most significant feature of this article, however, for future investigations of children's games is the researchers' adoption of both a projection and a socialization orientation toward the study of this behavior. In their conclusion, the authors suggested that they had advanced a theory of games that reconciles

> the classic theories of play as exercise (Groos 1901) and play as conflict (Freud 1920). . . . The theory implies (1) that . . . society induces conflict in children through its child-training processes; (2) that society seeks . . . to provide an assuagement of these conflicts by . . . [representing] their emotional and cognitive polarities in ludic structure; and (3) that through these models society tries to provide a form of buffered learning through which the child can make . . . step-by-step progress toward adult behavior. (1962:183–184)

This approach generated further subsystem validation studies. In these investigations, it was suggested that games serve as models of cultural power relationships and, in this capacity, serve as "buffered learning situations." In "Strategy in Games and Folk Tales" (1963), Roberts, Sutton-Smith and Kendon discussed how the strategic mode of competition is modeled in games of strategy and in folktales with strategic outcomes. In order to test relationships between cultural complexity, child-training variables and games and folktales, it was hypothesized that the strategic mode in folktales would occur in the

[25]The assumptions concerning relationships between child-training variables (e.g., responsibility training) and sex were made by Roberts and Sutton-Smith on the basis of studies by Sears, Maccoby, and Levin (1957) and Barry, Bacon, and Child (1957).

same general cultural setting as the strategic mode in games (p. 342). Previously games of strategy had been linked with the child-training variable of high obedience training and, likewise, had been found to be associated with "cultural complexity" (e.g., high political integration and high social stratification). The hypothesis was again tested in a manner similar to the original Roberts, Arth, and Bush (1959) study using material on folktales prepared by Irvin Child *et al.* (1958). For the purposes of this study, folktales that had "definite outcomes" (e.g., "the fortunes of a hero are followed through, either to triumph or defeat"; "where one individual or a group of individuals induce or restore a state of misfortune besetting a whole group") were treated as if they were games (p. 347). Based on a statistical analysis of this material, the hypothesis was confirmed.

In an attempt to replicate further and expand on their original hypotheses, a study of an elementary game of strategy (tick-tack-toe), as played by American school-aged boys and girls, was made by Sutton-Smith and Roberts (1967). In this investigation it was suggested that

> if games do in fact model various success styles . . . then those who are competent at these games should also reveal their type of success orientation in other forms of behavior. (p. 361)

Therefore, the researchers assumed that the various players' skill in playing the game of tick-tack-toe could be used "as an indirect means of inferring an hypothesized and underlying *elementary strategic competence*" (p. 361). This underlying pattern would be measured by specific tests for "automatization task persistence, pattern velocity, problem solving," and sociometric selection as idea leaders, ability at arithmetic and language, and general preference for games of strategy (p. 396). Four types of play styles were indicated, characterized as (1) the winning girl; (2) the winning boy; (3) the drawing girl; and (4) the drawing boy. The material collected supported the idea that "the game of Tick Tack Toe and the strategies adopted within this game . . . model related characteristics in the players" (p. 398). The evidence was most clear for the style of the "winning boy."

Other studies conducted by Roberts and Sutton-Smith in an effort to explicate further relationships between culture, child-rearing patterns, and games are : Sutton-Smith, Roberts, and Kozelka's "Game Involvement in Adults" (1963); Sutton-Smith and Roberts's, "Rubrics of Competitive Behavior" (1964); Roberts, Hoffman, and Sutton-Smith's "Pattern and Competence: A Consideration of Tick Tack Toe" (1965); and Roberts and Sutton-Smith's "Cross-Cultural Correlates of Games of Chance" (1966). In this latter article, the authors proposed a sequence of development for games in culture. It is suggested that, in earliest human societies, there were no games; physical-skill games were the first to be developed, followed by games of chance and, finally, games of strategy.

More recent studies by Roberts and Ridgeway (1969), Roberts and Forman (1971), and Barry and Roberts (1972) continue the investigation and explication of the conflict–enculturation hypothesis. In "Infant Socialization and Games of Chance" (1972), Barry and Roberts reported a series of relationships of games of chance with cultural, particularly child-training, variables based on a statistical analysis of a new sample of 186 societies compiled by Murdock and White (1969). The child-training measures developed by Barry and Paxson (1971) were used here. Examples of relationships reported are positive associations between games of chance and bodily restrictiveness (e.g., cradle boards or swaddling), social isolation, physical protectiveness, degree of training in responsibility and obedience, early age for modesty training, variable food resources, and land transport by animals or vehicles rather than humans. It is suggested that the "approach–avoidance" relationships proposed as necessary for game/model involvement by the conflict–enculturation hypothesis might be generated by certain of the child-rearing and other cultural characteristics found to be associated with games of chance or games of chance and physical skill (e.g., the high degree of bodily restrictiveness and social isolation in infancy, the high physical protectiveness and other mechanisms for strong social rewards present in these societies).

Criticisms and/or revisions and expansions of the "Roberts and Sutton-Smith" studies have been made by a variety of researchers. Georges (1969), for example, has suggested that the assertions made by these investigators have been based solely on information derived from observation and testing of American children and from data obtained from the Cross-Cultural Survey Files. He argued that there are very great problems in assuming that the material contained in these files is accurate, and likewise the coding and classification scheme utilized by the researchers is frequently ambiguous. It should be noted here, however, that Roberts and Sutton-Smith are very aware of such problems and discussed the limitations of this method in their various articles. Nevertheless, Georges criticized the investigators for not conducting observational cross-cultural studies. He stated that

> there are no indications in their publications that Roberts and Sutton-Smith
> have actually attempted to test these generalizations [conflict–enculturation
> hypothesis] cross-culturally. (p. 9)

Susanna Millar (1968) criticized the Roberts and Sutton-Smith studies in a similar fashion. In particular, she questioned their arguments as to causality, as portrayed in their suggestion that the frustration and anger aroused in children due to particular types of child-training (e.g., high obedience training) is displaced upon games and encourages involvement in particular types of games (e.g., the "unreal combat" of games of strategy), so that the child may still remain obedient in "real life":

> But even the most unequivocal association between variations in childhood training and certain types of games could give rise to no more than speculation about the direction of influence. Certain types of games might as easily be the cause of children being trained in certain ways as to result from it. . . . The findings do not necessitate an assumption of relief from inner conflict as the basis of involvement in a game, although they would be compatible with it. (pp. 207–208)

Rivka Eifermann has also criticized these studies in a fashion similar to Georges and Millar. However, she has also used the material collected in her large-scale study of Israeli children's play (1970, 1971a,b) to test the conflict–enculturation hypothesis. On the basis of this hypothesis, she predicted that rural children, with more opportunity to engage in the adult world (by doing tasks, etc.) than urban children, would develop less intense conflicts and, therefore, less interest in competitive games that model these conflicts. In analyzing her data, however, the opposite was found to occur. In discussing these findings, Sutton-Smith (in Herron and Sutton-Smith, 1971:268–269) argued that they do not contradict the conflict–enculturation hypothesis basically because Eifermann grouped all competitive games into one category rather than dividing them into the categories of physical skill, chance, and strategy.

Attempts at revisions and/or elaborations of the Roberts, Arth, and Bush (1959) classification scheme and scaling of social complexity have also been recently proposed. Ball (1972) has suggested that Roberts's (Roberts et al., 1959) original formulations concerning relationships between types of games and societal complexity are most generally associated with social organization (e.g., community size, complexity of class stratification, political integration) rather than economic organization (e.g., hunting-and-gathering versus fishing versus animal-husbandry versus agricultural societies). Revisions and/or testing of the original classification scheme have also been made (e.g., Ball, 1974; Royce, 1972). Royce's study is particularly interesting as he used information on Indonesian Sundanese children's games reported by Holtzappel (*Sundase Kinderspelen*, 1952) to examine the validity of both Roberts, Arth, and Bush's (1959) and Caillois's (1961) game classification systems. In the process, he presented a very useful comparative summary of the two systems, particularly in regard to their applicability to data on children's play, and he discussed material on the play of a specific group of children in an area of the world (Indonesia) from which there are few ethnographic reports on this behavior. On the basis of his analysis, he found Caillois's system preferable because it includes "non-competitive" games such as "make-believe" play and also vertigo *(ilinx)* games. Royce also suggested that Murdock's (1967) adoption of the Roberts, Arth, and Bush (1959) system of game classification in his overall classification of cultural groups excludes some very interesting games, such as the Tarahumara boys' game of making animal tracks with carved wooden sticks and then tracking them, "and also leads to the classification of certain cultures as 'gameless' though games (in Caillois's terms) are played" (p. 143).

The Roberts and Sutton-Smith studies have also influenced a number of cross-cultural studies of both sports and games. Günther Lüschen, in *The Cross Cultural Analysis of Sport and Games* (1970), included a number of articles reporting information on these activities by a variety of researchers. Many of these investigations have been influenced by the classification schema of Roberts, Arth, and Bush (1959), as well as the data source of the Human Relations Area File, although other conceptual and methodological frameworks are also employed.

May Seagoe reported information on her analysis of children's play as an indicator of cross-cultural and intracultural differences in Lüschen's volume (1970b:132–137). In this report, she compared Japanese and American children's play. In other reports, she presented information on differences in children's play in England, Norway, Spain, Greece, Egypt, and the United States (1971b) and in three American subcultures (white, Mexican-American, and black) (1971a). In these investigations, variation in children's "play socialization" (and the assumed "social complexity" of the play behavior) is determined by children's answers to a series of questions derived from a "play report" (e.g., "What do you spend most of your time playing at school, at home, at other places?" "What do you like to play most?" "What do you like to play least?", and the child was also asked to indicate for each response whether he/she played by him/herself, with grownups, with friends, on a team—see 1970a). Answers to these questions were rated using a developmental scheme that calls for "informal-individual play which is self-directed and not imitative of adults nor formally patterned" to be scored lowest while "cooperative-competitive play which is formally patterned toward team victory" is scored highest (see 1970:140). Differences in play noted and scored in this fashion were then associated with age, sex, type of schooling, rural-urban, cultural, and ethnic factors.

One of the most interesting findings reported in the 1971a study is the fact that the expected significant differences to occur between Mexican-American, white, and black "play socialization" scores did not occur except in the case of black girls. Differences between the white and

Mexican-American groups were slight, as were those for black boys. The black girls, however, "showed a rejection of play requiring high degrees of socialization three years earlier than other groups" (p. 169). Of course, there are many problems with such a study (including the way the play report was formulated, the scoring system devised, and the assumptions implicit in this system). Nevertheless, this information should be considered in relation to the play/imagination/culture question discussed in Chapter Six, where it was assumed that children from so-called "disadvantaged" groups (e.g., blacks) do not exhibit the same types of play behavior as white, middle-class children. Seagoe's findings do not appear to support this belief.

Sutton-Smith (1974b) has recently offered his own criticism of the Roberts and Sutton-Smith (and related) studies. He suggested that even though these investigations reopened the issue of play and games in anthropology, they ultimately represent more of an empirical than a theoretical breakthrough. Furthermore, he stated that perhaps the emphasis on the sociocultural functions of games ultimately served to reduce play phenomena to these more serious activities (p. 9). In this regard, then, he suggested that these investigations are, in the end, studies of play *contexts* (i.e., asserted relationships about psychogenic and sociogenic correlates of games) without much reference to play *texts* (p. 11).

An alternate view of this criticism can also be proposed, that is, that these studies (similar to the earlier approach of the diffusionists) tend to ignore not only text but also context. A "search and seize" methodology is characteristic of both schools, where games are pulled from their original sociocultural systems and placed in artificially constructed contexts for analysis (those set up by either statistical or diffusionist design). In the case of the cross-cultural quantitative studies, games and entire cultures are categorized and coded to make them available for statistical analysis in order to test associations between specific cultural variables and game types. This may be construed as a study of game or play contexts, in one sense of the term, but it does not analyze the game as it is actually played in its sociocultural context. A detailed examination of this context is ignored along with a consideration of specific texts because the investigators have chosen to adapt play to the requirements of a specific methodology (e.g., quantitative-statistical analysis) rather than adapting their methodology to the requirements of play.

With the above criticisms in mind, it is important to emphasize one of the most significant features of the Roberts and Sutton-Smith investigations. Along with turning anthropologists' attention toward the topic of play, this research is also significant for its attempt to study both the expressive and the formative or generative characteristics of play. This emphasis appears in other studies of play appearing in the 1960s. In "Games and Social Character in a Mexican Village" (1964), Michael Maccoby, Nancy Modiano, and Patricia Lander presented a report on children's games that was influenced by the above two researchers as well as by Caillois, Freud, Piaget, Erikson, and G. H. Mead.[26] In their study of children's games in a mestizo farming community in the Mexican state of Morales, the investigators chose to examine how interpersonal relationships are *expressed* in games, how games *influence* the development of social character, and also whether the introduction of a new game effects social change. The investigators were particularly interested in whether an analysis of games would provide them with information on how the character traits of cooperation, individualism, and rational authority develop. A description of the socioeconomic and value system of the villagers is also offered (e.g., sugar cane is grown under the direction of a large cooperative sugar mill; sharp differences of income exist; villagers are distrustful and hostile toward institutionalized authorities; there is a tendency to seek security in submission; and fatalistic attitudes dominate, which often lead to alcoholism and/or apathy).

Specific information on games was collected by participant observation, the administration of a formal questionnaire (questions concerning which games were played by boys, girls, both; which games were preferred and why), and the experimental introduction of new games. Five age periods are characterized: (1) dramatic and mimicry play are said to predominate in the play of children under 8 (e.g., dressing up kittens as babies, playing house, playing teacher, playing drunk); (2) physical skill games are played by younger (4–7) and older (8–12) children (e.g., climbing trees; using slingshots; playing *balero,* a cup-and-stick game; marbles; jump rope; bounce ball; and penny pitching, which combines skill, competition and chance); (3) central-person games are most popular in the 9–12 age group (e.g., *la rabia*—tag; *escondidas,* which is a version of hide-and-seek; *cuero que-mado,* a chasing game); (4) team sports are played between the ages of 12 and 16 (e.g., soccer—boys; volleyball—girls); (5) young men over the age of 16 play either basketball, cards, or billiards.

Differences in the enactment of the games by boys and girls illustrate differences in the social character development of the two sexes.

---

[26]More recently, Modiano has published an analysis of *Indian Education in the Chiapas Highlands* (1973), which includes lengthy descriptions of children's play (based largely on recollections of adults and other youths). Somewhat further afield from this topic is Maccoby's (1976) recent analysis of the "gamesman" approach of American corporate managers.

Most specifically, the way central-person games are played by village boys contrasts sharply with the way Western children play these games. The boys' games generally lack structure, are frequently violent, and portray authority only as an irrational punishing force where the central person has no authority and is chased by the group or, alternately, has full permission to punish the others who try to escape. The authors portrayed relationships between boys' games and social character in the following manner:

> A boy does not learn to disengage himself from authority, and egocentrism by cooperating with peers. . . . Authority remains dangerous and impulsive, a force he must escape or imitate. The central person is either chased or chases brutally. . . . In both games and village life the tendency is for atomism rather than cooperation, and the formation of a mass rather than individualism and respect for differences. (p. 159)

In contrast, the girls' games are more structured and orderly and less violent, and each player takes turns acting as the leader while players accept, rather than flee from, authority figures. The content of the games generally relates to danger from the male world and, particularly, the sexually predatory male. It is suggested that the symbolism of the girls' games, as well as their attitude toward authority, reflects the realities of village life for females.

The effects of the introduction of new games in the village are also discussed. The most interesting event described relates to one attempt to introduce a new central-person game—a variation of "Red Rover, Come Over." The "it" in this variation was called *jefe*, or the "chief of police," and the others were called "thieves," who were supposed to cooperate against *jefe*. Instructions were presented in Spanish to a classroom of third- and fourth-grade children by the investigator, who had lived in the village for two months prior to this "experiment." The various subversions and distortions of the game by the children clearly revealed their attitudes toward authority (see pp. 161–162). First, an attempt was made to combine boys and girls, but the girls left when *jefe* (a boy) did not call any girls' names. Next the boys picked up the various stones and pieces of wood that the investigator had used to mark the boundaries and began to use them as weapons for attacking, instead of just tagging, players. In this instance, the police chief punished anyone whom he caught very severely while the others fought back. When the researcher tried to calm the children after this first violent episode, and she reexplained the game to them, the "thieves" then decided that they should stand still and wait to be caught. Finally, in another version, the concept of the "it" was completely lost, and the group solidified to persecute the outsider. The girls, on the other hand, played in a much calmer fashion. However, no matter how many times the experimenter explained the procedures, it was always played as a game the purpose of which was to be chosen (caught) by the *jefe*. The girl who was not caught felt like an outcast instead of a winner.

SUMMARY

In the 1920s and 1930s, a new school of anthropological research—the culture and personality orientation—was developed in America by individuals such as Edward Sapir, Ruth Benedict, and Margaret Mead. In their early studies, the researchers sought to challenge the assumptions of Freud, Piaget, and others, as to the universal existence and biologically based nature of certain types of behaviors, feelings, and thoughts. Occasionally these investigators used the play or games of children to demonstrate their particular theses; however, these activities were generally ignored or only cursorily described.

In the 1930s and 1940s, a rapprochement with Freudian psychology occurred in anthropology, most specifically because of the influence of Abram Kardiner, Ralph Linton, and Cora DuBois. In the studies pioneered by these researchers, ethnographers were encouraged to collect and interpret projective material from their informants in order to answer certain questions regarding relationships between "basic personality structure" and "primary" and "secondary cultural institutions." Freud had earlier described the mastery-over-conflict and projection-eliciting character of children's play, and so certain culture and personality researchers developed an interest in this behavior. This is most evident in the doll play studies of Jules and Zunia Henry with Pilagá Indian children, and Géza Róheim with the Duau children of Melanesia. In these investigations, however, play was *used* only as a *context* for the investigation of other activities.

It was also at this time that two important studies presenting methodological innovations for the study of both children and play were made. Wayne Dennis's interest in natural observations of Hopi children's play behavior and his invention of a "play diary" and Gregory Bateson and Margaret Mead's use of still photography, film, and simultaneous field notes to record the behavior of both Balinese children and adults could potentially have revolutionized the study of non-Western children's play. Unfortunately, this did not happen. However, the work of Ralph Linton on the effect of culture on individual personality did inspire the extensive collection of the traditional play activities of African Luba, Sanga, and Yeke children by H. Centner.

More recently, a number of Western psychoanalytically oriented studies of children's play and fantasy behavior have been made by psychologists and psychiatrists. With certain exceptions (e.g., Winnicott), this research continues the Freudian tradition of using play to study other behaviors, and so the assumption that play is expressive but not generative of personality patterns has been perpetuated.

This view of play is also apparent in the studies of John W. M. Whiting and Irvin L. Child. These researchers have used statistical methods that necessitate the atomization of cultures for coding purposes (represented by the HRAF) for the testing of hypotheses derived from the psychoanalytic theories of Freud and the neobehaviorist learning theories of Hull, Dollard, Sears, and others. These studies continued to use the play-as-projection metaphor (when play is considered at all), and they influenced the research studies of Roberts, Arth, and Bush (1959) on the significance of games in culture.

In the *Six Cultures Project,* the most well-known production of the Whiting and Child research school, play was viewed as a projective system similar to art or religion. Investigators were encouraged to collect information on children's organized games and "recreations" following this model; however, for the most part, the ethnographers concentrated on the collection of information related to the important (and presumably generative) behavioral systems of succorance, nurturance, self-reliance, achievement, responsibility, obedience, dominance, sociability, and aggression. In the six ethnographies produced by this study, there are significant differences in the types and amount of play reported (e.g., Nyansongo versus Taira). However, what is most significant is that in only a few of the monographs are there detailed descriptions of an actual play event recorded for the children in the society. Generally, the ethnographers provided only lists of types of toys or types of games or, alternately, vague statements such as "the children go to the streets to play" (Minturn and Hitchcock, 1963:244). While the *Six Cultures Project* is certainly a landmark in the presentation of comparative ethnographic material on the subject of child-training practices, it is a disappointment for students of children's play.

More promising research, utilizing certain of the techniques and theories of the Whiting and Child approach, are the "Roberts and Sutton-Smith" studies. These investigations were inspired by the Roberts, Arth, and Bush (1959) article and, for the most part, were made during the 1960s and the early 1970s. Most specifically, these researchers attempted to establish relationships first between certain types of cultures and the presence or absence of certain types of children's competitive games and then between certain types of child-training variables, certain types of children's games, and certain types of cultures (i.e., the conflict–enculturation hypothesis). These relationships were tested by using HRAF material for the study of non-Western societies and experimental

data for the study of American culture. This research tradition has produced a number of studies (e.g., Roberts and Sutton-Smith, 1963, 1966;
Sutton-Smith and Roberts, 1967; Barry and Roberts, 1972). One of the
most significant observational investigations utilizing ideas from this
orientation and many other psychological theorists is Maccoby, Modiano, and Landers's (1964) analysis of games and their relation to the
development of social character in a Mexican village.

A number of researchers have criticized both the general Whiting
and Child school of culture and personality research and the specific
Roberts and Sutton-Smith studies of children's play (e.g., Georges,
Millar, Eifermann). Sutton-Smith, however, has presented the most
compelling criticism of these investigations by suggesting that this approach favors the study of the *contexts* of play to the exclusion of consideration of play *texts*. In this regard, this orientation is similar in focus to
that of the functionalist tradition. It is also possible to argue that these
are studies of artificially constructed contexts necessitated by the use of
statistical analysis.

The major significance of the Roberts and Sutton-Smith approach is
the researchers' recognition that play is both generative and expressive
of personality and culture. This view has helped to remove the biases of
earlier culture and personality researchers that caused them to see play
only as a context for the investigation of other activities. Because of these
biases, many anthropologists, like Little Hans's feared horses, were
wearing blinders when it came to the subject of play.

CHAPTER EIGHT

Saying Play: Communication Studies

"You are sad," the Knight said in an anxious tone: "let me sing you a song to comfort you. . . . The name of the song is called 'Haddock's Eyes.' "

"Oh, that's the name of the song, is it?" Alice said, trying to feel interested.

"No, you don't understand," the Knight said, looking a little vexed. "That's what the name is called. *The name really* is *'The Aged Aged Man.' "*

"Then I ought to have said 'That's what the song *is called'?" Alice corrected herself.*

"No, you oughtn't: that's quite another thing! The song *is called 'Ways and Means': but that's only what it's* called, *you know!"*

"Well, what is *the song, then?" said Alice, who was by this time completely bewildered.*

"I was coming to that," the Knight said. "The song really is 'A-sitting on a Gate': and the tune's my own invention."

Lewis Carroll *Through The Looking Glass, and What Alice Found*

The study of communication and control in men and machines, or cybernetics, developed in the late 1940s associated with the work of Norbert Weiner, Warren McCulloch, Heinz von Foerster, Julian Bigelow, and others. Norbert Weiner coined the term *cybernetics* from the Greek word *kubernetes* ("steersman") in order to designate this newly developing field, which brought together ideas from many disciplines (e.g., engineering, biology, physics) in one term. Central to this approach is the idea of feedback, which describes the principle of purposive or goal-directed behavior in systems[1] Related to this idea is the concept of *information*, which may be thought of as "the 'commodity' that circulates in a communication system, no matter what its physical form" (Rosenblith, 1967:27). Weiner believed that biological, mechanical, and social systems could all be understood as communication systems. And he specifically believed that cybernetic ideas were crucial to the understanding of society:

> This complex of behavior [communication and control] is ignored by the average man, and in particular does not play the role that it should in our habitual analysis of society; . . . I do not mean that the sociologist is unaware of the existence and complex nature of communications in society, but until recently he has tended to overlook the extent to which they are the cement which binds its fabrics together. (1954:39)

THE DIFFERENCE THAT MAKES A DIFFERENCE: GREGORY BATESON

In anthropology, Gregory Bateson was wrestling with issues that were ultimately able to be described in cybernetic terms as early as 1936. In his first monograph (*Naven*, 1936), Bateson examined the Naven ritual (a ceremony characterized by transvestism) of the Iatmul people of New Guinea from three different perspectives: structural (eidos), emotional (ethos), and sociological. In this analysis, the notion of *schismogenesis* was introduced and defined "as a process of differentiation in the norms of individual behavior resulting from a cumulative interaction between individuals" that promoted progressive change in the culture (pp. 175–177). However, increased "schismogenic tension" did not lead to the destruction of Iatmul society because, according to Bateson, this tension "set off" the Naven ceremonial (1958:289). As Bateson later realized, his discussion of schismogenesis was a depiction of the process of positive feedback, while the Naven ceremony was an example of negative feedback. In this way, Iatmul culture can be viewed as a self-corrective communication system.

In 1936, these cybernetic terms had not yet been developed, but Bateson was struggling with problems that he perceived in his own concepts (e.g., ethos, eidos, schismogenesis). The issue that he raised in his 1936 epilogue to *Naven* illustrates what has become one of Bateson's

---

[1]*Negative feedback* may be defined as a process whereby " 'mismatch' information into the systems behavior-directing centers reduces . . . the deviation of the system from its goal-states" (Buckley, 1967:53). *Positive feedback* is a similar process; however, in this case, information about deviation from an internal goal-state increases that deviation (see Maruyama, 1963).

major interests—the problem of levels of meaning and the fallacy of misplaced concreteness:

> there may be some among my readers who tend to regard such concepts as "structure" as concrete parts which "interact" in culture, and who find, as I did, a difficulty in thinking of these concepts as labels merely for points of view adopted by either the scientist or by the natives. (p. 262)

He went on to suggest that

> the habit of thought which attributes concreteness to aspects of phenomena is one which dies hard. The fallacy which Whitehead has pilloried has been an important principle or motif of European eidos, certainly since the days of Greek Philosophy. It has taken me over a year to drop the habit even partially, and I fear that many passages in the book may be still more or less infected with it, in spite of drastic revision. (p. 263)

Bateson returned to the problems of "labels" and "things" in the conclusion of his epilogue. Here he described the value of labels for "disentangling old ideas" and the problem of "jumbling." It was only later, as will be seen below, that he became interested in both the creative and the pathological aspects of "tangled" or "jumbled" labels:

> I am aware that there are dangers inherent in the use of labels, and that these little pieces of paper are only too liable to hide the things to which they are attached. But though labels must always be used with caution, they are useful things, and the whole of science depends on them. In this case, their use has been to help me to disentangle old ideas and to enable me to think in terms of one aspect of culture at a time instead of jumbling all the aspects together. (p. 279)

In the 1940s, Bateson continued his examination of self-corrective systems by discussing the pattern of an armaments race (1946a,b), and he also began to analyze the existence of levels of learning. In a 1942 commentary on a paper by Margaret Mead, Bateson coined the term *deutero-learning* to describe the process of *learning to learn*. He argued here that learning occurs at various levels and that this is true for both human and nonhuman animals. As an example of this process, he suggested that the Pavlovian dog learns to salivate when he hears a buzzer, but he also learns that he is operating in a "fatalistic" world, where one waits passively for rewards rather than engaging in action as would be the case in an "instrumental world." Another way to put this would be to say that the dog learns a specific *text* (i.e., a particular behavior), but he also learns a *context* for interpreting this text, which will be used for the interpretation of future texts.

By the late 1940s, Bateson had already examined many issues that were later developed, in the 1950s, into a comprehensive theory of communication (and epistemology) that tied together such seemingly unrelated phenomena as play, humor, psychotherapy, schizophrenia, hypnosis, and ritual. The themes evident in this early work (particularly

Naven), brought Bateson, in his own words, "to the edge" of cybernetic theory. When he returned to America following World War II, he became a participant in the now famous Macy conferences on cybernetics, which were also attended by Weiner, Bigelow, von Foerster, McCulloch, Hutchison, Margaret Mead, and others.[2] Bateson stated that his debt to the individuals involved in these conferences "is evident in everything that I have written since World War II" (1972:x).

Following this experience, Bateson began work at the Langley Porter Clinic with Jurgen Ruesch. The application of a cybernetic approach to the study of communication and the specific field of psychiatry is evident in their book *Communication: The Social Matrix of Psychiatry* (1951). It was also out of this collaboration that Bateson began a study of play between river otters, which will be discussed in detail shortly.

The themes of Bateson's research at this point may be summarized as follows. First, implicitly and explicitly, an emphasis is placed on the importance of considering the *relationship* between things (e.g., individuals, events, ideas) rather than the things themselves. In Bateson's terms, form, not substance, and context, not content, should be the primary focus for researchers (see, for example, his classification of symmetrical and complementary schismogenesis as a classification of relationships or contexts, 1936:190–197). One of Bateson's major interests is the study of evolution, and one of his clearest examples of the importance of considering relationships appears in his discussion of the evolution of the horse:

> the evolution of the horse from *Eohippus* was not a one-sided adjustment to life on grassy plains. Surely the grassy plains themselves were evolved *pari passu* with the evolution of the teeth and hooves of the horses and other ungulates. Turf was the evolving response of the vegetation to the horse. It is the *context* which evolves. (1972:155)

In the world of "form and communication," according to Bateson, there are no "things, forces or impacts," only differences and ideas: "A difference which makes a difference *is* an idea. It is a 'bit,' a unit of information" (1972:271–272).

A second stress is placed on the recognition that there are hierarchies or levels of difference. "There are differences between differences" because "every effective difference denotes a demarcation, a line of classification, and all classification is hierarchic" (p. 457). The description of an event is *different* than the event itself, as Bateson realized in *Naven*. According to Whitehead and Russell (1910–1913), a class of things is a different logical type than the members of the class. Or, as the White Knight tries to explain to Alice, the name of the song ("The Aged

---

[2]For an interesting recollection of these conferences by Bateson and Mead, see Stuart Brand's (1976) recent interview, "For God's Sake Margaret: Conversation with Gregory Bateson and Margaret Mead."

Aged Man") is different than the call-name of the name of the song ("Haddock's Eyes"), or than the call-name of the song ("Ways and Means"); and all of these are different than the song itself ("A-sitting on a Gate") (see Nagel, 1956).[3]

Finally, Bateson became interested in the "tangles" in the rules for making transforms of differences in communication. Because there are differences or discontinuities between classes and their members, it is possible for paradox to occur, and Bateson was very intrigued by this problem. However, he believed that it was first important to see if any nonhuman animals qualified their messages. Did they exhibit *any* awareness at all that they were, in fact, communicating?

PLAY AND PARADOX: THE MESSAGE "THIS IS PLAY"

In order to answer this question, Bateson had begun filming river otters in the Fleishhacker Zoo in San Francisco in the early 1950s. In 1952, he received a two-year grant from the Rockefeller Foundation to investigate paradoxes in communication, and by 1953, a research team had formed that included Jay Haley, John Weakland, and later, William Fry and Don Jackson.[4] The information used in the first year of this project was quite varied and included Bateson's study of otters' playing, a study of guide dogs for the blind, an analysis of a popular moving picture, a film on mongoloid children in a group, an analysis of humor and a ventriloquist and a puppet, and the speech of a schizophrenic patient (Haley, 1976:62).

In 1954, the group's developing theoretical orientation was expressed in two papers ("A Theory of Play and Fantasy," 1955, Bateson; "Paradoxes in Play, Fantasy and Therapy," 1955, Haley), which were presented by Haley at a meeting of the American Psychiatric Association in Mexico City. Haley also showed Bateson's film, *The Nature of Play—Part 1: River Otters*, at this meeting.[5] This orientation developed initially out of Bateson's research with the otters and, in particular, a study of

---

[3]In "The Philosopher's Alice in Wonderland," Roger Holmes suggested that Lewis Carroll was teasing the reader when the White Knight says, "The song really is 'A-sitting on a Gate,' " which is, after all, only another name. This is so because "to be consistent, the White Knight, when he had said the song *is* . . . , could only have burst into the song itself" (Holmes in Gardner, 1960:306).

[4]In this discussion of chronology and research team interests, I am using Haley's (1976) recently published, and very useful, history of the Bateson project.

[5]This movie is not commercially available, but it was shown recently in conjunction with Bateson's Keynote Address at The Association for the Anthropological Study of Play, 1977 Annual Meeting in San Diego, California. A description and discussion of the events recorded on this film appear in Bateson's article "The Message 'This is Play' " (1956). I have also included a brief discussion of this film in Chapter Twelve.

their play behavior. However, it brought together the previous themes of his research, stressing an analysis of how relationships are communicated, the classification of these messages, and the possibility that paradoxes may be generated by certain of these classifications.

The theory as it pertains to play, fantasy, and psychotherapy is discussed most specifically in Bateson (1955, 1956), Haley (1955), and the movie on river otters. In an earlier discussion of humor (Bateson, 1953), certain aspects of this theory are enumerated, and a more recent application of this approach to the study of humor is available by Fry (1963). In 1956, Bateson and his co-workers used this approach to examine patterns of communication in "schizophrenigenic" families. This analysis produced the well-known double-bind theory of schizophrenia (Bateson, Jackson, Haley, and Weakland, "Toward a Theory of Schizophrenia," 1956). Following the publication of this article a series of papers and articles were produced by members of the Bateson project and others interested in a systems, or communicational, approach to both the understanding and the treatment of mental illness. A recent compilation and evaluation of research on the double-bind thesis appears in Sluzki and Ransom (1976).

In the articles written in the early 1950s, Bateson suggested that human communication occurs at various levels of abstraction. As an example, he often cited the statement, "The cat is on the mat" (1953:1; 1955:39). At the denotative level, this message may relay an answer to the question, "Is the cat on the mat?" Following the work of McCulloch (see 1965), Bateson suggested that this *report* statement also contains a *command* or a stimulus that may urge the recipient of the message to pick the cat up, kick it, feed it, ignore it, etc. (1953:1). But there are other *implicit* levels of communication expressed in this message. At the metalinguistic level, the sound "cat" stands for any number of a certain class of objects, but this word or name itself "has no fur and cannot scratch" (1955:39). At the metacommunicative level, "the subject of discourse is the relationship between the speakers"; for example, "my telling you where to find the cat was friendly," or "this is play" (p. 39).

When messages are exchanged at various levels of abstraction, it is possible for paradoxes to be generated, because one message contradicts the other. Bateson knew that the problem of paradox in classification systems was a matter of great concern to philosophers and logicians. Whitehead and Russell (1910–1913) had dealt with this matter by arguing that a class of things is of a different level, or *logical type,* than the members of the class. In this way, they were able to avoid a number of paradoxes, particularly the "class of classes" paradox. Bateson discussed this problem in "The Message 'This Is Play' " (1956), which is a transcription of one session of the Second Conference on Group Processes sponsored by the Josiah Macy, Jr. Foundation.

Bateson: . . . let me put it to you like this: We live in a universe of name-ables [see Figure 19]. Within that universe we make classes. Let me make here the class of chairs. I now want you quickly, without thinking too much about it, to name for me some of the "not chairs." . . .

You have suggested "tables," "dogs," "people," "autos." Let me suggest one now: "tomorrow." Does it make you a little uncomfortable when I say tomorrow is not a chair?

A voice: Schizophrenic!

Bateson: Thank you. It would seem that there are two senses in which the term "not" is used. There are these things, which for lack of a better term I will call the proper ground for the class of chairs—the class of chairs being a figure as against that ground—and a second sense, in which the "not" indicates what I will call the improper non-chairs. Among these in the outer zone we have "tomorrow," and amongst other things—*the class of chairs* which evidently is not a chair. The nameable—the class of chairs—demarcated by inner line, is clearly not here where I have shown it, but out there among the "improper non-chairs."

We also have in the outer zone the class of non-chairs which evidently is one of the "not-chairs," and the moment we use the "not" in this improper sense, we are forced thereby into making a class a member of itself. The "class of non-chairs" is now one of its own members.

Fremont-Smith: Making a class a member of itself.

Bateson: The class of non-chairs is not a chair, is it?

Fremont-Smith: Therefore, it becomes a chair.

Bateson: No; it becomes an "improper non-chair." The class of improper non-chairs is an improper non-chair. Now, this is a matter which has bothered philosophers since 600 B.C. and which was seriously considered by Whitehead and Russell (1910–1913). Russell resolved the matter by saying that whenever we define a class, we must never include in the ground for that class anything of different "logical type" from the members of the class. That was excellent, and is a nice rule for scientific exposition. The definition of a class is a subjective process. (pp. 145–146)

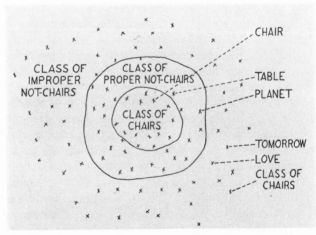

FIGURE 19. Bateson's "onionskin" diagram (G. Bateson, 1956:146).

There are other illustrations of paradoxes of this sort often referred to as Epimenides' paradox. For example, if a man says "I am lying," is this a true statement? If it is true, then it is false. Another example is diagrammed and discussed in Bateson's "A Theory of Play and Fantasy" (1955:44).

```
All statements within
this frame are untrue.
I love you.
I hate you.
```

Here it is obvious that the first statement contained in the frame is self-contradictory; that is, if the statement is true, it is false, and if it is false, then it is true. However, there are also two other statements bounded by this frame, and so, if the first is true, then the others must be false, and, likewise, if the first is false, then the others must be true (1955:44).

Bateson was intrigued by these paradoxes of self-reference and by Whitehead and Russell's solution to the logical problems they present. But did these problems of chairs, not-chairs, a class of improper not-chairs, and so on have anything at all to do with the world of human and nonhuman animal communication? Or were they only problems for mathematicians, logicians, philosophers, and linguists to worry about? Haley (1976:60) suggested that Bateson was possibly

> the first person to apply the theory of Logical Types to communication. For Russell and Whitehead, logical types were an aspect of the mathematical approach to classification systems, not a method of analyzing communication.

Bateson's realization that this theory could be applied to the understanding of human and other animal communication occurred initially in the early 1950s, when he began to investigate whether or not animals were aware that they were communicating. What he observed, when he began these studies, was the phenomenon of play:

> What I encountered at the zoo was a phenomenon well known to everybody. I saw two young monkeys *playing*; i.e., engaged in an interactive sequence of which the unit actions or signals were similar to but not the same as those of combat. It was evident, even to the human observer, that the sequence as a whole was not combat, and evident to the human observer that to the participant monkeys this was "not combat."
> Now, this phenomenon, play, could only occur if the participant organisms were capable of some degree of meta-communication, i.e., of exchanging signals which would carry the message "this is play." (1955:40)

According to Bateson, play can occur only among organisms able to metacommunicate and, therefore, able to distinguish messages of differing logical types. Therefore, an important stage of evolution must occur when organisms gradually cease to respond "automatically" to the "mood signs" of others and begin to recognize the sign as a signal "which can be trusted, distrusted, falsified, denied, amplified, corrected and so forth" (p. 40). It is at this point that the possibility of communicating at various levels of abstraction occurs, and play is an activity that illustrated to Bateson that both humans and some nonhuman animals have this capacity.

Metacommunicative messages act as "frames" or "contexts" providing information about how another message should be interpreted. In order to understand an action as play, it must be framed by the message "This is play." Bateson suggested that this message generates a paradox of the Russellian or Epimenides' type, wherein a negative statement contains an implicit negative metastatement (p. 41). Therefore, the message "This is play" states: "these actions, in which we now engage, do not denote what would be denoted by those actions which these actions denote" (p. 41). In a play fight, "the playful nip denotes the bite, but it does not denote what would be denoted by the bite" (p. 41). It is simultaneously a bite and a not-bite. In the above statement, the word *denote* is used in two senses, but they are treated as if they are synonymous. According to Bateson, this produces paradox and is inadmissible following the theory of logical types because the terms are used at differing levels of abstraction (p. 41). However, it is important to remember that these rules of logic are broken all the time in mammalian communication and are, in fact, necessary for the evolution of communication to occur:

> Our central thesis may be summed up as a statement of the necessity of the paradoxes of abstraction. It is not merely bad natural history to suggest that people might or should obey the Theory of Logical Types in their communications; their failure to do this is not due to mere carelessness or ignorance. Rather, we believe that the paradoxes of abstraction must make their appearance in all communication more complex than that of mood-signals, and that without these paradoxes the evolution of communication would be at an end. Life would be an endless interchange of stylized messages, a game with rigid rules, unrelieved by change or humor. (1955:50–51)

In Bateson's terms, the texts and contexts of play are intimately and systemically related and cannot be considered in isolation from one another. This relationship is most clearly expressed in Bateson's *metalogues*, in which the structure and content of a discussion are comments on one another (e.g., "About Games and Being Serious," "Why Do Things Have Outlines?", see 1972:3–58). But these issues are also raised in his analysis of what children learn by playing. Because play and learning are multileveled phenomena, analyses of texts (of the content of specific interactions) that do not consider context are invariably inaccurate. In fact, Bateson suggested that it is in play that one learns that there are frames or contexts of behavior:

> Someone has said that we know that play is important to children because it is in play that we learn role behavior. What I would like to say is that there is an element of truth in that, no doubt, but there seems to be a much more important truth in that it is by play that an individual learns that there are sorts and categories of behavior. . . . The child is playing at being an archbishop. I am not interested in the fact that he learns how to be an archbishop from playing the role; but that he learns that there is such a thing as a role. He learns or acquires a new view, partly flexible and partly rigid, which is introduced into life when he realizes that behavior can, in a sense, be set to a logical type or a style. It is not the learning of the particular style that you are playing at, but the fact of stylistic flexibility and the fact that the choice of style or role is related to the frame and context of behavior. And play itself is a category of behavior, classified by context in some way. (1956:148–149)

Play is not the only activity characterized by paradoxical metacommunication. Bateson (1955) discussed fantasy, ritual, threat, art, magic, psychotherapy, and the interesting case of schizophrenic communication (so-called word salad), which may be characterized by the absence of metacommunicative framing (p. 190, and later developed in Bateson *et al.*, 1956). In describing similarities between play and psychotherapy, Bateson made a very important distinction between these two activities and games. In games, the paradoxical reference system of play is embodied in a codified system of rules that organize the use of objects, space, and time, as well as player activities. Here it is not necessary for metacommunication to occur continually to define or "frame" the players' actions, as this is achieved by the game's explicit rule structure. In games, the ambiguity and paradox inherent in play, which necessitates constant metacommunication for maintenance of the event, has been "ruled" out:

> As we see it, the process of psychotherapy is a framed interaction between two persons, in which the rules are implicit but subject to change. Such change can only be proposed by experimental action, but every such experimental action, in which a proposal to change the rules is implicit, is itself a part of the on-going game. It is this combination of logical types within the single meaningful act that gives to therapy the character not of a rigid game like canasta, but, instead, that of an evolving system of interaction. The play of kittens or otters has this character. (1955:192)[6]

---

[6]This distinction between "rigid games" and "play" is also made in Bateson's metalogue "About Games and Being Serious" (1972:14–20) and also in his discussion (1955:50–51) included here of the importance of the paradoxes of abstraction in the evolution of communication.

This contrast between the rigidity of games and the flexibility of play is an important distinction and one that many researchers fail to make. The confusion between these two activities is compounded by the fact that *play* is frequently used as a verb, as in the statement "Let's play a game." It may be, however, that such a statement is itself a contradiction in terms. This possibility will be explored further in Chapter Eleven.

THE SINGLE SIGNAL

Bateson's theory of play has certainly advanced our understanding of this activity; however, his analysis has frequently been misunderstood. The most common mistake made is to assume that the message "This is play" is a single, static signal. In this instance, the message *is treated as if it is a thing* (rather than the result of a relationship), and researchers set about searching for *the* characteristic play signal of a particular species. The matter is further confused by the fact that certain animals appear to exhibit "single signals" (e.g., dogs spread their front legs forward in a bowing gesture and wag their tails as an invitation to play; see Bekoff, 1972, 1974). However, in play events, all behaviors are transformed in some way (e.g., they may be exaggerated or repeated) and continually marked (e.g., by a tail wag) as play. Attempts to turn this message into a *thing* always result in the separation *in time* of text and context; that is, the signal is said to be a context marker that occurs *prior* to the text (see Miller, 1973:90; Goffman, 1974:254; Turner, 1977:70). But it was Bateson's view that communication is always multileveled, and so the message "This is play" always acts as both a context and a text. It is important to emphasize here that these messages *are not delivered sequentially but simultaneously.* Another way of indicating this is to use Garvey's suggestion (see below) that "the saying is the playing," with the realization that this means that text and context cannot be separated.

One of the clearest examples of the confusion of these issues is found in Suzanne Chevalier-Skolnikoff's (1974) discussion of the primate play face. Here she examined Bateson's notion of metacommunication and in particular the idea that the primate play face is a metacommunicative signal. She suggested that while this view may be useful "on a descriptive level," it obscures "some of the more basic biological functions and causes of play" (p. 15). In addition, she believes that the idea of metacommunication may be unnecessary:

> The nonhuman primate play face is just one aspect of play that functions as a sign that a particular sequence is play behavior and not aggression. The *whole* play sequence differs from aggression, and the other functional behavior

> categories it may resemble . . . it consists of rapid shifts between motor patterns; it is re-ordered, exaggerated and fragmented. . . . Consequently, no meta-communicative signal is theoretically necessary to signal that a playful interaction is play. (pp. 18–19)

Chevalier-Skolnikoff argued that because the *whole sequence* is different in play, the idea of metacommunication is inappropriate. However, while she sees her discussion as a refutation of Bateson's views, it is really a reiteration of them.

The single-signal view results from the fact that researchers have not understood Bateson's idea of levels of communication. Related to this is also the fact that attention has been focused on the idea of the message as a context and not on what the message *says*. Because play actions are never quite what they seem to be (e.g., "This nip is not a bite"), metacommunicative messages must be contained in *every* action that is play. There can be no single signal.

Another problem with Bateson's view, and it is one that he is well aware of (1977), is the realization that the message "This is play" is itself play. The multiple and potentially conflicting layers of meaning in all communication are reflected by the complexity of play communication. We cannot, however, resolve the paradoxes and metaparadoxes that play gives rise to but only seek to understand them and their effect on and place in social life. This was, from the start, Bateson's only goal.

WINKING OR BLINKING? TEXT AND CONTEXT

Bateson's ideas on play were formulated, for the most part, on the basis of research with nonhuman animals (e.g., monkeys and otters). He recognized, however, that the possibilities for complications or, in Gilbert Ryle's terms, the difference between blinking, winking, parodying a wink, rehearsing a parody of a wink, and so on (see Geertz, 1973) was even greater among humans. Bateson's approach to the study of play as communication in specific and culture as communication in general has influenced, either directly or indirectly, many researchers concerned with the study of human interaction.

In the mid-1950s, Edward T. Hall began a systematic study of the subtleties and nuances of human communication. In his view, culture could best be conceptualized as a shared communicative system. Hall's analyses of nonverbal communication (e.g., paralinguistics, gestures, use of time) and particularly his investigations of different cultures' patternings of space (proxemics) are now well known (see particularly 1966). In the first presentation of this approach, *The Silent Language* (1959), Hall described his work with the linguist George Traeger and the development of the notion of primary message systems (PMS). These are cultural systems that have their foundation in a biological activity, are capable of analysis in their own terms, and yet are constituted in such a way as to reflect the rest of the cultural system and to be reflected in all of them. Ten primary message systems are described: (1) interaction; (2) association; (3) subsistence; (4) bisexuality; (5) territoriality; (6) temporality; (7) learning; (8) play; (9) defense; and (10) exploitation (use of materials) (pp. 45–62). The interlocking relationship of these systems with one another is most graphically illustrated in Hall and Traeger's "Map of Culture" (see pp. 174–175).

Although there are many questions that can be raised about this schema (e.g., Are these categories meaningful to the individuals of a specific culture or only to the researcher who devises them? Can all cultures be categorized in this fashion? Is play a *category* or a *mode* of behavior?), what is important to note is that the significance of *play in culture* and *culture in play* is specifically recognized. This is clearly revealed in the analysis and in the map diagram. For example, Hall suggested that,

> In the course of evolution, play has been a relatively recent and not too well understood addition to living processes. It is well-developed in mammals but not so easily recognizable in birds, and its role as an adaptive mechanism is yet to be pinned down. However, one can say that it is interwoven into all of the other PMS. (p. 57)

Stephen Miller (1973) has recently used Bateson's idea of metacommunication to develop a definition of play capable of encompassing all the various activities (e.g., playing puppies, playing house, playing games) referred to by this label. In this article, he reviewed material on the subject of both human and nonhuman play, considering reports on the various forms as well as presumed functional attributes of this behavior. Miller suggested that there are a number of patterns, or "motifs," to be found in all these diverse activities. In describing these motifs, he used Bateson's notion of frames to suggest that play is a *context* or mode of organization in which "ends are not obliterated" but do not, as is true for other behaviors, "determine the means" (p. 92). Play is also distinguished by a psychological process that Miller (borrowing from Lewis Carroll's poem "Jabberwocky") referred to as "galumphing," that is, "the voluntary placing of obstacles in one's path" (p. 92). In this article, Miller attempted to deal with one of the main "obstacles" presented to the student of play (i.e., how can we talk about the phenomenon of play when its manifestations appear to be so diverse?).

In a second article, written in 1974, Miller self-consciously "galumphed" through a discussion of "The Playful, the Crazy and the Nature of Pretense." Transforming ideas from cybernetics and, in particular, Bateson (1972), he suggested that pretense exists in a number of seemingly nonplayful areas, such as respiration circuitry. For example, in this system, CO_2 excess may be said to "stand for" the lack of O_2, which produces, according to Miller, a *double* feedback loop:

> The inner loop represents the flow of information about something *else*, some variable like CO_2 that does not have real consequences. . . . Now this relationship, in which one thing (amount of CO_2) is a representation . . . of something else (amount of O_2) but without the consequences of the latter, is precisely the relationship known as *pretending* . . . [in this case,] the "pretend" system exists in the body, while the "real" system is an abstraction that we observers construct when we ask questions about the purpose of breathing. (p. 34)

Miller went on to suggest that this form of pretense obtains in other relationships as well, for example, theory: data; myth: events; map: territory. Theories, for example, determine (as Bateson has also suggested, 1972) what data we will see and what data will be "noise," and inevitably play is involved in this process because we must pretend that some things are important while others are not. However, if we are flexible, our theories will change. According to Miller, because all theories are *caricatures,*

> it is inevitable that nonsupportive data will eventually squeak into the territory that the theory maps. . . . There is pressure on the theory to change or "adapt"—to be a better map of the territory. (p. 39)

Flexibility is the key word here, for Miller suggested that play produces flexibility and it is

> the reinterpretation of reality or the production of novelty [that] keeps us from becoming ossified and unable to deal with a changing world. Play enables us to rearrange our capacities so that they can be used in many different ways. (p. 35)

In other words, play transforms the familiar into the novel, while exploration transforms the novel into the familiar (see p. 48).

Erving Goffman has also been greatly influenced by Bateson, as evidenced by his discussion of "Fun in Games" in *Encounters* (1961) and more recently *Frame Analysis* (1974). In the first study, Goffman used games to discuss the nature of social encounters or focused gatherings, for example, a jury deliberating, lovemaking, and boxing. A key concept in this analysis is the notion that any social event of this sort is enclosed by a "membrane," "boundary," "gate," or, using Bateson's term, a "frame." Goffman described "rules of irrelevance" and "transformation rules" that are said to operate either to exclude properties out of a situation or to define how the "realized resources" of the encounter will be allocated and defined within the frame. He also discussed how a formalized game-theoretical model overlooks certain attributes of these events, most specifically the occurrence of "spontaneous involvement" (i.e., becoming totally engrossed in the activity) in games and other focused gatherings. In fact, it is this unselfconscious involvement that becomes the "fun" of the game, according to Goffman, because, ironically, when this happens, the encounter "can become real" to the participants (p. 80). As is typical of a Goffmanian analysis, "Fun in Games" is replete with descriptions of processes occurring in focused gatherings for which he has invented a name. He has therefore provided us with a discussion of "euphoria and dysphoria function," "incidents," "integrations," "flooding out," "flooding in," "tipping," "leaky words," "by-play," "postplay," "collusive by-play," and so on.

This approach was continued in *Frame Analysis* (1974), where Goffman described Bateson's and others' studies of play, and suggested that if one studies only monkeys and otters, there will not be many *other* phenomena that exhibit the transformational character of play. However, when we begin to examine humans,

> many different kinds of monkey business can be found. Keys abound. In addition to what an otter can do, we can *stage* a fight in accordance with a script, or *fantasize* one, or describe one *retrospectively*, or *analyze* one, and so forth. (p. 45)

The notion of keys and keying now becomes the central concept in frame analysis:

> I refer here to the set of conventions by which a given activity, one already meaningful in terms of some primary framework, is transformed into something patterned on this activity but seen by the participants to be something quite else. The process of transcription can be called keying. (p. 44)

Five types of "keys" are discussed here: make-believe, contests, ceremonials, technical redoings, and regroundings. While the discussion is interesting, we are lost again in a morass of "strips," the "astonishing complex," "muffings," "benign and exploitive fabrications," "scriptings," "evidential boundaries," "episoding conventions," "appearance formulas," "upkeying," "downkeying," "say fors," and so forth.

In both studies, these types of descriptions often point out some subtlety, nuance, or implicit aspect of interaction that may have previously been taken for granted. However, Goffman's constant name inventions turn his analysis of interaction and communication into a discussion of these *things* (e.g., "keys," "muffings," "strips") without a consideration of the relationships between them. In the end, then, interaction becomes atomized and reified as process is transformed into entity,[7] and the parts never coalesce into an understandable whole or

---

[7]See John Schwartzman, "Art, Science and Change in Western Society" (1977), for a discussion of this transformation in the development of art and science in Western society.

system. It is also important to note that Goffman uses a play/reality contrast that his analyses ultimately seem to contradict.

Sutton-Smith employed both Goffman and Bateson in his discussion of "Boundaries" (1971a). Here he suggested the importance of studying "the codes that govern entries and exits" in play and differential "ludic techniques" used by children "to cross such boundaries" (pp. 103–104). These techniques are viewed (after Bateson) as "metacommunications" such as play gestures, smiles, and giggling, as well as verbal announcements (e.g., "Look at me—I'm an airplane"), invitations, challenges, greetings, requests, and "special integrating techniques" (after Goffman). He discussed Gump's (Gump et al., 1955) studies, which show that these boundary techniques are more important for maintaining informal play than formalized games with rules. And he also suggested that individuals cross such "boundaries" with varying degrees of ease; that is, some do it easily, while others are unable to enter the play frame at all.

More recently, Sutton-Smith has proposed an approach to the study of both the texts and the contexts of play in his new book, *The Dialectics of Play* (1976b). Many of the ideas expressed here were presented in summary form in an earlier paper entitled "Towards an Anthropology of Play" (1974b). This paper is included, along with several others, in a series of readings that appear as part of the book. In this report, Sutton-Smith discussed the importance of considering the *antecedent* (e.g., biological predispositions, sociocultural context, previous exploratory activity, power relationships, signal activity—"metacommunications") and *postcedent* (e.g., the outcomes of novelty, flexibility, and revival) *contexts* of play and their relationship to cultural ideologies. The *textual* structures of play are described here from several perspectives. Cognitively, they are viewed as a form of abstraction (or "prototype") where "the child creates meaning and organization out of his prior experience," whereas conatively they are seen as a form of power reversal and affectively as a type of vivification experience (i.e., one feels totally involved, vital and vivid, as if one is "flowing") (1974b:14; 1976b:54–55, 78–83).[8]

In this work, Sutton-Smith particularly stressed the notion of reversal and reversibility. This is his reason for the use of the term *dialectics* in the book's title. Emphasis is given here to the view that "play is a reversal mechanism built in at birth which early in life permits the dissociation of instrumental from goal behaviors" (p. 1). In this book, two dialectics are discussed: (1) the *ludic dialectic,* which "refers to the relationship of play to its antecedents" (i.e., the antecedent contexts); and

---

[8]See Csikszentmihalyi (1975) for a discussion of the concept of "flow" in play and work.

(2) the *adaptive dialectic,* which relates to the function or outcome of play in cultural and biological life (i.e., the postcedent contexts) (p. 2). Sutton-Smith also offered a brief and concise structural definition of play as dialectic:

> Play is a subset of voluntary behaviors involving a selective mechanism which reverses the usual contingencies of power so as to permit the subject a controllable and dialectical simulation of the moderately unmastered arousal and reductions of everyday life, in a way that is alternately vivifying and euphoric. (pp. 5–6)

In all of these "post-Bateson" discussions, very little has been said about the *interpretation* of play texts or play contexts (i.e., how the player or the observer/researcher interprets behavior as play). Clifford Geertz not only has recently made this the central feature of his analysis of a form of Balinese play (1972), but he has also suggested that the interpretation of cultural texts may be viewed as *the* major activity of the ethnographer (1973):

> The culture of a people is an ensemble of texts, themselves ensembles, which the anthropologist strains to read over the shoulders of those to whom they properly belong. There are enormous difficulties in such an enterprise, methodological pitfalls to make a Freudian quake, and some moral perplexities as well. . . . But to regard such forms as "saying something of something," and saying it to somebody, is at least to open up the possibility of an analysis which attends to their substance, rather than to reductive formulas professing to account for them.
>
> As in more familiar exercises in close reading, one can start anywhere in a culture's repertoire of forms and end up anywhere else. One can stay . . . within a single, more or less bounded form and circle steadily within it. One can move between forms in search of broader unities or informing contrasts. One can even compare forms from different cultures to define their character in reciprocal relief. But whatever the level at which one operates, and however intricately, the guiding principle is the same: societies, like lives, contain their own interpretations. One has only to learn how to gain access to them. (1972:29)

In "Deep Play: Notes on the Balinese Cockfight" (1972), Geertz circled steadily within this particular cultural form, but he produced an analysis of both the cockfight and anthropology. This discussion is one of the few sustained commentaries on this activity available in the ethnographic literature on Bali (see also Bateson and Mead, 1942). According to Geertz, the cockfight is best thought of as a "focused gathering" in Goffman's terms; that is, it is neither an organized group nor a crowd.

The important thing, for the Balinese, is to make the cockfight "interesting" by creating a "deep" match. This is done by making the center bets (i.e., bets between the two cock owners) as large as possible in order to ensure that the cocks will be equally matched and that the outcome will be unpredictable. This, in turn, increases the volume of side bets, which, unlike center bets, are never for even money. However, it is not merely the size of the bets and the money that is exchanged that are important to the Balinese. What makes the cockfight "deep" is that it is a simulation of the Balinese social matrix, the "crosscutting, overlapping, highly corporate groups—villages, kingroups, irrigation societies, temple congregations, 'castes'—in which its devotees live" (p. 18).

It is within this system of group hierarchies, rivalries, and hostilities that the Balinese exist, and ordinarily the emotions attached to this system are enveloped "in a haze of etiquette, a thick cloud of euphemism and ceremony, gesture and illusion" (p. 25). However, in the cockfight, these potentially dangerous emotions and aggressions are expressed in the safety of the play form (they are *displayed*). Because it is framed as "only a cockfight," practical consequences are removed:

> the cockfight is "really real" only to the cocks—it does not kill anyone, castrate anyone, reduce anyone to animal status, alter the hierarchical relations among people, nor refashion the hierarchy; it does not even redistribute income in any significant way. (p. 23)

It is, finally, a social text characterized by "its use of emotion for cognitive ends," and according to Geertz, this textual quality is revealed only by a social semantic analysis:

> What sets the cockfight apart from the ordinary course of life, lifts it from the realm of everyday practical affairs, and surrounds it with an aura of enlarged importance is not, as functionalist sociology would have it, that it reinforces status distinctions (such reinforcement is hardly necessary in a society where every act proclaims them), but that it provides a metasocial commentary upon the whole matter of assorting human beings into fixed hierarchical ranks and then organizing the major part of collective existence around that assortment. Its function, if you want to call it that, is interpretive: it is a Balinese reading of Balinese experience; a story they tell themselves about themselves. (p. 26)

Geertz's textual analysis, then, is also a contextual interpretation. The cockfight is a social text that is a commentary on its larger sociocultural context. The Balinese are themselves both the subjects and the objects of this text and illustrate Jacques Ehrmann's very important suggestion that "players may be played; that, as an object in the game, the player can be its stakes and its toy" (1968:55).

There are very few studies available that describe children's play as a communication system. Three investigations are discussed here; one considers non-Western children's play, and the other two were conducted with American children.

SAYING PLAY: THE MESCALERO APACHE CHILD

Claire Farrer (1976) has recently described the play of Mescalero Apache schoolchildren, stressing how such play replicates the communication system or culture of the child. In a detailed comparison of how Anglo-American and Mescalero children play the game of "tag," she demonstrated how this activity may be seen "as a miniature communication system" (p. 90). For example, Anglo-American children spend a great deal of time negotiating the "it" role and also the specific rules. However, for Mescalero children, "verbal interaction is minimal," and so games may just spontaneously start when someone tags someone else, and when rules are broken, "there is no verbal correction" (p. 88).

Most importantly, the Anglo-American game is played *linearly*, as players chase one another along "horizontal, vertical or diagonal avenues," and when one's personal space is invaded by a touch, then a "tag" is said to have occurred (pp. 88–89). In contrast, for the Mescalero Apache child, *circularity* is crucial, and so the game is played on the jungle gym with the children in close contact with one another, moving clockwise so that a "tag" occurs "only when the 'it' person touches another's head (the preferred tag spot), shoulder, arm, or leg in a deliberate movement" (p. 88). Farrer described the importance of circularity to the Mescalero Apache in their traditional homes, their dance patterns (which are also clockwise), and in their consensual and egalitarian decision-making patterns (e.g., "no one is the obvious leader in a circle," p. 89). For all these reasons, Farrer suggested that the differences in Anglo-American and Mescalero children's play styles relate to differences in the basic tenets of these children's cultures, tenets that pattern particular communication styles:

> Each of these differences is predicated on an aspect of standard, adult, Mescalero behavior. The children are replicating, or acting out, basic tenets of the culture. They stress in their play the importance of contact, circularity, and learning by observation. They are making statements about standard communication patterns; when it is appropriate to speak and when to remain silent; to whom one speaks; and in what manner; and whether "speech" is verbal or non-verbal. Thus play is metacommunication. (pp. 88–89)

SAYING PLAY: THE AMERICAN PRESCHOOL CHILD

Recently two detailed studies of the make-believe or pretend communication of American preschool-aged children have appeared. The first study reported here was conducted by a psychologist, Catherine Garvey, in a research laboratory with middle-class nursery-school children. The second was conducted by the author in a day-care center located in a low-income, multiethnic community in Chicago. The two investigations were conducted independently; however, even though there are differences in research approach and population, there are interesting similarities in the findings reported.

Children's Play in a Research Laboratory: Organizing Transformations

Catherine Garvey has presented information on her research project in a number of reports (e.g., Garvey, 1974; Garvey and Berndt, 1975; Garvey, 1977). In this study, previously acquainted nursery-school children (3–5½ years old) were observed interacting with one another in a dyadic situation in a research laboratory. All of these interactions were videotaped. The children came from five different nursery schools and were accompanied to the laboratory by one of their teachers. All children were from middle-class professional families, and in all there were 21 girls and 15 boys observed.

In this project, Garvey was specifically interested in collecting information on how children communicate pretending, how they organize these play episodes in terms of plans, and what types of play roles and activities they most frequently adopt. *Pretend play* is defined here as an action involving "some transformation of the Here and Now in which the child is actually situated" (Garvey and Berndt, 1975:1). On the basis of her analysis, she proposed that there are at least five types of communication involved in pretending. The first type is called *negation of pretend*, whereby an ongoing pretend state is transformed back to the "here and now" (e.g., "I'm not the dragon anymore. Please don't push me 'cause I'm not the dragon anymore," p. 4). The second form of communication is labeled *enactment* and relates to the actions, gestures, attitudes, tone of voice, etc., exhibited by the player to signify his/her pretend identity. *Play signals,* such as giggling, grinning, winking, and so forth, are the third variety discussed, which are said to be markers of the adoption of a play orientation. *Procedural* or *preparatory behaviors* are also necessary so that objects may be apportioned correctly (e.g., "This is my telephone") and rights may be clarified (e.g., "I didn't get a turn"), and as general references to interaction (e.g., "Do you want to play with me?") (p. 5).

The fifth type of play communication is called *explicit mention of pretend transformations*. These verbal transformations occur in a variety of ways, and seven different categories or "explicit verbal techniques" are outlined. Players may (1) *mention their partner's role* (e.g., "Are you going to be a bride?"); (2) *mention their own role* (e.g., "I'm a work lady at work"); (3) *mention their joint roles* (e.g., "We can both be wives"); (4) *mention their partner's plan* (e.g., "Pretend you hated baby fish"); (5) *mention their own plan* (e.g., "I gotta drive to the shopping center"); (6) *mention their joint plan* (e.g., "We have to eat. Our dinner's ready"); (7) *transform objects* (e.g., "This is a train"; puts suitcase on sofa) or *invent objects* (e.g., "Now this is a cheese cake and this is ice cream"; points to empty places on plate) (p. 7).

The significance of schemata and plans as organizing features in the communication of pretending is also discussed. A *schema* is defined as "an abstract representation of dynamic relations and events from which more detailed plans, or action formats, can be derived" (p. 19). Schemata may be chosen because of the existence of "some object or event in the Here and Now, e.g., a telephone, a loud voice. Once cued, the action format is available for guiding the joint make-believe performance" (p. 20). It is suggested that, while these plans or formats are being "played out," they greatly affect the type of object and identity transformations to occur in the play event. These plans, however, are not "copied directly from any single adult model. Rather, bits and pieces of experience may have been grasped and conjoined in the process of the child's construction of the schema" (pp. 9–10). A number of schemata are described, and these are named using a linguistic analogy that treats them as if they are verblike: treat/heal; making a call; averting threat/danger (pp. 10–14). Other schemata that are briefly mentioned are cooking/baking; dining; packing; traveling; provisioning/shopping; and building/repairing.

According to Garvey, object transformations are frequently influenced or "directed" by the particular action format in use. These action formats, therefore, should be considered as the *context* of an object transformation or invention. In the averting threat/danger schema, the object may become the defender or the source of the threat, or it may be the instrument used for counteraction (pp. 14–15).

The identities and roles that children adopt are also influenced by specific action formats. Four different types of roles are discussed here: (1) *functional roles* are the agent, patient, beneficiary roles in a format (e.g., for the dining schema, it is necessary to have one who eats and one who serves); (2) characters may be *stereotypic* and therefore related to an occupation or an habitual action (e.g., cowboy, foreman, Indian chief) or *fictional*, stemming from stories, television, or oral tradition (e.g., Santa Claus, Hansel and Gretel, the Cookie Monster); (3) *relational roles* are familial roles—Mommy is server in dining schema; (4) *peripheral roles* are those individuals who are discussed or addressed but whose identity is not assumed by the player.

On the basis of this study, it was found that "a great deal of speech is devoted to creating, clarifying, or negotiating the social pretend experience" (p. 8). In fact, the average density of speech is reported to be "one utterance every four seconds" (Garvey, 1974:165). It is suggested that this speech is important because it may be that, for children of this age, "the saying is the playing" (Garvey and Berndt, 1975:9). This is an important statement, for it indicates that the researchers recognize the important relationship existing between play texts and play context. It may be that they are indistinguishable.

In an earlier article, Garvey (1974) presented information on the types of competencies that underlie children's social play behavior. First, it is necessary for players to be able to distinguish play and nonplay states and, therefore, to be able to recognize jointly when they are operating in a play state. Second, organizing rules for interaction must be abstracted, and these rules must be seen as mutually binding on the players. Finally, players must be able to identify a theme, contribute to its development, and agree that it is subject to modification.

In this discussion, *ritual play interactions* characterized by repetitive rhythmic exchanges are analyzed in terms of types of rules for taking turns (e.g., symmetrical versus asymmetrical distribution of turns) (p. 166). The manner in which repeatable units of interaction (called *rounds*) or sequences are built up is also discussed and illustrated. For example, a turn pattern where X says "Bye, Mommy" and Y says "Bye, Mommy" is a round demonstrating a symmetrical distribution of turns, and it may be repeated as is or modified (e.g., X: "Bye, Mommy"; Y: "Bye, Daddy") (pp. 166–167). In such a round sequence, roles may be symmetrical or asymmetrical, as when they are reversed. Two basic types of social interaction formats are exhibited in this material: (1) doing the same thing and (2) doing a complementary thing (pp. 175–176).

Garvey suggested that one reason children may enjoy practicing and repeating the social formats that she described is that this behavior involves the feature of control:

> Rapidly accumulating evidence on the sensitivity of young children to features of the human environment suggests that they would be ready and willing . . . to attempt control of the human environment and derive satisfaction from successful control of another's behavior. In the performances of ritual play such control is precise and knowledge of its success is immediate; furthermore the satisfaction derived is mutual, since each party is instrumental in eliciting and maintaining the responsive behavior of the other. (p. 179)

As will be seen in the next section, when children's transformations are analyzed from a "sideways" perspective, the issues of control and a related feature, *comment*, are particularly highlighted.

Children's Play in a Day-Care Center:
Sideways Transformations

In a recent study (1973, 1974, 1976b) of the make-believe play com-munication of a group of American preschool children, the author has also suggested the importance of interpreting play texts in specific social contexts.[9] This investigation was conducted in a day-care center located in a low-income, multiethnic community in Chicago. The researcher spent 1½ years (August 1971–December 1972) working as a participant observer in this context, collecting information on the topic of children's make-believe or sociodramatic play behavior. A variety of research methods were employed: (1) a diary record of each child's daily ac-tivities, relationships with peers, teachers, etc.; (2) field notes recording examples of specific play events occurring in the classroom; (3) inter-views with children and staff; (4) collection of children's drawings; (5) sociometric study; and (6) records of play events in still photography and on film (Super 8). (See Figures 20 and 21.)

The 23 children (13 boys, 10 girls) in this day-care-center classroom came predominantly from low-income families. Approximately 16 of the 22 families represented in this group had annual incomes below $7,500; 6 of these families reported an annual income under $5,000. Also many of these children (9) came from one-parent families, with the child living at home with his/her mother and generally one or more siblings.

The neighborhood in which the center was located is on Chicago's north side. This area has been a "port-of-entry" community for many years for various groups migrating and immigrating to Chicago. In the recent past, the area included a large number of Appalachian white and North American Indian residents, and currently the area has experi-enced rapid growth in its Latino and Asian populations. Over 50% of these children came from minority group families (e.g., Korean, Iranian, Filipino, Latino, South Asian, American black).

In this study, a view of play as communication (following Bateson, 1955, 1956) characterized by its production of paradoxical statements (e.g., "This nip is not a bite") about persons, objects, activities, and situations was adopted. Also, on the basis of the material collected in the classroom and following Geertz (1972) and Ehrmann (1971), it was pos-tulated that children's pretend play could be analyzed as a text in which players act as both the subjects and the objects of their jointly created play event. Therefore, in play *texts*, the players as *subjects* of these events

[9]This research was supported by grants received from the National Academy of Science, Division of Behavioral Sciences, and the Ford Foundation (Grant #710-0252). The com-plete results of this study are reported in Helen E. Beale (Schwartzman), *Real Pretending: An Ethnography of Symbolic Play Communication* (1973).

FIGURE 20. Children's play, Chicago (H. Schwartzman).

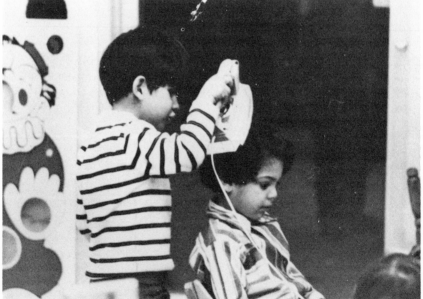

FIGURE 21. Children's play, Chicago (H. Schwartzman).

are able to interpret and comment on their relationships to each other (as these are developed in specific social *contexts* like a day-care center) as the *object* of their play. In this study, individuals' play styles were described in reference to the way they communicated their intention to act as both the subject and the object of their play. In these terms, in order to be a successful player, one must be able to communicate information that simultaneously (and paradoxically) defines one as a play *subject* (e.g., adopting the play role of a witch, mother, etc.) and as a person in the defining social context (e.g., the day-care center) and therefore a play *object*. For example, a child (Linda) must be able to communicate to other players that she is both *Linda* (i.e., a person who leads, dominates, and directs activities, as she is known for this in the general classroom setting) and *not-Linda* (i.e., a witch or a mother) in a play situation. In brief, the purpose of this study was to describe *play texts in context* and the *context in play texts*.

All investigations of children's play necessarily imply the existence of actual players. However, frequently this activity is discussed as if these players do not exist and instead we have only "Ss," or the player is eliminated entirely in an attempt to elucidate the structure and function of play or games in general. Of course, this happens because the investigator is concerned that his/her research findings do not reflect idiosyncratic or unique play styles or behaviors and are, in fact, generalizable to other players, other populations. However, by adopting an experimental or quasi-experimental approach, an important dimension of play has been neglected. This is so because, in experimental/laboratory situations, children are generally observed interacting with *strangers* (other children or other adults) in a *strange* situation (see Bronfrenbrenner, 1974). Garvey's research is significant in this regard because she studied previously acquainted nursery-school children, but still in the context of the laboratory. The laboratory, however, is not the place to produce generalizable findings on play, unless, of course, we wish only to generalize on how children play in unfamiliar situations.

This problem has concerned many, and the obvious solution is to study this behavior in a more "natural" and familiar setting for the child (e.g., a nursery school, a neighborhood). Unfortunately, what often happens in these instances is that the context is now familiar to the child and unfamiliar and uncomfortable for the researcher. To adjust to these circumstances, the investigator often uses tightly structured observation schedules (which arbitrarily designate and define what is and is not to be looked at and limit the observer's participation in the specific social context). And additionally, the researcher may not stay long in any one setting, moving from school to school, place to place, in an attempt to increase the sample size. All of these techniques ensure the researcher's collection of a great deal of presumably "objective" data, but they also limit his/her ability to develop any detailed knowledge about one specific social context.

The use of a participant-observation research methodology for the collection of detailed case-study material on specific cultures, subcultures, groups, or organizations is generally associated with the discipline of anthropology. By using this methodology in the study of children's play, it is possible to collect information on the social context of this activity that can be used to interpret play texts. In fact, this approach reveals a dimension of play that has not been disclosed in the experimental situation.

This dimension is referred to here as the *sideways* perspective of the child in play. For to the side of, or across from, one child there are often other children—his or her peers. Adopting this sideways perspective, it is proposed that make-believe play is itself a text or "a story the players tell themselves about themselves" (see Geertz, 1972). And it is in this way, as Ehrmann (1971) suggested, that the players may themselves become the "stakes" of their "game." However, in order for the textual, or sideways, dimension of play to be revealed, it is necessary to understand the social context of the players (e.g., the history of their relationships with one another in a particular setting). For example, it is necessary to know the variety of play statements (or types of play communication, after Garvey and Berndt, 1975) used by children in a specific social context to create, sustain, and eventually disband make-believe play events.

On the basis of my study, nine different types of *statements* (and this term is used to include both verbal and nonverbal behavior) were observed: (1) formation statements; (2) connection statements; (3) rejection statements; (4) disconnection statements; (5) maintenance statements; (6) definition statements; (7) acceptance statements; (8) counterdefinition statements; and (9) reformulation or disintegration statements. Of course, in one sense, many of these are definition statements involving, in Garvey's terms, "explicit mention of pretend transformations." However, each is used differently over the brief course of a group's history (i.e., they are dependent on the context of the play group), and also children employ them in a variety of ways (i.e., they are dependent on the context of the larger social group). There are other correspondences between these nine statements and Garvey's discussion of types of play communication. For example, disconnection statements often involve "negation of pretend"; all statements include nonverbal "enactment" in her terms, and many statements (e.g., connection or maintenance statements) would be called "procedural or preparatory behaviors" in her system. Examples of these statements will be briefly discussed below, followed by an analysis of a specific play event using this approach.

In order for a play event to occur, children must first communicate their intention to play to other children. This is accomplished in a variety of ways. Someone may say, "Let's play house" *(formation statement)*, and a particular group will form. However, it is important to remember that such a statement is usually directed to a specific child or group of children. As I discovered, the invitation to play, in the context of this day-care center, was not always extended to everyone in the immediate vicinity of the initiator. In fact, the very statement, "Let's play house," with eyes and body focused in the direction of a specific child or group can itself be a tactic used to exclude and/or offend another child or group, as well as an attempt to engage a particular child.

Once a group has formed, a child who wishes to play with this particular group must generally ask permission to do so (e.g., "Can I play with you?" "Can I be the goldfish?") *(connection statements)*. And the child must do this outside the defined play space. However, certain children, depending upon their position in the social context of the center (e.g., popular, sought-after, dominant, assertive), do not need to request such permission. These children may enter the group simply by defining themselves as part of it, by adopting a play role (e.g., "I'll be the princess") or defining a new activity for the group to respond to (e.g., "I'm cooking dinner") *(definition statements)*. In the day-care center only three children were allowed to employ this particular tactic. Other children who attempted this approach would be quickly rejected by the group ("You can't play here!") *(rejection statement)*. And, if this did not work, an appeal might be made to the teacher.

In asking permission to play, a child will frequently speak to a person in the group with whom he/she is on friendly terms. If this child wishes to include his/her friend in the group, a new role or activity may be defined for this person (e.g., "You can be the sister") *(connection statement)*. However, the group as a whole must agree to this new participant. If they do not, certain children at the center were adept at posing *tricks* as *connection statements* (e.g., "If I can play, I'll show you what's in my pocket"). Children may voluntarily part from a group at any time (e.g., "I'm not playing anymore," or "I'm not the sister anymore") *(disconnection statements)*.

In order to maintain a play group, it is necessary for the transformation of roles, objects, activities, etc., to be coordinated to some degree. In the day-care center, this was generally accomplished by one or possibly two children taking leadership responsibility for defining objects (e.g., "This is rice"), roles (e.g., "I'm the mother, and you can be the baby"), and activities (e.g., "I'm cooking in the kitchen") *(definition statements)*.

These definitions, however, can be either accepted (e.g., "OK, now I'm eating it") *(acceptance statement)* or challenged (e.g., "No, this is meat, not rice," or "I'm the father, not the baby") *(counterdefinition statements)*. The roles that children adopt, or are assigned, frequently reflect the authority structure of the play group (e.g., the mother dominates the baby and defines activities for him/her to engage in—e.g., "Now it's time for you to go to sleep"), and at the center, they often reflected the hierarchy of children outside the play sphere (e.g., those who frequently played "mothers" and "fathers" were often the most popular and desired "friends" in the classroom). In house play, the role of pet (e.g., "kitty," "doggie") was generally assumed by one of the more unpopular children in the group. However, in certain instances, one particularly dominant child would define herself in a submissive role (e.g., as sister or baby) or even as "not playing" (at which point she might move to some other area of the classroom) while actually continuing "to play" by carrying on a conversation across the room asking about the progression of the play activities (e.g., "Is dinner ready yet?"). In one instance, when a child came over to ask this child if she could play house with the two other girls who were busily "preparing dinner," she stated, "Don't ask me; I'm the sister. Ask Christine; she's the mother." However, she had defined the activities and roles for the players, and it was clear to everyone that even though she denied her role as player and as leader, she was both and had to be consulted.

In order for a play group to sustain itself over any period of time, situations that might potentially disrupt a play activity must be avoided or transformed into the play theme. For example, if a child falls down and hurts him/herself, the play will be stopped. However, in certain instances, if the accident is not severe it will become part of the play event (e.g., "Daddy hurt himself; quick, Mary, bring the bandages!") *(maintenance statement)*. Eventually the play event comes to an end by a child's or a teacher's initiation (e.g., "Let's not play this anymore") or, alternately, a new theme may be proposed (e.g., "Let's play cowboys now") *(disintegration* or *reformulation statement)*.

The most useful approach for gathering information on make-believe play for this particular project was to record field notes on a play group's activities during "free play" time in the classroom. On these occasions, I would situate myself in a place (e.g., block corner, doll house corner) where a play activity was already in progress or was about to be initiated. At this location, notes were taken as carefully as possible on the play situation as it was in the process of being created and constructed by the children. Often the children would ask what I was doing, and I would inform them that I was writing down "what they did and said." Occasionally I would ask them to clarify what a particular object stood for in the play situation, or what role such-and-such a person had in the play event, or why they were doing such-and-such. As I was, in fact, doing exactly what I claimed to be doing, this explanation of my activity seemed to be satisfactory both to the children and the staff.

Of the many make-believe play events that were recorded in this manner, one brief example is offered here. Date: 3/17/72; time: 3:30 P.M.–4:00 P.M.; place: block corner (see Figure 22):

> Thomas, Paul, and Karen are playing in the block corner. Sonia enters the area and asks if she can play with Thomas and Paul. They emphatically say "No!" Karen says "Yes! she can. I know, you marry me (pointing to Thomas) and Sonia can marry Paul." Thomas and Paul respond again: "No!" Karen replies "OK, I'll marry her and you can marry each other." Again they reject this proposal, but then they respond reluctantly, "OK, she can play." Karen says to Sonia, "We'll be nurses, and you sleep in the tent." Karen explains to Sonia where the "boat," "tent," "water," "quicksand" and "alligators" are. Linda comes in from playing in the outside yard. She observes the play

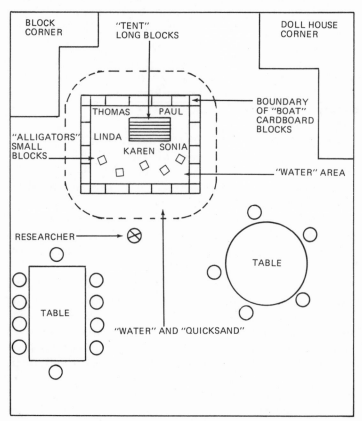

FIGURE 22. Spatial diagram for play event, Chicago (H. Schwartzman, 1973:240).

group briefly and then goes over to the block corner and falls in the designated "water" and "quicksand" area and screams: "Help! Something is biting my legs!" The group responds to Linda's action, and then Karen announces that "Captain Paul is dead!" At this point Thomas acts very upset and says forcefully (directing his statement to Paul, Karen, and Linda), "You guys never know what to do!" Karen leaves the group at this point and says, "I'm not playing anymore." (During this period, Sonia is busying herself in the "water" area, saying, "Oh, I've found a small snail," "Look, a baby alligator, a baby raccoon, a baby parakeet, a baby bird." She becomes absorbed in this activity and the rest of the group ignore her.) Thomas, Paul, and Linda shift their discussion to talk of "angels, wings, and heaven." At this point, Thomas, with very agitated body movements, falls to the ground, saying, "I'm dead." Linda responds to this by declaring that "Thomas is an angel." Paul now begins to fidget and act restless and states his desire to return to the original boat play theme. Linda responds by saying, "Well, I guess it was just a dream." The boat play theme is resumed.[10]

There are many things to be noted in this event (and this is actually only one part of a much longer incident). To begin with, this presentation itself is obviously an interpretation of the actual play event. However, I would argue that rather than attempting to deny or disguise the interpretive process involved in such a presentation, one should accept this as an intrinsic and basic part of the research process.[11]

In order to analyze the above text, it is important to know something about the history of these children's relationships with each other in the classroom. First, it is necessary to know that Thomas and Paul almost always play together as a dyad—with Thomas generally dominating Paul (i.e., he defines events and Paul accepts the definition). However, one would also have to know that Linda was *the* dominant child in the day-care center.[12] (This was expressed in play by her ability to enter almost any group without the formality of a request and then to establish control and leadership by assuming the defining and directing responsibility of the group.) It would also be important to know that Linda, Thomas, and Paul often played together, with Linda generally

---

[10]Along with this record of social situation and dialogue, a spatial diagram noting significant objects, boundaries, and player's definition of play area was also constructed.

[11]This focus on the interpretive process of social research studies grounds its claim for "historical" (as opposed to "scientific") objectivity (Palmer, 1969) in terms of the nature of intersubjective communication between one's informants (Hymes, 1974) and between researcher and informant (Fabian, 1971). For further elaboration of this approach with reference to social research in general, see Ricoeur (1971), with reference to research in anthropology, see Geertz (1973), and for studies of play, see Schwartzman (1974).

[12]Linda's "popularity" is inferred from the sociometric study (children's answer to the question, "Who are your favorite friends in the classroom?"), in which she was chosen 11 times and no other child was chosen more than 4 times, and from teacher and researcher observations.

operating in the leader role (i.e., defining the situation). Karen was also a participant in this play group, but often she was reluctant to accept Linda's dominance, and to establish her control of play groups, she would frequently bring in notoriously "submissive" (i.e., nonleader, nondirecting individuals) players such as Sonia. Karen was also very adept at employing "tricks" in order to define a situation as she wished it to be.

With this brief social history, it is now possible to begin to interpret these children's "sideways" transformations as illustrated by this text. Initially, Sonia enters the play area, but she does not move into the defined play space. Before she is able to move into this area, she makes a connection statement: "Can I play with you?" and she is immediately rejected by Thomas and Paul. However, Karen, who wishes to bring (or connect) Sonia into the play group, responds to this by suggesting a possible activity (marriage) whereby Sonia could be included in the group. This suggestion is again rejected by Thomas and Paul. Karen then employs what is referred to here as a *trick* (a type of connection statement) whereby she reformulates her original proposition, which, I would suggest, she most likely knew to be an unfavorable marriage alternative—"I'll marry her, and you marry each other"—to Thomas and Paul. This trick is attempted by Karen, expecting a rejection of her proposal but an acceptance of Sonia into the play group. Thomas and Paul do, in fact, respond by rejecting the proposal, but they do admit Sonia into the group ("OK, she can play"). Karen then assumes definition/ leader responsibilities in her relationship with Sonia as she defines their role as nurses and then explains what the play space and objects are in the play event.

When Linda enters the classroom, she immediately goes over to this particular group, as it is composed of individuals with whom she often plays. Linda almost always assumed a leader role in reference to this group, and so she does not need to make an explicit connection statement. Rather, she immediately defines an activity (keeping to the boat play theme) for the group to respond to as she falls in the "water," saying, "Help! Something is biting my legs!" The group responds to this action immediately and then Karen (who occasionally has difficulty accepting Linda's leader role) responds with a counterdefinition: "Captain Paul is dead!"

At this point, it should be noted that Thomas and Paul (particularly Thomas) Karen and Linda all have attempted to define activities for the group. Thomas appropriately responds to this potentially chaotic situation by saying, "You guys never know what to do," implying that the group will not be able to continue if everyone is defining activities and a permanent leader is not established. Shortly after this, Karen leaves the group by making a disconnection statement ("I'm not playing any-more") and thus eliminating herself as a possible contender for the leader role. Sonia, in the meantime, is engaged in her own play event, even though it is in the same play space, defining various objects and speaking to herself but not attracting the attention of the other players.

The play group discussion now shifts to talk of "angels, wings, and heaven," a different theme from the original boat play theme. At this point, Thomas falls down, saying, "I'm dead!" In fact, at this point Thomas is "dead" as a potential play group leader, and Linda now begins to exhibit control of the group by defining Thomas as an "angel." Also, in response to Paul's restlessness about returning to the boat play, Linda defines this whole sequence (whereby leadership shifts clearly to Linda) as a dream *(maintenance statement)*. Shortly after this, the group returns to the boat play theme, and Linda exhibits her now clearly es-tablished leader role by defining various activities for the group to en-gage in.

Garvey suggested that one "intrinsically satisfying feature of social play, which is present for each participant, is the feature of control" (1974:179). My own research indicates that the children at this day-care center were very much concerned with issues of control, dominance, and manipulation (apparently much more so than Garvey's children, where emphasis on reciprocity is more in evidence), and their play was both a reflection and an interpretation of these concerns. It was, in fact, a *commentary* on their own abilities at control in and out of play, their own particular interaction styles; and because these abilities and styles exist in and are influenced by social contexts, this play was also a commentary on the various types of relationships (e.g., symmetrical, asymmetrical) that they have experienced in these contexts. In play, specific attempts at control, and commentaries on the more general idea of control, are "displayed" because children are able to act as both the subjects and the objects of their event. This is likewise facilitated by the paradoxical qual-ity of play communication whereby objects, persons, and activities both *are and are not* what they seem to be.

An analysis of the range of play events that were collected during my research suggested that they could be grouped into a variety of *genres* (see Fabian, 1974). Each genre was distinguished by a particular type of authority structure. In some instances, these genres could be associated with a particular content or theme (e.g., "bad guys"), and in certain instances, these genres could also be associated with particular individual and group play styles. (These genres are in some ways similar to Garvey's discussion of play schemata, plans, or action formats; how-ever, there are important differences). Each of the identified genres may also be related to a particular type of relationship model that the child has experienced. Five types of genres were identified, and they are illustrated in Table 2.

It should be emphasized that the relationship models described here are not simply *imitated* by the children, but instead are *used* by them as formats for commentaries on their own relationships to each other. Therefore, certain children or groups of children were associated with certain types of play genres. For example, in the classroom, there existed a particular group of teacher-defined (and to some extent child-defined) "problem" or "disruptive" children (in this instance, they were all males). These boys frequently engaged in the genre "group confrontations," playing various versions of "good guys versus bad guys." As these activities generally involved chasing and sometimes the use of "guns" (both discouraged by the teachers for classroom play), it almost always led to a confrontation between teachers and children, or between this group of players and another group. In this way, this play was an effective comment on their defined role as "disruptive" children in the classroom, and, of course, this play also contributed to their image as "problem children." On the other hand, the genre "metacomplementary relationships" (see Watzlawick, Beavin, and Jackson, 1967:69) could incorporate any play theme (e.g., house, school) but was played only in a group that included Linda. An example of this type of play has already been discussed (e.g., Linda defines herself as "not playing" or in a subservient role but is, in fact, leading the group). This type of play was a complex commentary on Linda's leadership role in the classroom,

TABLE 2
Play Genres

Genre	Relationship Model	Play Theme
1. Asymmetrical dyads	Parent(s)–child Older sib–younger sib	Playing house
2. Asymmetrical group relationships	Teachers–children Older children–younger children	Playing school, Witch, Trains
3. Symmetrical dyads or groups	Friend–friend	Name game
4. Metacomplementary relationships	Relationship confusion, where relationship is defined as symmetrical but, in fact, is asymmetrical	—
5. Group confrontations	Bad guys versus good guys	Cowboys versus Indians, Batman

transformed in the play event by her definition of herself as a not-leader. However, because she was doing the defining, she was actually the leader, and, in fact, she was able to underline her position as such by engaging in this play form. The other genres described were not unique to any one particular play group, although, of course, there were certain differences in the style of play, depending upon which children were involved in the event.

In the process of playing, children learn that behavior is "con-texted" (e.g., there is a difference between play and nonplay), that con-texts influence the authority structure of relationships (e.g., there are differences between symmetrical and asymmetrical relationships), and that these relationships can be commented on (see Bateson, 1956). As children most generally experience hierarchical relationships in their families and at day-care centers, schools, etc., it is not surprising to find that they use these relationship models in play as a way to interpret and comment on their experience of their own relationships to each other. The types of power reversals that Sutton-Smith (1972b) has described for certain children's games may also be evident in this type of play. In all classroom contexts, teachers are clearly demarcated as *the* authority figure(s). They, in turn, frequently define all children as equal (e.g., "Everyone takes turns"). However, it is often clear to everyone involved that some children are more equal than others, and this is evidenced by the peer-group hierarchies that invariably develop in these contexts (as well as the existence of "teachers' pets"). Nevertheless, the "pretense" of equality is maintained in the classroom by the teacher(s), while the "reality" of the hierarchy is reflected only in the "pretense" of play, where the children are in control. At another level, it is possible to suggest (after Geertz, 1972) that these play texts are a commentary on the whole notion of hierarchical ranking as children experience it in their families, at school, and so on. By providing children with an opportun-ity for commentary or interpretation, play suggests the possibility of reinterpretation, challenge, and even change in relationships. Make-be-lieve play creates these possibilities because it is both a *text* and a *context*. This, then, is the beginning of humor, art, and all forms of social satire and critique and is perhaps the most significant feature of this play form.

SUMMARY

An interest in the subtleties and nuances of interaction has been expressed by most researchers discussed in this chapter. Gregory Bate-son was one of the first advocates of a view of culture as communication that stressed the importance of attending to the subtleties of human interaction. This is evident in his early books (e.g., *Naven*, 1936; *Balinese Character*, with Margaret Mead, 1942), where he demonstrated his reaction to the, at the time, popular theories of structural-functionalism (particularly Malinowski's approach). In *Naven*, Bateson also illustrated the development of concepts that prefigured certain aspects of cybernetic theory, later to be formulated by individuals such as Norbert Weiner and Warren McCulloch into an overarching theory of communication and control.

In the 1950s, Bateson developed his interest in levels of communication and the generation of paradoxes of abstraction (e.g., Epiminedes' paradox) into a comprehensive theory of communication (and epistemology), using play as a prototype. This theory has conceptually linked the study of such seemingly diverse phenomena as psychotherapy (Haley, 1963), schizophrenia (Bateson, Jackson, Haley, and Weakland, 1956), and humor (Fry, 1963). It was Bateson's view (see 1955, 1956) that play could occur only among organisms able to metacommunicate and, therefore, able to distinguish messages of differing logical types. These messages act as "frames" or "contexts" providing information about how another message should be interpreted. Therefore, in order for an organism to understand an action as play, it must be framed by the message "This is play." Bateson suggested that this message generates a paradox of the Russellian or Epimenedes type, wherein a negative statement contains an implicit negative metastatement (1955:180). In a play fight, for example, the message would be "This nip is not a bite." Bateson also emphasized the importance of distinguishing play and game communication—a discussion that will be taken up again in Chapter Eleven. In this theory of play, text and context are intimately and systemically related and cannot be considered in isolation from one another. This relationship is most clearly expressed in Bateson's metalogues (1972), where the structure and content of an interaction are comments on one another. This relationship has often been misunderstood by investigators who adopt a "single-signal" approach.

Because play illustrates the importance of such relationships and, in particular, the importance of context, it has been central to the development of theories of social interaction and communication. Bateson developed his views in studies of nonhuman animals (e.g., monkeys and otters), while others have applied and expanded this approach to produce analyses of human behavior (e.g., Goffman, 1962, 1974; also see Hall, 1959, 1966). Geertz in particular has demonstrated how social texts can be understood only in reference to their larger sociocultural context (this is the point of "thick description," 1973). He has also suggested that certain texts (e.g., the Balinese cockfight, 1972) may themselves be interpretive of their cultural context. Miller (1973, 1974) has specifically illustrated the nature of play frames or "motifs," while Sutton-Smith (1974b, 1976b) has proposed a detailed approach for the synthesis of studies of play texts and play contexts.

There are, at present, few observational studies of children available that incorporate a view of play as communication. Farrer's (1976) analysis of Mescalero Apache children's play applies this approach to the study of a group of American Indian children. Two detailed studies of the play communication of American preschool children have been made. Garvey and Berndt's (1975) analysis is significant for its enumeration of types of play communication and the collection and recording of detailed play events exhibited in a research laboratory. In these examples, it is clear, as Garvey emphasized, that for these children, "the saying is the playing." My own research (1973, 1976b) illustrates the importance of interpreting play texts in specific social contexts. The "sideways" approach that is described here was revealed only when the researcher became familiar with the social context of her informants. In this way, it was possible to see how play can be both a text and a context, on many levels, because a sideways view portrays the *texts in context and the context in the texts.*

The studies examined in this chapter illustrate a view of play as communication that provides us with new information about the nature of play and also many other activities. This is so because we have learned here that contrary to the belief that "the facts speak for themselves," it is more accurate to say that "speaking (i.e., communication) creates the facts"; and a view of play as communication creates new "facts" for researchers to investigate.

Minding Play: Structural and Cognitive Studies

> *"How* can *you go on talking so quietly, head downwards?"*
> *Alice asked, as she dragged him out by the feet, and laid him in a heap*
> *on the bank.*
> *The Knight looked surprised at the question. "What does it*
> *matter where my body happens to be?" he said. "My mind goes on*
> *working all the same. In fact, the more head downwards I am, the*
> *more I keep inventing new things."*
> Lewis Carroll, *Through the Looking-Glass, and What Alice Found There*

In 1954, the linguist Kenneth Pike enumerated a distinction between etic and emic statements derived from the difference, in linguistic analysis, between phonemic and phonetic units. Etic statements were said to be those whose validity could be verified by independent investigators using similar operations, analogous to the linguists' discrimination of phonetic units (e.g., the difference between aspirated and nonaspirated sounds). Emic statements were those categories and meanings perceived, articulated, and validated by the actors themselves, as in the specific system of sound contrasts that English speakers employ (the phonemic units) (see Harris, 1976:331–332; Langness, 1974:107–108; Pike, 1954:8–28). Pike's purpose in formulating this distinction was to suggest the need for a unified theory of the structure of human behavior that would incorporate both types of statements as research "standpoints." Unity in theory and methodology could best be achieved, according to Pike, by viewing language as behavior and in turn behavior as language. He suggested that language must be treated as human behavior, as a phase of an integral whole . . . [because] language behavior and non-language behavior are fused in single events, and . . . verbal and nonverbal elements may at times substitute structurally for one another in function. (1954:2)

Pike believed that games were excellent examples of "single events" that were experienced as "integrated wholes" by their participants. This is evident in the numerous discussions of games and sports that appear in his study (e.g., the party game "Under the Spreading Chestnut Tree," p. 1; water polo, p. 3; hopscotch, p. 14; cricket as compared with baseball, pp. 15–16; football, pp. 44–56). By using games as exemplars of social behavior, Pike was, it could be argued, extending his own metaphor of language as behavior to a view of language as a game. Pike did not specifically explore the value of this extension in his study, although there have been others, writing both before and after him, who have done so. For example, Pike noted that he first heard Sapir compare language to a game—tennis—in 1937 (1954:20). Wittgenstein (1953) is probably most well known for his use of the language-as-game—in this case, chess—metaphor.

The etic–emic distinction discloses both the general metaphor (i.e., sociocultural systems are treated as if they are language systems) and the specific terms in which many current anthropological discussions and controversies are cast.[1] In adopting this metaphor for the analysis of culture many anthropologists have joined with psychologists and others in a search for cognitive structures (i.e., patterns in relationships) that

[1]For an overview of the relationship between anthropology and linguistics, see Hymes (1964). Recently Harris (1976) has presented a review of the history of the etic–emic distinction in anthropology, which is useful although somewhat limited because of his behaviorist stance. The definitions of these terms that I have offered reflect, at least generally, the way in which they are currently used in anthropology. Harris (see 1968 and 1976) used the etic–emic division to criticize what he sees as the ethnographer's overemphasis on the study of *emic* (or "ideational") phenomena (i.e., the actors' statements about what they do) to the exclusion of consideration of *etic* (or "materialist") phenomena (i.e., "principles of organization or structure [about what individuals do] that exist outside the minds of the actors," 1976:331). However, according to Pike, etic units are *nonstructural* because they are devised by the investigator for comparative purposes, while emic units reflect the *actual structure* of the data because the investigation of these units is conducted "not in isolation but as a part of a total functioning componential system within a total culture" (1954:93). In Pike's terms "emic units and emic systems . . . are in some sense to be discovered by the analyst, not created by him," as are etic units and systems (p. 20). Harris appears to believe that the opposite is true, while Lévi-Strauss has offered perhaps the most sensible statement on these differences, suggesting that *etics* are "really nothing but the emics of the observer" (1974). However, it should be noted that Pike anticipated this type of criticism (see particularly 1954:9–10, 20–21).

are thought to be reflected in particular cultural productions.[2] A concern with form, pattern, contrasts, and relationships (i.e., "the difference that makes a difference") is characteristic of the structuralist approach, as it is also of the communication studies advocated by Bateson. This similarity (in interest but not in the specific approach adopted) is not surprising, given the fact that both Gregory Bateson and Claude Lévi-Strauss, the leading proponent of structural studies in anthropology, were greatly influenced by the development of communications theory in the late 1940s. Lévi-Strauss was also influenced by Jean Piaget's investigations of cognitive structures, and in anthropology he has led the way in the search for *universal* structures of the mind as these are reflected in myths and kinship and classification systems.[3]

[2]This is not to say that all anthropologists who adopt a linguistic model concern themselves with a search for cognitive categories or structures. The linguist Leonard Bloomfield, who greatly influenced the development of anthropological linguistics, explicitly rejected any form of "mentalism" focusing "on descriptive method per se" in terms of his "behaviorist orientation" (Hymes, 1964:11). On the other hand, Edward Sapir, who also influenced the development of this field, articulated and illustrated a much broader view of what the scope of anthropological linguistics could (and should) be. His interests included the study of language as an expression of individual personality, thoughts, and feelings, and his research specifically influenced the work of Pike and also Noam Chomsky (see Hymes, 1964).

[3]Lévi-Strauss's theories and analyses are so wide-ranging, often contradictory, and always controversial that they cannot possibly be considered in any detail here. Munroe Edmonson's (1973) recent review of *Man Naked* (1971) (the fourth volume in Lévi-Strauss's monumental *Mythologics*—which also includes I. *The Raw and the Cooked*, 1964; II. *From Honey to Ashes*, 1967; and III. *The Origin of Table Manners*, 1968) briefly detailed these characteristics. He suggested that Lévi-Strauss's structuralism is an exploration of "logics": "the logic of science, the logic of inquiry, the logic of myth, the logic of the observer, and the logic of the observed. In an inspired suspension of disbelief, he manages to cling to his original suspicion that all these logics are one, while . . . consciously enunciating formal properties of mythic thought altogether contradictory to such an assumption . . . . this ambiguity neatly reflects but does not resolve the profound ambivalence of contemporary anthropology towards objective and subjective fact (the celebrated etic–emic distinction)" (p. 375).

As is clear even from this quote, Lévi-Strauss's interest is in the study of cognition and intelligence, but he is not concerned with the "staging" of thought processes, as is Piaget. On the other hand, Lévi-Strauss does indicate that there is a difference between "primitive" and "civilized" thought and that these differences give rise to the view that "primitive" thinking is childlike. However, he suggested that because these distinctions are relative, it is also true that "For the primitive, the attitudes of the civilized man correspond to what we should call infantile attitudes" (1949:94). Lévi-Strauss used this idea to criticize Piaget's and other child psychologists' uncritical equation of "primitive thought" with the thought of "civilized" children (see 1949:84–97). A more detailed discussion of Lévi-Strauss's critique of Piaget is presented in Chapter Four. For Lévi-Strauss's elaboration of what may be seen as a playlike theory of "structuring," see his discussion of *bricolage* in *The Savage Mind* (1962). For an example of his analysis of adult games and ritual, see pp. 30–31, also in this book.

There are numerous expositions and critiques of Lévi-Strauss's structuralism. An

In contrast, ethnoscientists advocate a "new ethnography," also based on models derived from linguistics, logical analysis, and mathematics, but they search for *particularistic* structures that informants employ to structure specific cognitive domains. In these terms, culture resides in the mind of the informant, and the problem for the anthropologist is how to get into the mind and how to know when one has gotten there:

> As I see it, a society's culture consists of whatever it is one has to know or believe in order to operate in a manner acceptable to its members . . . culture is not a material phenomenon; it does not consist of things, people, behavior, or emotions. It is rather an organization of these things. It is the forms of things that people have in mind, their models for perceiving, relating and otherwise interpreting them. (Goodenough, 1964:36)

As this approach requires that the meaningful models or structures discovered be articulated and validated by informants, it is decidedly "emic" in orientation. However, Lévi-Strauss's approach may also be described as emic (see Harris, 1968), in that he is concerned with the study of mental phenomena, although he is not interested in the discovery of particularistic structures (or minds), because it is his belief that these models can always be reduced to one underlying structure (or Mind) and specifically to the logic of binary opposition.[4] In short, Lévi-Strauss is not interested in what informants think about what they do, because he already knows what they think (i.e., what they *really* think).

In comparing structural studies of children's play and games, two research approaches are evidenced, and these correspond in general to Pike's distinction between etic and emic "standpoints." A number of investigators focus on an analysis of the "intrinsic" elements existing within play or game texts assuming that these structures, as derived by the researcher, represent the "reality" of the game. More recently, a

---

interesting examination of Lévi-Strauss's theories in relation to his specific fieldwork experiences in South America (among the Cuduveo, Bororo, Nambikwara, and Tupi-Kawahib) is provided by Geertz (1973). Geertz also suggested that Lévi-Strauss's theories are themselves "very simple transformations" of the "same deep underlying structure: the universal rationalism of the French Enlightenment" (p. 356). For other commentaries, see Leach (1970), Harris (1968:464–513), Murphy (1971:157–205), and Wilden (1972:302–350). Wilden's critique is specifically directed toward Piaget but is applicable in part to Lévi-Strauss. Piaget's recent *Structuralism* (1970) is also a useful introduction to the topic and includes a discussion of Lévi-Strauss.

[4]Ethnoscientists, however, are also ultimately concerned with underlying (or deep) structures. Rather than focusing on the logic of binary opposition, the ethnoscientist attempts to uncover the underlying principles of ordering that generate particularistic orderings (e.g., Tzeltal classifications of plant terms). These ordering principles are generally discussed as (1) taxonomies; (2) paradigms; or (3) trees (see Tyler, 1969:25–26). According to Tyler, "it is in this limited sense [that] cognitive anthropology constitutes a return to Bastian's search for the 'psychic unity of mankind' " (1969:14).

number of investigators have suggested that the structures or units (i.e., the meaningful contrasts) of a game can be articulated *only* by the players themselves and that the researcher's job is only to record the informant's stated differences. These researchers may also be compared with regard to whether or not they associate game structures with cognitive structures (their own or the players'). In fact, neither approach is completely satisfactory because each believes that he/she has discovered *the* structural reality of play and games, associating it either with the player's perspective on the event (i.e., emic statements) or the "intrinsic" elements of the activity, which is another way of discussing the researcher's perspective (i.e., etic statements). As is typical of such contrasts, the truth most likely is somewhere in the middle.

THE PLAYER'S PERSPECTIVE

Ethnoscience, or cognitive anthropology, is one of the newest subdisciplines in anthropology. It is an approach dedicated to the development of rigorous standards of fieldwork that focus the ethnographer's attention on the collection of different peoples' "names" for the things in their environment and the examination of "how these names are organized into larger groupings" (Tyler, 1969:6). As is clear from Ward Goodenough's statement (quoted earlier), the cognitive anthropologist assumes that culture is not located in material things themselves but rather in the organization of these things that people have *in their mind* (i.e., their conceptual or cognitive models). According to Steven Tyler, anthropologists have traditionally

> been much more concerned with discovering what anthropology was than, for example, what an Eskimo was. In a sense anthropologists were studying only one small culture—the culture of anthropology. (1969:2–3)

It should be pointed out, however, that a concern with the "native's" point of view has always been a part of anthropology and that the "new ethnography" is only the most recent statement of this perspective.

The ethnoscientist's definition of culture has many implications for the study of children's play. In the first place, this approach stresses the importance of the player's understanding and interpretation of his/her activity. It is no longer the anthropologist who acts as analytic expert; instead it is the child, as player, who relates his/her knowledge of the play or game to the ethnographer. The child is the teacher; the researcher is the student. This emphasis on the child's-eye view has its parallels in other works, such as Mary Ellen Goodman's *The Culture of Childhood* (1970). However, as opposed to Goodman, who ranges broadly over various types of material written from numerous perspectives, cognitive anthropologists define their data and approach very narrowly. In fact, they have often been accused of researching only trivial subjects (see Berreman, 1966).

Ethnoscientists assume that *names* create order and therefore give meaning to the *things* in one's environment (Tyler, 1969:6). In order to discover the conceptual models of informants, the ethnoscientist investigates how individuals classify and categorize or code their names for things. Applied to the study of children's play, it is therefore possible to investigate only the players' terms and categories for play or games. If this is not a highly systematized and organized domain of the child's culture (or if the child cannot verbalize his/her terms), it cannot be studied by the ethnoscientist. It is also true that the nonverbal activities of the player, as well as the material implements used in (or produced by) the play event, cannot, in so far as they are not able to be verbalized by the informant, be investigated. Adopting this perspective, it is possible to suggest that Culin's (1907) monumental study of North American Indian games is really *not* a study of these societies' games at all. Instead, because he formulated a classification of gaming implements (i.e., material things) on the basis of his own or other ethnographers' descriptions and categories, the ethnoscientist would consider Culin's work to be a study of Western game models (i.e., the Western anthropologist's organization and classification of gaming implements). Suggesting this line of argument, von Glascoe (1976) has recently stated that an implicit assumption of researchers such as Culin is that

> games could be conceptualized and classified as completely unambiguous collections of rules and well defined playing strategies from all members' points of view. The basic underlying assumption of game taxonomists has been: one game, one interpretation. (p. 109)

Many other researchers have used Western schemas to interpret how non-Western individuals view game activities. For example, von Glascoe went on to suggest that the work of Roberts *et al.* (1959)

> has been predicated on Western European abstract conceptions such as probability theory and the maximization of expected values. Not only is it believed that members relate to games as clear cultural objects, but that they do so under Western European interpretations. (p. 109)

There are both advantages (i.e., the emphasis on the players' as opposed to the researcher's perspective) and disadvantages (i.e., what individuals say they do is not always what they actually do) to this approach. Unfortunately, because this is still a new field in anthropology, there are few ethnoscientific studies of children's play. There are, however, two interesting investigations available, which illustrate what one learns when the derivation and interpretation of meaningful structures (or contrasts) is treated not as a given, but as a problem, requiring careful and specific *eliciting* techniques that emphasize the point of view of the player.

Sue Parrott's "Games Children Play: Ethnography of a Second Grade Recess" (1972) is an example of the use of this approach for the study of American schoolchildren's conceptions of games and gaming. In this study, she described the significant categories (or conceptual models) used by a group of six second-grade boys to classify and organize their own play (or recess) activities.[5] This information was elicited in several interview sessions with the boys in which she focused on questions such as "What kinds of things do you do at recess?" Answers: "keep-away," "fire red," "suck icicles," "relay races," "splash someone," "play ditch," "flip someone," "fighting," "running around," "look under girls' skirts," etc. After accumulating a list of 30 different types of recess activities, Parrott then posed questions such as "What would you call fire red?" "Which two are most alike: chase, frisby, or ditch?"

On the basis of this questioning, Parrott determined that the boys classified their activities into three major categories: (1) "games" (e.g., keep-away, fire red, ditch, relay races); (2) "goofing around" (e.g., sucking icicles, running around, fighting); and (3) "tricks" (e.g., flipping someone, looking under a girl's skirt, splashing someone). By asking the boys to compare and contrast these various activities, Parrott was able to discern the "distinguishing features" of games versus goofing around versus tricks (although there was much variability and change even within this small group, as to which activities were classed where and why). The distinguishing features of "games," from the players' perspective, are described in terms of (1) types of boundaries; (2) types of penalties; (3) types of roles; (4) game outcome; (5) presence or absence of teams; and (6) rule structure. The basic features of "tricks" were more difficult to establish, but Parrott reported that they are characterized by (1) unexpectedness; (2) physical activity; (3) opposing forces; and (4) players' intentions. "Goofing around" is characterized, in comparison with games, by its lack of teams, rules, competition, or goals, and also by the fact that "you can do it alone" as opposed to "games," which "you cannot do alone." Obviously, the majority of these features were named by Parrott (e.g., game outcome, roles, player's intentions), as the children did not explicitly articulate the terms but only the *idea* of the contrast in statements such as the following where keep-away and relay races are compared in terms of types of penalties: "In keep-away you

[5]Recently Blanchard (1976) has used the techniques of ethnoscience to investigate differences in Choctaw and Anglo adolescent males' definitions of sports behaviors (e.g., basketball).

can do anythin' to the other guy, as long as you don't hurt him or do something the teacher don't like." "When we have relay races sometimes guys cheat by pushing the runner, but they get kicked out of the game for doing that" (p. 215). The features outlined by Parrott will be discussed again as they relate to categories used in other studies.

Christine von Glascoe (1975a,b, 1976; von Glascoe and Metzker, 1977) has presented one of the most detailed ethnoscientific studies of game classification systems available. In these reports, she concentrated specifically on an investigation of the patterning of game preferences for Yucatán children, adolescents, and adults. The overall thrust of this research is to question the "one game, one interpretation" view and thereby "to contribute evidence to the general thesis that games are multiply interpreted by members, regarding both interest and understanding" (1976:109).

Von Glascoe conducted her research in two communities in the Yucatán: Chelem Puerto, a community of subsistence-level fishermen and farmers, and Merida, where she studied white-collar workers. In comparing these communities, and also by comparing men with women, adolescents with children, adults with adolescents, and so forth within each community, von Glascoe discovered significant differences in terms of an individual's or a group's knowledge and organization of, as well as involvement with, games. For example, she reported that Chelem young boys classify the game *tinbomba* (which is a type of stick baseball) as similar to *canicas* (marbles) (von Glascoe and Metzker, 1977:2). However, adolescents tend to classify *tinbomba* with *béisbol* (baseball). These differences are illustrated in Figure 23. This figure also illustrates how ethnoscientists diagram and visualize their informants' classification systems. In constructing these "dendrograms," the games that are conceived by informants to be most similar to one another are placed at the lowest nodes of a particular branch (p. 10).

In these reports, von Glascoe noted many other types of differences. For example, she discovered that certain groups of people (e.g., children versus adolescents versus adults; girls versus boys) focus on different descriptive (i.e., "distinguishing") features of the general game domain. In the community of Chelem Puerto, she found that young girls emphasize the idea of directing game play actions toward other players and will focus only secondarily on nonpersonal actions of the game itself (e.g., jumping over lines) (p. 7). In contrast, young boys from Chelem Puerto stress the action of players as directed toward gaming implements, and they deemphasize the action of the player as directed toward other players. Other descriptive features outlined by Chelem Puerto informants and contrasted by von Glascoe according to age difference of informant and feature emphasis are configuration of players; naming of

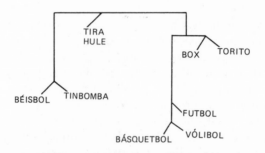

FIGURE 23. A game dendrogram from Chelem Puerto, showing the differential place-ment of *tinbomba* in the cognitive structuring of young boys versus adolescents (From von Glascoe and Metzger, 1977, Figure 1).

game implements; part of the body used; action of game implement (p. 6).

In "The Patterning of Game Preferences in the Yucatán" (1976), von Glascoe discussed the game interests and preferences of the females of Merida. Here she found that young girls report that they play games that they do not like, while some say that they like games that they do not play (p. 109). She also described how females' interests in particular games change as they move from childhood to adulthood. The use of different features by young girls, adolescent girls, and women for the comparison of one game with another is also illustrated. For example, young girls classify *adivinanzas* (riddles) as a "circle game," which in-volves "central figures"; however, adolescents place it in a larger class of games "played in social gatherings," and these games are said to "exer-cise the mind." Women emphasize the feature of "exercising the mind" and also call it "a scientific game" (p. 119). The addition or deletion of entire "classificatory sets" or "similarity clusters" (e.g., "ball games," "games played in couples") by certain age groups is also illustrated.

This research underlines the importance of collecting information from a variety of groups (age, class, sex, etc.) within the context (e.g., block, school, village, community), of a research study. Von Glascoe, adopting the ethnoscientists' perspective, suggested that the variable interpretations of games that she discovered illustrate the fact that "games, like all cultural objects, are what members can make of them in the context of other similar objects" (1975b:26). This variation suggests that games are themselves "opaque states of affairs" and that game involvement can therefore be viewed "as an investigation of this opacity" (von Glascoe and Metzker, 1977:1). In this way,

> The enactment of a game teaches people to focus their attention on a problematic state of affairs and, through influence and action, reduce the problematicalness to a consensually validated solution. (p. 1)

THE RESEARCHER'S PERSPECTIVE

In many early studies of play, an emphasis was placed on the collection and classification of game texts. Examples of these investigations (e.g., Babcock, 1888; Culin, 1907; Best, 1925) have already been discussed in Chapter Five. In these analyses, significant features of the play or game activity (from the researcher's point of view) were used to order and categorize the texts. This approach, which may be described as etic, has continued in more recent structural studies of children's play and games.

One of the most influential students of play in this century is the Dutch historian Johan Huizinga.[6] In *Homo Ludens* (1938), he inaugurated an anthropology of play that attempts to delineate the "play element" in culture and in particular in language, law, war, poetry, myth, philosophy, and art. In this book, Huizinga argued for the importance of understanding "what play is *in itself* and what it means to the player" (p. 2). In this case, the player and the researcher are one and the same, and so he offers his own description of what play *is*. In the first place, according to Huizinga, play is mind, not matter:

> But in acknowledging play you acknowledge mind, for whatever else play is, it is not matter. . . . Play only becomes possible, thinkable and understandable when an influx of *mind* breaks down the absolute determination of the

[6]See Norbeck (1976) for an extensive discussion and assessment of Huizinga's contribution to the anthropology of play.

cosmos. The very existence of play continually confirms the supralogical
nature of the human situation. Animals play so they must be more than
merely mechanical things. We play and know that we play, so we must be
more than merely rational beings, for play is irrational. (pp. 3–4)

Huizinga then enumerated what has become a classic and standard
definition of play:

> Summing up the formal characteristics of play we might call it a free activity
> standing quite consciously outside ordinary life as being "not serious," but at
> the same time absorbing the player intensely and utterly. It is an activity
> connected with no material interest, and no profit can be gained by it. It
> proceeds within its own proper boundaries of time and space according to
> fixed rules and in an orderly manner. It promotes the formation of social
> groupings which tend to surround themselves with secrecy and to stress
> their difference from the common world by disguise and other means. The
> function of play in the higher forms which concern us here can largely be
> derived from the two basic aspects under which we meet it: as a contest *for*
> something or a representation of something. These two functions can unite
> in such a way that the game "represents" a contest, or else becomes a contest
> for the best representation of something. (p. 13)

Roger Caillois, in *Man, Play, and Games* (1960), criticized and elaborated on Huizinga's definition. Most specifically, he suggested that it is
too narrow because it stresses only the competitive character of play. In
order to add to this definition, Caillois developed a classification scheme
that has influenced many play researchers. In this system, four types of
play are identified: *agôn* (competition); *alea* (chance); *mimicry* (simulation); and *ilinx* (vertigo). Superimposed on this scheme is a continuum
of ways of playing, which at one end is characterized by *ludus* (controlled and regulated play) and, at the other, *paidia* (spontaneous play).

Neither Huizinga nor Caillois concentrated on the specific study of
children's play; however, as has already been mentioned, their works
are frequently cited and have often provided guidance for students of
this topic. Jacques Ehrmann (1968) has made an excellent description and
critique of both authors' studies. In this analysis, Ehrmann examined the
Western bias and in particular the assumed "givenness" of the play–reality dichotomy, which he suggested is apparent in both Huizinga's and
Caillois's studies. According to Ehrmann,

> if the status of "ordinary life," of "reality," is not thrown into question in the
> very movement of thought given over to play, the theoretical, logical and
> anthropological basis on which this thinking is based can only be extremely
> precarious and contestable . . . we are criticizing these authors . . . for con-
> sidering "reality," the "real," as a *given* component of the problem as a
> referent needing no discussion. . . . They define play in opposition to, on
> the basis of, or in relation to this so called reality. (p. 33)

The tendency to assume that certain play elements or structures are
given or self-evident—or as in the case of both Huizinga and Caillois,

that play is naturally (as opposed to culturally) the opposite of work or seriousness—is evident in many recent structural studies of children's games and stories. Although the researchers employ a variety of structural models in their analyses, their investigations have been placed in this section because none of them employ the "player's perspective" in the construction of their categories or structural units. Instead they appear to assume that the player's perspective and their own are one and the same.

In "The Impact of Game Ingredients on Children's Play Behavior" (1959), Fritz Redl "takes apart" the game "beatle" in order to demonstrate an analytic approach that he developed in conjunction with Paul Gump and Brian Sutton-Smith. This system was used to examine games in terms of a series of "dimensions" or "ingredients" established by the investigators. Examples of these ingredients are challenge or theme; chance skill; competition; personalization of game props; potential sexualization range; outcome clarity; timing; role-taking factors; interdependence of players; pleasure–pain content of winning or losing; trust dependence; nature of obstacles; mirroring of life themes; and rule complexity.

The game "beatle" or "beedle" is a circle game that requires that one child holding a "beatle" (e.g., an object such as a stuffed sock) walk around a circle of players who are holding their hands behind their backs, and place the "beatle" in one of the other player's hands. The person who receives the beatle then begins to hit the player on his/her right, who runs away as fast as possible. The chase continues around the circle until the player being chased chooses to return to his/her place, at which point the player with the "beatle" gives it to someone else and the game continues. Redl stated that his interest in analyzing this game was to answer the question, "What is *in* this game?" and also to discuss its "potential impact on . . . players" (pp. 34–36). He also wished to emphasize the importance of games in the psychotherapeutic treatment of children.

This paper is a transcription of a discussion that occurred during one of the Macy conferences on group processes, and Redl stated that he chose the topic of games because of Bateson's (see 1956) earlier discussion on this subject, which also occurred during these conferences. Because of the context of the discussion, Redl was frequently interrupted in his presentation by requests for information and clarification as well as expressions of differing opinions by other participants. This was both an advantage and a disadvantage. On the one hand, it made the presentation of a coherent argument difficult; however, the participants often brought up important questions or points. Because of the multidisciplinary range of the participants (e.g., psychologists, anthropologists, ethologists, biologists) and also because many of the individuals on the panel had conducted their own research on play (e.g., Bateson, Birdwhistell, Bühler, Erikson), a number of important, as well as differing, issues were raised.

Redl's particular interest in the study of games is in the utilization of them in therapeutic settings. This led him to focus on an analysis of game "ingredients" in order to determine "what the game permits or demands" of individual players (p. 36). In his view, if clinicians have an understanding of these internal game ingredients, they will be able to determine what individual players exposed to specific types of games with particular "permissions" and "demands" will have to "handle" within themselves. The discussion of this idea, however, was very wide-ranging, covering such issues as the universality of these game elements or structures; the value of conducting "mental hygiene assessments" of game ingredients; the functions of games and what children learn in games; the evolution of game ingredients; status hierarchies and game status structures; the "fun" in games; play and games and physiological processes; and the difference between fantasy, play, and games.

Another issue raised by a number of participants was the question of whose perspective had been used in this analysis of game ingredients. The idea that researchers and clinicians may attend to, value, or emphasize one ingredient, while children may emphasize another, was discussed repeatedly. This argument is relevant to the contrast used in this chapter between the researcher's and the player's perspective; it is also relevant to the tendency to mix perspectives, as well as analytic levels, in the development of game structure or category lists. In commenting on this problem in Redl's system, Margaret Mead asked him the following very important question:

> Have you made a list showing *where* you are when you are making any one of these categorizations? . . . one minute you are looking at this as a therapist, . . . [then] as one of the boys, . . . [then] as a classifier of games, and the next minute you are handling the game as a microcosm of life. You have given us a mass of parameters, all taken from different positions. (p. 73)

Redl suggested that for his part he was interested in what a game is composed of, "its bones, its organs, its physiology" (p. 54). In his view, games exist as "structural entities" that can be analyzed as objects irrespective of the actions of particular players. While this may be possible to do, it is not possible to pretend that these "ingredients" or "structures" exist irrespective of the researcher who creates them. This is the point of Mead's comments. The fact that categorization systems, such as the one proposed by Redl, are frequently arbitrary and always open to discussion and debate is particularly well illustrated by this paper. This is so because it is a transcription of a discussion of one structural system (i.e., Redl's) by several researchers who differ with regard to how they would choose to categorize and analyze the specific game of beatle, as well as games in general.

A number of discussions of this particular system, and studies related to it, are available in Redl, Gump, and Sutton-Smith (1971); Redl and Wineman (1957); Gump and Yueng-Hung (1954); and Gump and Sutton-Smith (1955a,b). A more recent discussion of 10 significant game features (similar to the Redl system) is presented by Avedon (1971). Based on his study of New Zealand children's games, Sutton-Smith offered a structural analysis of the meaning of the game "bar the door" (or "red rover," "anty over") in "A Formal Analysis of Game Meaning" (1959a). This game is examined by analyzing its "five basic features" (also similar to Redl's ingredients), which are said to be (1) the game challenge; (2) player participation; (3) performance; (4) spatial scene; and (5) temporal structure.

"On Game Morphology: A Study of the Structure of Non-Verbal Folklore" (1964b), by Alan Dundes, is one of the first structural analyses of children's games attempted by an anthropologist. In this article, Dundes suggested that certain ordered units of action, or *motifemes*, may be isolated as "the minimum structural units" of both games and folktales (p. 276). In this, he follows the work of Vladimir Propp, who analyzed Russian fairytales in terms of the distribution of *functions* (i.e., "an act of a character, defined from the point of view of its significance for the cause of action," 1928:21) among the dramatis personae of a fairytale.[7] Propp offered single-word designations for each of the 32 functions that he isolated. For example, the function *interdiction* (II) refers to statements such as "you dare not look into this closet," which appear early in the story (pp. 26–27). Examples of other functions are violation (III); delivery (V); trickery (VI); villainy (VII); lack (VIIIa); departure (XI); lack liquidated (XIX); pursuit (XXI); solution (XXVI); transfiguration (XXIX); and punishment (XXX). According to Propp, functions are "stable, constant elements . . . independent of how and by whom they are fulfilled" (pp. 26–27). However, certain functions belong to the "sphere of action" of particular dramatis personae (e.g., villainy, struggle, and pursuit belong to the villain's sphere). Propp also emphasized that there are only a limited number of functions existent in the fairytale genre and that their sequence of occurrence is always the same, although all do not necessarily occur in each tale. Propp's interest in formulating this approach was to produce a "morphology" of these tales that would be "a description of the tale according to its component parts

---

[7]Dundes (1964a) has also adapted Propp's approach for use in the analysis of American Indian folktales.

and the relationship of these components to each other and to the whole" (p. 19).

Dundes began his examination of children's games by suggesting that verbal folklore and games (i.e., nonverbal folklore) are structurally similar. This is illustrated by an analysis of several children's games using Propp's notion of functions, which Dundes referred to as *motifemic* units.[8] There is, however, one important difference between games and folktales that Dundes outlined. In games, one finds that two sequences of action occur simultaneously, whereas in folktales, only one action sequence may be described at a time.

In the game "hare and hounds," four functions, or motifemes, are identified: lack, interdiction, violation, and consequence. According to Dundes, two action or motifemic sequences occur in this game. One action takes place "from the point of view of the Hounds, and the other from the perspective of the Hare" (p. 278). The "hounds" wish to catch the "hare," who is hiding and therefore missing *(lack)*. They must catch the hare before he/she reaches "home," which is a place designated and agreed upon by the players at the beginning of the game and therefore an agreed-upon *interdiction*. If the hounds do not catch the hare *(violation)*, they lose the game *(consequence)*. At the same time as this sequence is occurring, the hare is engaged in his/her own activity. The hare wishes to go home, which he/she *lacks*. However, in order to do this, the hare must run from the hiding place without being caught by the hounds *(interdiction)*. If this is not achieved *(violation)*, the hare loses the game *(consequence)* (see pp. 278–279).

An important difference between games and folktales must be noted here. As Dundes suggested, "in folktales the hero always wins and the villain always loses." In games, however, "the outcome is not so regular or predictable; sometimes the hare wins and sometimes the hounds win" (p. 279). Dundes illustrated the use of Propp's structural schema in the analysis of several other games—such as "steps" ("Mother, may I?"), "thimble in sight," and "the witch"—in this article.

[8]Colby (1970) has recently criticized Dundes's (1964a) adaptation of Propp's system and in particular his use of the term *motifeme*. In the first place, Colby argued that this term suggests that the units are motifs, which they are not, and, second, he stated that Dundes's analysis does not meet Propp's specifications. This is so because Dundes presented a number of schemes in his study that are illustrated by selected folktales from a number of *different* North American Indian cultures. In contrast, Propp's work was in one culture with one type of narrative event. Colby also criticized Dundes's use of Propp's scheme because "it is extremely limited and general," as evidenced by the two motifemic sequence lack/lack liquidated (p. 191). According to Colby, action sequences are never this short and simple. Finally, the move from equilibrium to disequilibrium, which Dundes suggested is characteristic of American Indian folktales (and also games), is actually a property of *all* folk narrative, according to Colby, because it represents "the movement from concern to reduction of that concern" (p. 191).

Recently, Sutton-Smith and a number of his students have initiated a series of structural analyses of children's fantasy narratives. The material for these studies was collected from children (ages 5–11) from classrooms in a New York City public elementary school. The children came predominantly from Anglo-American, middle-class professional families. In this research, children were asked to make up a story and to relate a recent dream, which the investigators (who came to be known as "storytakers") wrote down in a notebook (see Sutton-Smith *et al.*, 1975).[9] These investigators of children's imagination were themselves quite imaginative in their use of a variety of structural approaches for the interpretation of these stories. One similarity, however, is the researchers' concern with illustrating the development of *structural complexity* (as this is revealed by the story texts). In doing this, relationships are drawn between this complexity and the child's developing cognitive abilities.

In "Children's Narrative Competence: The Underbelly of Mythology" (1974a), Sutton-Smith utilized several structural models (e.g., Lévi-Strauss, 1955; P. and E. K. Maranda, 1971; Propp, 1928; Dundes, 1964a) to discuss the development of children's narrative competence. From Lévi-Strauss (1955), he developed the proposition that "children's stories will be analyzable in terms of a mediation between powers" (p. 3). And from the work of the Marandas, he suggested that between the ages of 5 and 10 years, children may be expected to develop through the following story stages: (1) one power overwhelms another; (2) a minor power responds but fails; (3) a minor power nullifies the original threat; and (4) the original circumstances of the threat are transformed.[10] On the basis of Dundes's (1964a) use of Propp's (1928) system to analyze North America Indian folktales in terms of "nuclear dyads" of functions (e.g., lack/lack liquidated; interdiction/violation), Sutton-Smith derived two more propositions. He suggested that (1) "children's stories are analyzable in terms of dyadic interactive units in which disequilibrium is followed by some sort of equilibrium" (e.g., lack/lack liquidated), and (2) "these dyadic units occur in a lawful sequence" (p. 4).

On the basis of his analysis of the story texts, Sutton-Smith concluded that the first proposition, involving mediation of powers, is not indicated. On the other hand, the four narrative levels suggested by the

---

[9]For an example of the use of these materials for the testing of Erik Erikson's developmental model, see Caring (1977).

[10]E. K. and P. Maranda (1971) suggested that in American culture children pass through the above levels during the course of their development. This idea was tested by telling children a tale and then asking them to retell it to the investigator. They reported that the results of this study showed that younger children *reduced* "the narrative structure of the input to their own level" (Sutton-Smith, 1974a:2).

Marandas do appear to be applicable, and he illustrated each level type with a story text and an age grouping. For the propositions derived from Propp and Dundes, Sutton-Smith found that the dyads lack/lack liquidated and villainy/villainy nullified are most commonly employed, and he suggested that they provide a "useful technique for analyzing the dynamic elements of narrative" (p. 16). There is also a sex difference reported in the use of these dyads, with girls favoring the lack/lack liquidated and boys the villainy/villainy nullified theme. There was, however, no evidence for the order of occurrence of these units in the texts.

A Proppian analysis of these story texts has also been undertaken by Botvin (1976). Here Propp's scheme (also Dundes, 1964a) was used as a way to delimit a series of seven levels of structural complexity found to be exhibited by these fantasy stories and also based on research in cognitive development and psycholinguistics:

> In each case the basic unit of analysis is an action or event and the basic structure is the dyad. Increasing structural complexity [is] . . . conceived in terms of the articulation and hierarchical organization of nuclear dyads as well as the integration of intermediary elements between the initial and final terms of the nuclear dyad. (p. 5)

On the basis of his analysis, Botvin suggested that the development of these structures is also highly correlated with chronological age. He illustrated these relationships by describing each proposed level and then offering an example of a representative story text. The development of structural complexity (as defined here) can best be described by comparing a "level-two" with a "level-six" story. The former are characterized by the presence of one dyad with no intervening elements. These stories are told by children between the ages of 4 and 5.

> Story: An astronaut went into space [departure] he was attacked by a monster [villainy]. The astronaut got in his spaceship and flew away [villainy nullified]. (p. 6)

In level-six stories, one finds "the single embedding of one dyadic structure within another," in which case "the main action of the narrative is interrupted by a subsequence of action"—the subplot (p. 8):

> Story: A man named Mr. Dirt lived in the country all by himself and owns a farm [initial situation]. One calf got away into the woods and headed for the mountains [lack]. So Mr. Dirt went up the mountain after the calf [departure, pursuit]. On the way a bear came after Mr. Dirt [villainy]. He ran up the tree [escape] and the bear climbed up the tree after him [pursuit]. Mr. Dirt threw his ax at the bear [counterattack] and hit the bear in the head. Blood poured out of his head [wound] and the bear fell down and died [villainy nullified]. A few minutes later the calf ran over to Mr. Dirt [find] and they went back to the farm [return, lack liquidated]. (pp. 8–9)

Level-seven stories are described as similar to level six, but characterized by the embedding of multiple dyadic structures. These stories are told most frequently by children who are over 11 years old.

In Abrams and Sutton-Smith (1977), an analysis of the development of "tricksters" in children's narratives (and also in children's favorite cartoon shows—e.g., Bugs Bunny) is presented. The investigators called their approach "genetic folklore" (adapting Piaget's term "genetic epistemology"). Four stages of trickster tales are enumerated, using the Maranda levels and a "trickster inventory": (1) the "stage of physical clumsiness" (5-year-olds); (2) the "stage of moronic self-defeat" (6- to 7-year-olds); (3) the "stage of the unsuccessful trickster" (7- to 8-year-olds); and (4) the "stage of the successful trickster" (9- to 11-year-olds). Two interpretations of these trickster narratives are offered. Following a socialization view, it is suggested that they may be used to master developmental tasks; however, they are also interpreted, after Sutton-Smith (1972b), as a form of symbolic inversion (see discussion of these two approaches in Chapter Six).

An analysis of these stories specifically using Piaget's schema of development was presented by Mahony (1976), who outlined a series of storytelling stages (e.g., free association, conserved main character, three-part story structure, formal creativity). Sutton-Smith also utilized Piaget's schema in "A Structural Grammar of Games and Sports" (1975b).[11] Here he attempted "to outline a sequence of structures as these occur developmentally, and as they may have occurred in human evolution" (p. 1). Sutton-Smith began by suggesting an analogy between games and Piaget's concept of structures. Games and logical structures exhibit qualities of wholeness, are self-regulating (and self-contained), and also have rules of transformation (p. 3; also see Piaget, 1970b). The purpose of this approach, however, is to use Piaget's concepts to construct a schema of the development of social interactional complexity in games and sports.

Sutton-Smith organized these activities into a trilevel sequence of social interaction and suggested that each level corresponds to shifts in logical thought, although each shift is said to precede the logical one by several years (p. 4). In this schema, the first level of games is referred to as Type A: Pastimes—characterized by conservation of role. Here "neither roles nor actions need to be internalized operations" because they are defined by traditional verses (pp. 5–6). Role and action reversals are built into the game (e.g., "farmer in the dell" or "ring around the

<hr />

[11]T. Stevens (1977) has also used a similar approach for the analysis of American adolescents' sports activities.

rosey"), and the only nonprescribed element is the choice of the next player. These are the types of games played by 4- to 5-year-olds.

Type B games are central-person games characterized by *primary interactions*, where players act upon each other in carrying out the reversible actions of the game. These actions are the "result of operations within . . . [the player's] own head, rather than any externally prescriptive statements" (p. 7). Two levels of games are outlined here: level 1 games are characterized by role reversals (e.g., "hide-and-seek"), and level 2 games include both role and action reversals (e.g., "frozen tag"). These games are said to be played most frequently until age 7, and Sutton-Smith suggested that they anticipate Piaget's stage of concrete operations.

Type C games are competitive games where *secondary interactions* are found (e.g., special types of interactions, such as signaling, are used to control the primary interactions of levels one and two). Two levels are found here: level 3 games are characterized by coordination of roles and actions (e.g., noncentral players may cooperate with one another against the central player, as in "dodge ball" or "bull in the ring"); and level 4 games include coordination within and between groups (e.g., "prisoner's base"). Type C games are played by children between the ages of 9 and 12 and are said to anticipate the child's capacity for making multiple classifications.[12]

Type D games are sports activities characterized by *tertiary interactions*, which involve a number of specialized interactions and roles whether *outside* (external to) the playing group (e.g., referees, umpires, score-keeper, audience) or *within* the playing group (e.g., pitcher, first baseman). Level 5 games are those where one finds external tertiary interactions; level 6 games are those where one finds coaches, referees, etc., and the defense team exhibits internal tertiary interactions (e.g., first, second, third basemen, pitcher). Finally, level 7 games are those where both attack and defense teams exhibit internal and external differentiation (e.g., football). These games are said to anticipate formal operations.

In attempting to use this system to speculate about the evolution of games, Sutton-Smith considered material from five different non-Western groups: Mbuti Pygmies; Australian aborigines; Mackenzie River Es-

[12]One wonders where or how Sutton-Smith would classify imaginative or make-believe play. The sophisticated cognitive and social capabilities that children display in this activity (e.g., discrimination between play and nonplay; simultaneous communication of both personal and play identity; negotiation of play roles, actions, situations, space, time) would seem to place it, at least, in Sutton-Smith's level three or four. The fact that this play requires that children exhibit such skills for the play event to "work" (e.g., as discussed by Sutton-Smith—reversible operations, multiple classification) does not mean that Piaget's operations are *anticipated* but rather that *they are already in evidence*.

kimos; North American Indian villagers (e.g., Shawnee, Iroquois, Cherokee); and Polynesians. These groups are considered in order of "increasing cultural complexity" derived from Murdock (1967) and Lomax and Berkowitz (1972).

The Mbuti Pygmies are said to exhibit some examples of level 3 games (played by children) and level 4 games (played by adults), while the Australian aborigines exhibit level 1–4 games and a few level 5 games. Sutton-Smith found that the Eskimos play a great number of "level four individual self-testing games" and also games that may be "an intermediate structure between level 4 and level 5" (p. 22). The North American Indian villagers exhibit an increase in level 5 games and some examples of levels 6 and 7. Finally, the Polynesian groups are said to show even more of an increase in level 5, 6, and 7 games and a great concern with sports activities in general.

These investigations by Sutton-Smith and his students are interesting and often innovative examples of the use of various types of structural models (e.g., Propp, Lévi-Strauss, P. and E. Maranda, Piaget) for the analysis of children's games and fantasy narratives. The investigators' eclecticism (within the structural framework) is noteworthy and points out the value of pursuing studies that recognize that there are multiple interpretations to be made of all "realities," even (or perhaps particularly) the realities of play. On the other hand, all of these researchers are interested in the *staging* of these structures in association with individuals' cognitive and social development and, in the case of Sutton-Smith (1975b), paralleling individual ontogeny with cultural evolution. This orientation must be considered in relation to the approach of the early evolutionists and the present-day developmentalists discussed in Chapter Four. The tendency to speak in terms of *higher and lower stages or levels* is exhibited in all these investigations. This view is particularly questionable, as has been said before, when talking about cultures. In associating the logic of games with cognitive capabilities, it is easy to draw the conclusion that those individuals in cultures that exhibit only "lower-level" games are able to think or conceptualize only at this level. It is not clear that Sutton-Smith wished to draw this conclusion, but others may choose to do so on the basis of statements such as the following:

> Clearly the tournaments and the referees and the helpers make these team games [of the Australian aborigines] into level five. We are at a higher level of complexity than the account of the Pygmy games. (1975b:21)

Even if words such as *higher* and *lower* are not meant to be applied to the thought of non-Westerners, the stage model lends itself to this imagery, and it should therefore be carefully and cautiously used by researchers.

MINDING PLAY: PIAGET VERSUS SUTTON-SMITH

Jean Piaget is one of the main proponents of a view of play as cognition. His analysis of the development of play phenomena, as presented in *Play, Dreams, and Imitation* (1951), has already been discussed in Chapter Four. A number of critiques of Piaget's theory of play are available (e.g., Gilmore, 1966; Millar, 1968; Singer, 1973); however, by far the most sustained and insightful analysis of Piaget's view has been formulated by Sutton-Smith (1966).[13] This critique is particularly interesting because it inspired Piaget to respond (1966), and this debate is reprinted in Herron and Sutton-Smith (1971:326–342) along with a reply by Sutton-Smith.

"In Piaget on Play: A Critique" (1966), Sutton-Smith suggested that in his theory of play, Piaget acts as if he had a "copyist epistemology," and because he shows a focal concern with directed thought (e.g., understanding the operations of the physical world) as opposed to undirected thought (e.g., understanding imaginative thought), he has been unable to account for play and has therefore reduced it to a function of cognition. Sutton-Smith argued that for Piaget, concepts are ultimately copies derived from "an external reality," and since play is said to *distort* this reality, it can have no constitutive role within thought. In short, "intelligence cannot proceed without imitation. It can proceed without play" (p. 329). Because Piaget cannot explain play in terms of his own system, Sutton-Smith asserted that he resorts to a series of affective explanations for this behavior (e.g., play functions to serve "ego continuity").

Piaget (1966) responded to this critique by stating that he does *not* exhibit a copyist epistemology, because it is his belief that "concepts are the expression of an assimilation by schemes of accommodation," whereby reality may be transformed without the necessity of submitting this transformation "to the criterion of objective fact" (p. 338). However, Piaget stressed that play in his system is never subordinated to "accommodative imitation" and cannot be reduced to such imitation because it is always "assimilation of reality to the self" (p. 338).

Sutton-Smith (1971b) replied to these comments by suggesting that Piaget had still not indicated what the vital cognitive *function* of play is in early childhood. Second, he stated that Piaget continued to focus on the way play corresponds with adaptive cognitive structures at various age

[13]A useful presentation and analysis of Piaget's often difficult and abstruse concepts is available by Ginsberg and Opper (1969). There are also several critiques of Piaget's general theory of intellectual development and his particular brand of structuralism that have been formulated by anthropologists or are relevant to anthropological concerns, for example, Lévi-Strauss (1949:84–97), T. Turner (1973), and Wilden (1972:302–350).

levels rather than on the structural uniqueness of particular play *transformations*. The result, according to Sutton-Smith, is that imagination is subordinated to reason (pp. 341–342).

PIAGET'S ASSIMILATION OF PLAY

According to Piaget, play acts are those characterized by "the primacy of assimilation over accommodation" when the child incorporates elements of the external world into his/her own schema, thus distorting "objective reality." This interpretation of play, however, is itself an example of theoretical assimilation, which suggests that contrary to Piaget's view, adults, as well as children, engage in symbolic play activities. Piaget exhibits this behavior by forcing the "realities" of play into his particular *theoretical schema*, and by so doing, he distorts, reduces, and ultimately disregards this activity.

Piaget's assimilation of play occurs in a variety of ways. Sutton-Smith suggested one of the most obvious by arguing that Piaget has subordinated imagination to reason (1971b:341–342). In *Genetic Epistemology* (1970a), Piaget clearly separated two modes of thought: the figurative aspect and the operative aspect. Examples of figurative functions are said to be "perception, imitation, and mental imagery" (or "symbols"). The figurative aspect "is an imitation of states taken as momentary and static" (p. 14). In contrast, operative thought "deals not with states but with transformations from one state to another," which occur either as actions "which transform objects or states themselves" or as intellectual operations that are "essentially systems of transformation" (p. 4). This form of thought relies upon "signs" (i.e., arbitrary, collectively, or culturally standardized tokens) as opposed to "symbols," which because of their personal, individual, and therefore idiosyncratic nature, play no role in cognitive development after early childhood (T. Turner, 1973:352). The primary role that *operative thought* plays in Piaget's system is clearly expressed in the following statement:

> Now, the figurative aspects are always subordinated to the operative aspects. Any state can be understood only as the result of certain transformations or as the point of departure for other transformations. In other words, to my way of thinking the essential aspect of thought is its operative and not its figurative aspect. (1970a:14–15)

Piaget's discussion of figurative thought, of course, denies the fact that symbolic forms such as myth, ritual, the arts, and also symbolic play and games, are often cultural or collective and therefore nonarbitrary in character (see T. Turner, 1973:352). However, Piaget has never been concerned with the social character of such forms, for he has concentrated on an analysis of the development of knowledge about objects in the physical world. This knowledge is acquired in the process of the individual's interaction with this environment. Piaget's approach is significant because he focuses on the *active*, as opposed to the *passive*, character of knowledge-acquiring systems, but he could just as well have been studying molluscs as children. In fact, his early studies in biology were of molluscs. In these investigations, Piaget was particularly impressed with the ability of these organisms to adjust to new environments. In an early experiment:

> Piaget placed some acquatic molluscs which had the normal elongated shape into the great lakes of Switzerland—bodies of water far more turbulent than their customary homes in the marshes of Europe and Asia. Through motorid adjustments during the period of growth to the rough movement of the water, a new breed of mollusc developed which was globular in shape and more resistant to the currents of the water. When this mollusc was placed into a calmer body of water, however, it retained the new, globular shape. Piaget interpreted this result as indicating that, rather than merely being subject to chance mutations, the structure of an organism has the potential to develop in diverse ways, depending on the eliciting circumstances of the environment. Adaptation to new conditions involves an *active* restructuring and accommodation to the environment on the part of the organism which may result in a lasting alteration of form. . . .
>
> By analogy, Piaget reasoned that an organism's intelligence was embodied in a series of structures with latent tendencies for development, which could be brought out by appropriate interaction with the environment. . . .
>
> Piaget, seeking the essential property or capacity of organisms, concluded that it was *action*. (Gardner, 1972:59)

This interest in action and its relation to intelligence was therefore developed very early in Piaget's studies. The part that figurative thought (i.e., "he reasoned by analogy") has to play in Piaget's thinking about this and other matters, however, has apparently escaped his notice. This occurs because, according to Piaget, knowledge results from actions performed on objects and over time the "systems of transformations," which are constructed on the basis of these actions, "correspond more or less adequately, to reality. Knowledge, then, is a system of transformations that become progressively adequate" (1970a:15). Because Piaget believes that figurative phenomena, and especially children's symbolic play, do not contribute significantly to the process of knowledge becoming "progressively adequate" (i.e., corresponding to reality), he can account for this activity only by offering a cathartic explanation for its existence (see also Sutton-Smith, 1966a). In Piaget's terms, children between the ages of 2 and 4 must begin to conform to social rules and in particular to the rules that language imposes. However, their ability to express in words the frustration and problems that they are experiencing at this time is quite limited. Symbolic play is one activity that does not demand such conformity. Instead, according to Piaget:

> The child can assimilate the external world almost directly into his own desires and needs with scarcely any accommodation. He can therefore shape reality to his own requirements. Furthermore, . . . he can act out the conflictual situations of real life in such a way as to ensure a successful conclusion in which he comes out the winner. . . . In brief, symbolic play, serving a necessary cathartic purpose, is essential for the child's emotional stability and adjustment to reality. (Ginsberg and Opper, 1969:80–81)

Symbolic play, however, does not serve a "necessary" cognitive purpose, as it cannot help the child construct "systems of transformations" that progressively correspond to reality, because according to Piaget, it distorts this reality.

Piaget's theory of child development portrays children (as well as researchers) as objects "in a world of objects which are there simply to be used and not also to be listened to and communicated with" (Wilden, 1972:327). This view disregards the effect of the sociocultural context on an individual's behavior at the very moment that it stresses the effect of the physical environment on these actions. The contradictions inherent in making this artificial dichotomy between physical and social context are most apparent in Piaget's view of "the research situation" created by the relationship set up between a questioner and a child. Anthony Wilden suggested that this relationship is, at the very least,

> ruled by the questioner's dominance, by conscious or unconscious assumptions about "intelligence" (i.e., performance) by the questioner's desire (or goal), and by the child's desire to satisfy the desire of the questioner (who also represents what both he and the child necessarily believe to be "adult reality"). (1972:319)[14]

Piaget, however, must assume that the data that he collects within this situation are not affected by the above features of the research relationship. Apparently children act and react only to their physical environment and not to their social context (at least not if it is a research situation). In Wilden's opinion, this leads to a confusing conclusion:

> the vaunted "biological" model of the "equilibrated interaction between organism and environment" . . . does not apply, in his view, to the relationship between child and questioner. (p. 320)

[14]An excellent example of the effect of "the research or testing situation" on the quantity and quality of a young black child's verbal behavior is presented by Labov (1972:205–213; see also Dickie and Bagur, 1972). Isaacs (see 1930:78–97) has offered probably the earliest and certainly one of the most interesting critiques of Piaget's interview/experimental techniques, suggesting that "his conclusions apply legitimately only to the particular conditions of his particular experiments" (p. 83). She specifically stressed the point that these were *unfavorable* "conditions" for the manifestation of children's ideas about or interest in causal explanations.

Not only does Piaget's theory of intelligence not account for the effect of the research relationship on a child's answers, but it also does not explain the researcher's actions as a theoretician where the "figurative aspect" of thought (i.e., use of analogies, metaphors, and models) is so important. Piaget has been able to assimilate play into his own schema (i.e., theory)—and yet not to realize that he has done this—because he wishes to study only the "operative aspect" of thought. Unfortunately, this leads him to disregard and thereby distort the significance of figurative thought exhibited in the reasoning of children and also of researchers. Piaget's general theory of intellectual development must therefore be judged as inadequate, because it is a theory that should be able to (but ultimately cannot) explain its own formulation.

PLAY AND LEARNING

Piaget is not the only researcher to have considered relationships between play and learning. There are a variety of studies available in which this topic is discussed. These can be divided into two basic types: (1) investigations that emphasize the deuterolearning qualities of play, and (2) investigations that emphasize the learning of specific contents in play. In Bateson's (1942) terms, deuterolearning is the process whereby an individual learns how to learn, also described as "Learning II" (see Bateson 1972:292–301), which can be contrasted with learning, simple learning, or "Learning I." A number of researchers have proposed somewhat similar contrasts, for example, Harlow's (1949) discussion of set learning versus single learning; Kohlberg's (1968) distinction between cognitive-structural change and specific learning. As I use these terms here, *deuterolearning studies* are those that emphasize the importance of play for facilitating or generating change in children's cognitive sets. *Specific learning studies* emphasize the ability of play to facilitate or generate the learning of specific cognitive skills within a given cognitive set.

The difference between these two types of investigations is illustrated in Bateson's discussion "The Message 'This Is Play' " (1956) (also discussed in Chapter Eight). In brief, Bateson proposed that play is an important learning arena because in play children learn "that behavior can be set to a logical type or to a style . . . and the fact that the choice of style or role is related to the frame or context of behavior" (p. 256). This is in contrast to the view that children learn and practice specific roles and/or skills in play. In other words, learning the specifics of particular roles or skills (specific learning) cannot occur until the idea of roles (which are, in fact, sets of relationships) and the related idea of context have been understood (deuterolearning). Most socialization studies, as discussed in Chapter Six, describe play as specific learning, whereas its more important "function" may be its role in deuterolearning.

Lev S. Vygotsky, the Russian psychologist, has presented an analysis of play that is representative of the first category of theories. Vygotsky was both an admirer and a critic of Piaget's early studies of language and thought (e.g., 1926, 1929). As a critic, he specifically questioned Piaget's view that the sequence of speech development proceeded from "non-verbal autistic thought through egocentric thought and speech to socialized speech and logical development" (1962:20). Instead Vygotsky proposed that the primary function of speech was communication, making the first speech of the child *necessarily* social or "socialized." He suggested that egocentric and then inner speech followed this early form of social communication, and it was also his view that "inner speech served both autistic and logical thinking" (p. 19). Sutton-Smith (1966a) has applied this argument to Piaget's view of play, suggesting that "children's play does not give way to intelligent adaptation, but becomes differentiated in a variety of ways" (p. 334).

In "Play and Its Role in the Mental Development of the Child" (1966), Vygotsky proposed his own theory of play and learning. Here he was reacting to what he believed to be the "terrible intellectualization of play," where the child is looked upon "as an unsuccessful algebraist who cannot yet write the words on paper, but depicts them in action" (pp. 6, 8). In contrast to this view, Vygotsky argued that a child's needs, incentives, and motives must be taken into account by play theorists. In this regard, it is his belief that play "is essentially wish fulfillment" arising from the "unsatisfied desires" of the child, which become generalized affects (pp. 8–9) (a view reminiscent of Freud). Play must also be distinguished from a child's other forms of activities, and Vygotsky suggested that one important feature is the fact that in play an *imaginary situation* is created by the child. (This is true for both sociodramatic play and also games, according to Vygotsky.)

Another characteristic that is also stressed is the rulebound nature of play, although these rules need not be explicit as is the case of games. In order to illustrate this quality, Vygotsky commented on an incident in which two sisters, aged 5 and 7, decided to play at being sisters, which was, of course, the "reality" of their relationship. When the sisters "play sisters," however, there is a difference:

> The vital difference in play . . . is that the child in playing tries to be a sister. In life the child behaves without thinking that she is her sister's sister. . . . In the game of sisters playing at sisters, however, they are both concerned with displaying their sisterhood; the fact that two sisters decided to play sisters makes them both acquire rules of behavior. (I must always be a sister in

. relation to the other sister in the whole play situation.) Only actions which fit
these rules are acceptable to the play situation. . . . What passes unnoticed
by the child in real life becomes a rule of behavior in play. (p. 9)[15]

Play is most important in the child's development, according to
Vygotsky, because it "liberates the child from situational constraints" (p.
11). In play, things and actions are not what they appear to be, and so in
imaginary situations "the child begins to act independently of what he
sees," and he/she begins to be guided by the *meaning* of the situation (p.
9). This is in contrast to the infant's behavior, which Vygotsky suggested
is very situationally constrained. Preschool children's play, however,
enables them to discover that "action arises from ideas rather than from
things," and so a stick as an object can become "a pivot for severing the
meaning of horse from a real horse" (p. 12). When this occurs, the
psychological structures that determine a child's relationship to "reality"
have been radically altered. Vygotsky depicted this new structure as a
fraction, with "meaning" as the numerator and the object as de-
nominator: $\frac{\text{meaning}}{\text{object}}$. Here "the semantic aspect—the meaning of the
word, the meaning of the thing—dominates and determines his [the
child's] behavior" (p. 13).

Play also liberates the child from actions that may be "completed
not for the action itself but for the meaning it carries" (p. 14). When the
child stamps on the ground and pretends to be riding a horse, meaning
is dominating the action, and this may also be depicted as a fraction:
$\frac{\text{meaning}}{\text{action}}$. This process gives the child "a new form of desires," according
to Vygotsky, which are related to this "fictitious" I (i.e., the child's role
in the game and its rules):

> Therefore, a child's greatest achievements are possible in play—achieve-
> ments which tomorrow will become his average level of action and his mo-
> rality. (p. 14)

Vygotsky also proposed that play is "the highest level of preschool
development" and that it is through play that the child "moves for-

---

[15]This description should be compared with the discussion of the author's research that
appears in Chapter Eight. Here it is suggested that children must be able to communicate
characteristics of the relationship being played (e.g., sisters, mother and father, parent
and child) that simultaneously communicate aspects of their own relationships to each
other (e.g., symmetrical, asymmetrical, metacomplementary). Play, therefore, enables
the child to learn (and also comment on) *rules for relationships*. It is not primarily an
activity that teaches the *content* of specific roles because it focuses on relationship forms.
This is the significance of the example of sisters "playing sisters," where the girls are
playing with the *idea* of "a relationship" and the *idea* of "context."

ward" or "jumps above the level of his normal behavior" (p. 15). This view is in opposition to Piaget's theory, where play is depicted as a distorting and compensatory activity. In contrast, Vygotsky believes that play is crucial to cognitive development because the process of creating imaginary situations leads to the development of abstract thought. This occurs because new relationships are created in play between meanings and objects and actions.

Current studies of Russian children's play "symbolics" have been recently reviewed by El'Konin (1971). The results of these investigations have been discussed in Chapter Six as they pertain to the issue of the cultural patterning of children's imaginative play behavior. The influence of adults in inspiring the child's play transformations is particularly stressed by El'Konin. In their examination of the functions of symbolization in play these researchers, following Vygotsky, stressed the importance of this activity to the development of abstract thought. Play is significant in this regard because in these symbolizations there occurs the "emancipation of the word from the thing," and in this way play becomes "a powerful means of the child's penetration into reality" (p. 320).

Sutton-Smith (1967) has also proposed a view of play as deutero-learning. In "The Role of Play in Cognitive Development" (1967), he suggested that the child's adoption of an "as if" attitude in play illustrates his/her ability to *conserve* imaginative identities even in the presence of contrary stimuli. However, according to Piaget, it is not until the ages of 5–7 years that children can conserve class identities of phenomena such as number, quantity, and space. If the "as if" attitude of play is viewed as a *representational set*, Sutton-Smith suggested, the ability to use such sets in play perhaps facilitates the adoption of representational categories at a later age. Following Vygotsky, it could be argued that this is an example of how play functions as "the highest level of preschool development."

A similar view of the relationship between play and learning is offered in the studies of Susan Isaacs (e.g., 1930, 1933), the well-known British child psychologist and educator. These works are excellent early attempts to integrate the study of cognition and affect (intellectual and social development). On the basis of her observations and recordings of children's behavior at the Malting House School for young children in Cambridge between 1924 and 1927, Isaacs argued that young children, when observed in both play and work activities at school, exhibit more sophisticated forms of thought than those which Piaget found in his more structured interviews. For example, she cited an instance of a child's (age 5:9) understanding of mechanical causality at an age when Piaget has suggested that children have *no* appreciation of this concept

as exhibited by their inability to explain the function of pedals for bicycles (i.e., they may draw pedals on a bicycle but do not show how they
connect with the machine). In this example, as luck would have it, she
was walking through the school with Piaget (who had come for a visit
and tour), and he asked her how the Malting children stood with regard
to their understanding of this concept. In order to illustrate their understanding, Isaacs walked over to a child who was sitting on a tricycle and
in the process of back-pedaling:

> I went to him and said, "The tricycle is not moving forward, is it?" "Of
> course not, when I'm back-pedaling," he said. "Well," I asked, "how does it
> go forward when it does?" "Oh, well," he replied, "your feet press the
> pedals, that turns the crank round, and the cranks turn that round" (pointing
> to the cog-wheel) "and that makes the chain go around, and the chain turns
> the hub round, and then the wheels go round—and there you are!" (1930:44)

Isaacs provided numerous examples of this sort (pp. 78–97),
suggesting that children are much more competent "thinkers" than
Piaget (and most other adults) realizes. One example of an adult's attempt to motivate a child by the use of magical thinking is particularly
amusing and also suggestive of the fact (noticed as well by Mead, 1932)
that adults teach children certain illogical forms of thought that must
later be unlearned. In this particular incident, a child (4:0) was told, in
order to encourage her to put on her coat, that if she did this, then her
mother (who was late) would "come quicker." The child responded by
describing this as a "silly" thing for an adult to say, although she was
not completely sure of this very accurate judgment because, after all, an
adult had said it: "Wasn't that silly? *That* couldn't make any difference,
could it?" (p. 84). And later she said, "It could only make us quicker
going home, couldn't it? But it couldn't make you quicker coming, could
it?" (p. 84).

Isaacs's view of play is discussed in both studies (1930, 1933). In
these works she suggested that play is simultaneously expressive of
children's concerns—and in this way enables them to achieve "mental
ease" (the psychoanalytic view) (see 1933)—and also serves as a vehicle
for learning (see 1930). Her view of "play as education" stresses the
importance of play for the development of manipulative skills and also
growth in discovery, reasoning, and thought (1933:425). Make-believe
play is particularly crucial, in her view, because it is here that children
take "the first steps toward that emancipation of meanings from the *here*
and *now* of a concrete situation, which makes possible hypotheses and
the 'as if' consciousness" (1930:104) a view that is similar to that advocated by Vygotsky, El'Konin, and also Sutton-Smith. Examples of other
studies of play's relation to cognition and motivation are available in a
reader edited by Almy (1968).

Jerome Bruner (also a critic of Piaget's stages) and his associates have recently conducted a series of empirical studies related to the subject of play and learning. For example, in a study of peek-a-boo, Bruner and Sherwood (1977) suggested that young infants already exhibit a wide variety of cognitive abilities (e.g., mastery, to some degree, of object permanence) and soon become very sensitive to the "rules of the game" (i.e., initial contact, disappearance, reappearance, reestablished contact). These rules are learned, according to the investigators, in a way that is characteristic of rule learning; that is, they are learned in a general form, with assignable roles, with permissable substitutions of moves and so forth (p. 277). In this study, six infants were seen over a period of 10 months (7–17 months of age), and spontaneously produced peek-a-boo games occurring between mothers and children were the subject of the investigation. The authors discussed the procedures established between mother and child for generating peek-a-boo games and the conversion of these procedures into rule structures. It is suggested that in these games the infant is learning "not only the basic rules of the game, but the range of variation that is possible within the rule set," and it is this emphasis on "patterned variation within a constraining rule set that seems crucial to the mastery of competence and generativeness" (p. 283). Additionally, it is proposed that peek-a-boo provides children with an opportunity for exploring the "boundary" between "real" and "make-believe" activities.

In another study, by Sylva, Bruner, and Genova (1977), the effect of play on preschool-aged children's problem-solving abilities is investigated. In this project, three groups of children were presented with a task: how to retrieve a piece of colored chalk placed inside a transparent box that was sitting on a table, but not within the child's reach. The children were told that they could not get up from the chair, but they could use any object that was on the table in front of them. There were three sticks and two C clamps on the table. Each group of children experienced a different "treatment" condition prior to the presentation of the problem in this project. Each group viewed one similar demonstration (i.e., an adult demonstrated one clamp tightened onto the middle of one long stick). After this demonstration, one group of children was allowed 10 minutes of free play with 10 sticks and 7 clamps—this was designated as the *play* group. A second group watched an adult demonstrate how to construct an elongated tool by rigidly joining two long sticks with clamps; this was the *observe* group. In the third group, no treatment followed the first demonstration; this was the *no-treatment* group.

The results of this study are very interesting, particularly because the children who observed the actual construction of the tool did not construct significantly more spontaneous solutions to the problem than did the play group (i.e., the observe group produced 15 solutions, whereas the play group produced 14 solutions). The no-treatment group was markedly different in this regard, evidencing only 3 solutions. There were other differences as well. For example, it is reported that each group approached the problem in unique ways. The play-group children were said to be

> eager to begin, continuous in their efforts to solve the problems and flexible in their hypotheses. In contrast, children who observed the principle first were prone to an "all or nothing approach." (p. 250)

The play group also exhibited more goal-directed behaviors and less frustration at failed attempts than either of the other groups. The researchers concluded that the play group's success in problem solving occurred because (1) solving problems requires self-initiative and these players were the only ones in the experiment whose actions were self-initiated; (2) tool invention requires serial ordering, and the play group was the only one with an opportunity to explore alternate orderings; and (3) play reduces stress and therefore frustration and fear of failure, which also contributed to the players' increased goal-orientation (p. 256).

On the basis of these types of studies, Bruner has suggested in a paper entitled "Play Is Serious Business" that play makes possible "the practice of subroutines of behavior, that later come together in useful problem solving" (1975:81). This is an example of the interpretation of play as an activity that may facilitate the learning and/or practice of specific behaviors.

Operating on the assumption that games can be used as *learning contexts*, a variety of researchers and educators have formulated specific "learning games" for the presentation of traditional classroom material (e.g., math, spelling, history, geography) (see Coleman, 1971; Humphry, 1975; also see Avedon and Sutton-Smith, 1971). Coleman (1971) specifically reported on the construction of games that "simulate complex activities in a society" for students (e.g., life-career games, family games, representative democracy game, community game, response and consumer game, p. 460). The use of games as a means for "diagnosing" a child's cognitive abilities (e.g., at reading and math) has also been suggested (see Humphry, 1976; and also Elmore and Gorham, 1957, and Richardson and Church, 1959, on proverb tests). These studies do not investigate, nor do they appear to assume, that child-structured play might be valuable as a learning experience in and of itself, prior to teacher or researcher interventions. These designated learning (or diagnostic) games, view play in a manner similar to many culture and personality researchers; that is, *play is used as a context* for the teaching or testing of nonplay behaviors.

There are, however, a number of things that children do learn from teacher-structured games, entertainments, and sports that are often not planned by the adult as part of the lesson. In fact, the terms "hidden curriculum" or "tacit lessons" (Gearing, 1973; Gearing and Tindall, 1973) have been proposed to describe these processes, but they are related to the forms of learning designated here as deuterolearning. Jules Henry (1963) produced some of the earliest studies of what American children actually learn in school. In his terms, it is the *noise* (or cultural drives, values, or orientations) and not the *formal subject matter* (e.g., math, spelling, history) that children learn in the classroom context. This learning occurs as well in the realm of structured play activities. For example, Henry (pp. 290–293) presented a discussion of what actually is learned by students during a typical music period. In the instance that he cites, the children were singing songs about Ireland while the teacher played the piano. However, during the singing, a number of children were searching through a song index looking for related songs, and when one was discovered, the child quickly raised a hand so that he/she could be the next one to name the song for the class to sing. The actual singing, according to Henry, was of "that pitchless quality always heard in elementary school classrooms," while the teacher may demonstrate a song by singing in a typically "off-key" fashion (p. 290).

The formal purpose of these song periods is to broaden the children's interests and to teach them something about music. But what else are the children learning? According to Henry, they are learning first of all to sing "like everybody else," which is in an off-key and tuneless style and which may not be the way the child actually hears the song. Most importantly, however, the children are learning the importance of competition and ambition, by searching for songs and then trying to get the teacher's attention so that the class can sing "their" song. Along with this, they are learning that it is all right to be distracted from the formal lesson in order to find a song and get one's way. Additionally, the children who do not learn the importance of all this competition, ambition, and distraction will quickly be scolded and derided by the teacher for not participating in the event, as measured by their eagerness to raise their hands. In fact, hand raising is, according to Henry, "the prime symbol of having learned what school is all about" (p. 291). And what it is all about is the transmission of cultural values and orientations, *not* formal learning[16]:

---

[16]Lewis Carroll presented an interesting commentary on the function of schools that is strikingly similar to Henry's observations. When Alice and the Mock Turtle discuss their respective schools in *Alice's Adventures in Wonderland*, the Mock Turtle's list of subjects

The first lesson a child has to learn when he comes to school is that lessons are not what they seem. He must then forget this and act as if they were. This is the first step toward "school mental health," it is also the first step in becoming absurd. (p. 291)

B. Allan Tindall (1975) has analyzed the "hidden curriculum" in sports (e.g., basketball) tournaments played by Ute and Mormon boys in a Utah high school. Here Tindall suggested that the tacit lesson of these events is about the relationship between man and man and "specifically that men are (and ought to be) controlled by other men" (e.g., teachers are controlled by principals; students are controlled by teachers; some students—team captains—control other students; all student players are controlled by the referee) (p. 3). The basketball tournaments played in this high school were organized by Anglo-Mormon principals and teachers as "educationally sound" events for their students. However, these contests were rejected by Ute students, who failed to come to school on the day of a playoff, or who forgot to bring their uniforms, or who refused to play on "their" team. These actions demonstrate, according to Tindall, the Ute boys rejection

of the major premise (lesson) being enacted [in these games]; that one man can control another. These students operate according to another premise, a premise which stresses individuality and the equality between men. Thus, they rejected the attempts by the principal, the teacher, or the captain to force them to play. In this rejection they were themselves providing lessons in appropriate behavior, but that lesson fell on deaf ears. (p. 4)

Studies of non-Western children's play that examine this as an activity that contributes to the development of either general or specific cognitive skills are very rare. In fact, there are few investigations available on the more general topic of the cultural context of cognition.[17] One exception to this is a project conducted in Liberia with the Kpelle by a group of ethnographic psychologists (see Gay and Cole, 1967; Cole, Gay, Glick, and Sharp, 1971). This research was designed specifically to examine relationships between culture and thought.

Although the above researchers were not particularly interested in

---

are at one and the same time puns on the "three Rs" and perceptive descriptions of the "hidden curriculum" of schools:

"I only took the regular course."
"What was that?" enquired Alice.
"Reeling and Writhing, of course, to begin with," the Mock Turtle replied, "and then the different branches of Arithmetic—Ambition, Distraction, Uglification, and Derision."

[17]Examples (e.g., Mead, 1932; Dennis, 1942) of research related to this issue, inspired by Piaget's studies of children's thought, have been discussed in Chapter Seven. Also see Price-Williams (1961) and Greenfield (1966) for studies of non-Western children's conservation of quantity and Jahoda (1958) for an investigation of West African children's concepts of immanent justice.

the topic of play and games, one of their associates—David Lancy—did have the opportunity to collect material on this aspect of Kpelle child and adult life (see particularly 1974 and 1975 and the discussion of Lancy's studies in Chapter Six). In "An Experimental Analysis of Riddles and Rule-Based Problem Solving" (1971), Lancy specifically discussed the relation of Kpelle riddles to problem-solving skills. In this paper, he described riddles that have no "right" answer. Instead, one person poses a riddle, and then anyone who wishes to may respond with an answer: "The correct answer is the one which seems most erudite and convincing as determined by consensus" (p. 2). A similar process occurs in the Kpelle jurisprudence system. In order to examine the context-based nature of this approach to riddle solving, Lancy formulated a riddle experiment. For example, he adapted a traditional Western problem to produce the following:

> A. Any time a rice farmer sees something in the bush it is his to keep.
> B. Sumo, the trapper, Flumo, the rice farmer and Goma Togba the hunter are walking in the bush beyond Kayata. They have been walking for three hours and since the sun is very hot they are tired. As they pass a clearing, Flumo spots a very large leopard. Sumo quickly makes a trap and with it catches the leopard. But the leopard is very angry and dangerous still, so Goma Togba must take his gun and kill it.
> C. Now, to which of these people does the leopard belong?
> D. Why? (p. 3)

Results from this experiment indicated that individuals who had not been exposed to Western schools ignored all stated rules and formulated lengthy and complex answers based on their own experience as well as material in the riddle. However, individuals who had been exposed to Western schools concentrated on the stated rule in formulating their answer. According to Lancy, these respondents "parroted" the rule back (e.g., "Well, you said that whatever a rice farmer sees in the bush is his to keep"), when asked for an explanation of their answer. It is significant to note here that Lancy left the question open as to which approach to riddle/problem-solving is "more intelligent":

> It might be interesting to speculate on which method of problem solution is more "intelligent," the traditional . . . method with its reliance on the individual's accumulated personal history versus the "modern" or scientific method which depends on the individual grasping some arbitrary externally-imposed rule, but I'll leave that to the reformers. The fact remains, however, that the drop-out rate in Liberian schools is enormous, and economic and social factors aside, it does seem reasonable to hypothesize that the difficulties associated with the change over to Western cognitive systems is partly responsible. (p. 7)

Unfortunately, while this research is significant because of its sensitivity to cultural matters, games (e.g., riddles) are treated as if they are a *context* only for the *expression* (and not the generation) of specific cognitive skills.

In another study reported by Eleanor Leacock, "At Play in African Villages" (1971), the potential of play for curriculum planning in Zambia is examined. Leacock was particularly interested in formulating educational experiences for children on the basis of their day-to-day activities, and specifically their play behavior. She suggested that in their play, children are already demonstrating their familiarity with a variety of concepts and behaviors (e.g., organization of roles and counting scores is demonstrated in games; ability to handle volume, area, and linear measurement is found in water play and play with tin cans and other objects; language is used in stories and songs; adult role play occurs in the "husband and wife" games; application of practical knowledge and technical skills is exhibited in the making and use of various toy objects; and various social and cognitive skills are exhibited in the children's version of *nsoro* or *mancala*).

In order to illustrate this argument, Leacock presented a description of girls' and boys' play activities observed in Matero, which is a large working-class suburb of Lusaka (the capital city of Zambia). She stated that boys are particularly ingenious in finding, collecting, and improvising various materials (e.g., wires, sticks, shoe-polish tins, cardboard) to produce see saws, poles for stilts, wagons, and miniature bicycles and cars. Another game, called *kapenta* (a fish dried for shipment) and described to Leacock by a 12-year-old girl, is an interesting comment on the multiple languages and dialects encountered in an urban context such as Lusaka. In this particular game, the players are selling *kapenta* and the plot develops in the following manner:

> One person in the game is Nsenga and the other Bemba [two of the many national groups in Zambia]. The Bemba sells the *kapenta* saying, "I am selling Kapenta." The Nsenga asks the Bemba what he is selling in Nsenga. The Bemba misunderstands, and a fight starts due to the misunderstanding of the languages. Someone who knows both languages comes to intervene in the fight between the two and explains what each one has said to the other. (p. 64)

All in all, this is an excellent brief ethnography of urban African children's play activities.

A recent study of natural indicators of cognitive development based on observations of rural Guatemalan children (Nerlove, Roberts, Klein, Yarbrough, and Habicht, 1974) also contains interesting information on play. In this research, the investigators suggested that there are natural indicators of differences in specific aspects of children's cognitive development. Furthermore they stated that children and adults can and do make judgments on the basis of these indicators, which "differentially affects the way in which children are socialized" (p. 266). Finally, it is proposed that associations between natural indicators (such as performance in a game) and performance on formal, but artificially constructed, psychological tests also exist. Two specific hypotheses are tested in this regard: (1) that self-managed sequences of behavior (at work or at play) will be related to analytic ability as measured on formal tests (e.g., adaptations of Embedded Figures Task, Matching Familiar Figures); and (2) that voluntary social activities will be related to language facility as measured in formal tests (e.g., adaptations of Peabody Picture Vocabulary Test, Verbal Analogies task) (see p. 287). In both cases, significant associations were found to obtain. The authors suggested that the indigenous "tracking" system that operates both consciously and unconsciously in a culture must be investigated if researchers wish to understand the complexity of a society's child-socialization practices. Additionally they believe that an understanding of this tracking or evaluative system might also be used to develop new programs and also tests in formal educational settings that would be experienced. as less alien by the child.

In relation to the concerns of this book, this article is significant because in order to explain their natural indicator approach, the authors presented a miniethnography of child life in the two rural Guatemalan villages of the study. Here specific attention was paid to both work and play activities as indicators of particular types of cognitive abilities (e.g., play is said to indicate self-managed sequencing of activity; play may require transformation of objects and/or social roles and communication of these transformations; play and games may also be indicators of the size of a child's "cognitive spatial map"). Once again, however, these researchers focused on the value of play as an *indicator*, not a *generator*, of children's cognitive abilities.

RHYMES AND REASONS: CHILDREN'S VERBAL PLAY

Even though infants play with language sounds long before they can speak recognizable words, the study of children's verbal play continues to be a neglected research topic. The field of speech play as the study of the variety of ways in which speech may be manipulated for its own sake (see Jakobson's 1960 definition of the "poetic function" of language) and recognized as play or art is a particularly impoverished research area in anthropology. This is due in large part to the fact that a researcher must be very familiar with a language before the subtleties and nuances of usage, tone, and so forth, on which much linguistic play depends, are understood. In a 1964 review of the anthropological study of verbal play, Dell Hymes observed the following:

> On the whole, studies with this specific orientation have been lacking in American linguistics and anthropology. Speech play and verbal art have come to attention mainly by obtruding upon the ordinary course of linguistic and ethnographic analysis and through the collection and analysis of texts. (p. 291)

Fortunately, an excellent survey of ethnographic studies of speech play has recently been presented by Barbara Kirshenblatt-Gimblett. In *Speech Play* (1976b) Kirshenblatt-Gimblett included a detailed review of the literature on this subject and also eight original articles discussing the following topics: play languages used by speakers of Cuna, French, and Javanese (J. Sherzer, pp. 19–36); play languages spoken by the Saramaka Maroons in Surinam (R. and S. Price, pp. 37–50); Zinacanteco joking strategies (V. Bricker, pp. 51–62); Texas children's traditional speech-play forms (M. Sanches and B. Kirshenblatt-Gimblett, pp. 65–110); a developmental–structural analysis of Ohio children's riddles (B. Sutton-Smith, pp. 111–120); verbal dueling games in Chamula, a Mayan Indian community located in the Chiapas Highlands of southern Mexico (G. Gossen, pp. 121–146); the use of a mnemonic word-play technique for the memorization of numbers in Japanese (A. Backhouse, pp. 149–162); and gnomic expressions in Samuel Beckett's novel *Molloy* (D. Sherzer, pp. 163–171).

Two comprehensive surveys of children's speech play are available in this book. In "Children's Traditional Speech Play and Child Language," Sanches and Kirshenblatt-Gimblett presented a review of studies of speech play in English. Here an examination of children's lore (i.e., traditions transmitted from child to child) and *not* nursery lore (i.e., traditions transmitted from adult to child) (see Opie and Opie, 1959:1) is presented. Also included in this volume is an extensive bibliographic survey of the literature on all forms of speech play by Kirshenblatt-Gimblett (pp. 179–222) (see Hymes, 1964:303–304, for an earlier discussion of this subject).

Sanches and Kirshenblatt-Gimblett offered a sociolinguistic analysis of children's speech play in their article, which is included in this volume. Here they specifically analyzed the differences that exist between these forms and adult verbal art. The authors argued that these differences can best be understood by examining the differences between adult and child language structures. In their view, a child's developing language system is not just quantitatively different than an adult's (e.g., children's language is syntagmatically shorter and less complex than adults'), but it is also qualitatively different (1976:76–77).[18] In the authors' opinion, child speech is characterized by emphasis on the phonological component of language, and it is this component that is "much more strongly organized than the syntactic, semantic, or sociolinguistic" (p. 77).

The authors illustrated their argument by comparing characteristics of children's speech play with adult verbal art productions. The limited nature of the child's developing syntagmatic organization is said to be exhibited by the relatively short length of their play utterances (which the authors reported range from 7 words or less to 60 or 70 words) as compared with adult productions, which can last for hours (p. 87). Additionally, stylistic devices that children use are much less complex and more often irregular than those of adults (e.g., children frequently use rhyming couplets as opposed to more complex rhyme schemes or stanzaic structures, p. 87). Examples of differences between child and adult productions in regard to use of concatenations, expansion, and also differences in the organization of the semantic system are also discussed.

The authors suggested that phonological structure may be the "strongest influence on the shape of early preferred children's speech play forms" (p. 92). This interest in playing with phonology (as opposed to semantics or syntax) reflects the fact that phonology is more developed in the child's language. Therefore, it is the state of the child's linguistic development that determines the nature of his/her speech-play productions. This concern with phonology is illustrated by distinguishing two types of nonsense rhymes. *Gibberish rhymes* are commonly used by children, and here "only the phonological rules are observed: the phonological sequences neither form units which have grammatical function nor lexemes with semantic reference" (p. 92). The following jump rope rhyme is an example of gibberish:

> *Inty, ninty, tibbety fig*
> *Deema dima doma nig*
> *Howchy powchy domi nowday*
> *Hom tom tout*
> *Olligo bolligo boo*
> *Out goes you.*
> (pp. 92–93)

Jabberwocky rhymes, on the other hand, are produced by adults and ob-

---

[18]For a recent review of studies of child language, see Blount (1975). Also see Keenen (1974) for a discussion of the playful character of early speech.

serve both phonological and syntactic rules. Lewis Carroll's poem entitled "Jabberwocky" is said to be the classic example of these rhymes:

> 'Twas brillig, and the slithy toves
> Did gyre and gimble in the wabe:
> All mimsy were the borogoves,
> And the mome raths outgrabe.
> (1871)

Numerous other examples of children's interest in phonological
structure, as reflected in their rhymes and verses, are offered. Adults are
seldom amused by these creations, but children repeat them endlessly
and apparently with great pleasure. For example, the simple question
"Did you ever in your life see the devil kiss his wife?" can become for the
child a hilarious exercise in phonological elaboration:

> Did you eever, iver, over,
> In your leaf, life, loaf,
> See the devil, divel, dovel,
> Kiss his weef, wife, woaf?
>
> No, I neever, niver, nover,
> In my leef, life, loaf,
> Saw the deevel, divel, dovel,
> Kiss his weef, wife, woaf.
> (p. 94)

Rhymes that play with words that are similar in sound but different
meaning also illustrate this interest in phonology:

> I scream,
> You scream,
> We all scream,
> For ice cream.
> (p. 95)

Children's puns are also influenced by this concern. In "true" puns,
according to the authors, "perfectly homonymous elements [must] be
used to produce two well-formed syntactic representations and thus two
possible semantic interpretations" (p. 96). For example,

$$\text{Many a blond } \genfrac{}{}{0pt}{}{(\text{dies})}{(\text{dyes})} \text{ by her own hand. (p. 96)}$$

In contrast, children's puns are created only on the basis of phonological
resemblence, while the grammatical functions of the lexemes eliminate
the ambiguity necessary for a true pun (pp. 95–96):

> Do you carrot all for me?
> My heart beets for you.

> *With your turnip nose.*
> *And your radish face*
> *You are a peach.*
> *Lettuce marry*
> *Weed make a swell pear.*
> (p. 95)

The authors also illustrated their argument by offering examples of older (over 8 years) children's speech play, where grammatical, and later semantic and sociolinguistic, concerns are dominant and length of utterance increases. For example, play with semantic relations is evidenced in the following rhyme repeated by an 11-year-old:

> *Ladies and jelly-beans, hobos and tramps,*
> *Cross-eyed mosquitos and bow-legged ants,*
> *I come before ye to stand behind ye,*
> *To tell ye something I know nothing about.*
> *There's going to be a ladies' meeting*
> *Friday, Easter Sunday.*
> *Men admitted free.*
> *Pay at the door.*
> *Pull up a chair and sit on the floor.*
> *We're going to talk about the four corners of the round table.*
> *When Columbus sailed the Missisolopy River in a punch bowl,*
> *With the Star Spangled Banana in one hand,*
> *And the Declaration of Indigestion in the other.*
> (pp. 103–104)

Also beginning at age 8 or 9, the development of parody rhymes of adult figures, institutions, or activities (see discussion of play as satire in Chapter Six) is said to occur.

There are a variety of other studies of children's verbal play available in the literature. A few of these investigations appear to corroborate the sociolinguistic–developmental analysis of Sanches and Kirshenblatt-Gimblett; however, for the most part, these studies have been made by collectors who have not provided information on the ages of their informants. These reports are briefly described below, organized roughly on the basis of developmental age and then on type of speech play described.

The speech play of very young children has only occasionally been investigated. Certainly one of the most intriguing studies made to date is the linguist Ruth Weir's analysis of her 2½-year-old son Anthony's bedtime monologues (*Language in the Crib*, 1962).[19] Although the extent

---

[19]For a discussion and comparison of adult babytalk (i.e., the style of speech that adults adopt in order to talk to infants) in six different languages, see Ferguson (1964).

and quality of Anthony's sound play may have been unusual, the importance of phonological structure for the generation of this speech play is well-illustrated by these productions and in Weir's analysis (p. 103, and also Sanches and Kirshenblatt-Gimblett, 1976:78). In illustrating the "linguistic sense in the child's nonsense," Weir focused on the importance of sound play for Anthony's productions. In one of the collected texts, Anthony made the following association:

> Babette
> Back here
> Wet

Weir suggested that Anthony was using the name *Babette* here because the syllables alliterate and have rhythm. In order to illustrate this, she analyzed the rest of the sequence in the following manner:

> *Back* of the next line repeats the alliterating /b/, followed not only by the same phoneme /E/ as in the second syllable of *Babette*, but also by the same phonetic variant [E] which again occurs in the third line, *wet*. The alveolar /t/ of the first line is changed to velar /k/ in the second, but /t/ reappears in the third line where the bilabiality of the preceding two initial /b/'s is again reflected in the glide /w/. (1962:105)

Weir also illustrated Anthony's play with grammatical patterns (e.g., noun substitution, pronominal substitution, verb substitution, plural formation). Roman Jakobson, in commenting on Anthony's productions in the introduction to this study, suggested that this bedtime play is strikingly similar to the grammatical and lexical exercises one finds in textbooks for self-instruction in foreign languages (p. 19). This is seen in productions such as the following: "What color—What color blanket—What color mop—What color glass. . . . Not the yellow blanket—the white. . . . It's not black—it's yellow. . . . Not yellow—red" (p. 19).

Chukovsky's analysis of the verbal play of Russian children (ages 2–5), discussed in Chapter Six, is (like Weir's) one of the few detailed examinations of very young children's speech-play activities. Garvey (1977:59–76) also presented an interesting analysis of American preschool-aged children's play with language and language forms on the basis of her research material, which has been discussed in Chapter Eight. Here she described various types of sound play, nonsense productions, and play with conversational forms. One of the most interesting examples described was produced by two children (boy 5:2, girl 5:4) and is characterized by rhyming and play with word shape and prosodic features. In this sequence, the children were wandering around the room while handling a variety of objects.

(In this text the symbols `\and\` indicate high falling and low falling pitch; `\and\` high rising and low rising; and `\and\` indicate high rising–falling and low rising–falling pitch, respectively.)

Boy

1. And when Melanie
   and . . . and you will be in
   here you have to be 'grand
   \mother 'grand ₍mother.
   'Right?

3. ₍Grand͡ mother grand͡ mother
   ₍grand ₍mother.

5. ₍Grand͡ mother ₍grand ₍mother
   ₍grand ₍mother.

7. ₍Momma.

10. 'Hey.

(laugh)

13. 'Peer.

15. ₍Pooper.

17. ₍Pooper. Now 'that's a . . .
    'that's a good ₍name.

Girl

2. I'll have to be ₍grand ₎momma
   ₍grand ₎momma 'grand ₍momma.
   (in distorted voice)

4. ₍Grand͡ momma ₍grand ₍momma
   ₍grand ₍momma.

6. ₍Grand͡ momma ₍grand ₍mother
   ₍grand ₍momma.

8. ͡Momma̍ I. . . . my ₍mommy
   ₍momma
9. ₍Mother ₍humpf.

11. 'Mother 'mear (laugh) 'mother
    'smear.

12. I said 'mother 'smear ₍mother
    ₍near ₍mother ₍tear 'mother 'dear.
    (laugh)

14. 'Fear.

16. 'What?

(pp. 68–69).

In my own research (e.g., Schwartzman, 1973), also with pre-school-aged children, a variety of speech-play forms were observed. These were designated as a specific *genre* of play called *name games*. Frequently these name games would spontaneously begin when the children were sitting at the classroom tables involved in some form of sedentary activity such as eating, drawing, painting, or pasteing. The following is an example of playful noun substitution.

Andrew (4:10): Today we're having   Sonia (5): No! Today we're having
pears for dessert.   pajamas for dessert.

A: No! Today we're having tables   S: No! Today we're having chairs
for dessert.   for dessert.

In *Children's Humor: A Psychological Analysis* (1954), Martha Wolfenstein described the development of children's styles of verbal humor interpreted from a psychoanalytic perspective. This research is based on interviews with 145 children from two New York City private schools. The children were between the ages of 4 and 17 and came predominantly from professional families. Wolfenstein suggested that the preschool-aged child's humor focuses on play with the ambiguity of words as particularly expressed in proper names. For example, she cited an instance in which she was introduced to a group of 5- and 6-year-olds, who immediately began to play on the last syllable of her name: "Stains!" "Everything you put on you stains!" (p. 75). Four-year-olds are said to specialize in making "a joke of shifting the reference of proper names, playfully asserting that Mary is Johnny and vice versa" (p. 19). An earlier form of this type of joke is said to be evidenced by 3-year-olds, who enjoy the practice of reversing sex, that is, calling a girl a boy and vice versa. At the age of 6 (the onset of latency), children begin to acquire a repertoire of joking riddles, according to Wolfenstein. These riddles are said to reflect their concern with smartness and dumbness, as they serve "the function of demonstrating that they are smart and the other fellow, who does not know the answer, is dumb" (p. 20). These riddles are themselves parodies of the question–answer format, and frequently the main protagonist is "the moron":

> Why did the moron tiptoe past the medicine cabinet? Because he didn't want to wake the sleeping pills. (p. 105)

> Why did the moron throw the clock out the window?
> Because he wanted to see the time fly. (p. 116)

Several of the joking riddles that Wolfenstein described are interesting comments on the historical era of her research and are therefore less commonly repeated today:

> Why did the moron put the TV on the stove?
> Because he wanted to see Milton Boil.
>   Or:
> Because he wanted to see Arthur Godfry.
>   Or:
> Because he wanted to see Hopalong Cassidy ride the range. (p. 101)

In adolescence a new form of humor becomes popular as anecdotes and comic mimicry replace joking riddles. At this stage, the joke teller impersonates the characters in the joke because he/she "does not need to dissociate himself from them as drastically as latency children do in the case of the moron" (p. 21). Following Freud's analysis of jokes (see 1905), Wolfenstein stated that the basic motive of children's humor is "the wish to transform a painful experience and to extract pleasure from it" (1954:18). In analyzing the devices children use to produce such transformations, she concentrated particularly on the relationship of children to adults and the disappointment, envy of size and power, and general "wish-to-be-grown-up" feelings that she assumes all children experience.

School-aged children's speech play has received considerably more research attention. The most detailed and extensive collection for this age group is certainly Iona and Peter Opies' analysis of British children's verbal play (The Lore and Language of Schoolchildren, 1959), which has been discussed in Chapter Five. There are, however, a number of other studies available, particularly of non-Western children's speech play, which can be described on the basis of the type of play discussed. In this brief survey, particular attention will be paid to how the various components of speech-play forms have been analyzed as communicative events by researchers (e.g., the participants, channels, codes, settings, message forms and genres, attitudes and contents, and the event; see Hymes, 1974:10).

Play Languages

This speech-play form has been defined by Sherzer (1976) as "the creation of a linguistic code based on the language usually employed by the participants and derived from the language by a series of definable rules" (pp. 19–20). Play languages therefore play with the shared linguistic code of a population, and generally this is done by producing phonological transformations of this code. Americans are probably most familiar with the term pig Latin for these languages (see Hirschberg, 1913; Berkovits, 1970), although they are also referred to as "secret languages" or "secret codes" (Opie and Opie, 1959), "disguised speech" (M. Haas, 1967), "linguistic games" (Burling, 1970), "ludlings" (Laycock, 1972), and "speech disguise" (Conklin, 1956) in the literature. Jargon, argots, slang, ceremonial languages, and dialect humor were also discussed as play languages by Kirshenblatt-Gimblett (1976a). Van Gennep (1908) presented one of the earliest theoretical appraisals of "special languages," while more recently, M. Haas (1967) and Laycock (1972) have offered taxonomies of these languages. Most researchers argue that this speech play is developed for the purpose of concealment and the resulting effect of creating an "in-group" and an "out-group" (although, as will be seen below, this is not always their purpose). Therefore the statuses of the participants, as well as the contexts in which the events occur, are important for analysis (see Conklin, 1964). In this regard, it is possible to suggest that children use play languages as a way to exclude adults from their activities and also to reverse the normal status hierarchy by making children the "in-group" and adults the "out-group."

Play languages have been reported in a variety of cultures and are probably much more widespread than the literature available indicates. Centner's (1962) discussion of secret languages in central Africa has already been described. Examples of other reports for African groups are Delafosse (1922), Trevor (1955), and Leiris (1948). Play languages are also described by Conklin (1964) for the Hanunoo in the Philippines; M. Haas (1969) for Burma; Richard and Sally Price (1976) for the Saramaka Maroons in Surinam; Pike (1945) for the Mixteco Indians; and Yakir (1973) for Israeli children.

Sherzer (1976) presented an interesting analysis of the significance of play languages, as used by children, for sociolinguistic studies. In this article, he described play languages from three different speech communities: Cuna, French, and Javanese. The Cuna data was collected on the islands of Mulatupu and Niatupu in San Blas, Panama, and a more extensive analysis is available in Sherzer (1970). Five play languages are described for Cuna speakers, who refer to this speech as *sorsik summakke* ("talking backwards") or *ottukkuar sunmakke* ("concealed talking"). One example of "talking backwards" requires that the speaker take the first syllable of a word and place it at the end of the word. A number of examples of word transformations produced by this one rule are offered:

> osi "pineapple"—sio
> ope "to bathe"—peo
> takke "to see"—ketak (1976:21)

According to Sherzer, Cuna children do not use these languages to keep secrets or conceal things from each other; instead he suggested that it seems to be a "form of linguistic play for play's sake" (p. 35).

The play language discussed for French speakers is a much more complicated example of code switching. This *langage à l'envers* (or "backwards language") is spoken by French adolescents and is therefore based on the colloquial slang that they speak. Additionally, when it is used by French gangs, the source words may be in the argot limited to the gang. In this case,

> a double code is involved: in order to decipher what is said in the play language, one must first move back up the play derivation rules to the source word and then translate the source word from the special gang argot, into standard French. (p. 34)

One example of this backwards language involves the switching of syllables and the deletion of function words (e.g., prepositions). For example, *peau de balle* ("nothing") becomes *balpeau; l'envers* ("backwards") becomes *verlan* (the name of the play language in the code); *mari* ("husband") becomes *rima;* and *cul* ("ass") becomes *luc* (p. 25). Other more complicated versions of *verlan* are also discussed.

Seven different types of Javanese play languages have been described by Sherzer. One type requires that "every vowel of the source word [be] . . . followed by a syllable which consists of *f* plus a repetition of the vowel" (p. 27). For example:

> aku arep tuku klambi ("I want to buy a dress") > afaku afarekep tufukifu klafambifi. (p. 27)

Another version is truly a backwards language, as every word is pronounced backwards:

> bocah iku dolanan asu ("The boy is playing with a dog") > hacob uki nanalod usa. (p. 29)

In analyzing these languages, Sherzer argued that play languages are important to study in and of themselves, but they also provide information on various issues in linguistics, sociolinguistics, and the ethnography of communication. For example, he suggested that these forms are particularly striking cases "of creativity in language use, especially when one considers that the play languages in question are usually played by relatively young children" (p. 31). The variation in speaking play languages that occurs also "strongly suggests the possibility that there is a corresponding variation in native speaker linguistic models," an issue of concern to both linguists and psychologists (pp. 32–33). Sherzer suggested that studies of play languages also provide investigators with information on the nature and learning of linguistic rules and also "the ethnographic patterns involved in speech use" (p. 36).

Verbal Dueling

Anthropologists have long been interested in formalized joking relationships (see Radcliffe-Brown, 1952; Douglas, 1968), which can range from mild teasing to full-scale verbal battles. For the most part, these studies have been concerned with *who* is doing the joking rather than how, about what, and why the joking occurs (Kirshenblatt-Gimblett 1976a:203). These studies have not been motivated by sociolinguistic concerns, and so attention has been paid only to the participants involved in the exchange and not to the forms of the messages, the permissible settings, or the channels and codes, which are also features of this activity. Ritualized insults or verbal duels engaged in by children or adolescents have been less frequently described in the ethnographic or folklore literature. However, there are several reports available that are significant, particularly Abrahams's (1962) study of "playing the dozens" in American black communities and Labov's (1974) more recent sociolinguistic analysis of "sounding" (also called "the dozens," "signifying," "chopping," "joining," and "woofing") as a speech event in the black English vernacular (BEV). Verbal dueling has most frequently been reported to occur among adolescent males, and its purpose is generally to establish a hierarchy or pecking order (see Abrahams, 1962; Gossen, 1976; Dundes, Leach, and Ozkök, 1970). This is in contrast to the privileged disrespect of joking relationships, which reverses or attacks the ordinary hierarchical relations of a society (see Douglas, 1968) also Kirshenblatt-Gimblett 1976a:204–205).

Dundes, Leach, and Ozkök (1970) presented an extensive account of the strategies used by Turkish boys (ages 8–14) in verbal contests, which are found throughout Turkey. In presenting this analysis, the authors commented that "it seems incredible that none of the anthropologists who have conducted fieldwork in Turkey have so much as mentioned the tradition" (p. 326). The goal of the duel "is to force one's opponent into a female, passive role," which is usually achieved by "casting him as a submissive anus" or less directly by disparaging or threatening the opponent's mother and sister (p. 326). Additionally, "the retort must rhyme with the immediately preceding insult," as in the following example:

> Speaker A *Ayi*
>   bear
> Speaker B *Sana girsin   keman yayi*
>   you to enter let it violin bow. (p. 327)

In this exchange "You bear" (connotation, "You clumsy, big, stupid animal") is said to be a commonly used insult in Turkey, and the authors stated that there are only two traditional retorts to this opening insult. The one demonstrated here translates as "May the bow of a violin enter your ass," in which *yayi* ("bow") rhymes with *ayi* ("bear") (p. 328). In this article, a variety of insult sequences or routines are described, and the strategies (i.e., choice of retort from traditional repertoire, response to "break elements" in opponents' statements, innovative retorts, and so forth) are also discussed.

Other reports available are Ayoub and Barnett's (1965) description of ritualized verbal insults used by a group of Anglo-American adolescents; Focks's (1958) description of verbal duels among the Waiwai; Devereaux's (1951) discussion of "friendly quarrels" among the Mohave; P. S. Stevens's (1976) discussion of Bachama song contests; and Eskimo song duels reported by Elliot (1960) and Chamberlain (1910).

Gossen's (1976) detailed description of the genre "truly frivolous talk" spoken in the Mayan community of Chamula (the language spoken is Tzotzil) is one of the most recent and most interesting descriptions of verbal dueling available. Duelers in Chamula are always males, generally between the ages of 12 and 35. Gossen reported, however, that he heard "feeble attempts" at duels from children as young as 2 or 3. At the age of 5 or 6, young boys are said to become more proficient in this game, but they are generally able only to repeat memorized sequences and so are quickly "beaten" by an older child who is able to handle improvisations. Gossen indicated that his own "level of competence in performing the genre was at about the level of a six year old" (pp. 142–143). The rules are somewhat similar to those described for Turkish duels, as they require "a minimum sound shift combined with a maximum derogatory or obscene attack on the opponent" (p. 129). Unlike Dundes, Leach, and Ozkök's (1970) examples, which were simulated duels (although based on the experience of Ozkök), Gossen presented one lengthy text of a dueling event that occurred during a fiesta and was recorded verbatim by a Chamula assistant. A brief excerpt (starting with the 14th exchange of this text, which included 65 exchanges) is included here, where boxes □ and arrows ↓ indicate the required sound continuity, and the translation and/or explanatory notes describe the necessary semantic continuity. The players were two 17-year-old boys, who were both bachelors and also close friends:

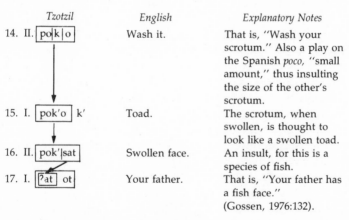

Tzotzil	English	Explanatory Notes
14. II. po|k|o	Wash it.	That is, "Wash your scrotum." Also a play on the Spanish *poco*, "small amount," thus insulting the size of the other's scrotum.
15. I. pok'o k'	Toad.	The scrotum, when swollen, is thought to look like a swollen toad.
16. II. pok'|sat	Swollen face.	An insult, for this is a species of fish.
17. I. ʔat ot	Your father.	That is, "Your father has a fish face." (Gossen, 1976:132).

According to Gossen, the humorous items of "truly frivolous talk," as demonstrated by these texts, relate to one theme: they all stress what the brother-in-law relationship (players assume a fictive brother-in-law relationship with one another) and the adult male sexual role should *not* be (p. 138). In this sense, then, these duels may also be seen as joking reversals or parodies of proper adult male behavior. Gossen also suggested that Chamula verbal dueling is important for the socialization process in general and for the learning of language in particular. Eloquence is highly valued in Chamula society, and "truly frivolous talk" as a secular genre helps to prepare players for mastery of the structures and rhythms of the formal genres: "language for rendering holy," "prayer," "true ancient words," and "song" (p. 143).

Riddles

Following Wolfenstein's suggestion, it is possible to view riddles as parodies of all question–answer message forms. The relationship that is most obviously being satirized is that between teacher and child, but this extends to all adult–child interaction. In "A Developmental–Structural Account of Riddles" (1976a), Sutton-Smith suggested that riddles are most likely to appear in cultural contexts in which adults quiz children orally and in which children are required to be attentive and responsive (p. 111). A recent cross-cultural analysis of riddles by Roberts and Forman (1971) appears to support this view, as riddles are found to exist in cultures that emphasize rote learning from authority figures and also oral interrogation of children by these figures. Sutton-Smith proposed in his study that riddles are "fun" for children because "their incongruities model, in a safe way, the larger process of adult interrogation and ambiguity" (1976a:111). A riddle is defined as "a puzzling question with an arbitrary answer," but this definition is also expanded in a variety of ways (p. 115; also see p. 119). On the basis of his collection of a large sample of Ohio children's riddles, Sutton-Smith proceeded to analyze this material by using Piaget's categories of classification. Here Sutton-Smith was particularly concerned with examining how the specific semantic devices of riddles "give the riddler the materials for his exercise of arbitrary power in the rhetorical context" (p. 113). In this way, seven different types of riddles are discussed: preriddles ("Why did the man chop down the chimney?" "He needed the bricks"); implicit reclassifications or homonymic riddles ("Why did the dog go out in the sun?" "He wanted to be a hot dog"); riddle parodies ("Why did the chicken cross the road?" "He wanted to get to the other side"); inverted relationships ("What does one flea say to another as they go strolling?" "Shall we walk or take the dog"); explicit reclassifications or homonymic oppositional riddles ("What has an ear but cannot hear?" "Corn"); classifications on the basis of noncritical attributes ("White inside and red outside?" "An apple"); and multiple classifications ("What is the difference between a teacher and an engineer?" "One trains the mind and the other minds the train").

Riddles have been analyzed and categorized by a number of other researchers. For example, Georges and Dundes (1963) distinguished types of riddles on the basis of whether they are "metaphorical" or "literal" and "oppositional" or "nonoppositional." Gowlett (1968) has used this scheme to classify Lozi riddles. More recently, Abrahams and Dundes (1972) have expanded on this classification scheme. Structural analyses of the relationship between the riddle and its answers have been presented by Hamnett (1967), E. K. and P. Maranda (1971), Todorov (1973), and Bailey (1974). Examples of studies concentrating on children's riddles are Shultz (1974) for Canadian children; Weiner (1970) for Massachusetts children; McDowell (1974) for Mexican-American children; Lancy (1973) and Kulah (1973) for Kpelle children; and Isbell and Fernandez (1977) for Quechua-speaking adolescents in the south central highlands of Peru.

Vocabulary Games

Speech play can frequently serve an important language-learning function. Mary Haas presented an important analysis of this play form in a non-Western culture in her article "Thai Word Games" (1964). Here she described two types of games that help to enlarge the children's vocabulary either in Thai (identical-initial-syllable game) or in English (rhyming-translation game). The first game is played by younger children in the following manner. One child picks a word, such as *sabaaj* ("to be well, comfortable"), and the other player(s) must then repeat other *sa-* words, such as *sabuu* ("soap") and *saduag* ("to be convenient"). The game can be complicated by specifying syllable (e.g., *kra-*) and also reference (e.g., birds and animals). The rhyming-translation game is played by older children. In this game, the players can begin with either an English or a Thai word. If a Thai word is chosen, the player must give the English translation, and the next player must produce a Thai word that rhymes with the English translation. For example,

| 1st player: | "kob" | pleewaa (means) | "frog" |
| 2nd player: | "hòog" | pleewaa (means) | "spear" |

(p. 302)

In both games, "losers" are players who cannot supply the required word when their turn arrives.

Children's number games and counting-out rhymes have also been the focus of a number of collections. For example, studies are available by Boyce and Bartlett (1940), Gullen (1950), Bolton (1888), Goldstein (1971), and Brewster (1939).

Narratives

Children's stories and storytelling devices have recently been analyzed by a number of researchers. Several of these studies (e.g., Sutton-Smith, 1974a; Botvin, 1976) have already been discussed; however, there are some interesting investigations of non-Western children's stories also available. One particularly intriguing narrative form found only among Uupik-speaking Eskimos of Southwestern Alaska is referred to as "storyknifing" (Oswalt, 1964; Ager, 1974, 1975). Ager presented a description of the performance context, types, and styles of knife stories and their game features in "Play as Folklore: An Alaskan Eskimo Example" (1975). These stories are told by girls between the ages of 5 and 13 while they are sitting in a circle, using a knife to draw the setting, characters, objects, actions, etc., on the ground in the mud or snow. For example, a house may be drawn in "blueprint style" and various objects will be designated and catalogued: "Here's the bed; here's the table" and so forth (p. 16). As the story develops, the narrator uses her knife to draw new objects or characters or to indicate actions such as walking or talking. Three different categories of tales are recognized: (1) old-time tales; (2) "scary" stories; and (3) made-up stories or everyday happenings (p. 17). Ager reported that creative and innovative stories that captivate an audience because of the plot and/or the storyteller's style and voice inflection are highly valued by these Eskimo girls.

Oswalt's (1964) earlier analysis of Eskimo girls' storyknife tales includes presentations of 41 complete texts and also illustrations for 9 of the stories. The plots of these knife stories are more traditional and conventional than those found in Ager's more recent research. The moral for these tales is "obey your elders," and for a Yuk girl this meant "obey your grandmother" (who was traditionally responsible for the child's education). In these stories, a plot generally develops in which a grandmother tells a granddaughter *not* to do something or go somewhere, but the granddaughter does so anyway, and the grandmother dies.

Examples of other studies of children's narratives have been presented by Ames (1966), Pitcher and Prelinger (1963), and Wolfenstein (1954); and specific sociolinguistic analyses are offered by Sacks (1972), Watson (1972), and Watson-Gegeo and Boggs (1977) (the last two reports are investigations of Hawaiian children's stories). Examples of children's speech-play forms that are not discussed in this chapter are jump rope rhymes (see Chapter Five) and puns, tongue twisters, word puzzles, nicknames, curses, and obscenities (see Kirshenblatt-Gimblett, 1976a).

SUMMARY

Beginning in the 1950s and continuing to the present, anthropologists have increasingly adopted linguistic metaphors for their analyses of culture. In utilizing this approach, ethnographers assume that culture is to be found in the minds (cognitive models or mental structures) of their informants. These structures are discovered in a variety of ways, for example, from an analysis of people's names for things and the organization of these names into larger groupings, or from an examination of structures as these are reflected in mythic texts and kinship or classification systems.

Kenneth Pike's distinction between etic and emic units of analysis can be used to clarify the difference between studies that adopt the "native" or internal emic perspective and those that utilize external or etic criteria. This contrast can be used to differentiate the variety of structural analyses of children's play and games that are available. Studies that focus solely on the player's perspective (the emic view) are relatively rare. Recently, however, interesting investigations have been made by researchers employing the approach of ethnoscience for a study of American (Parrott, 1972) and Yucatán (e.g., von Glascoe, 1975a,b) children's games. Examples of structural studies of play or games where the significant features of the game have been formulated by the researcher (the etic view) are much more numerous. Huizinga's (1938) classic definition and Caillois's (1961) well-known categorization of play and games both exemplify this approach in their delineation of "play elements" (Huizinga) and "play types" (Caillois). More recent structural analyses of children's games and narratives (e.g., Redl, 1959; Dundes, 1964b; Sutton-Smith, 1974a, 1975b; Botvin, 1977; Abrams and Sutton-Smith, 1977) also illustrate this orientation. In these studies, children play the games or tell the stories, which the researchers then proceed to examine or "dissect." In these instances, children do not analyze, categorize, or otherwise comment on their own games or stories.

The structural analyses of certain anthropologists converge, in part, with many psychologists' interest in the study of cognition. Jean Piaget has created a field, which he calls "genetic epistemology," to designate his research on the development of intelligence in children. In Piaget's theory, play acts are characterized by assimilation, as opposed to accommodation, which is the other pole of his cognitive dialectic. In this schema, play is viewed as a behavior that distorts "objective" reality, and therefore, according to Piaget, it serves an expressive but not a generative role in the constitution of thought in the child. Piaget's theory of play is particularly interesting for consideration here not because it adds significantly to our understanding of relationships between play and learning, but because it provides us with a unique perspective on a researcher-at-play.

A variety of views as to the relationship between play and learning have been proposed. These studies emphasize either the deuterolearning qualities of play (e.g., learning new relationships between meanings and objects, Vygotsky, 1967; learning the idea of frames or contexts, Bateson, 1956; learning representational sets, Sutton-Smith, 1967); or the learning of specific contents or skills (e.g., problem-solving skills, Sylva, Bruner, and Genova, 1976). Recently, a few studies of non-Western societies have appeared in which games are viewed as contexts for the display or expression of certain cognitive skills (e.g., Lancy, 1971; Leacock, 1971; Nerlove et al., 1975). These studies appear to grant play only an expressive role in the development of these skills. In this way, these investigations are similar to those of the culture and personality researchers discussed in Chapter Seven, who viewed play as expressive of children's feelings and personalities. Also following in this tradition are a number of researchers and educators who advocate using explicitly designed educational games as teaching (e.g., Coleman, 1971) or as learning diagnostic contexts.

Studies of Western children's verbal play have been formulated only rarely by psychologists, although there are several descriptive reports (i.e., text collections) available in the folklore literature. Studies of non-Western children's play have also been neglected by anthropologists; however, this may be accounted for in part by the language problem. Fortunately, a few psychologists (e.g., Sutton-Smith, 1976a) and anthropologists (e.g., Sanches and Kirschenblatt-Gimblett, 1976) have recently developed an interest in the study of children's speech play. Many of these recent investigations employ linguistic or sociolinguistic models in their analysis of this linguistic phenomenon, and emphasis is placed on the study of texts in context. One of the best examinations of young children's speech play has been formulated by a linguist, using her 2½-year-old son as her informant (Weir, 1962). A variety of forms of older children's speech play exist, and these have been described and analyzed by several researchers (e.g., secret languages, verbal dueling, riddles, vocabulary games, and narratives and stories).

The approach of structuralist and cognitive play researchers is extremely varied. These investigations do, however, converge on one point, and that is that play is a phenomenon of the mind. In this case, mental structures may be reflected in the words or categories that players use to describe their own activities, or that researchers use to describe these players' actions. Play is also viewed as cognitive activity that may be expressive or generative of both general and specific cognitive skills. This orientation is significant because it suggests that the perspective or viewpoint adopted in a study (i.e., the player's or the researcher's) is extremely important. On the whole, this research tradition has focused on analyses of play texts and their "dissection," but there are also many studies available that examine play contexts (particularly psychological functions). In minding play, however, many researchers have developed the White Knight's habit of standing or falling "head downwards" for much too long. In the process, they have *assimilated* play to their own brand of structural/cognitive theories (which are, of course, their "inventions") rather than *accommodating* to the "realities" of play.

CHAPTER TEN

Defining Play: Ecology, Ethology, and Experiments

> *"When I use a word,"* Humpty Dumpty said, *in rather a scorn-ful tone, "it means just what I choose it to mean—neither more nor less."*
> *"The question is,"* said Alice, *"whether you* can *make words mean so many different things."*
> *"The question is,"* said Humpty Dumpty, *"which is to be mas-ter—that's all."*
> Lewis Carroll, *Through the Looking-Glass, and What Alice Found There*

It has recently become fashionable for researchers to bemoan the lack of an operational definition for play. For example, John Buettner-Janusch, in commenting on the published series of papers delivered at the 1973 American Anthropological Association meetings on the topic "The Anthropological Study of Human Play" (see Norbeck, 1974b) made the following statement:

> I want to know several things which the participants, the authors, have not told us. First, I want to know if they are able to construct an operational definition of play. I do not see any such definition in the papers and I am convinced that such a definition is essential. (p. 94)

And in a recent survey of psychological studies of play and exploration, Weisler and McCall (1976) suggested that there has been a form of scientific "stagflation" in the literature dealing with these topics, whereby the number of articles has increased yearly but there has been a "recession" in the production of knowledge. According to these authors,

> This state of affairs derives at least in part from a lack of precise definitions of concepts and from a near total absence of comprehensive theory. Indeed,

almost every review of this area begins with an apology for not being able to objectively define the concepts to be discussed—exploration or play. (p. 492)

This "definitional problem" has concerned many, and some researchers, exasperated by their own or others' attempts to formulate *the* definition of play, have suggested that it be eliminated as a useful category of investigation. Schlosberg argued as early as 1947 that "the category of 'playful activity' is so loose that it is almost useless for modern psychology" (p. 215), and Berlyne suggested in a 1969 review of studies of laughter, humor, and play that "Psychology would do well to give up the category of play in favor of both wider and narrower categories of behavior" (p. 843). In fact, it is possible to suggest that these researchers' exasperation with and characterizations of the "state" of the research literature on play are themselves the best definitions of this subject (as well as evidence that something is actually *there*), for they complain that the category is too "loose" (Schlosberg, 1947) or that the studies are "a discordant polyphony" (Berlyne, 1969), a "cognitive haze" (Gramza, 1972), "unsystematic" (Weisler and McCall, 1976) or "fuzzy" (Buettner-Janusch, in Norbeck, 1974b). Perhaps play's evasion of investigators' attempts to capture it definitionally is itself a suggestive clue as to what its nature may be.

There are, however, a number of investigators who do believe that play can be objectively defined. Although these studies are quite varied, interest in the formulation of a definition of play is a common concern of the researchers to be discussed in this chapter. Ecological researchers, for example, examine the effect of play environments on a child's play activities, and they attempt to construct environmental/material definitions. More recent ethological researchers have searched for behavioral definitions of play that are describable in anatomical terms and therefore allow for interspecies comparisons. There are also several recent experimental studies available characterized by their interest in the formulation of an objective, and therefore measurable, definition of play. All of these studies typify the *etic* approach as described by M. Harris, because they are investigations "of principles of organization or structure that exist outside the minds of the actors" (1976:331). These investigations (as is typical of all experimental studies or research that seeks to emulate the experimental approach) are formulated on the basis of the researcher's, and not the player's, interests and perspective.

ENVIRONMENTAL DEFINITIONS: TOYS AND NICHES

In the 1930s, a number of observational and experimental studies were conducted emphasizing the importance of investigating ecological, or play context, variables. For example, Van Alstyne (1932) noted, in a study of preschool-aged children's use of play materials, that play objects such as dishes, dolls, wagons, and telephones encourage conversation between children, whereas materials such as clay, scissors, puzzles, and books foster a more passive type of cooperation. Parten (1933) also investigated the use and choice of play materials and play activities evidenced by a group of preschool children by using a one-minute time-sampling technique. She found that these children most frequently played in groups of two, that the size of the play groups increased with age, that two-thirds of the groups were unisexual, and that "playing house" was the most social type of play engaged in by these children (i.e., it required complex social adjustments, negotiations, and cooperation), while sand play and constructive work with clay, paper, beads, and paints involved the children in parallel and generally nonsocial play activities (p. 95.). A similar study conducted by Updegraff and Herbst (1933) suggested, however, that play with clay produced more sociable and cooperative behavior than play with blocks.

It was also during this period that investigations began to be made of the effect of playground designs on children's play activities. For example, Johnson (1935) found that playgrounds with less equipment encouraged both social contact and conflict among children, whereas playgrounds with more equipment encouraged individual play and discouraged both social contact and conflict. A number of playground and play-material design studies are currently available (e.g., Chase et al., 1977; Gramza, 1970). In response to these investigations, it is interesting to note that Scholtz and Ellis (1975) found in a study of American 4- and 5-year-old children's preferences for toys and peers that, after repeated exposure to a particular play environment (i.e., specifically designed toys and play equipment), the children became bored with the toys and increasingly preferred to play with their peers. Perhaps material objects, no matter how well they are designed, can never be as interesting or novel as the presence of another person.

Other studies of relationships existing between play setting and play activity have been reported by Gump and Sutton-Smith (1955a) and Gump, Schoggen, and Redl (1963). In the latter report, an interesting analysis comparing the play of one boy—Wally—in his home and also in a camp environment is presented. The authors suggested here that the differences that they observed in Wally's play behavior in these two contrasting settings "were the result of environmental differences" (1963:179). They reported that Wally's "watching play time" was facilitated by the presence of a television in his home, whereas at camp this watching time occurred less frequently because the camp "did not have the necessary behavior objects or props to support extended watching" (p. 181). Investigative and exploratory activities, however, increased in the camp context because of the novelty of the woods as compared to the relative lack of novelty available in the home and neighborhood environment.

Examples of other recent studies utilizing this ecological perspective are available in works by Barker and Wright (1966), Shure (1963), and Doyle (1976). Doyle used the concept of an ecological niche in his study of American preschool children to differentiate between *single-niche play settings* (i.e., those that encourage solitariness or competitiveness by the presence of "props" such as puzzles and bicycles) and *multiple-niche play settings* (i.e., those that foster sociality and cooperativeness by the presence of props such as teeter-totters). Doyle suggested that if preschools wish to emphasize sociality, cooperation, and sharing and to deemphasize antisocial behavior such as name calling, competition, quarreling, and fighting, then the number of multiple-niche settings should be increased while the number of single-niche settings should be reduced. On the other hand, it could be argued that competition *is* a social skill in American society and that a reduction in settings that encourage this behavior (while pleasing to teachers and reformers) is not (at least, not at this point) in tune with cultural realities.

American children's preferences for sex-typed toys has already been briefly discussed in Chapter Six. However, an interesting study by Rheingold and Cook entitled "The Contents of Boys' and Girls' Rooms as an Index of Parents' Behavior" (1975) is important to mention here. In this research, an inventory was conducted of the private rooms of 96 children (aged 1–6) of American upper-middle-class families, and it was found that parents continue to create sex-stereotyped environments for their children. For example, the researchers found that boys' rooms contained more toy animals and objects related to "science" (e.g., magnets, puzzles, spaceships), while girls' rooms contained more dolls (particularly female and baby dolls) as well as doll houses, stoves, tea sets, etc., and frequently these rooms were decorated with floral wallpaper, ruffles, lace, and frills. Most striking of all was the difference in the number of vehicles found in boys' rooms (375) in comparison to girls' (17). None of the girls in this sample, no matter what their age, owned a wagon, bus, motorcycle, boat, or trailer. (Perhaps this suggests that girls, in the parents' opinion, are not going anywhere.) Rheingold reported, however, that in her laboratory, young girls spent as much time playing with trucks and other vehicles as boys. It appears that these parents were creating environments that reflected their own interests, which were not necessarily those of their children.

Relationships between "play milieu" and Danish personality have recently been investigated by Robert Anderson and Edna Mitchell (1977). This work emphasizes the uniformities in children's play environments that currently exist in Denmark because of factors such as general access to toy shops; the prevalence of nursery schools, parks, and playgrounds (particularly the well-known "adventure play-grounds"); and the small size of the country. Uniformities and differences existing in the play milieu of Danish children growing up at the turn of the century are also examined. The effect of these play uniformities on the patterning of Danish personality is suggested here, but the research is directed toward identifying the "cultural mechanisms that produce uniformity in play" (p. 3).

While researchers continue to argue over whether or not play is the "serious business" of children, it is unquestionably the serious business of toy manufacturers. In the United States, retail toy sales were reported at $4.8 billion for the 1974–1975 year (Mitchell and Anderson, 1977:45). In an important study of the toy industry in the United States and Denmark, Mitchell (1977; Mitchell and Anderson, 1977) found that toy manufacturers take their business so seriously that it is often difficult to talk to them because they assume that researchers are spies from other companies attempting to steal new product designs. In fact, the researchers were attempting to examine how marketing practices and also manufacturer and store-owner play preferences and values influence the play milieu of American and Danish children. Because toy store owners purchase their toys through jobbers with international connections, the toys available to Danish children are also found in almost all Western European countries (and often these are copies of American manufactured toys, such as "Barbie" and "Ken" dolls). There are still, however, a number of toys (generally wooden cars, trucks, and other objects) characteristic of Denmark and Scandinavia, although these have become increasingly expensive to manufacture and are rapidly being replaced by plastic toys.

The personal values and preferences of Danish toy store owners and managers are said still to exert some influence on a store's inventory. This is most evident in the refusal to stock guns, war, or other violence-related toys. This voluntary censorship is not exercised by American store owners and managers. Sex stereotyping of toys is, however, apparent in the types of toys manufactured and in their display in stores in Denmark, although to a lesser degree than is found in the United States. For example, "masculine" toys such as model kits, cars, and building sets are grouped together in one section of a store that is staffed by male personnel, while dolls and other "feminine" items are placed in another section and sold by women. The importance of orienting a store toward the adults' interests, as opposed to the child's, is apparently recognized by store owners and managers. One manager observed that playthings were one of the few businesses to sell to the giver and not to the user, which meant that he had "to consider what adults want to buy rather than what children want or need." Managers also suggested that "parents, rather than children, classify toys in sex-stereotyped categories" (Mitchell and Anderson, 1977:46). These observations appear to be supported by Rheingold and Cook's (1975) study discussed earlier.

The effect of the Danish policy of regulated advertising is also discussed as a factor influencing the child's play environment. The differences between the United States and Denmark are particularly striking in this regard, as television and radio advertisements of products are not allowed in Denmark, which means that toys can be advertised only in newspapers and mail catalogs. In the United States, however, more than $100 million a year is spent specifically on television advertisements of toys, producing a situation (according to one study) where programs for children under 12 may be interrupted by commercials as frequently as every 2.9 minutes (Mitchell, 1977:194).

Mitchell and Anderson commented specifically on what they see as the rapidly occurring worldwide homogenization of toys. This has created the possibility that soon children everywhere will be "playing with identical mass-produced toys most of which reflect the values and preoccupations of Western Industrial Society" (Mitchell, 1977:196). The impact of consumer action groups in the United States on toy manufacturers' product designs and advertising policies is also briefly examined in this report.

Ecological researchers assume that, if a child is in a researcher-defined play "niche," "environment," or "milieu" or is handling a researcher-defined play object, then the child must be playing. Of course, the child may actually be exploring the setting or object or thinking of something else—to name only two possibilities. It is therefore highly important for researchers to begin to examine how children actually do play with objects, persons, or environments and what this process entails. Do minimally structured, highly ambiguous toys or objects produce more imaginative play actions (as opposed to some other form of activity), or does the reverse occur? In a study by Pulaski (1970), it was found that children measured as "high in fantasy," using Singer's (see 1973) rating scales, preferred minimally structured toys (e.g., clay and blocks), whereas children measured as "low in fantasy" preferred highly structured toys (e.g., dolls and trucks). Pulaski also reported that children aged 5–8 produced more pretend or imaginative stories when toys were minimally structured.[1] Studies of younger children (2-year-

[1]American toy manufacturers have apparently decided, however, that children in this age group prefer (or should prefer) highly structured and realistic toys and dolls, for example, baby dolls that walk and talk, eat and wet, and clutch and "won't let go," or the "Growing Up Skipper" doll, who develops breasts when her arm is rotated, or the possibly more far-fetched "Dr. Steel," who delivers killer karate chops.

olds), however, suggest that this relationship may be reversed. Greta Fein (1975) analyzed play as the process whereby children make object and activity substitutions or transformations (e.g., the child pretends to drink from a cup or pretends to feed a toy horse). Pretense is discussed here as a symbolic transformation that permits one thing to be treated *as if* it is another. Fein suggested that when objects are "highly prototypical" (e.g., a "cuplike" cup or a detailed miniature representation of a horse), some transformational activity is still necessary in the play use of the objects. For example, a cup must be treated as if it is full, or an inanimate horse must be treated as if it is animate (p. 295). However, when material is less prototypical, more substitution/transformations are required. In this study, she found that

> an easy transformation (toy animal to living animal) can support a more difficult one (empty shell to full cup) and that with such support the functional relation between two objects can be maintained. The principle appears to be that the process whereby one thing is used to symbolize another initially requires a relatively prototypical context which serves to anchor the transformation. (p. 295)

At this age, therefore, more-structured toys (highly prototypical or realistic) appear to increase instances of pretending and also facilitate pretending with less-structured toys.

BEHAVIORAL DEFINITIONS: CHILD ETHOLOGY

The ethological studies of both nonhuman animals and humans appear to offer researchers an approach that is at once both evolutionary and objective in orientation. The now-classic studies of Konrad Lorenz and Niko Tinbergen examined specific behaviors in terms of their physiological, ontogenetic, and evolutionary causation (Crook and Goss-Custard, 1972:278). Ethological researchers also emphasize the importance of investigating the function of a behavior in its naturally occurring social and ecological context. To this end, ethological methods stress the importance of a preliminary descriptive and observational (or "naturalistic") phase of research, at which time simple observable features of behavior are recorded (preferably in anatomical terms) in order to "objectively" define and test the validity of particular categories of behavior and also to generate hypotheses regarding the causation and function of particular behaviors (see Blurton Jones, 1972b:4; Crook and Goss-Custard, 1972:278–279).

Advocates for the use of this method as applied to the study of human behavior (see Eibl-Eibesfeld, 1970) and particularly child behavior (see Blurton Jones, 1972b; McGrew, 1972) argue that it will produce more valid and reliable comparisons of human activity with that of nonhuman animals (particularly nonhuman primates). Charles Darwin's (1872) description of laughter and smiling is an early example of the type of behavioral description that ethologists strive to develop in their research studies:

> The sound of laughter is produced by a deep inspiration followed by short, interrupted, spasmodic contractions of the chest, and especially the diaphragm . . . the mouth is open more or less widely, with the corners drawn much backwards, as well as a little upwards; and the upper lip is somewhat raised. (Darwin, quoted in Berlyne, 1969:796)

More recently, Smith and Connolly (1972) have formulated the following anatomical definitions of laughter and smiling in their study of preschool-aged children's play:

> *Smile*—Corners of mouth withdrawn and turned upwards. . . . No audible vocalization.
> *Laugh*—Open-mouthed smile together with audible vocalization (rapid or staccato explusions of breath). (p. 78)

Given their skepticism concerning the "meaning and reality" of major categories of behavior (see Blurton Jones, 1972a:4–5), ethologists would naturally be distrustful of the category of play. According to Blurton Jones, ethologists ask a number of questions about behavior categories, such as "What do we mean by this?" "How do we know when we see it?" "Is it one thing or more than one or nothing at all?" (p. 17). As already mentioned, some researchers have argued that play is, in fact, "nothing at all," a "wastebasket category" held together by investigators' ignorance as to its function in context (see Schlosberg, 1947). Beach (1945) discussed what has become one of the most widely quoted examples of this ignorance. Fishes of the family Belonidae were seen to "exhibit a curious habit of 'leaping' over free-floating objects such as sticks and straws," and researchers (e.g., Gudger, cited in Beach, 1945:531), not knowing what to make of this activity, described it as "a playful response lacking in any practical outcome" (p. 531). Later, however, it was found that this habit was actually very useful because it enabled the fishes to dislodge parasites from their undersides. Therefore, so the argument goes, if the behavior is functional and useful, it cannot be play.

Caroline Loizos (1967), in a well-known review of studies of play behavior in the higher primates, presented a more positive solution to this definitional problem. She suggested that the word *play* can best be understood as "a useful shorthand description of a characteristic motor quality common to behavior occurring in certain situations" (p. 227). Loizos argued that one of the most noticeable characteristics of play "is that it is behavior that borrows or adopts patterns that appear in other contexts where they achieve immediate and obvious ends" (p. 228; see also Lorenz's 1956 description of play fighting). While these motor patterns may be adopted or borrowed, they are also "qualitatively distinct" from their "originally motivated contexts" (i.e., their source). This distinctiveness derives from the way these patterns may be altered in the play context. Loizos suggested six different ways this may occur: (1) a behavioral sequence may be reordered; (2) movements may be exaggerated; (3) movements may be repeated more than is normally the case; (4) a sequence may be broken off or fragmented, irrelevant activities may be introduced, and later the sequence will be resumed; (5) movements may be exaggerated and repeated; and (6) individual movements in a sequence are not completed, and this incomplete element may be repeated (p. 229). More recently, Peter Reynolds (1976) has suggested, following Loizos's argument, that play is behavior performed in the "simulative mode." However, Sade (1973) has suggested that, for rhesus monkeys, there is a postural component present in play interactions (i.e., rotation of the head or torso in the transverse plane), which appears to be unique to play. One interpretation of this finding, according to Sade, is that "play should be considered a mood in its own right and not simply derived from other aspects of behavior" (p. 541).

Loizos (1967) suggested that researchers are, for the most part, the only individuals perplexed by the problem of *defining* play, as most others (human and nonhuman animal alike) "know it when they see it" (see also Mason, 1965; Miller, 1973). Assuming that play does have survival value (and therefore is *not* useless), the more difficult problem is establishing what its consequences, benefits, or functions are.[2] In this book, I have discussed a number of proposed theories of play's function (see particularly Chapter Six). For her part, Loizos argued that play is crucial for primate development, particularly in regard to its value for practicing adult behaviors. Dolhinow and Bishop repeated this theme in their review entitled "The Development of Motor Skills and Social Relationships among Primates through Play" (1970). Bekoff (1972, 1974) also believes that play is important for the development of social interaction in mammals (he has specifically studied the play behavior of canids, e.g., dogs, wolves, and foxes).[3] Harlow's studies (Harlow and Harlow,

----

[2]Exploration and play are not commonly found in the lower vertebrates and tend to be most clearly associated with mammals, particularly the carnivores and primates (Baldwin and Baldwin, 1977:393; also see Welker, 1961). This would seem to indicate that these behaviors do have survival value, at least for specific orders of mammals.

[3]All of these studies—Loizos, Dolhinow and Bishop, Bekoff—should be consulted for specific references to the growing number of research studies of nonhuman animal, and particularly nonhuman primate, play.

1965; 1969; Harlow and Suomi, 1971) are also often cited as evidence of play's significance for social development, as this research indicates that rhesus monkeys who are deprived of social interaction with their mothers and peers evidence various forms of personality derangement or maladjustment, but when these same infants are allowed to participate in only 18 minutes per day of peer-group play, the effects of their isolation are overcome and they develop into normal adults.

Countering these glowing accounts of the adaptive value and functions of play are recent studies discussing the disadvantages and maladaptive consequences of play for players (e.g., in play and exploration, individuals can be led into dangerous or risky situations—increasing their chances of falling or vulnerability to predators) (see Baldwin and Baldwin, 1977) and for researchers (see Lazar and Beckhorn, 1974, who argued that the study of play "interferes" with answering important questions about the development of social behavior).

In the midst of these debates, a number of researchers have begun to use the methods of ethology to examine the general behavior of children. Child ethologists such as Blurton Jones (1967, 1972a,b) and Smith and Connolly (1972) have specifically examined the play behavior of children in an attempt to answer many of the questions posed in the above discussion. In "An Ethological Study of Some Aspects of Social Behavior of Children in Nursery School" (1967), Blurton Jones specifically examined English children's "rough-and-tumble" play behavior, which he suggested is almost identical to the rough-and-tumble category of play observed in rhesus monkeys by Harlow and Harlow (1962).[4] According to Blurton Jones, this type of play consists of seven movements: running; chasing and fleeing; wrestling; jumping up and down with both feet together; beating with an open hand without actually hitting; beating each other with an object without hitting; and laughing (1967:45). These are the observable "action patterns" or "fixed action patterns" associated with this behavior, and there are important similarities between these patterns and those found in actual fighting behavior. However, there are also important differences. For example, in a serious fight, beating with clenched fists occurs in conjunction with fixating, frowning, and shouting or screaming, but in a play fight, open-handed beats occur with jumping and laughing (p. 451). Additionally, the roles of players (e.g., chaser and chased) alternate rapidly, which is not the case in serious fights. In a more recent discussion of

[4]Aldis (1975) has recently published an extensive analysis of play fighting or rough-and-tumble forms of play in children and nonhuman animals, and Symons presented a specific examination of the social function of aggressive play in rhesus monkeys in his recent book entitled *Play and Aggression* (1977).

"Categories of Child–Child Interaction" (1972a), Blurton Jones retested his 1967 behavior groupings (including the pattern of rough-and-tumble play), again with a group of British children. In this study, similar behavior clusters were found to occur, and a more detailed discussion of age, sex, and familial variables is presented (e.g., older children engaged in more bouts of rough-and-tumble play than younger ones).

In an interesting ethological analysis of infancy and early childhood of the !Kung Bushmen (or Zhun/twasi), Melvin Konner (1972) stated that the components of rough-and-tumble play reported by Blurton Jones (e.g., chasing, fleeing, laughing, jumping, object beats) occur in this culture only when children attempt to annoy large animals (such as dogs) or try to kill smaller ones (see p. 299). Adult–child rough-and-tumble play bouts do occur here; however, child–child rough-and-tumble play takes place only infrequently and then in a highly stylized form unless there are a number (e.g., five or six) of same-age children together in a camp. In these instances, Konner reported that the play patterns are similar to those recorded for British children. A variation of rough-and-tumble play that Konner called "gentle and tumble" does occur more regularly for 1- to 5-year-old Bushmen children. The components of this play form are mutual touching, tangling of legs, clinging, and rolling while lying on the ground. There is also an absence of laughing while movements are slow, and the players seldom stand up during this activity.

Peter Smith and Kevin Connolly (1972) presented information on the play behavior of a sample of 40 British preschool-aged children attending three different day nurseries. Also included here is a useful review and methodological critique of the early ecological studies in comparison with more recent ethological investigations. In this article, as is frequently the case for most child ethological studies, behaviors (e.g., talking, smiling, standing, crying, laughing, fighting) are defined according to facial expressions, vocalizations, body posture, and motor patterns, and they are recorded in the context of the children's free play period (p. 76). Recognizing the difficulty of rigidly defining play behavior, the investigators chose instead to describe it as presumably occurring when the child is in contact with play objects (e.g., toys, apparatus such as slides, books, etc.) or is engaging in fantasy play (e.g., pretending to be dead) (p. 80). This approach to the problematic definition of play is often adopted by child ethologists (see for example Leach, 1972:273). Different types of play have also been defined by Smith and Connolly (e.g., self, parallel, and group play). The behaviors defined and recorded in the above fashion are examined in relation to data collected on age, sex, family structure, environmental settings, and other variables. On the basis of their analysis, the investigators reported, for example, that (1) social play and talking occurred more frequently in the older group; (2) talking and sucking behaviors were more frequent among girls, whereas play horses and rough-and-tumble play were more frequent among boys; (3) outdoors there was more running, laughing, and rough-and-tumble play and less aggressive behavior (pp. 81–82).

The child ethologists' interest in formulating behavioral definitions of play on the basis of careful observations conducted in naturally occurring contexts is significant. However, there are serious problems with the way child ethologists conceptualize the activities of both children and researchers. This approach requires the adoption of a metaphor for children that treats their behavior as if it is directly equivalent to the actions of monkeys and other nonhuman primates, and even to that of nonmammals. For example, Blurton Jones (1967) asserted:

> It became obvious that one can study human behavior in just the same way as Tinbergen . . . and others have studied gulls, and Van Hoof . . . and others have studied non-human primates. (p. 437)

This assumption of equivalence is also reflected by the fact that behaviors that the ethological investigator wishes to study are, whenever possible, defined in anatomical terms as has been illustrated in the above discussion. These definitions are used in order to allow for interspecies comparisons of behavior. The child's use of language (when recognized at all) is generally defined as "talk" (i.e., the occurrence of recognizable word utterances). What the child "says" is often presented only in terms of the frequency of the "talk" and rarely in terms of the content of what is "said." It is assumed that this content will be "primitive" and "limited," and, indeed, this is why children's behavior is seen as more directly comparable to that of nonhuman primates. However, as the studies of Washoe indicate (e.g., Gardner and Gardner, 1971) chimpanzees can learn and use a form of language (although to what extent is still a matter of debate; see Blount, 1975). It has also been found that chimpanzees can create imaginary play situations for themselves by constructing imaginary toys (see Hayes, 1976) or using objects as if they are something else (e.g., using a nail to represent a needle; see Gardner and Gardner, 1971). There will certainly continue to be arguments about the symbolic sophistication of chimpanzees and monkeys; however, there is no question as to the symbolic sophistication of even very young humans. To "pretend" otherwise, in order to view children as if they are monkeys or seagulls, is itself an illustration of the power of play. Additionally, this attempt to study children as if they are monkeys disregards a basic part of the child's social context and appears to be in direct contradiction to the ethologists' desire to study behavior in naturally occurring contexts.

In order to study children from what is thought to be a more "objec-tive" vantage point, the child ethologist also adopts a metaphor for conceptualizing his/her own "investigative" activity. This approach re-quires the researcher to adopt what can be called a "quiet as a mouse" presence in the research situation. In order to foster this image, the investigator assumes a passive and unresponsive attitude toward the children involved in a study. For example, Smith and Connolly (1972) stated that "observations were recorded on standard record sheets by one observer, who remained passive to any approaches by the children" (p. 76) (see also Blurton Jones 1967:440). In another study designed to test the effect of different observer styles (passive, smiling, smiling and talking) on children's reactions, Connolly and Smith (1972) described the passive observer as follows:

> At nursery A the observer assumed a totally passive attitude to the child; he adopted a neutral expression at all times and did not look at the children (apart from the glances necessary for observation), smile, talk or make any other overt responses. (p. 165)

The researchers reported that this style elicited the least approach re-sponses, and it is obvious why this would be so—for who would want to have anything to do with such an obviously inhuman individual ("a mouse not a man"). Child ethologists, however, believe that this style places them in a very advantageous position because once this metaphorical transformation has occurred, they will then be free to ob-serve and record the children's behavior in a detached and unobtrusive and therefore objective manner. In this way, it is felt that this style does not affect the occurrence of "natural" behaviors (once the children be-come accustomed to the researcher's presence). Other techniques, such as the use of one-way mirrors and videotape equipment, for observation and recording of data are also associated with this research tradition. All of these efforts, however, only disguise the part that researchers have to play in the research context and serve only to make it an unnatural and artificial context. Researchers who *pretend that they do not exist* produce studies that are neither ethologically nor ecologically sound. This methodological pretense is typical of experimental studies, but ethologists see themselves as offering researchers an alternative to the traditional experimental orientation (see Crook and Goss-Custard, 1972:278–279). In many important and generally unrecognized ways, however, I suggest that this is *not* the case.

The orienting metaphors of child ethology studies have been criti-cally examined here because it is believed that there are more appro-priate metaphors available for use in conceptualizing the activities of both children and researchers. It is also possible to argue that, if such an examination does not occur within the field of child ethology, this approach will ultimately eliminate itself because it will be hard to justify continually the use of a method that is guided by two metaphors that relegate both children and researchers to silence.

PLAY AND EXPLORATION

Ethologists are concerned with defining and examining units, sequences, and categories of behavior in order to question the validity of certain categories and to develop more objective measures and definitions of particular forms of behavior. Play has always been a problematic category for researchers, and one reason for this is that it is so frequently confused with other activities.

Exploration is one such behavior. In an important series of studies utilizing both ethological and experimental methods, Corinne Hutt (e.g., 1966, 1970a,b, 1975, 1977) has examined relationships between play and exploration. In the most widely quoted study, "Exploration and Play in Children" (1966), a new toy was constructed in order to investigate the exploratory activities of a group of 3- to 5-year-old British children. Sounds and lights were built into this unusual-looking toy, which could be activated by the child as he/she examined the object (e.g., if a lever was pressed one way, a green light might go on, or if pressed in the other direction, a buzzer might sound). Hutt stated that the majority of the 128 children involved in this study exhibited a fairly similar pattern in their interaction with this object. Initially they would approach and inspect the toy with varying degrees of tentativeness, and during this time, their posture and expression was one of concentration. Following this, the child would begin to use the toy playfully, and during this period, they exhibited a relaxed posture and expression. According to Hutt, this change from exploration to play can be characterized as follows:

> The quest changed from inquiry to invention and the child no longer asked himself "What does this *object* do?" but "What can *I* do with this object?" And while investigation declined with time, playful activity increased to a peak before declining. (1977:35)

On the basis of these studies, Hutt suggested that exploration may actually be seen to consist of two different classes of behavior, referred to as *specific* and *diversive* exploration. Specific exploration "seeks to reduce uncertainty and hence arousal or activation produced by . . . novel or complex stimulation"; whereas diversive exploration is an attempt "to vary stimulation in order to sustain a certain level of activation" (1966:248). According to Hutt, play exhibits more similarity to this latter form of exploration; however, because of the failure of investigators to distinguish between these two forms of exploration, the behaviors of exploration and play have often been confused. Hutt also argued that "specific exploration is obligatory while diversive exploration is optional and idiosyncratic" (1977:35).

One of the most interesting findings of this research indicates, in Hutt's opinion, that premature play with the toy precludes further learning about the object. For example,

> a boy having found the bell and incorporated it in a game in which he ran round the room filling a truck and ringing the bell twice each time, failed to find out about the buzzer. Learning during the playful phase, therefore, was largely accidental. If, during such play, the child chanced upon the lever movement which operated the buzzer, then a further period of exploration would ensue. Thus, playful behavior may actually preclude learning, in the sense of acquiring information from a novel or unfamiliar source. (1977:36)

Hutt's interpretation of this finding is, however, somewhat questionable. For instance, why is this boy's game, which incorporates both a mechanical toy and a truck into a new activity, not also a form of learning (e.g., learning that he can act on a mechanical object as much as it can act on him)? (This may be a very important thing for all children growing up in Western industrial societies to learn.) Dolhinow and Bishop (1970:170) also criticized Hutt's interpretation, suggesting that it does not apply to nonhuman primates because, while observers may feel that an animal is not learning anything new in a play event, the animal may, in fact, be learning a number of things that the observer cannot measure. This, of course, is also the case in studies of human children. In responding to Dolhinow and Bishop's criticism, however, Hutt (1977) complained that it is based only on "intuitive inferences" and is therefore "pure conjecture."

In order to discriminate further between specific and diversive exploration, Hutt has more recently (see 1975, 1977) conducted a series of studies in which young (2 years) children's heart-rate changes were monitored while they were engaged in various activities with specific toys. The experiment proceeded in three stages: (1) the play phase (the children were given three toys to play with); (2) the exploratory phase (the children were given a novel toy instead of a familiar one); and (3) the problem phase (the children were given a six-piece form-board puzzle to solve). Hutt stated that the behavioral manifestations of play and problem solving were quite different; for example, smiles and looking around occurred during play and not during problem solving. Exploration and problem solving were more similar to one another, although there were more instances of "examination and visual inspection" during exploration (1977:38). The heart-rate variability associated with these activities also helped the researcher to discriminate between them.

During relaxed and restful activity, heartbeats are "choppy" and irregular when written out on a paper tracer (cardiotachograph), but this choppiness or *variability* is suppressed when an individual is engaged in mental activity (see p. 37). In this experiment, Hutt found that heart-rate variability "was greatest during play and least during problem-solving," while during exploration, variability was less than for play and similar to that for problem-solving (p. 38). Hutt suggested that these measures indicate "that when a child is playing he is engaged in less mental effort, he is more relaxed and less attentive to external sources of stimulation" (p. 39).

With this evidence in hand, Hutt moved on to formulate a taxonomy of play that distinguishes between what she refers to as *epistemic behavior* (i.e., behavior concerned with acquiring knowledge and information and cued from an external source of stimulation) and *ludic behavior* (i.e., behavior that is playful, highly mood-dependent, and not necessarily cued from external sources) (p. 39). Problem solving of jigsaw puzzles and so forth, as well as exploratory activity and "productive" behavior (e.g., constructing a sand castle or learning to ride a bike), are all forms of epistemic behavior, according to Hutt. In contrast, ludic behavior forms are discussed as symbolic play (e.g., pretense with objects or roles) and repetitive play, which may contain new features mixed with the repetition of previously acquired skills. Hutt also included in her taxonomy a third subdivision, called *games with rules.*

Hutt related these above distinctions to Berlyne's (1960, 1966) theory of arousal. According to Berlyne, high and low levels of arousal potential ("arousal potential is directly proportional to intensity of a stimulus and inversely proportional to the duration of exposure to the stimulus source," p. 43) are mildly aversive for organisms, and, when either of these states occurs, the "organism will engage in those responses which will result in a return to arousal tonus" (Hutt 1977:43). In cases of high arousal, an avoidance response may occur, but when an individual attempts to reduce "the uncertainty and cognitive conflict" associated with this state, responses that are termed *exploratory*, in Hutt's system, may be said to take place. When arousal potential is moderate, productive and problem-solving activities are evidenced. As arousal potential decreases, enjoyment appears, and, with further decreases, symbolic play for children or reverie for adults occurs. Because minimal levels of arousal potential are also aversive, individuals will attempt "to optimize arousal by engaging in instrumental responses to obtain changes in stimulation" (Hutt 1977:43).

Hutt's view of the function of play is also related to Berlyne's theory. She suggested that play functions for particular species (i.e., those in which survival pressures are not too great and those that have a prolonged period of infancy) "to keep neural and behavioral systems primed and active in the absence of alternative stimulation" (pp. 46–47). Adopting this approach, the characteristic features of play behavior are explained in the following manner:

> Since such behaviors have no explicitly utilitarian function, they are invested with properties which serve to distinguish them from more goal-oriented behavior, such as exaggerations, galumphing, and caricatures. (p. 47)

Arousal theory has been used by a variety of researchers in their studies of exploration and play. For example, Ellis has employed this idea in his numerous experimental studies reported in *Why People Play* (1973), while an experiential adaptation of this model has been formulated by Csikszentmihalyi (1975; Csikszentmihalyi and Bennett, 1971). In this latter report, play is defined "as a state of experience in which the actor's ability to act matches the requirements for action in his environment," and it is differentiated from anxiety (where requirements outnumber one's ability) and boredom (where requirements are two few for one's ability) (Csikszentmihalyi and Bennett, 1971:45). Examples of other studies specifically concerned with the topic of exploration or the relationships between play and exploration are found in: Barnett (1958); Berlyne (1960, 1966, 1969); Collard (1971); McCall (1974); Nunnally and Lemond (1973); Piaget (1951); and Welker (1961).

BEHAVIORAL DEFINITIONS: EXPERIMENTAL STUDIES

Experimental studies of children's play have been made, for the most part, by psychologists. A number of these studies have already been discussed in this and other chapters. There are also several reviews of experimental and psychological studies of play available: for example, Britt and Janus (1941); Berlyne (1969); Millar (1968); Bruner (1972); and, most recently, Weisler and McCall (1976) and Hutt (1977). Singer (1973) and J. Singer and D. Singer (1976) have also presented useful reviews covering the specific topic of experimental studies of children's make-believe play, while Klinger (1971) presented a review of psychological theories of play and fantasy. The Weisler and McCall (1976) review includes discussion of both exploration and play and concentrates specifically on attempts to define and measure these concepts as well as to investigate their functions. Exploration is defined here as behavior characterized by "relatively stereotyped perceptual motor examination of an object, situation or event the function of which is to reduce subjective uncertainty (i.e., acquire information)" (p. 493). The adaptive value of exploration as it involves responding to changes in one's context appears to be obvious. In certain instances, according to the authors, it is also a high-priority behavior superseding basic/biological functions such as eating, drinking, or eliminating (p. 494).

The definition and measurement of play is a much more problematic issue for researchers (and this is particularly true for psychological researchers, who are invariably unhappy with any description that sounds "subjective"). Weisler and McCall offered the following definition, recognizing that, in their terms, it is both "subjective" and "ambiguous":

> Play consists of behaviors and behavioral sequences that are organism dominated, behaviors that appear to be intrinsically motivated and apparently performed for "their own sake" and that are conducted with relative relaxation and positive affect. (p. 494)

In contrast to exploration, the adaptive value of play is not obvious to investigators, who typically describe it as "purposeless" and "without consequence." In conjunction with this, play is an activity that, according to Weisler and McCall, has "a relatively low priority in the habit hierarchy" and therefore occurs only when "the organism feels safe and sated with respect to basic needs" (p. 295).

A number of explanations of play's function (e.g., as socialization, satirization, projection, communication, learning) have been discussed in this book. Recent psychological studies offer a number of other explanations, which will be briefly mentioned here. Several studies conducted by Harriet Rheingold (e.g., Rheingold and Eckerman, 1969; Rheingold and Samuels, 1969; Corter, Rheingold, and Eckerman, 1972) suggest that infants are more likely to leave their mother in the presence of novel toys, or that they may delay following their mother as she leaves a room when such toys are available. Therefore it has been argued that play may encourage the process of detachment of infant from mother. Konner (1972, 1975) made a similar suggestion based on his analysis of Bushmen children's multiaged play groups. Haley (1973) has also argued that children who are overly dependent on their mothers cannot (or will not) engage in peer play. On the other hand, it is also true that mothers and children do play together, and there have been several recent studies of mother–child play (see, for example, Stern's 1974 study of the facial, vocal, and gaze behavior exhibited by American, white, middle-class mothers and infants at play).

It has also been suggested that play may serve the goal of "effectance" in White's (1959) terms, allowing the child to control and manipulate objects, situations, and other individuals and to develop competencies in these areas (see also the studies in Almy, 1968). Ross, Goldman, and Hay (1977) documented the social interaction competencies displayed by infants in their "games" with mothers, strangers, and peers, while research by Mueller and Lucas (1975) is particularly concerned with the examination of children's developing social skills in peer play. These authors suggested that a transition occurs around age 2, at which time children's object-centered actions in play become peer-centered, but in these instances peers are treated and manipulated *as if* they are objects.

This research on peer-group play should, however, be read in conjunction with Konner's (1975) cross-cultural and cross-species examination of the existence of peer groups. He stated that children's peer groups are not generally found in hunting-and-gathering societies (because of the small group size and the long birth spacing), and he suggested that researchers' ideas about peer relations in infancy

> are almost entirely an artifact of laboratory investigations of child care conditions in advanced industrial states. In this context we can begin to understand the bizarrely inept form of social behavior which we know in the laboratory and nursery as "parallel play" and "collective monologue." (p. 122)[5]

Konner and also Patricia Draper (1976) have suggested that the existence of small multiaged children's groups (as opposed to peer groups) among the !Kung Bushmen clearly influences their play behavior. Most specifically, it makes competition between players difficult if not altogether impossible:

> Team sports are . . . unrealistic. Not only can the children not fill out a team; but the players are at such different levels of motor skill, motivation and cognitive development that it is difficult and unrewarding to play a game involving intense competition, rules, and fairly complex strategy. (pp. 202–203)

Experimental studies of children's imaginative play have recently been reviewed by Jerome and Dorothy Singer (1976), and there is also an excellent review in J. Singer's earlier book *The Child's World of Make-Believe* (1973). In this latter study, techniques for measuring children's "imaginative predisposition" using psychological tests (e.g., Holtzman Inkblot, Barron Inkblot, Torrence Just-Suppose) and a self-report interview (questions are simple and straightforward, such as "What is your favorite game?") are discussed in detail. Also included here is a discussion of observation and recording techniques useful for the study of imaginative play and also a description of observer ratings of "imaginativeness," "affect," "concentration," "mood" (a "mood checklist" is presented), and "aggression" as exhibited in play situations.

The Singers view play as a type of *autotelic* ("self-motivated") (see

---

[5]It should be noted here, however, that it is not at all clear that we do see these "bizarre forms" in the nursery or preschool. See, for example, Isaacs (1930, 1933).

Klinger, 1971, or Csikszentmihalyi, 1975) activity that is crucial to children's cognitive and affective development. In this regard, they suggested that play is important in the development of (1) imagery skills (see also Fein, 1975); (2) verbal fluency and divergent thinking (see also Garvey, 1977; Guilford, 1967; Wallach, 1971; and discussion below on creativity); (3) the ability to discriminate between reality and fantasy (see also Garvey, 1974); (4) a heightened sense of self-awareness (see also Singer, 1966; Sutton-Smith and Rosenberg, 1967); (5) self-entertainment and waiting skills (see also Singer, 1961); and (6) positive affect (see also Biblow, 1973; Rosenhan, Underwood, and Moore, 1974).

The Singers' works (see particularly J. Singer, 1973; D. and J. Singer, 1976) also emphasize the importance of play training programs for increasing children's imaginative abilities (and with this the assumed positive benefits discussed above). The use of these techniques to correct imaginative play "deficits" thought to be found among some non-middle-class children has already been examined and critiqued in Chapter Six.

Recent experimental studies have also continued the tradition of *using* play or game activities for the investigation of other behaviors. Several of these studies have tested the cooperativeness or competitiveness exhibited by children from a number of different cultures on the Madsen (1971) cooperation board (e.g., comparisons have been made between Maori and Pakeha children in New Zealand, Thomas, 1975; kibbutz and urban Israeli children, Shapira and Madsen, 1969; Anglo-American and urban Mexican and village Mexican children, Madsen and Shapira, 1970; Australian European and Australian aborigine children, Sommerlad and Bellingham, 1972; and Blackfoot Indian and urban Canadian children, Miller and Thomas, 1972). The most interesting finding reported in these studies is that children in all of the nonurbanized, nonwesternized cultures played the board game in a more cooperative manner than their urban and more westernized peers.

Examples of recent *uses* of children's play, games, or stories for the diagnosis and psychotherapeutic treatment of children are found in Gardner (1971), Winnicott (1971), and Kritzberg (1975) (also see the discussion of the play therapy tradition in Chapter Seven).

PLAY AND CREATIVITY

While play has frequently been confused with exploration, it has also often been associated with an equally nebulous and perplexing concept: creativity. A number of researchers have suggested this association (e.g., Piaget, 1951; Bruner, 1962; Lieberman, 1965, 1977; Sutton-

Smith, 1966a, 1967; Klinger, 1971; Dansky and Silverman, 1973; Singer, 1973; Feitelsen, 1972; Feitelsen and Ross, 1973). In a 1965 study conducted by J. Nina Lieberman, it was found that teachers' ratings of American middle-class children's "playfulness" (said to consist of the qualities of spontaneity, manifest joy, and sense of humor) were highly correlated with children's divergent-thinking abilities (ideational fluency, spontaneous flexibility, and originality) as measured by tests adapted from Torrence and Guilford and by use of the Monroe Language Classification Test. In another study, Lieberman (1967) suggested that the "playfulness" quality of play, which she described as the major element of play and for which she has developed identification and measurement instruments, developmentally transforms itself "into a personality trait of the player in adolescence and adulthood" (1977:23). In *Playfulness: Its Relationship to Imagination and Creativity* (1977), Lieberman reiterated her view that "the play element in play is playfulness," and she presented her rationale and research methods for studying the *how* and not the *why* of play. Also included here are descriptions of both her "playfulness" rating scale (used in the study of preschool children) and her "playfulness–nonplayfulness" rating scale (used in the study of adolescents). Related to these studies by Lieberman is research reported by Schaefer (1969), who found that high school students evaluated by teachers as "creative" were differentiated most clearly from their "noncreative" classmates in terms of their report that they had an imaginary companion or playmate during childhood.

Dansky and Silverman (1973) have specifically investigated the effects of play on a group of American middle-class and upper-middle-class children's associative fluency. In this research, children who were allowed to play freely with four different objects (a pile of paper towels, a screwdriver, a pile of paper clips, and matchboxes) scored higher on an alternate-uses test that involved these objects than children who watched an experimenter perform various tasks with the objects (imitation group) or children in a control group. The children who played with the objects named more nonstandard uses for each object than children in either the imitation or the control group. Examples of these uses, as noted by the investigators, included the observations that you could "wrap (a paper towel) around a bunch of paper clips and throw it," or you could use an empty matchbox to "put sand in it for a little house for ants." There were also the somewhat more fantastic suggestions that the matchbox could be used either as "a little TV" or "a big swimming pool"; for the screwdriver, one child reported that "If you turn it like this, it will be a merry-go-round" (p. 42). Dansky and Silverman stated that "In general, the children seemed capable of imagining that an object could become almost anything they would like it to be" (p. 42).

Jerome and Dorothy Singer (1976) have suggested that the study of play is a particularly important research area for psychologists to pursue because it is possible to observe "in miniature the origins of many of the basic capacities for imagination that characterize the adult" (p. 5). Both Singer (1966) and Klinger (1971) have formulated studies of certain of these abilities (i.e., daydreaming and fantasy, respectively) and their expression in childhood, adolescence, and, particularly, adulthood. Unfortunately, while many researchers have suggested associations between these behaviors and also expressions of creativity by adults and children's play, few investigators have systematically examined these relationships (but see the above studies) or their implications for the theoretical play that researchers should exhibit in their studies, particularly their studies of play. Singer (1976), however, suggested something of this sort in his analysis of Vico's view of the importance of human imagination:

> We should take his [Vico's] advice and rely more freely on our own direct experience of ourselves, our memories, fantasies, and dreams, as well as sensitive understandings of the thoughts and actions of others in order to build better models of the human imagination and of social interaction. (p. 726)

And Konrad Lorenz (1976) suggested a direct link between play and scientific research:

> All purely material research conducted by a human scientist is pure inquisitive behavior—appetitive behavior *in free operation*. In this sense, it is *play behavior*. All scientific knowledge—to which man owes his role as master of the world—arose from playful activities conducted in a free field entirely for their own sake. . . . Anybody who has seen in his own activities the smooth transition from inquisitive childhood play to the life-work of a scientist could never doubt the fundamental identity of play and research. (p. 95)

SUMMARY

The recent studies of ecological, ethological, and experimental researchers have focused primarily on formulating *the* operational definition of play. Specific emphasis has been given in this research to the use of observable environmental and/or behavioral criteria in the development of such a definition. This approach has been adopted in order to ensure the objectivity of the research study and to correct for past definitions that have been too "loose," "fuzzy," and "unsystematic" and that are thought to represent a "discordant polyphony." In fact, however, these characterizations of the problems encountered in defining play are actually appropriate definitions for this subject.

Ecological researchers have emphasized the importance of investigating environmental-context variables (e.g., play materials and toys, the play "niche" or "milieu"), but frequently this has resulted in the exclusion of detailed reports of play texts. Nevertheless, there are important factors to be considered here, as evidenced particularly by studies such as Pulaski's (1970) and Fein's (1975) on the effect of highly realistic versus minimally structured toy objects on children's play behavior. The research of Anderson and Mitchell (1977; Mitchell, 1977; Mitchell and Anderson, 1977) also suggests a new and important area of investigation for ecological researchers to follow, as it may be that toy manufacturers exhibit one of the strongest and most pervasive influences on Western, and increasingly non-Western, children's play and games.

The ethological researchers' interest in formulating behavioral definitions of play on the basis of careful and systematic observations conducted in "naturally occurring contexts" is also a significant new trend in play studies. Again, however, these researchers tend to concentrate on the examination of play context variables to the exclusion of the collection and analysis of specific play texts. In conducting their observations, ethological researchers unfortunately appear to want to remove themselves from the actual research context by acting as passive or unresponsive observers or by using one-way mirrors or videotape techniques. In regard to this approach, I have suggested that researchers who attempt to study children's play in "naturally occurring contexts" must recognize the part they have "to play" in such contexts, and if they do not, then the investigation is neither ethologically nor ecologically sound.

Experimentalists have frequently *used* play as a context (i.e., a testing ground) for the study of other aspects of children's behavior. Recently, however, a number of studies have appeared that use play as a testing ground but also make it the subject of the test. An important series of studies utilizing both ethological and experimental methods has been made by Corinne Hutt, who has attempted to disentangle and examine relationships between exploration and play. Another interesting series of experimental studies, specifically of children's make-believe play, has been formulated by Jerome and Dorothy Singer and their colleagues. Here an attempt has been made to discuss and also to provide methodological solutions for the observation and recording of imaginative play and the measurement of individual children's "imaginative predispositions." The Singers, along with other researchers such as Lieberman, and Dansky and Silverman, have also attempted to investigate relationships between play and creativity or "divergent" thinking. This is an extremely important area of research that needs to be greatly expanded in the future. It may be that by understanding the *process* and the *products* of children at play, we will also gain a better understanding of adults at research.

CHAPTER ELEVEN

Conclusion: New Metaphors for Old

A certain amount of attention has been paid of late years to the subject of the games of primitive peoples, but so far we are only in the preliminary stage of the inquiry; indeed, a vast deal more evidence must be collected before sound generalizations can be made. A few suggestions have been thrown out by various students which must be regarded more as trial hypotheses than as definite conclusions, indeed they should be looked upon rather as "kites."

A. F. C. Haddon, 1902

A. F. C. Haddon made the above statement over 75 years ago, and today we are still flying theoretical "kites" in the study of play—only now there are more of them. This is as it should be because play requires a multiperspective approach (a number of trial balloons) and resists any attempts to define it rigidly (and thereby ground it). In this book, the development and proliferation of anthropological theories of children's play has been traced from evolutionism to ethology. In the process, we have surveyed anthropologists' metaphors for play, for children, and for culture. This book was written as a critical survey of the ethnographic literature on children's play and also as a study of the development of anthropology as a discipline. In this way, I have attempted to illustrate how the discipline of anthropology provides students of play with a broadened perspective on their topic and also to suggest that the study of play provides anthropologists with a new perspective on their discipline. Here I have argued that play is not a peripheral or tangential subject to be investigated in the ethnographer's "spare time" but a topic of central importance whose study can only improve our understanding of the anthropological enterprise.

325

Anthropology was formulated, in part, as a way to make the *familiar* (our actions) *novel* by making the *novel* (others' actions) *familiar*.[1] Therefore, anthropologists were from the start both playful and exploratory in their theoretical and geographical interests. Early in the discipline's development, however, ethnographers became attached to various definitions of culture that were used to transform other peoples' novel actions into expected, predictable, and most importantly, *familiar* stages, traits, structures, patterns, domains, behaviors, and so forth. Anthropologists began to take these transformations (i.e., theories of culture) very seriously, and fieldwork became the ethnographer's trademark.

In the process of "working" on other cultures, anthropologists neglected the study of play. This is reflected in the discipline's history in a variety of ways. In the first place, anthropologists forgot about their original interest in transforming familiarity into novelty because all of their theories were geared toward transforming novelty into familiarity. A paradox soon developed, as recognized by Roy Wagner in his excellent book *The Invention of Culture* (1975), whereby anthropologists, in their theoretical "inventions," began to define man as basically conservative and uncreative. For example, many diffusionists believed that humans were by nature uninventive creatures given to borrowing rather than creating their cultures, while structure functionalists examined how societies maintained sameness rather than how they might produce differences and novelty. Naturally (and culturally) anthropologists would be perplexed by the phenomenon of play, and so they were led to ignore it (as they did their own theoretical inventions) or to preserve, categorize, socialize, pattern, or structure it—once again turning the novel into the familiar. In this book, I have attempted to question several of these familiar theories by suggesting transformations of them. In other words, I have been searching for "new metaphors for old" in the study of children's play.

In contrast to most researchers, I believe that current studies of play suffer from too much definitional familiarity. Although investigators may differ greatly on the specifics of their theories and the particular outcomes that they may advance regarding the "functions" or "benefits" of play, there is general agreement on a number of issues. Play is first of all assumed to be pleasurable and enjoyable, to be characterized by freedom and spontaneity, and to elicit active (as opposed to passive) engagement by players. Second, it is generally assumed that

---

[1]See S. N. Miller (1974:48) for a discussion of play as the reinterpretation of something familiar into something novel. For an examination of the transformation of "novelty" into "expectation" in terms of information theory, see Shands (1967), and for a discussion of the transformation of "expectation" into "novelty" in reference to postmodern fiction, see J. Schwartzman (1977).

play is unproductive and without "real" consequence in life—its motivations are said to be intrinsic as opposed to extrinsic. Finally, it is believed that play occurs in a separate space and time from other activities and that it is marked by an awareness of a "second reality" that is experienced as "make-believe" and "illusory." In conjunction with these views, it is also generally thought that games are more conventionalized, formalized, or institutionalized forms of play (see Garvey, 1977:104). Games are characterized by explicit rules that must be clearly articulated, understood, and accepted by all participants for the event to "work." Games are not, however, necessarily characterized by the production of a differential outcome.

There is nothing to be found in the anthropological literature to suggest that play is not pleasurable or enjoyable except the realization that this is not *always* the case, and, of course, it is also true that activities that are generally understood to be not-play are also pleasurable and enjoyable. This means that we cannot be satisfied with definitions or theories that argue in a curiously tautological fashion that "the play element in play is playfulness" (or joy or pleasure or fun). Although difficult to deny, this approach gets us nowhere. The fact that play requires *active* engagement by players seems also obvious, and yet this criterion has frequently been overlooked by researchers who focus either on the collection and categorization of texts or the analysis of contexts. When actual players have been placed (or put back) in the equation, as in the communication studies, the relationships existing between play texts and contexts have come into sharper focus. One reason that players have been ignored is that games (and not play) have been the most frequent subject of research studies, and games can be described and understood generally without reference to individual players. An understanding of game rules provides one with an understanding of the event, and too much spontaneity or individuality (i.e., too much play) can spoil the game for all participants. This may mean that, in order fully to understand play, we will have to separate it clearly from games. Games *rule* out the ambiguity, spontaneity, and flexibility characteristic of play, and it may be that it is only our language that is playing tricks on us when we are led to say that we "play games." This may actually be a contradiction in terms, a possibility that should be explored in further studies.

While everyone can agree on the fact that play is enjoyable, it is not at all clear that play is unproductive and without consequence. This view draws on the play-work dichotomy of Western cultures, which I have argued is not a contrast to be found in all human societies; nor is it one that accurately reflects the situation even in the West. If play is an orientation, mode, context, or frame that can be adopted for marking behavior in *any* situation (as has been repeatedly suggested by the research reviewed here), then it is possible for play to occur in the presumably productive sphere of "work." In fact, for some kinds of work (e.g., theory "building," artistic endeavors), play may be seen to enhance "productivity" because of its relation to "creativity."[2] But play is also productive in other ways; most especially it gives shape (i.e., it generates) and also expression to a child's developing emotional–social and cognitive systems. Children at play learn how to be sensitive to the effects of context and the importance of relationships; they develop the capacity to adopt an "as if" set toward objects, actions, persons, and situations; and they continually explore the possibilities of interpretation and reinterpretation and with this the creation of new pos ibilities. These abilities are certainly all of great consequence to the individual and to society.

If play is a mode, as opposed to a category, of activity, then clearly this challenges the traditional view that play occurs in a separate time and space, because, by adopting this approach, it can be seen that play can occur at any time or place. This argument relates also to what is perhaps the most perplexing problem of play: its relationship to nonplay. Catherine Garvey suggested that play is systematically related to what is not-play (1977:5). But what characterizes this relationship? Many researchers have suggested that play creates a separate "reality" characterized either by illusion or by imitation. For example, children's play is often viewed as a *distortion* of reality (i.e., the adult's view of the world) that functions to compensate children for the fact that they cannot be adults, but over time, these "illusions" increasingly come to correspond to "real" reality as play development is conceptualized as the unfolding of stages that move children from play → games → reality. In contrast to this view, it is argued here that play creates and contains its own "reality," which is characterized by *allusion* to, not distortion of, events. Over time, the content and process of these allusions may shift, but these changes can in no way be charted by the construction of linear stages.

The collections and categorizations of play and game texts that many researchers have offered treat play as if it is a form of social formaldehyde capable of preserving past societies' actions. However, play is an activity that is very much alive and characterized always by *transformation* and not preservation of objects, roles, actions, and so forth. By emphasizing the preservative quality of play texts, researchers

---

[2]The importance of imagination and the use of metaphors and analogies in the construction of scientific theories have been discussed by a number of researchers; see, for example, Black (1962), Hesse (1966), Turbayne (1970), and V. Turner (1974a).

have ignored the transformative quality of play contexts. And, similarly, by emphasizing the socialization function of play contexts, researchers have ignored the satirical, critical, and interpretive qualities of play texts.

Socialization theories also invoke what is perhaps the most common view of play's relationship to nonplay. This is expressed in the view of play as imitation of other (nonplay) activities. These explanations continually fail to describe this relationship because they all disregard the very important fact that these "imitations" are *purported* imitations that are purported by specific individuals (i.e., players) in specific situations. Richard Ohmann (1971) has recently developed this idea of purported imitation in his discussion of the nature of literary works, but it is applicable to play as well. He suggested that

> a literary work *purportedly imitates* (or reports) a series of speech acts, which in fact have no other existence. By doing so, it leads the reader to imagine a speaker, a situation, a set of ancillary events, and so on. (p. 14)

It is this "purporting" that creates the possibility for the reversals and satire, critique and commentary that some researchers have suggested is characteristic of play's relationship to nonplay.

Finally, play is also, and always, a defining activity, which is perhaps why it is itself so difficult to define. Because of this quality, play requires *interpretation* and resists operationalization. The study of play, perhaps more than any other topic, requires that researchers adapt themselves to the character of their subject and not the reverse. Researchers who have a compulsion for organization, predictability, and exacting definitions and methodologies produce only illusory theories and explanations, which distort play and fool only researchers. On the other hand, investigators who are more tolerant of disorganization, unpredictability, and loose and fuzzy definitions and methodologies are more likely to produce theories that allude to play (and this is the *best* we will ever do) and help to elucidate the nature of foolishness.

Anthropologists are well equipped to contribute to these studies, as our approach has always been "loose" and therefore flexible (it has to be when you study people on their own terms and in contexts that are familiar to them and strange to the researcher). As this method was developed in the past for the investigation of "exotic" peoples, it can easily be adapted for the investigation of what is still an exotic subject matter. My personal list of research that I would like to do or see done is the following:

1. It is imperative that anthropologists begin to produce "ethnographies of children's play" that are both textual and contextual in orientation. Currently there are few such studies available, and therefore almost all theorizing about play has been done on the basis of studies of

Western middle-class children. Because of this lack of information, differences between Western and non-Western (or middle-class and non-middle-class) children's play are often interpreted as evidence of deficiency rather than variation in play styles. As anthropologists know from their studies of other topics, such views generally last only as long as there is a deficiency of rich ethnographic material.

2. Studies of the varying and widening contexts of children's play (e.g., play in the immediate family or in the compound, village, neighborhood, school) should be made in order to explore not only how these particular contexts affect play texts but also how texts may both comment on and critique as well as transform contexts. Adopting this latter focus, the "games of order and disorder" that symbolically invert the social order, as Sutton-Smith has suggested, should be investigated to determine the nature and degree of their existence in other cultures.

3. Studies of relationships between play and sex roles, occupational roles, and cognitive skills are all important to pursue in attempting to determine what children actually learn in play. Do they, in fact, learn specific social roles and skills, or are they more generally "learning to learn" (Bateson, 1942)?

4. Cross-cultural studies focusing on developmental issues should be formulated specifically to put Piaget's and others' theories of play "stages" to the ethnographic test. In regard to these investigations, it is important to note that there is a particular lack of information on early infant play in the ethnographic literature.

5. Finally, research on the various forms of children's verbal play (e.g., riddles, puns, secret languages) and their cultural distribution should also be formulated. It would be particularly interesting to examine here the possibility that all (or most) types of children's speech play are parodies of adult–child communication events and adult–child relationships (as riddles may be viewed as parodies of the question–answer event typically found in schools and symbolic of the teacher–child relationship).

In conclusion, a brief summary of the new metaphors for old that have been delimited here would seem to be in order. In brief, play is an orientation or framing and defining *context* that players adopt toward something (an object, a person, a role, an activity, an event, etc.), which produces a *text* characterized by allusion (not distortion or illusion), transformation (not preservation), and *"purported* imitation" of the object, person, role, etc. In this way, play gives shape as well as expression to individual and societal affective and cognitive systems. These are play's products, and they are extremely consequential.

If this is our definition of play, then how can it be used to evaluate the discipline of anthropology? In the past, as has been illustrated here, anthropologists' theories of culture have determined their metaphors (or lack thereof) for play. Perhaps it is time for a change, and in fact many researchers have already begun to think about "reinventing" anthropology (e.g., Hymes, 1969), while others (e.g., Wagner, 1975) have suggested that invention is itself the key to understanding the relationship between the "culture" of anthropologists and the "culture" of our informants. I believe that the above definition of play can serve as well as a definition for anthropology. Is this not a discipline that requires the adoption of a contextual orientation for the interpretation of specific objects, persons, roles, and events (i.e., cultures); which produces particular types of texts (i.e., ethnographies) characterized by allusion (and hopefully not illusion), transformation (not preservation—although it has been this in the past), and *purported imitation* of these "cultures"? In our studies, we attempt both to shape and to give expression to individual and societal affective and cognitive systems. If these are the goals that motivate our "works," then perhaps we have always been *at* play—flying kites in many places.

CHAPTER 12

Selected References and Films

There are a number of important references on the general topic of play as well as the specific field of children's play that researchers interested in this subject should consult. The surplus-energy theory advanced by Schiller (1875) and H. Spencer (1873) in the 19th century, as well as Groos's (1898, 1901) survey of "animal" and "man" play studies written at the turn of the century, are all worthy of consideration by students interested in understanding the historical context out of which most 20th-century theories of play developed. Ariès (1962) and Stone (1971) enlarged this perspective in their discussions of the emergence of children and children's play in Western societies. The interpretive works of Huizinga (1938) and Caillois (1961), although not specifically concerned with children's play, are also important reading for play researchers.

A number of survey books, articles, readers, and bibliographies have recently appeared on the specific topic of children's play. One of the best in this regard is Herron and Sutton-Smith's *Child's Play* (1971). This book contains a useful collection of many of the most important articles written over the years on this subject. The experimental, ecological, psychoanalytic, cognitive, and developmental perspective are all included in this work, as is the Sutton-Smith/Piaget debate, but many of the more recent studies available are not reported here. However, reviews by Sutton-Smith (1975a) and J. L. and D. Singer (1976) cover several of the more recent studies. Sutton-Smith's *The Folkgames of Children* (1972a) provides a useful and needed compilation of many of his most significant publications on this topic. Included here in its entirety is his 1959 study of *The Games of New Zealand Children*, as well as examples of many of the Roberts and Sutton-Smith research projects. *The Dialectics of Play* (1976b) contains Sutton-Smith's most current theoretical statement on play as well as a number of his recent short papers on this subject, which are published here as a series of readings.

In Goodman's *The Culture of Childhood* (1970), a brief survey of anthropological studies of children's play, games, and humor is available. A discussion of anthropological studies of play is also available in Dolhinow and Bishop (1970) and in several studies by Norbeck (1969, 1971, 1974a,b). Norbeck's 1971 discussion appears in a *Natural History* special supplement devoted to the topic of play. Articles by other play researchers (e.g., Leacock, Sutton-Smith) are also included here. The proceedings of the first two annual meetings of The Association for the Anthropological Study of Play (TAASP) have recently been published, and they include a number of articles reporting current research in this area. *The Anthropological Study of Play: Problems and Prospects* (Lancy and Tindall, 1976) is the first proceedings volume, and it contains a number of articles on children's play that have been discussed in this book (e.g., Lancy, Rosenstiel, Schwartzman and Barbera, von Glascoe). The second volume, *Studies in the Anthropology of Play: Papers in Memory of B. Allan Tindall* (Stevens, 1977), also includes several articles on children's play as well as Sutton-Smith's keynote address to the members of the organization, entitled "Play, Games and Sports: Socialization or Innovation?" A recent review of anthropological studies of children's play is also available by Schwartzman (1976a). An earlier article by Mergen discussing "The Discovery of Children's Play" (1975) surveys and analyzes both historical and some ethnographic material on this subject.

Millar's *The Psychology of Play* (1968) is an excellent resource for students of play, because until recently many of the most significant studies of children's play have been made by psychologists. Singer (1973) included an excellent history and summary of theories of imaginative play, and Ellis presented a discussion of both "classical" and "modern" theories in his book *Why People Play* (1973). Garvey's new book, *Play* (1977), is also a useful and well-written introduction to the field that contains a survey of recent studies (mostly by psychologists) of children's play, focusing on play with motion, with objects, with language, with social materials, and with rules. Bruner, Jolly, and Sylva's *Play: Its Role in Development and Evolution* (1976) is *the* most comprehensive reader on play available, and it is therefore an important and necessary resource for students of this subject. Included here are articles on the evolution of play in animals and men, play with objects and tools, play and the social world, and play and the world of symbols.

The most extensive bibliography on children's play has been compiled by Herron *et al.* (1967), although it now needs to be updated. This resource contains psychological, psychiatric, anthropological, and sociological references. A more recent bibliography of children's play studies has been prepared by Schwartzman, "Works on Play: A Bibliography" (1977b). Sleet has also prepared a general play bibliography, *Interdisciplinary Research Index on Play: A Guide to the Literature* (1971). Avedon and Sutton-Smith's *The Study of Games* (1971) offers selected bibliographies on general studies of children's games, children's games in specific cultures, singing games, string-figure games, and a reference list of studies of children's games published in languages other than English between 1955 and 1965.

Finally, less extensive bibliographies on children's games in folklore and anthropological sources are available by Daiken (1950) and Hymes (1964:303–304). A comprehensive bibliographic survey of studies of speech play, including children's speech play, is available in Kirshenblatt-Gimblett's new book, *Speech Play* (1976a). A recent bibliographic compilation of studies of traditional games, including children's play, in Mexico has been prepared by Scheffler (1976).

FILMS ON CHILDREN'S PLAY

Baobab Play. 1974. Photographed and directed by John K. Marshall. 8 minutes. Rental $12, purchase $100.

Playing with Scorpions. 1973. Photographed and directed by John K. Marshall. 4 minutes. Rental $10, purchase $50.

Children Throw Toy Assegais. 1974. Photographed and directed by John K. Marshall. 4 minutes. Rental $10, purchase $50.

Tug of War. 1974. Photographed and directed by John K. Marshall. 6 minutes. Rental $10, purchase $80.

The Lion Game. 1973. Photographed and directed by John K. Marshall. 4 minutes. Rental $10, purchase $50.

Arrows. 1975. Film by Timothy Asch and Napoleon A. Chagnon. 10 minutes. Rental $12, purchase $110.

Children's Magical Death. 1975. Film by Timothy Asch and Napoleon A. Chagnon. 7 minutes. Rental $10, purchase $85.

Tug of War. 1975. Film by Timothy Asch and Napoleon A. Chagnon. 9 minutes. Rental $15, purchase $100.

Sandbox-Hazels. 1978. Photographed and directed by John K. Marshall and Roger Hart. 15 minutes. Rental $15, purchase $150.

Debree's Treehouse. 1978. Photographed and directed by John K. Marshall and Roger Hart. 15 minutes. Rental $15, purchase $150.

Sandbanks. 1978. Photographed and directed by John K. Marshall and Roger Hart. 15 minutes. Rental $15, purchase $150.

All films are 16mm color with synchronous sound and were produced by and are available from: Documentary Educational Resources, Inc., 24 Dane Street, Somerville, Massachusetts 02143.

Information on children's play appears in two forms in the anthropological literature. The fact that young humans play in one way or another in all societies of the world is illustrated by the numerous descriptions of this activity that appear in ethnographies. The second type of literature available consists of attempts on the part of investigators to formulate theories of play (e.g., Bateson, 1955, 1956; Roberts and Sutton-Smith, 1962). Fortunately, a third source of information has recently become available in the form of films made by ethnographers, specifically on the subject of children's play. The films listed above depict the activities of children at play in three very different societies: the !Kung Bushmen of South West Africa (now Namibia), the Yanomamö Indians of southern Venezuela, and white, middle-class children in Vermont, USA. In developing this series, Documentary Educational Resources (DER) offers students and researchers a unique opportunity to visually observe and compare children's play behavior in three different sociocultural contexts. These films would also be very useful in courses on child socialization and child development and psychology, as they illustrate aspects of non-Western children's behavior that until recently have been depicted only by verbal descriptions and still photos.

All of the above films are short, ranging in length from 4 to 15 minutes, and, therefore, it is necessary to have some familiarity with the ethnographic literature on the society (e.g., Lorna Marshall's *The !Kung of Nyae Nyae*, 1976; Napoleon Chagnon's *Yanomamö: The Fierce People*, 1968; and possibly John and Ann Fischer's *The New Englanders of Orchard Town, U.S.A.*, 1963 for the Vermont films), and it would also be useful to view these films in conjunction with others that are available on the culture (e.g., for the Bushmen, *The Hunters*, and for the Yanomamö, *The Yanomamö: A Multi-Disciplinary Study*).

The Bushmen films *(Baobab Play, Playing with Scorpions, Children Throw Toy Assegais, Tug of War, and The Lion Game)* are excellent depictions of the multiage composition of these children's social groups and its impact on their play. In *Baobab Play*, a group of 10 to 17 year-old boys throw sticks, berries, leaves, and so forth at each other from various positions in a large baobab tree and on the ground. These activities, however, are not performed in a competitive or aggressive manner. Sides or teams are not established, and there are no winners or losers as might be the case in American games such as cops and robbers or cowboys and Indians. Draper (1976) and Konner (1972) have both suggested that Bushmen children play in multiaged play groups because there are seldom large numbers of same-age children together in one context because of the small size of !Kung bands and the practice of lengthy birth spacing (three years). According to Draper, these ecological constraints help to produce a situation where meaningful competition cannot occur because, in order for a game to be competitive, players must be evenly matched. The noncompetitive and nonaggressive nature of Bushmen children's play is also supported by an ideological system that places a negative value on any kind of violence or competition between individuals or bands.

These values are also illustrated in *Children Throw Toy Assegais*. Here a group of boys throw small toy spears (assegais) at a tree in an attempt to develop their own throwing skills. The boys watch to see if their spear sticks into the tree, but they do not compete with each other or develop throwing contests where there are specifically designated winners and losers.

In contrast, the film *Arrows* depicts a group of Yanomamö boys engaged in a mock battle with each other using blunt, but still dangerous, arrows as weapons. The Yanomamö values of ferocity, aggression, and competition between individuals and groups are clearly demonstrated here. The parents' encouragement of these play battles is also illustrated by scenes that show their response as they sit on the sidelines watching the activity. These scenes are reminiscent of the kind of parental encouragement and vicarious enjoyment of competition that one witnesses during American Little League games. The dangers and risks inherent in a Yanomamö battle, even when it occurs as a play event, are demonstrated when an accident takes place at the end of the film (one child is hit in the eye with an arrow).

Although Bushmen children do not fight with or compete against each other, they do engage in some forms of play that expose them to environmental risks and that can be said to "bait nature." In *Playing with Scorpions*, a group of young children pick up scorpions and hold them on or near their own or others' arms and legs. The children know that scorpions cannot sting without striking, and so they are taking calculated risks in this game. The film shots portray the children's reactions in this game quite well, and even though the film is quite short, it is not for the squeamish.

In contrast to the aggression depicted in *Arrows*, the game of *Tug of War* as played by the Yanomamö seems remarkably free from aggression, competition, or interest in winning, perhaps because it is played here by the women and the children and not the men. The film was made on a rainy day, and the two "sides" slosh back and forth with each group appearing to enjoy being "taken." In the Bushmen film *Tug of War*, two groups of boys between the ages of 8 and 15 vie for a piece of rubber hose. In this instance, there are sides in the game (a situation not found in other Bushmen games), but again, there is no interest demonstrated in winning or losing.

The Vermont films illustrate one form of children's play sometimes referred to as *construction play*. These films are particularly useful in their depiction of how children both learn and express in play their culture's ideas about man's relation to nature. This point can also be illustrated by comparing the Vermont with the Bushmen films. *Sandbox-Hazels, Debree's Treehouse,* and *Sandbanks* all illustrate the American (and generally Western) view that "nature" exists to be reconstructed, rearranged, or "tamed" by man. This can be seen, for example, by comparing *Debree's Treehouse* with *Baobab Play.* In the former, the tree is hardly recognizable, as it has been transformed into a "treehouse," which has been constructed with boards, saws, hammers, and nails and which one enters by climbing a ladder. The children are very serious and pragmatic about their production, and their speech is focused on commands ("Nail this!") and requests ("Will you hand me the saw?"). In *Baobab Play,* the tree is unchanged by the children's play, as it is presumably respected or, at least, appreciated for the shade it provides on hot days. The children climb up, down, and around in this large tree without ladders or other apparatus and proceed to throw sticks, berries, and so forth at each other in a playful and generally inefficient manner. *Sandbanks* is perhaps the best film in the Vermont series, and it is an excellent documentation of American children's construction play. Here a large group of boys and girls concentrate on the construction of a dam to be dug out of a large sandbank. A dam, of course, is an excellent symbol of Western man's rearrangement and redirecting of nature, and the children approach their "task" with all the tools at hand—digging into the sandbank with coffee cans, shovels, buckets, and so forth. At the end of the film, the result of their work/play is shown as it is admired by the children. *Sandbox-Hazels* depicts two boys' construction of a highway in a sandbox. This is the least interesting of the Vermont films, although the boys' interaction with each other and with their cars (as they simulate motor noises) is intriguing to watch. I believe that this film could be shortened to 5 or 10 minutes with no loss of information. Unfortunately, all three of the Vermont films include a large number of tight, closeup shots that are not well balanced by shots that pan the entire play construction and that would give the viewer a better perspective on what is actually being constructed by the children. Nevertheless, the films are striking depictions of the Western view of man *versus* nature, which has increasingly come to haunt our culture. In these films, we see both the creative and the potentially destructive results of this world view, for here we see the beginnings of both skyscrapers and strip mining. If future films are planned for the Vermont series, I believe that ones illustrating American children's competitive games (e.g., possibly a Little League game) and make-believe role play (e.g., playing house or doctor) could be successfully contrasted with several of the Bushmen and Yanomamö films.

The film that best depicts non-Western children's imaginative role play is *Children's Magical Death.* This is a film of Yanomamö boys re-creating (and at times seeming to satirize) the behavior of their fathers and older brothers when they act as shamans *(shabori)*, who attempt either to cure sick children or to "kill" enemies spiritually. In Yanomamö society, shamans achieve these ends by taking a drug *(ebene)*, which is blown into their nostrils through a long, hollow tube. After taking the drug, the shaman goes into a trance and begins chanting and calling on spirits *(hekura)* to effect their cures or kills. This process is graphically depicted in the film *Magical Death*, which should definitely be seen in conjunction with *Children's Magical Death*. In the film, the children pretend to be shamans by blowing ashes into each other's nostrils through hollow stalks of grass and then chanting, dancing, and acting as if they are under the influence of the drug *ebene*. In this film, subtitles that translate a portion of the children's speech are included. These subtitles are useful for understanding the children's designation and interpretation of their behavior; however, one wishes that more translations had been offered here as well as in all of the other films. The subtitles also illustrate the multileveled nature of this play event, as we are made aware of the children's consciousness of the cameraman (as when one child comments to the other, "Brakiva!—That cameraman looks horny") and seeming interest in playing to the camera (this is also demonstrated visually) in the midst of their playing at being shamans (a role and activity that also has many playful features). At the conclusion of the film, the children attempt to cure a "sick" boy who is lying on a hammock, but this quickly turns into what looks like a lampooning of the whole event, as they end this activity by laughing, giggling, and falling over each other in the hammocks and on the ground.

The only Bushmen film that depicts a form of imaginative role play is *The Lion Game*. Here a group of boys ranging in age from 6 to 20 create a make-believe lion hunt. The young boys pretend to be the "dogs" who nip and bark at the lion (played by a young man in his early 20s), while the older boys act as the "hunters." The "hunters" pretend to shoot the lion with imaginary "carbines." After they make their "kill," the hunters begin to roll over the "carcass," but the lion springs back to life and begins to attack his killers as the game begins again. Finally, the hunters successfully kill the lion, and one of the younger children is brought close to the carcass in an effort to convince him that this time the lion is "really dead." As Seth Reichlin (1974) observed in his film notes for this particular movie, *The Lion Game* is a satire of Bantu hunting practices and *not* an imitation of Bushmen hunting techniques. The !Kung do not use guns and do not hunt lions or eat their meat. The movie is excellently filmed (and the pace is quite rapid at times), although it is quite short. The film is most notable for its depiction of the cleverness of the children in constructing their play satire (particularly their sound effects, i.e., skillful simulations of the dogs' yelping and barking and the lion's noises and actions).

OTHER FILMS OF INTEREST TO PLAY RESEARCHERS

Pizza Pizza Daddy-O. 1969. Written and directed by Bess Lomax Hawes and Robert Eberlein. 18 minutes. Rental $14, purchase $145. Produced at the Department of Anthropology, San Fernando Valley State College, Northridge, California. Available from University of California, Extension Media Center, Berkeley, California 94720. Film is 16mm, black-and-white with synchronous sound.

This film depicts a group of fourth-grade Afro-American girls playing singing games on a school playground in Los Angeles. In introducing and commenting on these singing games, the narrator adopts a diffusionist–particularist perspective that stresses the British origin of the lexical content of many of the games and the African origin of the games' stylistic features, particularly the musical and kinesic elements. Singing games are today played only infrequently by Anglo-American children (see Sutton-Smith and Rosenberg, 1961), and when they are, it is generally at the initiation of a teacher or some other adult. It is therefore possible to suggest that, at least in the United States, this play form has become the "exclusive cultural property of Black American children, both urban and rural" (Hawes, 1969:1). In the film, two game spatial patterns are illustrated: the ring and the parallel line. In both instances, one player initiates the action and the song, which is then repeated by the other players acting in unison, and so the game proceeds in a call–response fashion. The filmmakers have stated that the players organized and directed themselves in the enactment of the song games that are shown here, and the film depicts the various and subtle ways players make room for each other and move and adjust to each other's presence and actions. Unfortunately, since the filmmakers concentrated on the filming of the actual game in process, there is not much material on pregame negotiations, decisions, jockeying for leader position, and so forth. The importance of these activities for a successful game production, however, is apparent in the film, and it would have been useful to include some information on the girls' relations to one another. Eight song games are recorded in the film: "My Boyfriend Gave Me a Box," "This-a-Way Valerie," "When I Was a Baby," "Imbileenie," "This-a-Way Batman," "Mighty Mighty Devil," "My Mother Died," and the game from which the movie takes its name, "Pizza Pizza Daddy-O."

This is an excellent film and a must for use in any course on children's play as well as classes in child socialization and child development and psychology. This film would also be extremely useful for courses and/or research in spatial and movement analysis (e.g., proxemics and kinesics) and also sociolinguistic studies.

The Nature of Play—Part I: River Otters. 1954. Produced by Gregory Bateson. 16 mm, black-and-white with sound. Not commercially available.

This film was produced by Gregory Bateson as part of his inquiry into the nature of animal communication. In the early 1950s, Bateson was particularly interested in discovering whether or not animals qualified their messages in some fashion that would indicate that they had some awareness of their signaling process. In order to investigate this topic, Bateson began a study of river otters in the Fleishhacker Zoo in San Francisco and became especially intrigued by their play behavior. The film *River Otters* is one of the first recorded discussions of Bateson's ideas about the nature of play and paradox and, more specifically, his examination of the importance of the message "This is play." The difficulties and possibilities for misinterpretation of metacommunicative statements such as "This is play" are related here to the phenomenon of schizophrenia. In this film, Bateson has discussed in detail changes in the otters' play behavior as it was recorded over a period of time in the zoo. Initially the otters engaged in solitary play activities; however, one day Bateson lowered a piece of paper on a string to the otters after their meal. The otters immediately came over to this new "toy," and a rough-and-tumble conflict developed between them that Bateson stated was clearly not a "real fight." The next day and throughout the entire summer of 1953, the otters engaged in active and sustained rough-and-tumble play with each other, and one of these bouts is illustrated in the movie. In the fall, a chasing game developed between the otters that replaced the wrestling. By December, however, the chasing diminished, and at the end of the year, the otters had returned to their original solitary and noninteractive state. Bateson suggested in the film that "by presenting the otters with a toy which was *not* food, a context was created for interaction which was not combat." He went on to suggest that the dramatic change in the otters' behavior may have been the result of this kind of "psychotherapeutic" experience or intervention. An interesting discussion of this movie and its implications for the study of play is available in Bateson (1956, beginning on p. 175). Until this film becomes commercially available, this discussion stands as the most extensive and useful description of the movie. *River Otters* was shown recently at the 1977 meetings of The Association for the Anthropological

Study of Play (TAASP) in San Diego, and individuals attending the meeting were fortunate in being able both to view the film and to hear Bateson comment on and answer questions about it.

Trobriand Cricket: An Ingenious Response to Colonialism. 1973. Director and anthropological consultant, Jerry W. Leach. Filmmaker, Gary Kildea. Color, 54 minutes. Rental $33, purchase $515. Distributed by University of California, Extension Media Center, Berkeley, California 94720.

This film illustrates the Trobriand Islanders transformation of the notoriously reserved British game of cricket (introduced at the turn of the century by missionaries) into an exuberant, sensual, and also political event. It is an excellent depiction of the sophistication, ingenuity, and creativity of individuals from traditional cultures, and as such, it portrays behaviors that are strangely ignored by many ethnographers who seem to believe that "natives" exposed to Western beliefs and practices will always mindlessly adopt and accept them. Annette Weiner (1977) discussed this topic in her recent review of the movie:

> When a group of elders describe the way villagers were determined to "rubbish" (i.e., throw out) the British game and make cricket a Trobriand contest, their words speak of cricket, but the camera beautifully communicates to us the unique strength and resiliency of these people in the face of European dominating influences. (p. 506)

Trobriand Cricket is an excellent film with multiple uses. For courses on play, games, or sports, it specifically illustrates the importance of analyzing the transformative (as opposed to preservative) qualities of play. This film would also be useful in general and introductory anthropology courses, as it vividly demonstrates the importance of the concept of culture (when it is viewed as a dynamic as opposed to a static system) for interpreting our own and other's actions.

Movies available from the collection of Audio Visual Services, 17 Willard Building, The Pennyslvania State University, University Park, Pennsylvania 16802. (Unseen by reviewer.) Films are 16 mm, color or black-and-white with sound; and they are listed below with a distributor code and catalog number for reference purposes.

E383   Baga (Guinea Coast). Mankalla game. 1960. 11 minutes. Rental $7.50.

E384   Baga (Guinea Coast). Children's game. 1960. 3½ minutes. Rental $5.50.

E1823   !ko Bushmen (South Africa, Kalahari Desert). The //oli leapfrog game of men (grasshopper). 1971. Color. 3 minutes. Rental $6.80.

E1826   !ko Bushmen (South Africa, Kalahari Desert). Men's game *xhana*. 1970. Color. 4 minutes. Rental $6.80.

E1831   !ko Bushmen (South Africa, Kalahari Desert). Stick catapulting game of men, *ebi*. 1970. Color. 5 minutes. Rental $6.80.

E2024   !ko Bushmen (South Africa, Kalahari Desert). Women playing the ball game *dam*. 1970. Color. 7 minutes. Rental $9.50.

10434   Boy's Game (IFF). Boys from the Pushtu tribe of Badakhstan in Northeastern Afghanistan play games that involve hopping on one leg. Produced by Julien Bryan. 1968. Color, natural sounds only. 5 minutes. Rental $8.00.

10440   Buzkashi (IFF). Equestrian team competition of Pashtu men trying to drag a carcass into a goal. Produced by Julien Bryan. 1968. Color, natural sounds and music. 9 minutes. Rental $8.50.

E1295   Miao (Tak-Province, Thailand). Spinning game, *tau dumlu*. 1964–1965. Color. 2 minutes. Rental $6.80.

E1296   Miao (Tak-Province, Thailand). Badminton game, *tau mdi*. 1964/65. Color. 4 minutes. Rental $6.80.

E1297   Miao (Tak-Province, Thailand). Game of darts, *saba*. 1964/65. Color. 4 minutes. Rental $6.80.

E1298   Miao (Tak-Province, Thailand). Ball and spinning games on New Year. 1964–1965. Color. 6 minutes. Rental $10.25.

E1294   Miao (Tak-Province, Thailand). Boys' running game, *tsa-ge*. 1964–1965. Color. 4 minutes. Rental $6.80.

10905   Spear Making; Boys' Spear Fight (UCEMC). Australian aborigine boys play with toy spears. 1965. 10 minutes. Rental $7.00.

E994   Waurá (Upper Xingú, Brazil) *Javari*, mock battle. 1964. Color. 11 minutes. Rental $13.25.

E995   Waurá (Upper Xingú, Brazil). Wrestling match. 1964. Color. 5½ minutes. Rental $6.80.

E116   Krahó (Tocantin, Brazil). Ritual relay races. 1949. Color. 5 minutes. Rental $6.80.

E865   Krahó (Tocantin, Brazil). String games. 1964. Color. 5½ minutes. Rental $6.80.

E1323   Krahó, (Tocantin, Brazil). Making toys from palm leaves. 1965. Color. 11 minutes, Rental $13.25.

919.8-2   Angotee, Story of an Eskimo Boy (BFI). Movie follows the life of an Eskimo boy from birth to maturity—includes boys' games. 1953. 31 minutes. Rental $16.

30227   Children Adrift (MGHT). A day in the life of a boy in the Paris slums. 1962. 26 minutes. Rental $10.50.

20443   Spanish Children (EBEC). Activities of a boy and his sister during harvest time in a mountain village of southern Spain. 1965. Color. 16 minutes. Rental $11.00.

E1148   Baden, West Germany. "Cart wheeling" in Buchenbach. 1966. 17 minutes. Rental $9.50.

E789   Baden, West Germany. Boys' games at Pentecost in Fussbach. 1964. 5 minutes. Rental $5.50.

E1867   Portugal. Quarterstaff game at Basto. 1970. Color. 8 minutes. Rental $10.25.

10589   Game of Staves (UCEMC) (North American Indians). Pomo boys play variation of dice game using 6 staves and 12 counters. 1962. Color. 10 minutes. Rental $8.50, sale $130.00.

E875   Nonouti (Micronesia, Gilbert Islands). Children's games. 1963. 3 minutes. Rental $10.25.

E936   Nonouti (Micronesia, Gilbert Islands). Plaiting a ball. 1963. 3 minutes. Rental $5.50.

E876   Nonouti (Micronesia, Gilbert Islands). Ball games of girls, *warebwi*. 1963. 1½ minutes. Rental $5.50.

E877   Onotoa (Micronesia, Gilbert Islands). Hitting-stick game, *bwerea*. 1964. Color. 3 minutes. Rental $6.80.

E878   Nonouti (Micronesia, Gilbert Islands). Rock-hauling game, *katua*. 1963. 4½ minutes. Rental $5.50.

E879   Nonouti (Micronesia, Gilbert Islands). Ball game of men, *boiri*. 1963. 3 minutes. Rental $6.80.

E880   Nonouti (Micronesia, Gilbert Islands). Fabrication of a ball with a stone core. 1963. 6 minutes. Rental $6.30.

E881   Nonouti (Micronesia, Gilbert Islands). Ball game of men, *oreano*. 1963. 3 minutes. Rental $6.80.

E882   Nonouti (Micronesia, Gilbert Islands). Cockfight. 1963. Color. 3 minutes. Rental $6.80.

E883   Tabiteuea (Micronesia, Gilbert Islands). String games. 1963. 8½ minutes. Rental $6.30.

E884   Onotoa (Micronesia, Gilbert Islands). String games. 1964. 8½ minutes. Rental $6.30.

E885   Niutao (Polynesia, Ellice Islands). String games. 1963. 6 minutes. Rental $6.30.

E420   Niutao (Polynesia, Ellice Islands). Contests and games. 1960. 6½ minutes. Rental $6.30.

References

Abrahams, R. D., 1962. Playing the dozens. *Journal of American Folklore, 75,* 209–220.

Abrahams, R. D. (Ed.), 1969. *Jump-Rope Rhymes: A Dictionary.* Austin: University of Texas Press.

Abrahams, R. D., and Dundes, A., 1972. Riddles. In *Folklore and Folklife: An Introduction,* R. M. Dorson (Ed.). Chicago: University of Chicago Press, pp. 129–143.

Abrams, D. M., and Sutton-Smith, B., 1977. The development of the trickster in children's narrative. *Journal of American Folklore, 90,* 29–47.

Ager, L. P., 1974. Storyknifing: An Alaskan girls' game. *Journal of the Folklore Institute* (Indiana University), *11.*

Ager, L. P., 1975. Play as folklore: An Alaskan Eskimo example. *The Association for the Anthropological Study of Play Newsletter, 2*(3), 16–18.

Ager, L. P., 1976. The reflection of cultural values in Eskimo children's games. In *The Anthropological Study of Play: Problems and Prospects,* D. F. Lancy and B. Allan Tindall (Eds.). Cornwall, N.Y.: Leisure Press, pp. 79–86.

Aldis, O., 1975. *Play Fighting.* New York: Academic Press.

Alexander, F., 1958. A contribution to the theory of play. *Psychoanalytic Quarterly, 27,* 175–193.

Almy, M. (Ed.), 1968. *Early Childhood Play: Selected Readings Related to cognition and motivation.* New York: Simon and Schuster.

Ames, L. B., 1966. Children's stories. *Genetic Psychological Monographs, 73,* 337–396.

Ammar, H., 1954. *Growing Up in an Egyptian Village.* London: Routledge and Kegan Paul.

Ammons, R. B., 1950. Reactions in a projective doll-play interview of white males two to six years of age to differences in skin color and facial features. *Journal of Genetic Psychology, 76,* 323–341.

Ammons, R. B., and Ammons, H. S., 1959. Parent preferences in young children's doll-play interviews. *Journal of Abnormal and Social Psychology, 44,* 490–505.

Anderson, R. T., and Mitchell, E. M., 1977. Play and Personality in Denmark. Paper presented at the joint meeting of the American Ethnological Society and The Association for the Anthropological Study of Play, San Diego, California, April.

Anna, M., 1930. The mueso game among the Basoga. *Primitive Man, 11,* 71–74.

Appleton, L. E., 1910. *A Comparative Study of the Play Activities of Adult Savages and Civilized Children.* Chicago: University of Chicago Press.

Ariès, P., 1962. *Centuries of Childhood.* New York: Vintage Books—Alfred A. Knopf.

Ashton, E. H., 1952. *The Basuto.* London: Oxford University Press, 1967 ed.

Aufenanger, H., 1958. Children's games and entertainments among the Kumngo tribe in central New Guinea. *Anthropos, 53,* 575–584.

Aufenanger, H., 1961. A children's arrow-thrower in the central highlands of New Guinea. *Anthropos, 56,* 633.

Avedon, E. M., 1971. The structural elements of games. In *The Study of Games,* E. Avedon and B. Sutton-Smith (Eds.). New York: John Wiley, pp. 419–426.

Avedon, E., and Sutton-Smith, B. (Ed.), 1971. *The Study of Games.* New York: John Wiley.

Axline, V. M., 1947. *Play Therapy.* New York: Ballantine, 1969 ed.

Ayoub, R., and Barnett, S. A., 1965. Ritualized verbal insult in white high school culture. *Journal of American Folklore, 78,* 337–344.

Babcock, W. H., 1888. Games of Washington children. *American Anthropologist, 1,* 243–284.

Babcock-Abrahams, B., 1975. *The Reversible World: Essays in Symbolic Inversion.* Ithaca, N.Y.: Cornell University Press.

Bach, G. R., 1946. Father fantasies and father typing in father-separated children. *Child Development, 17,* 63–80.

Bacon, M. K., Barry, H., III, and Child, I. L., 1965. A cross-cultural study of drinking: II. Relations to other features of culture. *Quarterly Journal of Studies on Alcohol,* Supplement 3, 29–48.

Bailey, N., 1974. Structural aspects of the Anglo-Saxon riddle. *Semiotica, 10,* 143–175.

Baker, H. J., 1913. *Children of Rhodesia.* London: Charles H. Kelly.

Baldwin, J. D., and Baldwin, J. I., 1977. The role of learning phenomena in the ontogeny of exploration and play. In *Primate Bio-Social Development,* S. Chevalier-Skolnikoff and F. Poirier (Eds.). New York: Garland, pp. 343–406.

Ball, D., 1972. The scaling of gaming. *Pacific Sociological Review, 15,* 277–294.

Ball, D., 1974. Control vs. complexity—Continuities in the scaling of gaming. *Pacific Sociological Review, 17,* 167–184.

Barker, R., and Wright, H. F., 1966. *One Boy's Day.* Hamden, Conn.: Archon.

Barnett, S. A., 1958. Exploratory behavior. *British Journal of Psychology, 49,* 289–310.

Barnouw, V., 1973. *Culture and Personality.* Homewood, Ill.: Dorsey Press, rev. ed.

Barry, H. A., III, Bacon, M. K., and Child, I. L., 1957. A cross-cultural survey of some sex differences in socialization. *Journal of Abnormal and Social Psychology, 55,* 327–332.

Barry, H. A., III, Bacon, M. K., and Child, I. L., 1967. Definitions, ratings, and bibliographic sources for child-training practices in 110 cultures. In *Cross-Cultural Approaches,* C. S. Ford (Ed.). New Haven Conn.: HRAF Press, pp. 293–331.

Barry, H. A., III, and Paxon, L. M., 1971. Infancy and early childhood: Cross-cultural codes 2. *Ethnology, 10,* 466–508.

Barry, H. A., III, Roberts, J. M., 1972. Infant socialization and games of chance. *Ethnology, 11,* 296–308.

Barsamian, G., and Clapp, B., 1974. Child ethology: Turning TV on the kids. Paper presented at Annual Meeting of the Central States Anthropological Society, Chicago, Ill.

Barton, F. R., 1908. Children's games in British New Guinea. *Journal of the Royal Anthropological Institute, 38,* 259–279.

Bascom, W., 1969. *The Yoruba of Southwest Nigeria.* New York: Holt, Rinehart and Winston.

Bateson, G., 1936. *Naven.* Stanford, Calif.: Stanford University Press, 1958 ed.

Bateson, G., 1942. Social planning and the concept of deutero-learning. *Conference on Science, Philosophy and Religion, Second Symposium.* New York: Harper and Row. Reprinted in *Steps to an Ecology of Mind,* 1972. New York: Ballantine, pp. 159–176.

Bateson, G., 1946a. The pattern of an armaments race, Part I: An anthropological approach. *Bulletin of the Atomic Scientists, 2*(5 and 6), 10–11. Reprinted in *Personal Character and Cultural Milieu,* 1948, D. G. Haring (Ed.). Syracuse, N.Y.: Edwards Brothers, pp. 85–88.

Bateson, G., 1946b. The pattern of an armaments race, Part II: An analysis of nationalism. *Bulletin of Atomic Scientists*, 2 (7 and 8), 26–28. Reprinted in *Personal Character and Cultural Milieu*, D. G. Haring (Ed.). Syracuse, N.Y.: Edwards Brothers, pp. 89–93.

Bateson, G., 1953. The position of humor in human communication. In *Circular Causal and Feedback Mechanisms in Biological and Social Sciences; Transactions of the Ninth Conference*. H. von Foerster (Ed.). New York: Josiah Macy, Jr. Foundation, pp. 1–47.

Bateson, G., 1955. A theory of play and fantasy. In *American Psychiatric Association, Psychiatric Research Reports*, II, December. Reprinted in *Steps to an Ecology of Mind*, 1972, New York: Ballantine, pp. 177–193.

Bateson, G., 1956. The message "this is play." In *Group Processes: Transactions of the Second Conference*. New York: Josiah Macy, Jr. Foundation, pp. 145–242.

Bateson, G., 1958. *Epilogue to Naven*. Stanford, Calif.: Stanford University Press, 2nd ed.

Bateson, G., 1972. *Steps to an Ecology of Mind*. New York: Ballantine Books.

Bateson, G., 1977. Play and paradigm. The keynote address delivered at the Third Annual Meeting of The Association for the Anthropological Study of Play, San Diego, California, April 6–9.

Bateson, G., Jackson, D., Haley, J., and Weakland, J., 1956. Toward a theory of schizophrenia. *Behavioral Science*, 1, 251–264. Reprinted in *Steps to an Ecology of Mind*, 1972, New York: Ballantine, pp. 201–227.

Bateson, G., and Mead, M., 1942. *Balinese Character: A Photographic Analysis*. New York Academy of Sciences, Special Publication, Volume II.

Beach, F. A., 1945. Current concepts of play in animals. *American Naturalist*, 79, 523–541.

Béart, Ch., 1955. *Jeux et jouets de l'ouest africain*, II, Dakar, IFAN.

Beckwith, M. W., 1922. *Folk-games of Jamaica*. Publication of the Folklore Foundation, Vassar College, No. 1.

Bekoff, M., 1972. The development of social interaction, play, and metacommunication in mammals: An ethological perspective. *The Quarterly Review of Biology*, 47, 412–434.

Bekoff, M., 1974. Social play and play soliciting in infant canids. *American Zoologist*, 14, 323–340.

Belo, J., 1937. Balinese children's drawings. *Djawa*, 17.

Belo, J., 1953. *Bali; Temple Festival*. Locust Valley, N.Y.: J. J. Augustin.

Belo, J., 1960. *Trance in Bali*. New York: Columbia University Press.

Benedict, R., 1934. *Patterns of Culture*. Boston: Houghton Mifflin.

Beran, J. A., 1973a. Characteristics of children's play and games in the southern Philippines. *Silliman Journal*, 20, 100–113.

Beran, J. A., 1973b. Some elements of power in Filipino children's play. *Silliman Journal*, 20, 194–207.

Bereiter, C., and Engelmann, S., 1966. *Teaching Disadvantaged Children in the Pre-School*. Englewood Cliffs, N.J.: Prentice-Hall.

Berkovits, R., 1970. Secret languages of school children. *New York Folklore Quarterly*, 26, 127–152.

Berlyne, D. E., 1960. *Conflict, Arousal and Curiosity*. New York: McGraw-Hill.

Berlyne, D. E., 1966. Curiosity and exploration. *Science*, 153, 25–33.

Berlyne, D. E., 1969. Laughter, humor, and play. In *Handbook of Social Psychology*, vol. 3, 2nd ed., G. Lindzey and E. Aronson (Eds.). Reading, Mass.: Addison-Wesley, pp. 795–852.

Berndt, R. M., 1940. Some aboriginal children's games. *Mankind*, 2, 289–293.

Berne, E., 1964. *Games People Play*. New York: Grove Press.

Bernstein, B., 1966. Elaborated and restricted codes: Their social origins and some consequences. In *The Ethnography of Communication*, J. Gumperz and D. Hymes (Eds.). Special publication, *American Anthropologist*, 66, part 2.

Berreman, G., 1966. Anemic and anetic analysis in social anthropology. *American Anthropologist, 68,* 346–354.

Best, E., 1925. *Games and Pastimes of the Maori.* Dominion Museum Bulletin, No. 8.

Biblow, E., 1973. Imaginative play and the control of aggressive behavior. In *The Child's World of Make-Believe,* J. L. Singer (Ed.). New York: Academic Press, pp. 104–128.

Bidney, D., 1967. *Theoretical Anthropology.* New York: Schocken Books.

Black, M., 1962. *Models and Metaphors.* Ithaca, N.Y.: Cornell University Press.

Blanchard, K., 1976. Team sports and violence: An anthropological perspective. In *The Anthropological Study of Play: Problems and Prospects,* D. F. Lancy and B. Allan Tindall (Eds.). Cornwall, N.Y.: Leisure Press, pp. 94–108.

Blount, B. G., 1975. Review article: Studies in child language, An anthropological view. *American Anthropologist, 77,* 580–600.

Blurton Jones, N., 1967. An ethological study of some aspects of social behavior of children in nursery school. In *Primate Ethology,* D. Morris (Ed.). Garden City, N.Y.: Doubleday, pp. 437–463, 1969 ed.

Blurton Jones, N., 1972a. Categories of child–child interaction. In *Ethological Studies of Child Behaviour,* N. Blurton Jones (Ed.). Cambridge, England: Cambridge University Press, pp. 97–127.

Blurton Jones, N. (Ed.), 1972b. *Ethological Studies of Child Behaviour.* Cambridge, England: Cambridge University Press.

Boas, F., 1888. The game of cat's cradle. *International Archiv für Ethnographie, 1,* 538–539.

Bohannan, L., and Bohannan, P., 1953. *The Tiv of Central Nigeria.* London: International Institute (West. Af., Part 8, in Ethnog. Survey of Af.).

Bohannan, P., 1963. *Social Anthropology.* New York: Holt, Rinehart and Winston.

Bohannan, P., 1965. The Tiv of Nigeria. *Peoples of Africa,* J. Gibbs (Ed.). New York: Holt, Rinehart and Winston, pp. 513–546.

Bohannan, P., and Bohannan, L., 1958. A source notebook on the Tiv life cycle. *Three Source Notebooks in Tiv Ethnography.* New Haven, Conn.: Human Relations Area Files.

Bolton, H. C., 1888. *The Counting-Out Rhymes of Children: Their Antiquity, Origin, and Wide Distribution.* London: Elliot Stock.

Bolton, H. C., 1891. Some Hawaiian pastimes. *Journal of American Folklore, 4,* 21–26.

Botkin, B., 1937. *The American Play-Party Song.* Lincoln: The University of Nebraska Press.

Botvin, G. J., 1977. A Proppian approach to the analysis of children's fantasy narratives. In *Studies in the Anthropology of Play: Papers in Memory of B. Allan Tindall,* P. Stevens (Ed.). Cornwall, N.Y.: Leisure Press.

Boyce, E. R., and Bartlett, K., 1940. *Number Rhymes and Finger Plays.* London: Pitman.

Brand, S., 1976. For God's sake, Margaret: Conversation with Gregory Bateson and Margaret Mead. *Co-Evolution Quarterly, 10,* 32–44.

Brewster, P. G., 1939. Rope-skipping, counting-out and other rhymes of children. *Southern Folklore Quarterly, 3,* 173–184.

Brewster, P. G., 1944. Two games from Africa. *American Anthropologist, 46,* 268–269.

Brewster, P. G., 1945a. Johnny on the pony, A New York State game. *New York Folklore Quarterly, 1,* 239–240.

Brewster, P. G., 1945b. Some unusual forms of hopscotch. *Southern Folklore Quarterly, 9,* 229–231

Brewster, P. G., 1948. Forfeit games from Greece and Czechoslovakia. *Hoosier Folklore, 8,* 76–83.

Brewster, P. G., 1949a. Some Hungarian games. *Southern Folklore Quarterly, 13,* 175–179.

Brewster, P. G., 1949b. Some traditional games from Roumania. *Journal of American Folklore, 59,* 114–124.

Brewster, P. G., 1951. Four games of tag from India. *Midwest Folklore, 1,* 239–241.

Brewster, P. G., 1952, *Children's Games and Rhymes*. The Frank C. Brown Collection of North Carolina Folklore, *1*, 32–219. Durham, North Carolina: North Carolina University Press.

Brewster, P. G., 1953. *American Nonsinging Games*. Norman: University of Oklahoma Press.

Brewster, P. G., 1955. A collection of games from India, with some notes on similar games in other parts of the world. *Zeitschrift für Ethnologie, 80,* 88–102.

Brewster, P. G., 1956. The importance of the collecting and study of games. *Eastern Anthropologist, 10,* 5–12. Reprinted in *The Study of Games*, E. Avedon and B. Sutton-Smith (Eds.). New York: John Wiley, pp. 9–17.

Brewster, P. G., 1957. Some games from Czechoslovakia. *Southern Folklore Quarterly, 21,* 165–174.

Brewster, P. G., 1959. Three Russian games and their Western and other parallels. *Southern Folklore Quarterly, 23,* 126–131.

Brewster, P. G., 1960. A sampling of games from Turkey. *East and West* (Rome), *11,* 15–20.

Britt, S. H., and Balcom, M. M., 1941. Jumping-rope rhymes and the social psychology of play. *Journal of Genetic Psychology, 58,* 289–305.

Britt, S. H., and Janus, S. Q., 1941. Toward a social psychology of human play. *Journal of Social Psychology, 13,* 351–384.

Bronfrenbrenner, U., 1974. Developmental research, public policy, and the ecology of childhood. *Child Development, 45,* 1–5.

Browne, R. B., 1955. Southern California jump-rope rhymes: A study in variants. *Western Folklore, 14,* 3–22.

Bruner, J. S., 1962. *On Knowing*. Cambridge, Mass.: Harvard University Press.

Bruner, J. S., 1972. Nature and uses of immaturity. *American Psychologist, 27,* 687–708.

Bruner, J. S., 1975. Play is serious business. *Psychology Today, 8,* 81–83.

Bruner, J. S., Jolly, A., and Sylva, K. (Eds.), 1976. *Play: Its Role in Development and Evolution*. New York: Basic Books.

Bruner, J. S., and Sherwood, V., 1976. Peekaboo and the learning of rule structures. In *Play: Its Role in Development and Evolution*, J. Bruner, A. Jolly, and K. Sylva (Eds.). New York: Basic Books, pp. 277–285.

Buckley, B., 1966. Jump-rope rhymes—Suggestions for classification and study. *Keystone Folklore Quarterly, 11,* 99–111.

Buckley, W., 1967. *Sociology and Modern Systems Theory*. Englewood Cliffs, N.J.: Prentice-Hall.

Bühler, C., 1930. *The Mental Development of Children*. New York: Harcourt.

Bühler, C., 1935. *From Birth to Maturity*. London: Kegan, Paul.

Burling, R., 1970. *Man's Many Voices*. New York: Holt, Rinehart and Winston.

Burridge, K. O., 1957. A Tangu game. *Man, 57,* 88–89.

Cable, M., 1975. *The Little Darlings: A History of Child Rearing in America*. New York: Charles Scribner's Sons.

Caillois, R., 1961. *Man, Play, and Games*. New York: The Free Press.

Caplan, F., and Caplan, T., 1973. *The Power of Play*. Garden City, N.Y.: Anchor Press/Doubleday.

Caring, M., 1977. Structural parallels in dreams and narratives. In *Studies in the Anthropology of Play: Papers in Memory of B. Allan Tindall*, P. Stevens (Ed.). Cornwall, N.Y.: Leisure Press.

Carroll, L., 1865. *Alice's Adventures in Wonderland*. London: Macmillan.

Carroll, L., 1871. *Through the Looking-Glass, and What Alice Found There*. London: Macmillan.

Cavallo, D., 1976. Social reform and the movement to organize children's play during the progressive era. *History of Childhood Quarterly, 3.*

Centner, T., 1962. *L'enfant africain et ses jeux.* Elisabethville: CEPSI.

Chagnon, N., 1968. *Yanomamö: The Fierce People.* New York: Holt, Rinehart and Winston.

Chamberlain, A. F., 1901. *The Child: A Study in the Evolution of Man.* London: Charles Scribner.

Chamberlain, A. F., 1910. Nith-songs. In *Handbook of American Indians North of Mexico,* Bulletin 30, part 2, F. W. Hodge (Ed.). Washington, D. C.: Smithsonian Institution.

Chaplan, J. H., 1956. A note on Mancala games in northern Rhodesia. *Man, 56,* 168.

Chase, J. H., 1905. Street games of New York City. *Pedagogical Seminary, 12,* 503–504.

Chase, R. A., Williams, D., Welcher, D. W., Fisher, J. J., and Gfeller, S. F., 1977. Design of Learning Environments for Infants. Presentation at the Panel on Play and Learning sponsored by Johnson and Johnson, New Orleans, La., March.

Cheska, A., 1975. Stewart Culin: An early ethnologist of games. In *The Association for the Anthropological Study of Play Newsletter, 2,* 4–13.

Cheska, A., 1977. Native American Games as Strategies of Societal Maintenance. Paper presented at the joint meeting of the American Ethnological Society and The Association for the Anthropological Study of Play, San Diego, California, April.

Chevalier-Skolnikoff, S., 1974. The primate play face: A possible key to the determinants and evolution of play. In *The Anthropological Study of Human Play,* E. Norbeck (Ed). Rice University Studies, vol. 60, pp. 9–29.

Child, I. L., Storn, T., and Veroff, J., 1958. Achievement themes in folk tales related to socialization practice. In *Motives in Fantasy, Action, and Society,* J. W. Atkinson (Ed.). Princeton, N.J.: Van Nostrand.

Chukovsky, K., 1963, *From Two to Five,* translated and edited by M. Morton. Berkeley: University of California Press.

Cohen, M., 1942. Causation and its application to history. *Journal of the History of Ideas, 3,* 12–29.

Colby, B. N., 1970. The description of narrative structures. In *Cognition: A Multiple View,* P. Garvin (Ed.). New York: Spartan, pp. 177–192.

Cole, M., Gay, J., Glick, J. A., and Sharp, D. W., 1971. *The Cultural Context of Learning and Thinking.* New York: Basic Books.

Coleman, J. S., 1971. Learning through games. In *The Study of Games,* E. Avedon and B. Sutton-Smith (Eds.). New York: John Wiley, pp. 69–70.

Collard, R. R., 1971. Exploratory and play behaviors of infants reared in an institution and in lower and middle-class homes. *Child Development, 42,* 1003–1015.

Conklin, H. C., 1956. Tagalog speech disguise. *Language, 32,* 136–139.

Conklin, H. C., 1964. Linguistic play in its cultural context. In *Language in Culture and Society,* D. Hymes (Ed.). New York: Harper and Row, pp. 295–300.

Connolly, K., and Smith, P. K., 1972. Reactions of pre-school children to a strange observer. In *Ethological Studies of Child Behaviour,* N. Blurton Jones (Ed.). Cambridge, England: Cambridge University Press, pp. 157–172.

Cooper, J. M., 1949. A cross-cultural survey of South American Indian tribes: Games and gambling. *Bureau of American Ethnology,* Bulletin No. 143, pp. 503–524. Washington, D. C.: Government Printing Office.

Corter, C. M., Rheingold, H. L., and Eckerman, C. O., 1972. Toys delay the infant's following of his mother. *Developmental Psychology, 6,* 138–145.

Covarrubias, M., 1938. *The Island of Bali.* New York: Knopf.

Cox, J. H., 1942. Singing games. *Southern Folklore Quarterly, 6,* 183–261.

Crombie, J. W., 1886. History of the game of hop-scotch. *Journal of the Royal Anthropological Institute, 15,* 403–408.

Crook, J. H., and Goss-Custard, J. D., 1972. Social Ethology. In *Annual Review of Psychology*, vol. 23, P. H. Mussen and M. R. Rosenzweig (Eds.). Palo Alto, Calif.: Annual Reviews, Inc., pp. 182–312.

Crosswell, T. R., 1898. Amusement of Worcester school children. *The Pedagogical Seminary*, 6, 314–371.

Csikszentmihalyi, M., 1975. *Beyond Boredom and Anxiety*. San Francisco: Jossey-Bass.

Csikszentmihalyi, M., and Bennett, S., 1971. An exploratory model of play. *American Anthropologist*, 73, 45–58.

Culin, S., 1891. Street games of boys in Brooklyn. *Journal of American Folklore*, 4, 221–237.

Culin, S., 1894. Mancala, The national game of Africa. *Annual Report of the United States National Museum*, Washington, D. C.: Government Printing Office.

Culin, S., 1895. *Korean Games, with Notes on the Corresponding Games of China and Japan*. Philadelphia: University of Pennsylvania Press. Republished in 1958 as *Games of the Orient*, Rutland, Vermont: Charles Tuttle.

Culin, S., 1898. Chess and playing cards. *Annual Report of the United States National Museum*. Washington, D. C.: Government Printing Office.

Culin, S., 1899. Hawaiian games. *American Anthropologist*, 1, 201–247.

Culin, S., 1900. Philippine games. *American Anthropologist*, New Series, 2, 643–656.

Culin, S., 1903. America, the cradle of Asia. *American Association for the Advancement of Science Proceedings*, 52, 449–501.

Culin, S., 1907. *Games of North American Indians*. 24th Annual Report, Bureau of American Ethnology. Washington, D. C.: Government Printing Office. Republished in 1975, New York: Dover.

Curtis, H. S., 1915. *Education through Play*. New York: Macmillan.

Daiken, L. H., 1950. Children's games: A bibliography. *Folklore*, 61, 218–222.

Daniel, Z. T., 1892. Kansu: A Sioux game. *American Anthropologist*, 5, 215–216.

Dansky, J. L., and Silverman, I. W., 1973. Effects of play on associative fluency in preschool children. *Developmental Psychology*, 9, 38–43.

Darwin, C., 1872. *The Expression of the Emotions in Man and Animals*. London: Murray.

Delafosse, M., 1922. Langage secrète et langage conventionnel dans l'Afrique noir. *L'Anthropologie*, 32, 83–92.

de Mause, L. (Ed.), 1974. *The History of Childhood*. New York: The Psychohistory Press.

Demos, J., 1970. *A Little Commonwealth: Family Life in Plymouth Colony*. London: Oxford University Press.

Dennis, W., 1940. *The Hopi Child*. New York: Appleton-Century. Reprinted 1972 by Arno Press, New York.

Dennis, W., 1942. Piaget's questions applied to a child of known environment. *Journal of Genetic Psychology*, 60, 307–320.

Dennis, W., 1943. Animism and related tendencies in Hopi children. *Journal of Abnormal and Social Psychology*, 38, 31–36.

Dennis, W., and Russell, R. W., 1940. Piaget's questions applied to Zuni children. *Child Development*, 11, 181–187.

Deutsch, M., et al., 1967. *The Disadvantaged Child*. New York: Basic Books.

Devereux, G. A., 1951. Mohave Indian verbal and motor profanity. In *Psychoanalysis and the Social Sciences*, vol. 3, G. Róheim (Ed.). New York: International Universities Press, pp. 99–127.

Dewey, J., 1909. *School and Society*. Chicago: University of Chicago Press.

Diamond, S., 1974. Introduction. *Doll Play of Pilagá Indian Children*. New York: Vintage.

Dickie, J., and Bagur, J. S., 1972. Considerations for the study of language in young low-income minority group children. *Merrill-Palmer Quarterly of Behavior and Development*, 18, 25–38.

Dolhinow, P. J., and Bishop, N., 1970. The development of motor skills and social relationships among primates through play. In *Minnesota Symposia on Child Psychology,* vol. 4, J. P. Hill (Ed.). Minneapolis: University of Minnesota Press, pp. 141–198.

Dorsey, J. O., 1891. Games of Teton Dakota children. *American Anthropologist, 4,* 329–346.

Douglas, M., 1968. The social control of cognition: Some factors in joke perception. *Man, 3,* 361–375.

Douglas, N., 1916. *London Street Games,* 2nd ed. London: Chatto and Winders.

Doyle, P. H., 1976. The differential effects of multiple and single niche play activities on interpersonal relations among preschoolers. In *The Anthropological Study of Play: Problems and Prospects,* D. F. Lancy and B. Allan Tindall (Eds.). Cornwall, N.Y.: Leisure Press, pp. 189–197.

Draper, P., 1975. Cultural pressure on sex differences. *American Ethnologist, 2,* 602–616.

Draper, P., 1976. Social and economic constraints on child life among the !Kung. In *Kalahari Hunter-Gatherers,* R. Lee and I. DeVore (Eds). Cambridge, Mass.: Harvard University Press, pp. 199–217.

DuBois, C., 1944. *The People of Alor.* Minneapolis: University of Minnesota Press.

Dundes, A., 1964a. *The Morphology of North American Indian Folktales.* Helsinki, Finland: FF Communications, #195.

Dundes, A., 1964b. On game morphology: A study of the structure of non-verbal folklore. *New York Folklore Quarterly, 20,* 276–288.

Dundes, A., 1964c. Texture, text, and context. *Southern Folklore Quarterly, 28,* 251–265.

Dundes, A., Leach, J. W., and Ozkök, B., 1970. Strategy of Turkish boys' verbal dueling rhymes. *Journal of American Folklore, 83,* 325–349.

Dunlap, H. L., 1951. Games, sports, and other vigorous recreational activities and their function in Samoan culture. *Research Quarterly, 22,* 298–311.

Edel, M. M., 1957. *The Chiga of Western Uganda.* New York: Oxford University International African Institute Press.

Edmonson, M. S., 1967. Play: Games, gossip and humor. In *Handbook of Middle American Indians,* R. Wauchope (Ed.). Austin: University of Texas Press, pp. 191–206.

Edmonson, M. S., 1973. Book review of Lévi-Strauss's Mythologiques, L'homme nu. *American Anthropologist, 75,* 374–378.

Ehrmann, J., 1968. Homo ludens revisited. *Yale French Studies, 41,* 31–57.

Eibl-Eibesfeldt, I., 1970. *Ethology: The Biology of Behavior.* New York: Holt, Rinehart and Winston.

Eifermann, R., 1970. Cooperation and egalitarianism in kibbutz children's games. *Human Relations, 23,* 579–587.

Eifermann, R., 1971a. *Determinants of Children's Game Styles.* Jerusalem: Israel Academy of Sciences and Humanities.

Eifermann, R., 1971b. Social play in childhood. In *Child's Play,* R. Herron and B. Sutton-Smith (Eds.). New York: John Wiley, pp. 270–297.

Elder, J. D., 1965. *Song Games from Trinidad and Tobago,* Publication of the American Folklore Society, vol. 16.

El' Konin, D., 1971. Symbolics and its functions in the play of children. In *Child's Play,* R. Herron and B. Sutton-Smith (Eds.). New York: John Wiley, pp. 221–230.

Elliott, R. C., 1960. *The Power of Satire.* Princeton, N.J.: Princeton University Press.

Ellis, M. J., 1973. *Why People Play.* Englewood Cliffs, N.J.: Prentice-Hall.

Elmore, C. M., and Gorham, D. R., 1957. Measuring the impairment of the abstracting function with the proverb test. *Journal of Clinical Psychology, 13,* 263–266.

Ember, C. R., 1973. Feminine task assignment and the social behavior of boys. *Ethos, 1,* 424–439.

Emerson, J. S., 1924. Hawaiian string games. *Folklore,* Vassar College Publication, No. 5.

Erasmus, C. J., 1950. Patolli, pachisi and the limitation of possibilities. *Southwestern Journal of Anthropology, 6*, 369–387. Reprinted in *The Study of Games*, 1971, E. M. Avedon and B. Sutton-Smith, (Eds.). New York: John Wiley, pp. 109–129.

Erikson, E. H., 1940. Studies in the interpretation of play: Part I. Clinical observations of play disruption in young children. *Genetic Psychology Monographs, 22*, 557–671.

Erikson, E. H., 1941. Further exploration in play construction: Three spatial variables in their relation to sex and anxiety. *Psychological Bulletin, 38*, 748.

Erikson, E. H., 1943. *Observations on the Yurok: Childhood and World Image*. University of California Publications in American Archaeology and Ethnology, *35*, No. 10.

Erikson, E. H., 1951. Sex differences in play configurations of pre-adolescents. *American Journal of Ortho-Psychiatry, 21*, 667–692. Reprinted in *Child's Play*, 1971, R. Herron and B. Sutton-Smith (Eds.). New York: John Wiley, pp. 126–144.

Erikson, E. H., 1963. *Childhood and Society*. New York: W. W. Norton.

Evans, P., 1955. *Jump Rope Rhymes*. San Francisco: The Porpoise Bookshop.

Fabian, J., 1971. Language, history and anthropology. *Philosophy of the Social Sciences, 1*, 19–47.

Fabian, J., 1974. Genres in an emerging tradition: An anthropological approach to religious communication. In *Changing Perspectives in the Scientific Study of Religion*, A. W. Eister (Ed.). New York: John Wiley, pp. 249–272.

Farrer, C. R., 1976. Play and inter-ethnic communication. In *The Anthropological Study of Play: Problems and Prospects*, D. F. Lancy and B. Allan Tindall (Eds.). Cornwall, N.Y.: Leisure Press, pp. 86–92.

Fein, G., 1975. A transformational analysis of pretending. *Developmental Psychology, 11*, 291–296.

Feitelson, D., 1954. Patterns of early education in the Kurdish community. *Megamot, 5*, 95–109.

Feitelson, D., 1959. Some aspects of the social life of Kurdish Jews. *Jewish Journal of Sociology, 1*, 201–216.

Feitelson, D., 1972. Developing imaginative play in preschool children as a possible approach to fostering creativity. *Early Child Development Care, 1*, 181–195.

Feitelson, D., and Ross, G. S., 1973. The neglected factor—play. *Human Development, 16*, 202–223.

Ferguson, C. A., 1964. Baby talk in six languages. In *The Ethnography of Communication*, J. Gumperz and D. Hymes (Eds.). Special Issue *American Anthropologist*, Part 2, *66*, 103–114.

Fernandez, J., 1974. The mission of metaphor in expressive culture. *Current Anthropology, 15*, 119–145.

Fife, A. E., 1946. Rope skipping rhymes collected at Greensboro, North Carolina. *Journal of American Folklore, 59*, 321–322.

Firth, R., 1930. A dart match in Tikopia: A study in the sociology of primitive sport. *Oceania, 1*, 64–96.

Fischer, J., and Fischer, A., 1963. The New Englanders of Orchard Town, U.S.A. In *Six Cultures: Studies of Child Rearing*, B. Whiting (Ed.). New York: John Wiley, pp. 869–1010.

Fock, N., 1958. Cultural aspects and social functions of the "oho" institution among the Waiwai. Proceedings of the Thirty-Second International Congress of Americanists, Copenhagen: Munksgaard, pp. 136–140.

Ford, R., 1904. *Children's Rhymes, Games, and Songs*. Paisley, Scotland: Alex Gardner.

Fortes, M., 1938. Social and psychological aspects of education in Taleland. *Africa*, Supplement to vol. 11, no. 4. Reprinted in *From Child to Adult*, 1970, J. Middleton (Ed.). Garden City, N.Y.: Natural History Press, pp. 14–74.

Freud, A., 1946. *The Psychoanalytical Treatment of Children*. New York: Schocken, 1964 ed.

Freud, S., 1900. *The Interpretation of Dreams*, vol. 4 and 5 of The Standard Edition of the Complete Psychological Works, J. Strachey (Ed.). London: Hogarth Press, 1953 ed.

Freud, S., 1905. *Jokes and Their Relation to the Unconscious*. J. Strachey (Trans.). New York: W. W. Norton, 1963 ed.

Freud, S., 1909. *Analysis of a Phobia in a Five Year Old Boy*, vol. 10 of the Standard Edition of the Complete Psychological Works of Sigmund Freud. London: Hogarth.

Freud, S., 1918. *Totem and Taboo*. New York: New Republic.

Freud, S., 1920. *Beyond the Pleasure Principle*, J. Strachey (Trans.). New York: W. W. Norton. 1976 ed.

Freud, S., 1928. *The Future of an Illusion*. New York: Doubleday, 1957 ed.

Freyberg, J., 1973. Increasing the imaginative play of urban disadvantaged kindergarten children through systematic training. In *The Child's World of Make-Believe*, J. L. Singer (Ed.). New York: Academic Press, pp. 129–154.

Fry, W. F., Jr., 1963. *Sweet Madness: A Study of Humor*, Palo Alto, Calif.: Pacific Books.

Garcia, L. I., 1929. Children's Games. *Mexican Folkways, 5*, 79–85.

Garcia, L. I., 1932. Children's games. *Mexican Folkways, 7*, 63–74.

Gardner, B. T., and Gardner, R. A., 1971. Two-way communication with an infant chimpanzee. In *Behavior of Nonhuman Primates*, vol. 4, A. Schrier and F. Stolinitz (Eds.). New York: Academic Press, pp. 117–184.

Gardner, H., 1972. *The Quest for Mind*. New York: Knopf.

Gardner, M., 1960. *The Annotated Alice*. New York: Clarkson N. Potter.

Gardner, R., 1971. *Therapeutic Communication with Children: The Mutual Storytelling Technique*. New York: Science House.

Garvey, C., 1974. Some properties of social play. *Merrill-Palmer Quarterly, 20*, 163–180.

Garvey, C., 1977. *Play*. Cambridge, Mass.: Harvard University Press.

Garvey, C., and Berndt, R., 1975. The Organization of Pretend Play. Paper presented at the Annual Meeting of the American Psychological Association, Chicago, Ill. September.

Gay, J., and Cole, M., 1967. *The New Mathematics and an Old Culture*. New York: Holt, Rinehart and Winston.

Gearing, F., 1973. Hidden Curriculum. Paper presented to the Northeastern Regional Conference of the University Council for Educational Administration, Buffalo, N.Y., April.

Gearing, F., and Tindall, B. A., 1973. Anthropological studies of the educational process. *Annual Review of Anthropology, 2*, 95–105.

Geertz, C., 1972. Deep play: Notes on the Balinese cockfight. *Daedalus, 101*, 1–37.

Geertz, C., 1973. *The Interpretation of Cultures*. New York: Basic Books.

Georges, R. A., 1969. The relevance of models for analyses of traditional play activities. *Southern Folklore Quarterly, 33*, 1–23.

Georges, R. A., and Dundes, A., 1963. Toward a structural definition of the riddle. *Journal of American Folklore, 76*, 111–118.

Gesell, A., 1946. *The Child from Five to Ten*. New York: Harper.

Gesell, A., 1948. *Studies in Child Development*. New York: Harper.

Gilmore, J., 1966. Play: A special behavior. In *Current Research in Motivation*, R. N. Haber (Ed.). New York: Holt, Rinehart, pp. 343–355.

Gilmore, M. R., 1926. Some games of Arikara Children. *Indian Notes, 3*, 9–12.

Ginott, H., 1965. *Between Parent and Child*. New York: Avon Books.

Ginsburg, H., and Opper, S., 1969. *Piaget's Theory of Intellectual Development*. Englewood Cliffs, N.J.: Prentice-Hall.

Gladwin, T., and Sarason, S. B., 1953. *Truk: Man in Paradise*. New York: Viking Fund Publications in Anthropology, No. 20.

Goffman, E., 1961. *Encounters*. Indianapolis: Bobbs-Merrill.

Goffman, E., 1974. *Frame Analysis*. New York: Harper and Row.

Goldberg, S., and Lewis, M., 1969. Play behavior in the year-old infant: Early sex differences. *Child Development, 40,* 21–31.

Goldings, H. J., 1974. Jump-rope rhymes and the rhythm of latency development in girls. *The Psychoanalytic Study of the Child, 29,* 431–450.

Goldstein, K. S., 1971. Strategy in counting out: An ethnographic folklore field study. In *The Study of Games,* E. Avedon and B. Sutton-Smith (Eds.). New York: John Wiley, pp. 167–178.

Gomme, A. B., 1894. *The Traditional Games of England, Scotland and Ireland,* vol. 1. London: Nutt.

Gomme, A. B., 1898. *The Traditional Games of England, Scotland and Ireland,* vol. 2. London: Nutt.

Gomme, A. B., and Scarp, C. J., 1909. *Children's Singing Games.* London: Novello.

Goodenough, W. H., 1964. Cultural anthropology and linguistics. In *Language in Culture and Society,* D. Hymes (Ed.). New York: Harper and Row, pp. 36–39.

Goodman, M. E., 1970. *The Culture of Childhood.* New York: Teachers College Press.

Gossen, G. H., 1976. Verbal dueling in Chamula. In *Speech Play,* B. Kirshenblatt-Gimblett (Ed.). Philadelphia: University of Pennsylvania Press, pp. 121–146.

Gould, R., 1972. *Child Studies Through Fantasy.* New York: Quadrangle.

Gowlett, D. F., 1968. Some secret languages of children in South Africa. *African Studies, 27,* 135–139.

Gramza, A. F., 1970. Preferences of preschool children for enterable play boxes. *Perceptual and Motor Skills, 31,* 177–178.

Gramza, A. F., 1972. A measured approach to improvement of play environments. *JOHPER, Leisure Today, 43* (June).

Granqvist, H., 1975. *Birth and Childhood among the Arabs.* New York: AMS Press.

Greenfield, P. M., 1966. On culture and conservation. In *Studies in Cognitive Growth,* J. S. Bruner *et al.* (Eds.). New York: John Wiley, pp. 225–256.

Griaule, M., 1935. *Jeux et divertissements abyssins,* Paris.

Griaule, M., 1938. *Jeux Dogons,* Travaux et Mémoires de l'Institute d'Ethnologie, vol. 32, Paris.

Grief, E. B., 1976. Sex role playing in pre-school children. In *Play: Its Role in Development and Evolution,* J. S. Bruner, A. Jolly, and K. Sylva (Eds.). New York: Basic Books, pp. 385–391.

Groos, K., 1898. *The Play of Animals.* London: Chapman and Hall.

Groos, K., 1901. *The Play of Man.* New York: Appleton.

Guilford, J. P., 1967. *The Nature of Human Intelligence.* New York: McGraw-Hill.

Gulick, L. H., 1920. *A Philosophy of Play.* New York: Charles Scribner's Sons.

Gullen, F. D., 1950. *Traditional Number Rhymes and Games.* Publications of the Scottish Council for Research in Education, no. 32. London: University of London Press.

Gump, P. V., Schoggen, P., and Redl, F., 1963. The behavior of the same child in different milieus. In *The Stream of Behavior,* R. Barker (Ed.). New York: Appleton-Century-Crofts, pp. 169–202.

Gump, P. V., Schoggen, P. H., Sutton-Smith, B., Schoggen, M., and Goldberg, T., 1955. Wally O'Neil at Home (vol. 1), Wally O'Neil at Camp (vol. 2), Wayne State University Library Manuscript.

Gump, P. V., and Sutton-Smith, B., 1955a. Activity-setting and social interaction. *American Journal of Orthopsychiatry, 25,* 755–760. Reprinted in *Child's Play,* 1971, R. Herron and B. Sutton-Smith (Eds.). New York: John Wiley, pp. 96–102.

Gump, P. V., and Sutton-Smith, B., 1955b. The "it" role in children's games. *The Group, 17,* 3–8.

Gump, P. V., and Yueng-Hung, M., 1954. Active games for physically handicapped children. *Physical Therapy Review, 34,* 171–174.

Haas, M., 1964. Thai word games. In *Language in Culture and Society,* D. Hymes (Ed.). New York: Harper and Row, pp. 301–303.

Haas, M., 1967. A Taxonomy of Disguised Speech. Paper presented to the Linguistic Society of America.

Haas, M., 1969. Burmese disguised speech. *Bulletin of the Institute of History and Philology (Academia Sinica 39,* part 2), 277–285.

Haddon, A. C., 1902. Australian children's games. *Nature, 66,* 380–381.

Haddon, A. C., 1903. A few American string figures and tricks. *American Anthropologist, 5,* 213–223.

Haddon, A. C., 1908. Notes on children's games in British New Guinea. *Journal of the Royal Anthropological Institute, 38,* 289–297.

Haddon, K., 1917–1918. Some Australian string figures. *Proceedings of Royal Society of Victoria, 30,* 121–136.

Haley, J., 1955. Paradoxes in play and fantasy and psychotherapy. *Psychiatric Research Reports,* December.

Haley, J., 1963. *Strategies of Psychotherapy.* New York: Grune and Stratton.

Haley, J., 1973. Strategic therapy when a child is presented as the problem. *Journal of Child Psychiatry, 4,* 641–659.

Haley, J., 1976. Development of a theory: A history of a research project. In *Double Bind: The Foundation of the Communicational Approach to the Family.* New York: Grune and Stratton, pp. 59–104.

Hall, C. S., and Lindzey, G., 1957. *Theories of Personality.* New York: John Wiley.

Hall, E. T., 1959. *The Silent Language.* Garden City, N.Y.: Doubleday.

Hall, E. T., 1966. *The Hidden Dimension.* Garden City, N.Y.: Doubleday.

Hall, G. S., 1904. *Adolescence,* vol. 1. New York: D. Appleton.

Hall, J., 1941. Some party games of the great Smoky Mountains. *Journal of American Folklore, 54,* 68–71.

Hallowell, A. I., 1955. *Culture and Experience.* Philadelphia: University of Pennsylvania Press.

Halpert, H., 1945. Children's rimes from New Hampshire. *Journal of American Folklore, 58,* 349–351.

Hamnett, I., 1967. Ambiguity, classification and change: The function of riddles. *Man, 2,* 379–392.

Handelman, D., 1975. Expressive interaction and social structure: Play and an emergent game form in an Israeli social setting. In *Organization of Behavior in Face-to-Face Interaction,* A. Kendon and M. Ritchie Key (Eds.). The Hague: Mouton, pp. 389–414.

Handelman, D., 1977a. Play and ritual: Complementary frames of meta communication. In *It's a Funny Thing, Humor,* A. J. Chapman and H. Foot (Eds.). London: Pergamon, pp. 185–192.

Handelman, D., 1977b. *Work and Play among the Aged: Interaction, Replication and Emergence in a Jerusalem Setting.* Assen/Amsterdam: Van Gorcum.

Harlow, H. F., 1949. The formation of learning sets. *Psychological Review, 56,* 51–65.

Harlow, H. F., and Harlow, M. K., 1962. Social deprivation in monkeys. *Scientific American, 207,* 136.

Harlow, H. F., and Harlow, M. K., 1965. The affectional systems. In *Behavior of Nonhuman Primates,* vol. 2, A. M. Schrier, H. F. Harlow, and F. Stollnitz (Eds.). New York: Academic, pp. 287–334.

Harlow, H. F., and Harlow, M. K., 1969. Effects of various mother–infant relationships on rhesus monkey behaviors. In *Determinants of Infant Behavior,* vol. 4, B. M. Foss (Ed.). London: Methuen, pp. 15–35.

Harlow, H. F., and Suomi, S. J., 1971. Social recovery by isolation-reared monkeys. *Proceedings of the National Academy of Science, 68,* 1534–1538.

Harney, W., 1952. Sport and play amidst the aborigines of the Northern Territory. *Mankind, 4,* 377–379.

Harris, M., 1968. *The Rise of Anthropological Theory.* New York: Thomas Y. Crowell.

Harris, M., 1976. History and significance of the emic/etic distinction. In *Annual Review of Anthropology,* B. J. Siegel et al. (Eds). Palo Alto, Calif.: Annual Reviews, Inc., pp. 329–350.

Harris, T., 1968. *I'm OK, You're OK.* New York: Harper and Row.

Harrison, H. S., 1947. A bolas-and-hoope game in East Africa. *Man, 47,* 153–155.

Hartmann, H., and Kris, E., 1945. The genetic approach in psychoanalysis. *The Psychoanalytic Study of the Child, 1,* 11–30.

Hassrick, R., and Carpenter, E., 1944. Rappahannock games and amusements. *Man, 17,* 29–39.

Hawes, B. L., 1969. Pizza pizza daddy-o. Film notes. Berkeley: University of California Extension Media Center.

Hawthorne, R., 1966. Classifying jump-rope games. *Keystone Folklore Quarterly, 11,* 99–111.

Hayes, C., 1976. The imaginary pulltoy. In *Play: Its Role in Development and Evolution,* J. Bruner, A. Jolly, and K. Sylva (Eds.). New York: Basic Books, pp. 534–536.

Henry, J., 1963. *Culture against Man.* New York: Vintage Books, 1965 ed.

Henry, J., and Henry, Z., 1944. *Doll Play of Pilagá Indian Children.* New York: American Orthopsychiatric Association. Republished in 1974. New York: Vintage-Random House.

Herron, R. E., Haines, S., Olsen, G., and Hughes, J., 1967. *Children's Play: A Research Bibliography.* Champaign: University of Illinois Motor Performance Laboratory, Children's Research Center.

Herron, R. E., and Sutton-Smith, B. (Eds.), 1971. *Child's Play.* New York: John Wiley.

Hesse, M. B., 1966. *Models and Analogies in Science.* Notre Dame, Ind.: University of Notre Dame Press.

Hilger, I. M., 1951. Chippewa child life and its cultural background. *Bureau of American Ethnology,* Bulletin No. 146. Washington, D.C.: Government Printing Office.

Hirschberg, L. R., 1913. Dog Latin and sparrow languages used by Baltimore children. *Pedagogical Seminary, 20,* 257–258.

Hocart, A. M., 1909. Two Fijian games. *Man, 9,* 184–185.

Hodge, F. W., 1890. A Zuni foot-race. *American Anthropologist, 3,* 227–231.

Hogbin, H. I., 1946. A New Guinea childhood: From weaning till the eighth year in Wogeo. *Oceania, 16,* 275–296.

Holtzappel, H. A., 1952. *Sundase Kinderspelen,* 2 vols., Ph.D. Thesis, Leuven, Belgium.

Honigmann, J. J., 1976. *The Development of Anthropological Ideas.* Homewood, Ill.: Dorsey Press.

Hostetler, J., and Huntington, G., 1971. *Children in Amish Society: Socialization and Community Education.* New York: Holt, Rinehart and Winston.

Howard, D., 1958a. Australian "hoppy" hopscotch. *Western Folklore, 17,* 163–175.

Howard, D., 1958b. The games of knucklebone in Australia. *Western Folklore, 17,* 34–44.

Howard, D., 1959. Ball bouncing customs and rhymes in Australia. *Midwest Folklore, 9,* 77–87.

Howard, D., 1960a. Marble games of Australian children. *Folklore, 71,* 165–179.

Howard D., 1960b. The "toodlembuck"—Australian children's gambling device and game. *Journal of American Folklore, 73,* 53–54.

Hsu, F. L. K., 1963. *Clan, Caste and Club.* New York: Van Nostrand, Reinhold.

Huizinga, J., 1938. *Homo Ludens.* Boston: Beacon, 1955 ed.

Humphrey, J. H., 1975. Child Learning through Active Play. Paper presented at the

presented at the Second Annual Meeting of The Association for the Anthropological Study of Play, Atlanta, Ga., March 31–April 3.

Lancy, D., and Tindall, B. A. (Eds.), 1976. *The Anthropological Study of Play: Problems and Prospects.* Cornwall, N.Y.: Leisure Press.

Landauer, T. K., and Whiting, J. W. M., 1962. Infantile stimulation and adult stature of human males. *American Anthropologist, 66,* 1007–1028.

Landy, D., 1959. *Tropical Childhood: Cultural Transmission and Learning in a Rural Puerto Rican Village.* New York: Harper and Row, 1965 ed.

Langness, L. L., 1974. *The Study of Culture.* San Francisco: Chandler and Sharp.

Lansley, K., 1968. A Collection and Classification of the Traditional Melanesian Play Activities with a Supplementary Bibliography. M.A. Thesis, University of Alberta, Edmonton.

Lantis, M., 1946. *Eskimo Childhood and Interpersonal Relationships.* Seattle: University of Washington Press, 1960 ed.

Laycock, D., 1972. Towards a typology of ludlings, or play-languages. *Linguistic Communications, Working Papers of the Linguistic Society for Australia, 6,* 61–113. Clayton, Victoria: Monash University.

Lazar, J. W., and Beckhorn, G. D., 1974. Social play or the development of social behavior in ferrets *(Mustela putorius). American Zoologist, 14,* 405–414.

Leach, E., 1970. *Claude Lévi-Strauss.* New York: The Viking Press.

Leach, G. M., 1972. A comparison of the social behavior of some normal and problem children. In *Ethological Studies of Child Behaviour,* N. Blurton Jones (Ed.). Cambridge, England: Cambridge University Press, pp. 249–281.

Leacock, E., 1971. At play in African villages. *Natural History,* December, Special Supplement on Play, pp. 60–65.

Leakey, L. S. B., 1938. A children's game: West Australia and Kenya. *Man, 38,* 176.

Lehrs, M., 1969. *Late Gothic Engravings of Germany and the Netherlands.* New York: Dover.

Leighton, D., and Kluckhohn, C., 1947. *Children of the People.* New York: Farrar, Straus, and Giroux, 1974 ed.

Leiris, M., 1948. La langue secrète des Dogons de Sanga. *Soudan Français,* Travaux et Mémoires de l'Institut d'Ethnologie, 50. Paris: Université de Paris.

Leis, P., 1972. *Enculturation and Socialization in an Ijaw Village.* New York: Holt, Rinehart and Winston.

Lesser, A., 1933. *The Pawnee Ghost Dance Hand Game: A Study of Cultural Change.* Columbia University Contributions to Anthropology, *16.*

Lever, J., 1974. *Games Children Play: Sex Differences and the Development of Role Skills.* Ph.D. Thesis, Yale University, New Haven, Conn.

Lever, J., 1975. *Sex-Role Socialization and Social Structure: The Place of Complexity in Children's Games.* Paper presented at the Annual Meeting of the Pacific Sociological Association, Victoria, B.C.

Levin, H., and Wardwell, E., 1971. The research uses of doll play. In *Child's Play,* R. Herron and B. Sutton-Smith (Eds.). New York: John Wiley, pp. 145–184.

LeVine, R. A., 1973. *Culture, Behavior and Personality.* Chicago: Aldine.

LeVine, R., and LeVine, B., 1963. Nyansongo: A Gusii community in Kenya. In *Six Cultures: Studies of Child Rearing,* B. Whiting (Ed.). New York: John Wiley, pp. 19–202.

Lévi-Strauss, C., 1949. *The Elementary Structures of Kinship.* Boston: Beacon Press.

Lévi-Strauss, C., 1955. The Structural Study of Myth. *Journal of American Folklore, 78,* 428–444.

Lévi-Strauss, C., 1962. *The Savage Mind.* Chicago: University of Chicago Press, 1966 ed.

Lévi-Strauss, C., 1964. *The Raw and the Cooked.* Paris: Plon.

Lévi-Strauss, C., 1967. *From Honey to Ashes.* Paris: Plon.

Lévi-Strauss, C., 1968. *The Origin of Table Manners.* Paris: Plon.

Lévi-Strauss, C., 1971. *Man Naked*. Paris: Plon.

Lévi-Strauss, C., 1974. Structuralism and Ecology. In *Readings in Anthropology, 1975–76*, A. Weiss (Ed.). Guilford, Conn.: Dushkin, pp. 226–233.

Levy, D. M., 1937. Sibling rivalry. *American Orthopsychiatry Association Research Monographs*, No. 2.

Lieberman, J. N., 1965. Playfulness and divergent thinking: An investigation of their relationship at the kindergarten level. *Journal of Genetic Psychology, 107*, 219–224.

Lieberman, J. N., 1967. A developmental analysis of playfulness as a clue to cognitive style. *The Journal of Creative Behavior, 1*, 391–397.

Lieberman, J. N., 1977. *Playfulness: Its Relationship to Imagination and Creativity*. New York: Academic Press.

Linton, R., 1945. *The Cultural Background of Personality*. New York: D. Appleton Century.

Loizos, C., 1967. Play behavior in higher primates: A review. In *Primate Ethology*, D. Morris (Ed.). Garden City, N.Y.: Doubleday Press, pp. 226–282, 1969 ed.

Lomax, A., and Berkowitz, N., 1972. The evolutionary taxonomy of culture. *Science, 177*, 228–239.

Lorenz, K., 1956. Plays and vacuum activities. In *L'instinct dans le comportement des animaux et de l'homme*, M. Autuori *et al.* (Eds.). Paris: Masson.

Lorenz, K., 1976. Psychology and phylogeny. In *Play: Its Role in Development and Evolution*, J. Bruner, A. Jolly, and K. Sylva (Eds.). New York: Basic Books, pp. 84–95.

Lowenfeld, M., 1935. *Play in Childhood*. New York: John Wiley, 1967 ed.

Lowie, R., 1920. *Primitive Society*. New York: Boni and Liveright.

Lurie, N. O., 1971. Matilda Coxe Evans Stevenson. In *Notable American Women*, vol. 3, E. T. James (Ed.). Cambridge, Mass.: Harvard University Press, pp. 373–374.

Lüschen, G. (Ed.), 1970. *The Cross-Cultural Analysis of Games*. Champaign, Ill.: Stipes.

McCall, R. B., 1974. Exploratory manipulation and play in the human infant. *Monographs of the Society for Research in Child Development, 39*, No. 155.

McCulloch, W., 1965. *Embodiments of Mind*. Cambridge, Mass.: MIT Press.

McDowell, J. H., 1974. *Interrogative Routines in Mexican-American Children's Folklore*. Working Papers in Sociolinguistics, no. 20, Austin, Texas: Southwest Educational Development Educational Laboratory.

McGhee, Z., 1900. A study in the play life of some South Carolina children. *The Pedagogical Seminary, 7*, 459–478.

McGrew, W. C., 1972. *An Ethological Study of Children's Behavior*. New York: Academic Press.

McPhee, C., 1938. Children and music in Bali. *Djawa, 18*, 1–15.

Maccoby, E. E., 1959. Role-taking in childhood and its consequences for social learning. *Child Development, 30*, 239–252.

Maccoby, M., 1976. *The Gamesman*. New York: Simon and Schuster.

Maccoby, M., Modiano, N., and Lander, P., 1964. Games and social character in a Mexican village. *Psychiatry, 27*, 150–162.

Mackay, R., 1974. Conceptions of children and models of socialization. *Ethnomethodology*, R. Turner (Ed.). Harmondsworth, England: Penguin, pp. 180–193.

Madsen, M. C., 1971. Developmental and cross-cultural differences in the cooperative and competitive behavior of young children. *Journal of Cross-Cultural Psychology, 2*, 365–371.

Madsen, M. C., and Shapira, A., 1970. Cooperative and competitive behavior of urban Afro-American, Anglo-American, Mexican-American, and Mexican village children. *Developmental Psychology, 3*, 16–20.

Mahony, D., 1977. A Piagetian analysis of children's fantasy narratives. In *Studies in the Anthropology of Play: Papers in Memory of B. Allan Tindall*, P. Stevens (Ed.). Cornwall, N.Y.: Leisure Press.

Maier, H. W., 1965. *Three Theories of Child Development*. New York: Harper and Row.

Malinowski, B., 1922. *Argonauts of the South Pacific*. New York: Dutton.

Malinowski, B., 1927. *Sex and Repression in Savage Society*. London: Routledge and Kegan Paul, 1953 ed.

Malinowski, B., 1929. *The Sexual Life of Savages in North-Western Melanesia*. New York: Harcourt Brace.

Malinowski, B., 1944. *A Scientific Theory of Culture*. New York: Oxford University Press, 1960 ed.

Maloney, V. G., 1944. Jumping rope rhymes from Burley, Idaho. *Hoosier Folklore Bulletin, 3*, 24–25.

Manning, F. E., 1973. *Black Clubs in Bermuda*. Ithaca and London: Cornell University Press.

Maranda, E. K., and Maranda, P., 1971. *Structural Models in Folklore and Transformational Essays*. The Hague: Mouton.

Maranda, P., and Maranda, E. K., 1971. *Structural Analysis of Oral Tradition*, University of Pennsylvania Publications in Folklore and Folklife, no. 3, Philadelphia: University of Pennsylvania Press.

Maretzki, T., and Maretzki, H., 1963. Taira: An Okinawan village. In *Six Cultures: Studies of Child Rearing*, B. Whiting (Ed.). New York: John Wiley, pp. 363–539.

Marshall, L., 1976. *The !Kung of Nyae Nyae*. Cambridge, Mass.: Harvard University Press.

Martin, G., 1931. Somali game. *Journal of the Royal Anthropological Institute, 61*, 499–511.

Martin, R., 1937. Babies' rattles from 2600 B.C. and other ancient toys. *Field Museum News* (Chicago), *8*, 5.

Maruyama, M., 1963. The second cybernetics: Deviation-amplifying mutual causal processes. *American Scientist, 51*, 164–179.

Maryott, F., 1937. Nebraska counting-out rhymes. *Southern Folklore Quarterly, 1*, 39–62.

Mason, W. A., 1965. Determinants of social behavior in young chimpanzees. In *Behavior of Nonhuman Primates*, vol. 2, A. M. Schrier, H. F. Harlow, and F. Stollnitz (Eds.). New York: Academic Press, pp. 335–364.

Maude, H. C., 1958. String figures from the Gilbert Islands. *Polynesian Society Memoirs, 13*, 1–161.

Mayer, P. (Ed.), 1970. *Socialization: The Approach from Social Anthropology*, A. S. A. Monograph #8. London: Tavistock.

Mead, G. H., 1934. *Mind, Self, and Society*. Chicago: University of Chicago Press.

Mead, M., 1928. *Coming of Age in Samoa*. New York: Morrow, 1973 ed.

Mead, M., 1930. *Growing Up in New Guinea*. New York: Morrow, 1975 ed.

Mead, M., 1932. An investigation of the thought of primitive children with special reference to animism. *Journal of the Royal Anthropological Institute, 62*, 173–190. Reprinted in *Personalities and Cultures*, 1967, R. Hunt (Ed.), Garden City, N.Y.: Natural History Press, pp. 213–237.

Mead, M., 1933. The primitive child. In *A Handbook of Child Psychology*, C. Murchison (Ed.). Worcester, Mass.: Clark University Press, pp. 909–926, 1967 ed.

Mead, M., 1935. *Sex and Temperament*. New York: Dell, 1963 ed.

Mead, M., 1939. *From the South Seas*. New York: Morrow.

Mead, M., 1956. *New Lives for Old*. New York: Dell, 1966 ed.

Mead, M., 1963. Socialization and enculturation. *Current Anthropology, 4*, 184–188.

Mead, M., 1972. *Blackberry Winter*. New York: Pocket Books, 1975 ed.

Mead, M., and Macgregor, F. C., 1951. *Growth and Culture: A Photographic Study of Balinese Childhood*. New York: G. P. Putnam's Sons.

Mensing, A., 1943. Jumping rope jingles from Bloomington, Indiana. *Hoosier Folklore Bulletin, 2*, 48–49.

Mergen, B., 1975. The discovery of children's play. *American Quarterly, 27*, 399–420.

Mergen, B., 1977. Work and Play in Shipyard Culture. Paper presented at the Third

Annual Meeting of The Association for the Anthropological Study of Play, San Diego, California, April 6–9.

Middleton, J. (Ed.), 1970. *From Child to Adult.* Garden City, N.Y.: Natural History Press.

Millar, S., 1968. *The Psychology of Play.* Harmondsworth, England: Penguin.

Miller, A. G., and Thomas, R., 1972. Cooperation and competition among Blackfoot Indian and urban Canadian children. *Child Development, 43,* 1104–1110.

Miller, N., 1928. *The Child in Primitive Society.* New York: Brentano.

Miller, S. N. (now S. Nachmanovitch), 1973. Ends, means, and galumphing: Some leitmotifs of play. *American Anthropologist, 75,* 87–98.

Miller, S. N. (now S. Nachmanovitch), 1974. The playful, the crazy, and the nature of pretense. In *The Anthropological Study of Human Play,* E. Norbeck (Ed.). Rice University Studies, vol. 60, pp. 31–51.

Mills (Howard), D. (Ed.), 1944. *Folk Rhymes and Jingles of Maryland Children.* Frostburg, Md.: State Teachers College.

Milojkovic-Djuric, J., 1960. The Jugoslav children's game "most" and some Scandinavian parallels. *Southern Folklore Quarterly, 24,* 226–234.

Minturn, L., and Hitchcock, J., 1963. The Rājpūts of Khalapur, India. In *Six Cultures: Studies of Child Rearing,* B. Whiting (Ed.), pp. 203–361. New York: John Wiley.

Minturn, L., and Lambert, W., 1964. *Mothers of Six Cultures: Antecedents of Child Rearing.* New York: John Wiley.

Mistry, D. K., 1958. The Indian child and his play. *Sociological Bulletin* (Bombay), *7,* 137–147.

Mistry, D. K., 1959. The Indian child and his play. *Sociological Bulletin* (Bombay), *8,* 86–96.

Mistry, D. K., 1960. The Indian child and his play, *Sociological Bulletin* (Bombay), *9,* 48–55.

Mitchell, E., 1977. The business of toys: A cross-cultural perspective. *Claremont Reading Conference 41st Yearbook,* Claremont, Calif., pp. 189–199.

Mitchell, E., and Anderson, R. T., 1977. Toys in cultural perspective: Denmark and the United States. *Childhood Education, 54,* 45–48.

Modiano, N., 1973. *Indian Education in the Chiapas Highlands.* New York: Holt, Rinehart and Winston.

Monroe, W. S., 1904. Counting out rhymes of children. *American Anthropologist, 6,* 46–50.

Mook, M. A., 1935. Walapai ethnography: Games. *Memoirs of the American Anthropological Association, 42,* 167–173.

Mora, G., 1976. Vico and Piaget: Parallels and differences. *Social Research* (Special Issue, Vico and Contemporary Thought, 2), *43,* 698–712.

Morgan, E. S., 1944. *The Puritan Family: Religion and Domestic Relations in Seventeenth Century New England.* New York: Harper and Row.

Morgan, L. H., 1877. *Ancient Society.* Chicago: Charles H. Kerr and Company.

Mouledoux, E., 1977. The development of play in childhood. In *Studies in the Anthropology of Play: Papers in Memory of B. Allan Tindall,* P. Stevens, (Ed.). Cornwall, N.Y.: Leisure Press.

Moustakas, C. E., 1953. *Children in Play Therapy.* New York: McGraw-Hill.

Mueller, E., and Lucas, T., 1975. A developmental analysis of peer interaction among toddlers. In *Peer Relations and Friendship,* M. Lewis and L. Rosenblum (Eds.). New York: John Wiley, pp. 223–257.

Murdock, G. P., 1957. World ethnographic sample. *American Anthropologist, 59,* 664–687.

Murdock, G. P., 1967. *Ethnographic Atlas.* Pittsburgh: University of Pittsburgh Press.

Murdock, G. P., and White, D. R., 1969. Standard cross-cultural sample. *Ethnology, 8,* 329–369.

Murphy, R. F., 1971. *The Dialectics of Social Life.* New York: Basic Books.

Nagel, E., 1956. Symbolic notation, haddock's eyes, and the dog-walking ordinance. In

The World of Mathematics, vol. 3, J. R. Newman (Ed.). New York: Simon and Schuster, pp. 1878–1900.

Nerlove, S. B., Roberts, J. M., Klein, R. E., Yarbrough, C., and Habicht, J. P., 1974. Natural indicators of cognitive development: An observational study of rural Guatemalan children. *Ethos, 2,* 265–295.

Newell, W. W., 1883. *Games and Songs of American Children,* expanded 1903. New York: Dover, 1963 ed.

Newell, W. W., 1906. Notes on the interpretation of European song-games. *Boas Anniversary Volume,* pp. 404–409.

Nisbet, R. A., 1969. *Social Change and History.* Oxford and New York: Oxford University Press.

Norbeck, E., 1969. Human play and its cultural expression. *Humanitas, 5,* 43–55.

Norbeck, E., 1971. Man at play. *Natural History,* December, Special Supplement on Play, pp. 48–53.

Norbeck, E., 1974a. Anthropological views of play. *American Zoologist, 14,* 267–273.

Norbeck, E. (Ed.), 1974b. *The Anthropological Study of Human Play.* Rice University Studies, vol. 60, no. 3, Summer.

Norbeck, E., 1976. The study of play—Johan Huizinga and modern anthropology. In *The Anthropological Study of Play: Problems and Prospects,* D. F. Lancy and B. Allan Tindall (Eds.). Cornwall, N.Y.: Leisure Press, pp. 1–10.

Nunnally, J. C., and Lemond, L. C., 1973. Exploratory behavior and human development. In *Advances in Child Development and Behavior,* vol. 8, H. W. Reese (Ed.). New York: Academic Press, pp. 59–109.

Nydegger, W., and Nydegger, C., 1963. Tarong: An Ilocos barrio in the Philippines. In *Six Cultures: Studies of Child Rearing,* B. Whiting (Ed.). New York: John Wiley, pp. 693–867.

Ohmann, R., 1971. Speech acts and the definition of literature. *Philosophy and Rhetoric, 4,* 1–19.

Olofson, H., 1976. Playing a kingdom: A Hausa meta-society in the walled city of Zaria, Nigeria. In *The Anthropological Study of Play: Problems and Prospects,* D. F. Lancy and B. Allan Tindall (Eds.). Cornwall, N.Y.: Leisure Press, pp. 156–164.

Opie, I., and Opie, P., 1959. *The Lore and Language of School Children.* Oxford, England: Oxford University Press.

Opie, I., and Opie, P., 1969. *Children's Games in Street and Playground.* Oxford, England: Oxford University Press.

Opler, M., 1946. *Childhood and Youth in Jicarilla Apache Society.* Los Angeles: The Southwest Museum.

Ortner, S. B., 1974. Is female to male as nature is to culture. In *Woman, Culture and Society,* M. Z. Rosaldo and L. Lamphere (Eds.). Stanford, Calif.: Stanford University Press, pp. 67–87.

Osgood, C., 1959. Games of the Orient: Korea, China, Japan. *American Anthropologist, 61,* 536–537.

Oswalt, W., 1964. Traditional storyknife tales of Yuk girls. In *Proceedings of the American Philosophical Society, 108,* 310–336.

Palakornkul, A., 1971. Some linguistic games in Thai. In *A Collection of Linguistic Games* (Penn-Texas Working Papers in Sociolinguistics, 2), J. Sherzer *et al.* (Eds). Austin: University of Texas, pp. 25–31.

Palmer, R. E., 1969. *Hermeneutics.* Evanston, Ill.: Northwestern University Press.

Parley, P., 1833. *Juvenile Tales.* Philadelphia.

Parrott, S., 1972. Games children play: Ethnography of a second-grade recess. In *The Cultural Experience,* J. Spradley and D. McCordy (Eds.). Chicago: Science Research Associates, pp. 207–219.

Parsons, E. C., 1930. Ring games and jingles in Barbados. *Journal of American Folklore, 43,* 326–329.

Parten, M., 1933. Social play among preschool children. *Journal of Abnormal and Social Psychology, 28,* 136–147. Reprinted in *Child's Play,* 1971, R. Herron and B. Sutton-Smith (Eds.). New York: John Wiley, pp. 83–95.

Payne, L. W., 1916. Finding list for Texas play-party songs. *Folklore Society of Texas, 1,* 35–38.

Peller, L. E., 1954. Libidinal phases, ego development and play. In *The Psychoanalytic Study of the Child, 9,* 178–198.

Perry, W. J., 1923. *Children of the Sun.* London: Methuen.

Piaget, J., 1926. *The Language and Thought of the Child.* New York: Harcourt, Brace.

Piaget, J., 1928. *Judgment and Reasoning in the Child.* New York: Harcourt, Brace.

Piaget, J., 1929. *The Child's Conception of the World.* New York: Harcourt, Brace.

Piaget, J., 1930. *The Child's Conception of Physical Causality.* New York: Harcourt, Brace.

Piaget, J., 1932. *The Moral Judgment of the Child.* New York: Free Press, 1965 ed.

Piaget, J., 1951. *Play, Dreams and Imitation in Childhood.* New York: W. W. Norton, 1962 ed.

Piaget, J., 1966. Response to Brian Sutton-Smith. *Psychological Review, 73,* 111–112. Reprinted in *Child's Play,* 1971, R. Herron and B. Sutton-Smith (Eds.). New York: John Wiley, pp. 337–339.

Piaget, J., 1970a. *Genetic Epistemology.* New York: Columbia University Press.

Piaget, J., 1970b. *Structuralism.* New York: Basic Books.

Piers, M. W., 1972. *Play and Development.* New York: W. W. Norton.

Pike, K. N., 1945. Mock Spanish of a Mixteco Indian. *International Journal of American Linguistics, 11,* 219–224.

Pike, K. N., 1954. *Language in Relation to a Unified Theory of the Structure of Human Behavior.* Glendale, Calif.: Summer Institute of Linguistics, Part I.

Pinon, R., 1965. *Chansons populaires de la Flandre Wallone.* Bruxelles: Commission Royale Belge de Folklore.

Pitcher, E. G., and Prelinger, E., 1963. *Children Tell Stories: An Analysis of Fantasy.* New York: International Universities Press.

Pope, H. C., 1956. Texas Rope Jumping Rhymes. *Western Folklore, 15,* 46–48.

Powdermaker, H., 1945. Review of *The People of Alor. American Anthropologist, 47,* 155–161.

Powell-Cotton, P. H., 1931. A Mancala board called songo. *Man, 31,* 133.

Price, R., and Price, S., 1976. Secret play languages in Saramaka: Linguistic disguise in a Caribbean Creole. In *Speech Play,* B. Kirshenblatt-Gimblett (Ed.). Philadelphia: University of Pennsylvania Press, pp. 37–50.

Price-Williams, D. R., 1961. A study concerning concepts of conservation of quantities among primitive children. *Acta Psychologica, 18,* 297–305.

Propp, V., 1928. *Morphology of the Folktale.* Austin: University of Texas Press, 1968 ed.

Pukui, M. K., 1943. Games of my Hawaiian childhood. *California Folklore Quarterly, 2,* 205–220.

Pulaski, M. A., 1970. Play as a function of toy structure and fantasy predisposition. *Child Development, 41,* 531–537.

Pulaski, M. A., 1973. Toys and imaginative play. In *The Child's World of Make-Believe,* J. L. Singer (Ed.). New York: Academic Press, pp. 74–103.

Radcliffe-Brown, A. R., 1952. *Structure and Function in Primitive Society.* New York: Free Press, 1968 ed.

Radcliffe-Brown, A. R., 1957. *A Natural Science of Society.* Glencoe, Ill.: Free Press.

Ramson, J. E., 1946. Children's games among the Aleut. *Journal of American Folklore, 59,* 196–198.

Randolph, V., 1929. The Ozark play party. *Journal of American Folklore, 43,* 201–232.

Randolph, V., 1953. Jump rope rhymes from Arkansas. *Midwest Folklore, 3,* 77–84.

Raum, O. 1940. *Chaga Childhood*. London: Oxford University Press.

Read, K. E., 1959. Leadership and Consensus in a New Guinea Society. *American Anthropologist, 61*, 425–436.

Read, M., 1968. *Children of Their Fathers: Growing Up among the Ngoni of Malawi*. New York: Holt, Rinehart and Winston.

Reany, M. J., 1916. *The Psychology of the Organized Group Game*. Cambridge, England: Cambridge University Press.

Redl, F., 1959. The impact of game ingredients on children's play behavior. *Transactions of the Fourth Conference on Group Processes*. New York: Josiah Macy, Jr. Foundation, pp. 33–81.

Redl, F., Gump, P., and Sutton-Smith, B., 1971. The dimensions of games. In *Child's Play*, R. Herron and B. Sutton-Smith (Eds.). New York: John Wiley, pp. 408–418.

Redl, F., and Wineman, D., 1957. *The Aggressive Child*. Glencoe, Ill.: Free Press.

Reichlin, S., 1974. Film Notes for *The Lion Game*. Somerville, Mass.: Documentary Educational Resources.

Reynolds, P., 1976. Play, language and human evolution. In *Play: Its Role in Development and Evolution*, J. Bruner, A. Jolly, and K. Sylva (Eds.). New York: Basic Books, pp. 621–635.

Rheingold, H., and Cook, K., 1975. The contents of boys' and girls' rooms as an index of parents' behavior. *Child Development, 46*, 459–463.

Rheingold, H. L., and Eckerman, C. O., 1969. The infant's free entry into a new environment. *Journal of Experimental Child Psychology, 8*, 271–283.

Rheingold, H. L., and Samuels, H. R., 1969. Maintaining the positive behavior of infants by increased stimulation. *Developmental Psychology, 1*, 520–527.

Rich, G. W., 1976. *Core Values, Organizational Preferences and Children's Games in Akureyri, Iceland*. Anthropology Ph.D. Thesis, University of California, Davis.

Rich, G. W., 1977. Games and Values in Iceland. Paper presented at the Third Annual Meeting of The Association for the Anthropological Study of Play, San Diego, California, April 6–9.

Richardson, C., and Church, J., 1959. A developmental analysis of proverb interpretation. *Journal of Genetic Psychology, 94*, 169–179.

Ricoeur, P., 1971. The model of the text: Meaningful action considered as a text. *Social Research*, pp. 529–562.

Riessman, F., 1964. The overlooked positives of disadvantaged groups. *Journal of Negro Education, 33*, 225–231.

Ritchie, J., 1957. *Childhood in Rakau: The First Five Years*, Victoria University Publications in Psychology #10, Wellington, New Zealand.

Robert, J. M., Arth, M. J., and Bush, R. R., 1959. Games in culture. *American Anthropologist, 61*, 597–605.

Roberts, J. M., and Forman, M. L., 1971. Riddles: Expressive models of interrogation. *Ethnology, 10*, 509–533.

Roberts, J. M., Hoffman, H., and Sutton-Smith, B., 1965. Pattern and competency: A consideration of Tick Tack Toe. *El Palacio, 72*, 17–30.

Roberts, J. M., and Ridgeway, C., 1969. Musical involvement and talking. *Anthropological Linguistics, 1*, 223–246.

Roberts, J. M., and Sutton-Smith, B., 1962. Child training and game involvement. *Ethnology, 2*, 166–185.

Roberts, J. M., and Sutton-Smith, B., 1966. Cross-cultural correlates of games of chance. *Behavior Science Notes, 1*, 131–144.

Roberts, J. M., Sutton-Smith, B., and Kendon, A., 1963. Strategy in games and folk tales. *Journal of Social Psychology, 61*, 185–199.

Robinson, C., 1977. Social Adaptation of Vietnamese Refugee Children through Play.

Paper presented at the Third Annual Meeting of The Association for the Anthropological Study of Play, San Diego, California, April 6–9.

Robinson, C., 1978. Sex-Typed Behavior in Children's Spontaneous Play. In *The Association for the Anthropological Study of Play Newsletter, 4,* 14–17.

Róheim, G., 1941. Play analysis with Normanby Island children. *American Journal of Orthopsychiatry, 11,* 524–529.

Róheim, G., 1943. Children's games and rhymes in Duau (Normanby Island). *American Anthropologist, 45,* 99–119.

Róheim, G., 1950. *Psychoanalysis and Anthropology, Culture, Personality, and the Unconscious.* New York: International Universities Press.

Romney, K., and Romney, R., 1963. The Mixtecans of Juxtlahuaca, Mexico. In *Six Cultures: Studies of Child Rearing,* B. Whiting (Ed.). New York: John Wiley, pp. 541–691.

Rosaldo, M. Z., and Lamphere, L. (Eds.), 1974. *Woman, Culture and Society.* Stanford, Calif.: Stanford University Press.

Rosenberg, B. G., and Sutton-Smith, B., 1960. A revised conception of masculine–feminine differences in play activities. *Journal of Genetic Psychology, 96,* 165–170.

Rosenblith, W. A., 1967. Afterword. In *The Human Use of Human Beings: Cybernetics and Society,* N. Weiner (Ed.). New York: Avon Books.

Rosenhan, D., Underwood, B., and Moore, B., 1974. Affect moderates self-gratification and altruism. *Journal of Personality and Social Psychology, 30,* 546–552.

Rosenstiel, A., 1976. The role of traditional games in the process of socialization among the Motu of Papua, New Guinea. In *The Anthropological Study of Play: Problems and Prospects,* D. F. Lancy and B. Allan Tindall (Eds.). Cornwall, N. Y.: Leisure Press, pp. 52–58.

Ross, H. S., Goldman, B. D., and Hay, D. F., 1977. Features and Functions of Infant Games. Presentation at Panel on Play and Learning, sponsored by Johnson and Johnson, New Orleans, La., March.

Roth, W. E., 1902. Games, sports, and amusements. *North Queensland Ethnography,* Bulletin no. 4.

Rowell, M. K., 1943. Pamunky Indian games and amusements. *Journal of American Folklore, 56,* 203–207.

Royce, J., 1972. Validation of game classification models against children's games. *Anthropos, 67,* 138–151.

Royce, J., 1973. Guide to notation of games observation. *Anthropos, 68,* 604–610.

Ruesch, J., and Bateson, G., 1951. *Communication: The Social Matrix of Psychiatry.* New York: Norton, 1968 ed.

Sacks, H., 1972. On the analyzability of stories by children. In *Directions in Sociolinguistics: The Ethnography of Communication,* J. Gumperz and D. Hymes (Eds.). New York: Holt, Rinehart and Winston, pp. 325–345.

Sade, D. S., 1973. An ethogram for rhesus monkeys. 1. Antithetical contrasts in posture and movement. *American Journal of Physical Anthropology, 38,* 537–542.

Sahlins, M. D., and Service, E. R., 1960. *Evolution and Culture.* Ann Arbor: University of Michigan Press.

Salter, M. A., 1967. *Games and Pastimes of the Australian Aboriginal.* Edmonton: University of Alberta Printing Department.

Salter, M. A., 1974. Play: A Medium of Cultural Stability. Paper presented at the International Seminar on the History of Physical Education and Sport, Vienna, Austria, April 17–20.

Sanches, M., and Kirshenblatt-Gimblett, B., 1976. Children's traditional speech play and child language. In *Speech Play,* B. Kirshenblatt-Gimblett (Ed.). Philadelphia: University of Pennsylvania Press, pp. 65–110.

Sanderson, M. G., 1913. Native games of Central Africa. *Journal of the Royal Anthropological Institute*, 43, 726–736.

Schaefer, C. E., 1969. The self-concept of creative adolescents. *Journal of Psychology*, 72, 233–242.

Scheffler, L., 1976. The study of traditional games in Mexico: Bibliographical analysis and current research. In *The Anthropological Study of Play: Problems and Prospects*, D. F. Lancy and B. Allan Tindall (Eds.). Cornwall, N.Y.: Leisure Press, pp. 58–66.

Schiller, F., 1875. *Essays, Aesthetical and Philosophical*. London: George Bell.

Schlosberg, H., 1947. The concept of play. *Psychological Review*, 54, 229–231.

Scholtz, G. I. L., and Ellis, M. J., 1975. Repeated exposure to objects and peers in a play setting. *Journal of Experimental Child Psychology*, 19, 448–455.

Schwartzman (Beale), H. B., 1973. *Real Pretending: An Ethnography of Symbolic Play Communication*. Anthropology Ph.D. Thesis, Northwestern University, Evanston, Ill.

Schwartzman, H. B., 1974. Re-"Metaphorizing" the Study of Children's Symbolic Play Activity. Paper presented at the 53rd Annual Meeting of the Central States Anthropological Society, Chicago, March 27–30.

Schwartzman, H. B., 1976a. The anthropological study of children's play. *Annual Review of Anthropology*, B. Siegel *et al.* (Eds.). Palo Alto, Calif.: Annual Reviews, Inc., pp. 289–328.

Schwartzman, H. B., 1976b. Children's play: A sideways glance at make-believe. In *The Anthropological Study of Play: Problems and Prospects*, D. F. Lancy and B. Allan Tindall (Eds.). Cornwall, N.Y.: Leisure Press, pp. 198–205.

Schwartzman, H. B., 1977a. Organizational Dancing: How Play Works in a Community Mental Health Center. Paper presented at the Third Annual Meeting of The Association for the Anthropological Study of Play, San Diego, Calif., April 6–9. To appear in *Play: Anthropological Perspectives*, M. A. Salter (Ed.). Cornwall, N.Y.: Leisure Press.

Schwartzman, H. B., 1977b. Works on play: A bibliography. In *Studies in the Anthropology of Play: Papers in Memory of B. Allan Tindall*, P. Stevens (Ed.). Cornwall, N.Y.: Leisure Press.

Schwartzman, H. B., and Barbera, L., 1976. Children's play in Africa and South America: A review of the ethnographic literature. In *The Anthropological Study of Play: Problems and Prospects*, D. F. Lancy and B. Allan Tindall (Eds.). Cornwall, N.Y.: Leisure Press, pp. 11–21.

Schwartzman, J., 1977. Art, science, and change in Western society. *Ethos*, 5, 239–262.

Seagoe, M. V., 1970a. An instrument for the analysis of children's play as an index of degree of socialization. *Journal of School Psychology*, 8, 139–144.

Seagoe, M. V., 1970b. Children's play as an indicator of cross-cultural and intra-cultural differences. In *The Cross-Cultural Analysis of Sport and Games*, G. Lüschen (Ed.). Champaign, Ill.: Stipes.

Seagoe, M. V., 1971a. Children's play in three American subcultures. *Journal of School Psychology*, 9, 167–172.

Seagoe, M. V., 1971b. A comparison of children's play in six modern cultures. *Journal of School Psychology*, 9, 61–72.

Searcy, A., 1965. *Contemporary and Traditional Prairie Potawatomi Child Life*. Lawrence, Kans.: University of Kansas Press.

Sears, R. R., 1950. Relation of Fantasy Aggression to Interpersonal Aggression. *Child Development*, 21, 5–6.

Sears, R. R., 1951. Effects of frustration and anxiety on fantasy aggression. *American Journal of Orthopsychiatry*, 21, 498–505.

Sears, R. R., Maccoby, E. E., and Levin, H., 1957. *Patterns of Child Rearing*. Evanston, Ill.: Row, Peterson.

Sears, R. R., Pintler, M., and Sears, P. S., 1946. Effect of father separation on pre-school children's doll play aggression. *Child Development, 17*, 119–243.

Sebeok, T. A., and Brewster, P. G., 1958. *Studies in Cheremis: Games.* Bloomington, Ind.: Indiana University Press.

Sexton, A., 1971. *Transformations.* Boston: Houghton Mifflin.

Shands, H., 1967. Novelty as object. *Archives of General Psychiatry, 17*, 1–4.

Shapira, A., and Madsen, M. C., 1969. Cooperative and competitive behavior of kibbutz and urban children in Israel. *Child Development, 40*, 609–617.

Sherzer, J., 1970. Talking backwards in Cuna: The sociological reality of phonological descriptions. *Southwestern Journal of Anthropology, 26*, 343–353.

Sherzer, J., 1976. Play languages: Implications for (socio) linguistics. In *Speech Play*, B. Kirshenblatt-Gimblett (Ed.), Philadelphia: University of Pennsylvania Press, pp. 19–36

Shoemaker, N., 1964. Toys of Chama (Eseejja) Indian children. *American Anthropologist, 66*, 1151–1153.

Shultz, T. R., 1974. Development of the appreciation of riddles. *Child Development, 45*, 100–105.

Shure, M., 1963. Psychological ecology of a nursery school. *Child Development, 34*, 979–992.

Signorney, L. H., 1838. *Letters to Mothers.* Hartford, Conn.: Hudson and Skinner.

Singer, D. G., and Singer, J. L., 1977. *Partners in Play.* New York: Harper and Row.

Singer, J. L., 1961. Imagination and waiting ability in childhood. *Journal of Personality, 29*, 396–413.

Singer, J. L., 1966. *Daydreaming: An Introduction to the Experimental Study of Inner Experience.* New York: Random House.

Singer, J. L., 1973. *The Child's World of Make-Believe: Experimental Studies of Imaginative Play.* New York: Academic Press.

Singer, J. L., 1976. Vico's insight and the scientific study of the stream of consciousness. *Social Research* (Special Issue, Vico and Contemporary Thought, 2) *43*, 715–726.

Singer, J. L., and Singer, D., 1976. Imaginative play and pretending in early childhood: Some experimental approaches. In *Child Personality and Psychopathology*, vol. 3, A. Davids (Ed.). New York: John Wiley.

Singer, M., 1961. A survey of culture and personality theory and research. In *Studying Personality Cross-Culturally*, B. Kaplan (Ed.). Evanston, Ill.: Row, Peterson, pp. 9–90.

Sleet, D., 1971. *Interdisciplinary Research Index on Play: A Guide to the Literature.* Ann Arbor, Mich.: University Microfilms International.

Sluzki, C. E., and Ransom, D. C. (Eds.), 1976. *Double Bind: The Foundation of the Communicational Approach to the Family.* New York: Grune and Stratton.

Smilansky, S., 1968. *The Effects of Sociodramatic Play on Disadvantaged Preschool Children.* New York: John Wiley.

Smilansky, S., 1971. Can adults facilitate play in children? Theoretical and practical considerations. In *Play: The Child Strives toward Self-Realization.* Washington, D.C.: National Association for the Education of Young Children, pp. 39–50.

Smith, G. E., 1928. *In the Beginning: The Origin of Civilization.* New York: Morrow.

Smith, P. K., and Connolly, K., 1972. Patterns of play and social interaction in pre-school children. In *Ethological Studies of Child Behaviour*, N. Blurton Jones (Ed.). Cambridge, England: Cambridge University Press, pp. 65–95.

Sommerlad, E. A., and Bellingham, W. P., 1972. Cooperation–competition: A comparison of Australian European and aboriginal school children. *Journal of Cross-Cultural Psychology, 3*, 149–157.

Sonnenberg, M., 1955. Girls jumping rope. *Psychoanalysis, 3*, 59–60.

Speck, F. W., 1944. Catawba games and amusements. *Primitive Man, 17*, 19–28.

Spencer, F. C., 1899. *Education of the Pueblo Child: A Study in Arrested Development.* Columbia University Contributions to Philosophy, Psychology, and Education, New York.

Spencer, H., 1873. *The Principles of Psychology,* vol. 2. New York: D. Appleton.

Spiro, M. E., 1958. *Children of the Kibbutz.* New York: Schocken, 1965 ed.

Spock, B., 1946. *Baby and Child Care.* New York: Simon and Schuster.

Statistical Abstract of the United States, 1972. 93rd Annual Edition, U.S. Department of Commerce, Washington, D.C.: Government Printing Office.

Stearns, R. E. C., 1890. On the Nishinam game of "ha" and the Boston game of "props." *American Anthropologist, 3,* 353–358.

Stephens, W. N., 1962. *The Oedipus Complex: Cross-Cultural Evidence.* Glencoe, Ill.: The Free Press.

Stern, D., 1974. Mother and infant at play: The dyadic interaction involving facial, vocal and gaze behaviors. In *The Effect of the Infant on Its Caregiver,* M. Lewis and L. Rosenblum (Eds.). New York: John Wiley, pp. 187–213.

Stevens, P., 1976. Social and judicial functions of Bachama song-contests. In *The Anthropological Study of Play: Problems and Prospects,* D. F. Lancy and B. Allan Tindall (Eds.). Cornwall, N.Y.: Leisure Press, pp. 164–171.

Stevens, P., (Ed.), 1977. *Studies in the Anthropology of Play: Papers in Memory of B. Allan Tindall.* Cornwall, N.Y.: Leisure Press.

Stevens, T., 1977. Cognitive structures in sports tactics. In *Studies in the Anthropology of Play: Papers in Memory of B. Allan Tindall,* P. Stevens (Ed.). Cornwall, N.Y.: Leisure Press.

Stevenson, M. C., 1883. *Fifth Annual Report of the Bureau of American Ethnology.* Washington, D.C.: Government Printing Office.

Stevenson, M. C., 1903. Zuni Games. *American Anthropologist, 5,* 468–497.

Stone, G. P., 1971. The play of little children. In *Child's Play,* R. Herron and B. Sutton-Smith (Eds.). New York: John Wiley, pp. 4–14.

Storey, K. S., 1976. Field study: Children's play in Bali. In *The Anthropological Study of Play: Problems and Prospects,* D. F. Lancy and B. Allan Tindall (Eds.). Cornwall, N.Y.: Leisure Press, pp. 66–72.

Stumpf, F., and Cozens, F. W., 1947. Some aspects of the role of games, sports, and recreation activities in the culture of modern primitive peoples: The New Zealand Maoris. *Research Quarterly, 18,* 198–218.

Stumpf, F., and Cozens, F. W., 1949. Some aspects of the role of games, sports, and recreation activities in the culture of modern primitive peoples: The Fijians. *Research Quarterly, 20,* 2–20.

Sunley, R., 1955. Early nineteenth century American literature on child rearing. In *Childhood in Contemporary Cultures,* M. Mead and M. Wolfenstein (Eds.). Chicago: University of Chicago Press, pp. 150–167.

Sutton-Smith, B., 1951a. The meeting of Maori and European cultures and its effects upon the unorganized games of Maori children. *Journal of the Polynesian Society, 60,* 93–107. Reprinted in *The Folkgames of Children,* 1972. Austin: University of Texas Press, pp. 317–330.

Sutton-Smith, B., 1951b. New Zealand variants of the game buck-buck. *Folklore, 63,* 329–333.

Sutton-Smith, B., 1952. The fate of English traditional games in New Zealand. *Western Folklore Quarterly, 11,* 250–253.

Sutton-Smith, B., 1953a. The game rhymes of New Zealand children. *Western Folklore, 12,* 14–24.

Sutton-Smith, B., 1953b. Marbles are in. *Western Folklore, 12,* 186–193. Reprinted in *The Folkgames of Children,* 1972. Austin: University of Texas Press, pp. 455–464.

Sutton-Smith, B., 1953c. The traditional games of New Zealand children. *Folklore, 64,* 411–423.

Sutton-Smith, B., 1959a. A formal analysis of game meaning. *Western Folklore, 18,* 13–24. Reprinted in *The Folkgames of Children,* 1972. Austin: University of Texas Press, pp. 491–505.

Sutton-Smith, B., 1959b. *The Games of New Zealand Children.* Berkeley: University of California Press. Reprinted in *The Folkgames of Children,* 1972. Austin: University of Texas Press, pp. 5–257.

Sutton-Smith, B., 1959c. The kissing games of adolescents in Ohio. *Midwest Folklore, 12,* 189–211. Reprinted in *The Folkgames of Children,* 1972. Austin: University of Texas Press, pp. 465–490.

Sutton-Smith, B., 1966a. Piaget on play: A critique. *Psychological Review, 73,* 104–110. Reprinted in *Child's Play,* 1971, R. Herron and B. Sutton-Smith (Eds.). New York: John Wiley, pp. 326–336.

Sutton-Smith, B., 1966b. Role replication and reversal in play. *Merrill-Palmer Quarterly of Behavior and Development, 12,* 285–298. Reprinted in *The Folkgames of Children,* 1972. Austin: University of Texas Press, pp. 416–432.

Sutton-Smith, B., 1967. The role of play in cognitive development. *Young Children, 22,* 361–370. Reprinted in *Child's Play,* 1971, R. Herron and B. Sutton-Smith (Eds.). New York: John Wiley, pp. 252–260.

Sutton-Smith, B., 1968. The folkgames of American children. In *Our Living Traditions: An Introduction to American Folklore,* T. Coffin (Ed.). New York: Basic Books.

Sutton-Smith, B., 1971a. Boundaries. In *Child's Play,* R. Herron and B. Sutton-Smith (Eds.). New York: John Wiley, pp. 103–106.

Sutton-Smith, B., 1971b. A reply to Piaget: A play theory of copy. In *Child's Play,* R. Herron and B. Sutton-Smith (Eds.). New York: John Wiley, pp. 340–342.

Sutton-Smith, B., 1972a. *The Folkgames of Children.* Austin: University of Texas Press.

Sutton-Smith, B., 1972b. Games of Order and Disorder. Paper presented at the Annual Meeting of the American Anthropological Association, Toronto, Canada, December. Reprinted in *The Dialectics of Play,* 1976. Schorndoff, West Germany: Verlag Hoffman.

Sutton-Smith, B., 1972c. The two cultures of games. In *The Folkgames of Children.* Austin: University of Texas Press, pp. 295–311.

Sutton-Smith, B., 1974a. Children's Narrative Competence: The Underbelly of Mythology. Paper presented at the Annual Meeting of the American Folklore Society, Oregon, November.

Sutton-Smith, B., 1974b. Toward an anthropology of play. *The Association for the Anthropological Study of Play Newsletter, 1,* 8–15. Reprinted in *The Dialectics of Play,* 1976. Schorndoff, West Germany: Verlag Hoffman.

Sutton-Smith, B., 1975a. Current Research and Theory on Play, Games and Sports. Paper presented to the first National Conference on Mental Health Aspects of Sports Exercise and Recreation, American Medical Association, Atlantic City, N.J.

Sutton-Smith, B., 1975b. A Structural Grammar of Games and Sports. Paper presented at the International Society for the Sociology of Sport, Heidelberg, October.

Sutton-Smith, B., 1976a. A developmental structural account of riddles. In *Speech Play,* B. Kirshenblatt-Gimblett (Ed.). Philadelphia: University of Pennsylvania Press, pp. 111–119.

Sutton-Smith, B., 1976b. *The Dialectics of Play.* Schorndoff, West Germany: Verlag Hoffman.

Sutton-Smith, B., 1977. Play, games and sports: Socialization or innovation? In *Studies in the Anthropology of Play: Papers in Memory of B. Allan Tindall,* P. Stevens (Ed.). Cornwall, N.Y.: Leisure Press.

Sutton-Smith, B., Abrams, D., Botvin, G., Caring, M., Gildesgame, D., and Stevens, T.,

1975. The importance of the storytaker: An investigation of imaginative play. *Urban Review, 8,* 82–95.

Sutton-Smith, B., and Roberts, J. M., 1964. Rubrics of competitive behavior. *Journal of Genetic Psychology, 105,* 13–37.

Sutton-Smith, B., and Roberts, J. M., 1967. Studies in an elementary game of strategy. *Genetic Psychology Monographs, 75,* 3–42.

Sutton-Smith, B., and Roberts, J. M., 1970. The cross-cultural and psychological study of games. In *The Cross-Cultural Analysis of Games,* G. Lüschen (Ed.). Champaign, Ill.: Stipes, pp. 100–108.

Sutton-Smith, B., Roberts, J. M., and Kozelka, R. M., 1963. Game involvement in adults. *Journal of Social Psychology, 60,* 15–30.

Sutton-Smith, B., Roberts, J. M., and Rosenberg, B. G., 1964. Sibling association and role involvement. *Merrill-Palmer Quarterly, 10,* 25–38.

Sutton-Smith, B., and Rosenberg, B. G., 1961. Sixty years of historical change in the game preferences of American children. *Journal of American Folklore, 74,* 17–46. Reprinted in *The Folkgames of Children,* 1972. Austin: University of Texas Press, pp. 258–294.

Sutton-Smith, B., and Rosenberg, B. G., 1967. The dramatic boy. *Perceptual and Motor Skills, 25,* 247–248.

Sutton-Smith, B., Rosenberg, B. G., and Morgan, E. F., Jr., 1963. Development of sex differences in play choices during preadolescence. *Child Development, 34,* 119–126. Reprinted in *The Folkgames of Children,* 1972. Austin: University of Texas Press, pp. 405–415.

Sutton-Smith, B., and Savasta, M., 1972. Sex Differences in Play and Power. Paper presented at the Annual Meeting of the Eastern Psychological Association, April. Reprinted in *The Dialectics of Play,* 1976, Schorndoff, West Germany: Verlag Hoffman.

Sylva, K., Bruner, J. S., and Genova, P., 1976. The role of play in the problem-solving of children 3–5 years old. In *Play: Its Role in Development and Evolution,* J. Bruner, A. Jolly, and K. Sylva (Eds.). New York: Basic Books, pp. 244–257.

Symons, D., 1977. *Play and Aggression.* New York: Columbia University Press.

Terman, L. M., 1926. *Genetic Studies of Genius,* vol. 1. Stanford, Calif.: Stanford University Press.

Thomas, D. R., 1975. Cooperation and competition among Polynesian and European children. *Child Development, 46,* 948–953.

Tindall, B. A., 1975. Ethnography and the hidden curriculum in sport. *Behavioral and Social Science Teacher, 2*(2).

Todorov, T., 1973. Analyse du discours: L'example des devinettes. *Journal de Psychologie Normale et Pathologique, 1–2,* 135–155.

Trevor, J. C., 1955. Backwards languages in Africa. *Man, 55,* 111.

Tucker, A. N., 1933. Children's games and songs in the southern Sudan. *Journal of the Royal Anthropological Institute, 63,* 165–187.

Turbayne, C., 1970. *The Myth of Metaphor.* Columbia: University of South Carolina Press.

Turnbull, C., 1961. *The Forest People.* New York: Simon and Schuster.

Turner, T., 1973. Piaget's structuralism. *American Anthropologist, 75,* 351–373.

Turner, V., 1969. *The Ritual Process: Structure and Anti-Structure.* Chicago: Aldine.

Turner, V., 1974a. *Dramas, Fields and Metaphors.* Ithaca, N.Y.: Cornell University Press.

Turner, V., 1974b. Liminal to liminoid in play, flow, and ritual: An essay in comparative symbology. In *The Anthropological Study of Human Play,* E. Norbeck (Ed.). Rice University Studies, vol. 60, pp. 53–92.

Turner, V., 1977. Process, system, and symbol: A new anthropological synthesis. *Daedalus* (Summer), pp. 61–80.

Tyler, S. A. (Ed.), 1969. *Cognitive Anthropology.* New York: Holt, Rinehart and Winston.

Tylor, E. B., 1871. *Primitive Culture: Researches into the Development of Mythology, Philosophy, Language, Art and Custom,* 2 vols. London: J. Murray, 1903 ed.

Tylor, E. B., 1879a. The history of games. *The Fortnightly Review, 25,* 735–747. Reprinted in *The Study of Games,* E. M. Avedon and B. Sutton-Smith (Eds.). New York: John Wiley, pp. 63–76.

Tylor, E. B., 1879b. On the game of patolli in ancient Mexico, and its probable Asiatic origin. *Journal of the Royal Anthropological Institute of Great Britain and Ireland, 8,* 116–131.

Tylor, E. B., 1896. On American lot-games as evidence of Asiatic intercourse before the time of Columbus. Supplement to *International Archiv für Ethnographie, 9,* 56–66. Reprinted in *The Study of Games,* 1971, E. M. Avedon and B. Sutton-Smith (Eds.). New York: John Wiley, pp. 77–93.

Updegraff, R., and Herbst, E. K., 1933. An experimental study of the social behavior stimulated in young children by certain play materials. *Journal of Genetic Psychology, 42,* 372–391.

Van Alstyne, D., 1932. *Play Behavior and Choice of Play Materials of Pre-School Children.* Chicago: University of Chicago Press.

Van Gennep, A., 1908. Essai d'une théorie des langues spéciales. *Revue des Etudes Ethnographiques et Sociologiques, 1,* 327–337.

Van Zyl, H. J., 1939. Some of the commonest games played by the Sotho people of northern Transvaal. *Bantu Studies, 13,* 292–305.

Voget, F. W., 1975. *A History of Ethnology.* New York: Holt, Rinehart and Winston.

von Glascoe, C., 1975a. *The Case for Multiple Game Cognitions in the Yucatán.* Anthropology Ph.D. thesis, University of California, Irvine.

von Glascoe, C., 1975b. Evidence for multiple cognitive realities in Yucatec game cognition. Social Sciences Working Paper, 78b. To appear in *Boas, Sapir, Whorf Revisited: Cultural Meaning in Grammar and Lexicon,* M. Mathiot (Ed.). The Hague: Mouton (in press).

von Glascoe, C., 1976. The patterning of game preferences in the Yucatán. In *The Anthropological Study of Play: Problems and Prospects,* D. F. Lancy and B. Allan Tindall (Eds.). Cornwall, N.Y.: Leisure Press, pp. 108–123.

von Glascoe, C., and Metzger, D. G., 1977. Game Cognition and Game Preference in the Yucatán. Paper presented at the American Ethnological Society meetings, San Diego, Calif., April 6–9.

Vygotsky, L. S., 1962. *Thought and Language.* Cambridge, Mass.: MIT Press.

Vygotsky, L. S., 1967. Play and its role in the mental development of the child. *Soviet Psychology, 5,* 6–18.

Waelder, R., 1933. The psychoanalytic theory of play. *Psychoanalytic Quarterly, 2,* 208–224.

Wagner, R., 1975. *The Invention of Culture.* Englewood Cliffs, N.J.: Prentice-Hall.

Walker, J. R., 1906. Sioux games, II. *Journal of American Folklore, 19,* 29–36.

Wallach, M., 1971. *The Intelligence/Creativity Distinction.* New York: General Learning Press.

Watson, K. A., 1972. The Social Context of Narrative Performance among Hawaiian Children: A Sociolinguistic Approach. Paper presented at the Annual Meeting of the American Anthropological Association, Toronto.

Watson, W., 1953. Play among children in an East Coast mining community. *Folklore, 64,* 397–410.

Watson-Gegeo, K. A., and Boggs, S. T., 1977. From verbal play to talk story: The role of routines in speech events among Hawaiian children. In *Child Discourse,* S. Ervin-Tripp and C. Mitchell-Kernan (Eds.). New York: Academic Press, pp. 67–90.

Watt, W., 1946. Some children's games from Tanna, New Hebrides. *Mankind, 3,* 261–264.

Watzlawick, P., Beavin, J. H., and Jackson, D. D., 1967. *Pragmatics of Human Communication*. New York: W. W. Norton.

Weber, M., 1920. *The Protestant Ethic and the Spirit of Capitalism*. New York: Charles Scribner's Sons, 1958 ed.

Weiner, A. B., 1977. Review of film, "Trobriand Cricket: An ingenious response to colonialism." *American Anthropologist, 79,* 506–507.

Weiner, M., 1970. The riddle repertoire of a Massachusetts elementary school. *Folklore Forum, 3,* 7–38.

Weiner, N., 1954. *The Human Use of Human Beings: Cybernetics and Society*. New York: Avon Books, 1967 ed.

Weir, R., 1962. *Language in the Crib* (Janua Linguarum, Series maior 14). The Hague: Mouton.

Weisler, A., and McCall, R. B., 1976. Exploration and play. *American Psychologist, 31,* 492–508.

Welker, W. I., 1961. An analysis of exploratory and play behavior in animals. In *Functions of Varied Experience,* D. W. Fiske and S. R. Maddi (Eds.). Homewood, Ill.: Dorsey Press, pp. 175–226.

Whelen, B., 1976. *A Baby, Maybe?* Indianapolis, Ind.: Bobbs-Merrill.

White, R. W., 1959. Motivation reconsidered. The concept of competence. *Psychological Review, 66,* 297–333.

White, S., 1976. Developmental psychology and Vico's concept of universal history. *Social Research* (Special Issue, Vico and Contemporary Thought, 2) *43,* 659–671.

Whitehead, A. N., and Russell, B., 1910–1913. *Principia Mathematica,* 3 vols. Cambridge, England: Cambridge University Press.

Whiting, B. B., 1950. *Paiute Sorcery*. New York: Viking Fund Publications in Anthropology, No. 15.

Whiting, B. B. (Ed.), 1963. *Six Cultures: Studies of Child Rearing*. New York: John Wiley.

Whiting, B. B., and Edwards, C. P., 1973. A cross-cultural analysis of sex differences in the behavior of children aged 3–11. *Journal of Social Psychology, 91,* 171–188.

Whiting, B. B., and Whiting, J. W. M., 1975. *Children of Six Cultures: A Psycho-Cultural Analysis*. Cambridge, Mass.: Harvard University Press.

Whiting, J. W. M., 1941. *Becoming a Kwoma*. New Haven, Conn.: Yale University Press.

Whiting, J. W. M., 1964. Effects of climate on certain cultural practices. In *Explorations in Cultural Anthropology: Essays in Honor of George Peter Murdock,* W. H. Goodenough (Ed.). New York: McGraw-Hill, pp. 511–544.

Whiting, J. W. M., and Child, I. L., 1953. *Child-Training and Personality: A Cross-Cultural Study*. New Haven, Conn.: Yale University Press.

Whiting, J. W. M., Child, I. L., and Lambert, W. W., 1966. *Field Guide for a Study of Socialization*. New York: John Wiley. Written with the field teams for the *Six Cultures Series.*

Whiting, J. W. M., Kluckhohn, R., and Anthony, A., 1958. The function of male initiation ceremonies at puberty. In *Readings in Social Psychology,* E. Maccoby, T. Newcomb, and E. Hartlay (Eds.). New York: Henry Holt, pp. 359–370.

Wilden, A., 1972. *System and Structure*. London: Tavistock.

Williams, T. R., 1969. *A Borneo Childhood: Enculturation in Dusun Society*. New York: Holt, Rinehart and Winston.

Winnicott, D. W., 1971. *Playing and Reality*. New York: Basic Books.

Wishy, B., 1968. *The Child and the Republic*. Philadelphia: University of Pennsylvania Press.

Wissler, C., 1926. *The Relation of Man to Nature in Aboriginal America*. New York: Oxford University Press.

Withers, C., 1947. Current events in New York City children's folklore. *New York Folklore Quarterly, 3,* 213–222.

Withers, C., 1963. Introduction. W. W. Newell's, 1883, *Games and Songs of American Children*. New York: Dover.

Wittgenstein, L., 1953. *Philosophical Investigations*, 3rd ed. New York: Macmillan.

Wolfenstein, M., 1954. *Children's Humor: A Psychological Analysis*, Glencoe, Ill.: Free Press.

Wolfenstein, M., 1955. Fun morality: An analysis of recent American child-training literature. In *Childhood in Contemporary Cultures*, M. Mead and M. Wolfenstein (Eds.). Chicago: University of Chicago Press, pp. 168–178.

Wolford, W. J., 1916. *The Play Party in Indiana*. Indianapolis: Indiana Historical Commission.

Yakir, R., 1973. Secret languages of Israeli children. In *Language-Behavior Papers*, no. 2. Jerusalem, Israel: Language-Behavior Section, The School of Education of the Hebrew University and the Ministry of Education and Culture, pp. 29–39.

Zoete, B. de, and Spies, W., 1937. *Dance and Drama in Bali*. New York: Harper.

Index

Page numbers in italic refer to figures

Abrahams, R.D., 36, 91, 294
Accommodation/Assimilation, 52, 268–271, 299, 301
Adult games and play, 14, 30, 35, 42n, 54, 101, 198
Aleut, 36
Alorese, 33, 143–145
Anderson, R., 305–307, 324
Animistic thought of children, 58, 138–140, 139n–140n
Arapesh, 140–141
Archaic illusion, 57
Ariès, P., 2n, 9–15
Arousal, 315
  theory of, 317–318
Art, 224n, 245, 326n
Arrested development, 22
Associative fluency, 322
Australia, 32, 74, 85, *86*, 87, 108, 267
Australian Aborigine, 32, 74–77, *75*, *76*, 108, 267
Autocosmic play, 50, 149, 162–163, *164*–*165*

Babcock, W.H., 36, 70–71
Bali, Balinese, 22, 33, 160–163, *164*, *165*, 166, 226–227
Barnouw, V., 142, 143n, 153, 179, 180–182
Bascom, W., 8

Bateson, G., 20, 33, 160–163, *164*, *165*, 166, 196n, 211–226, 213n, 214n, *219*, 232, 246, 250, 272, 340–341. *See also* Definition of play
Beach, F.A., 309
Beale, H. *See* Schwartzman
Beatle, 259
Behavioral systems, 180, 182, *183*
Benedict, R., 23, 207
Berlyne, D.E., 302, 317–318
Best, E., 5, 32, 77–79, 77n
Black English Vernacular (BEV), 121, 123, 294
Blurton Jones, N., 24, 308–309, 311–313
Boas, F., 21, 64–65, 77n, 136n
Bohannan, P., 5, 29n
Bohannan, L., 29n
Boomerangs, 76–77
Boys' gangs, 73
Brewster, P.G., 30, 36, 79. *See also* Classification of games
Bruner, J., 277–278, 321, 333
Burridge, K.O., 27–28
Bushmen. *See* !Kung Bushmen

Caillois, R., 202–203, 258, 299, 332
Carroll, L. 9, 27, 41, 59, 61, 98, 135, 210, 214, 248, 279n, 302
Catharsis. *See* Play as catharsis

Cat's cradle. *See* String figures
Centner, H., 166–169, 171–173
Chaga, 37, 104–106
Chamula, 34, 295–296
Chelem Puerto, 255–257, *256*
Cheska, A., 30n, 63n, 64, 66, 108n
Child, I.L., 21, 24, 180
Childhood
    concepts of in American history,
        14–20, 14n
    concepts of in Western European
        history, 9–14, 10n, *10, 11*
    innocence, 14–15, 18
    separate status of, 19
    studies of by anthropologists, 10,
        20–26
    topics for study of, 137
China, 19, 30
Chukovsky, K., 25, 131
Classification of games (Brewster),
    80–82; (Sutton-Smith), 83
Classification of rhymes (Opie), 89
Classification of street games (Opie),
    89–91
Cockfighting, 162, 226–227, 246
Cole, M. *et al.*, 22, 58, 280
Comparative method, 43n
Competition, 28n, 106, 193–194, 197,
    203, 305, 320–321, 335–337. *See
    also* Winning-losing in games
Conflict-enculturation hypothesis,
    198–199, 202
Counting-out rhymes, 36, 92, 297
Cross-Cultural Survey File (HRAF), 179,
    181, 197, 201
Csikszentmihalyi, M., 4n, 5, 225n, 318,
    321
Culin, S., 5, 30, 32, 33, 35–36, 63–64,
    66, 72, 253
Cultural complexity, association with
    play and games, 192–193, 198,
    203–204
Cultural evolution
    premises of, 41–42
    stages of, 42, *43*
    as a game, 44
Cultural relativism, 136, 180
Culture, definition of (Tylor), 61
Culture versus nature, 136–137, 152
Cybernetics, 210–213, 222

Darwin, C., 41, 70n, 309
Daydreams, 323

Definition of games (Roberts), 196–197
Definition of play (Bateson), 217–218;
    (Huizinga), 258; (Schwartzman),
    330; (Sutton-Smith), 226
Denmark, 305–307
Dennis, W., 10, 20, 35, 139n-140n,
    156–160, *158*
Deprivation/Deficiency Theories,
    120–124, 134, 321, 330
Deutero-learning, 212, 272–273, 279, 300
Dolls-indigenous
    of Pilagá, 150 n
    of Hopi, *158*
    small animals used as, 159
    of Luba, Sanga, Yeke, 169, *170*
Doll play studies, 149–150
    of Duau children, 153–155, 155n
    of Maori children, 155
    of Pilagá children, 150–152
    of Puerto Rican children, 155
Dorsey, O., 5, 35, 71–72
Dreams, 263, 323
Duau, 32, 153–155
DuBois, C., 23, 33, 143, 144–145
Dundes, A., 4n, 261–262, 294

Ehrmann, J., 227, 232, 237, 258
Eifermann, R., 38, 55, 106–107, 120, 202
El'Konin, D., 117, 275
England, 14n, 16, 30, 87–91, *91*, 311–318
Erikson, E. H., 13n, 49–50, 148–149,
    162–163, 263n
Eskimo, 36, *73*, 267, 298
Ethnoscience, 251–257, 251n, 299
Etic-emic distinction, 248–249, 249n,
    251–252, 299

Fabian, J., 241n, 243
Fein, G., 308, 321
Figurative thought, 269–270
Fischer, A., 182, 188–189, 193, *194*
Fischer, J., 182, 188–189, 193, *194*
Flow/flowing, 225, 225n
Folktales, 183, 197, 199, 200, 261n,
    262
Fortes, M., 23, 102–104
Fox and chickens, 90, *91*
Frame, 217–219, 223–224, 246, 327
France, *11*, 13n, 16, 292
Freud, A., 149n
Freud, S., 15, 20, 23–24, 48–49, 48n,
    59, 142, 145–146, 153

Friendship groups
  in Tarong, 195
  in Mexico, 195–196
  See also Peers
Fun morality, 16–19

Galumphing, 222
Game questionnaire, 39
Game preferences, 34, 84–85, 255–257
Games, as distinct from play, 218–220,
  219n, 246, 327
Garvey, C., 228–231, 236, 243,
  289–290
  definition of pretend play, 229, 333
  types of play communication, 229–230
Geertz, C., 161n, 226–227, 232, 241n,
  245, 251n
Genetic epistemology, 57–58, 269, 299
Gesell, A., 18, 20
Goffman, E., 223–225
Goodenough, W., 251–252
Goodman, M. E., 10, 25, 131, 252
Gomme, Lady A. B., 5, 45–46, 68
Gossen, G., 34, 295–296
Gould R., 175–176
Groos, K., 100, 332
Guatemala, 282–283
Gusii, 119, 182, 184–186, 192–193

Haas, M., 31, 291, 297
Haddon, A. C., 31–32, 74n, 325
Hall, E. T., 221–222
Hall, G. S., 21–22, 46–48, 59
Handelman, D., 5
Harris, M., 2n, 249, 251
Henry, J., 34, 150–152, 279–280
Henry, Z., 34, 150–152
Hidden curriculum, 279–280
History of anthropology, 2, 2n
Hitchcock, J., 31, 182, 190
Hopi, 35, 156–160, 158
Hopscotch, 38, 85, 86, 87, 92
Howard, D., 32, 85, 86, 87
Huizinga, J., 257–258, 299, 332. *See also*
  Definition of play
Human Relations Area Files (HRAF). *See*
  Cross-Cultural Survey File
Humor, 212, 214–215, 218, 245–246
  children's speech play, 290–298
Hutt, C., 315–318. *See also*
  Taxonomy of play
Hymes, D., 249n, 250n, 284, 291, 331

Imaginative play, 66n, 116, 118, 120,
  139n, 140, 191, 204, 266n, 307
  films of, 337–339
  See also Sociodramatic play; Pretend
    play; Symbolic play; Make-believe;
    Play tutoring; Play interventions
Imaginative predisposition
  measurements, 320
Imitation and Play, 23, 31, 52, 55, 74,
  100–105, 116, 118, 131, 268, 329
India, 30, 31, 182, 190–191
Infants
  babytalk of parents, 287n
  play of, 277, 319–320
  lack of cross-cultural studies of, 330
  sex differences in play of, 114
  speech play of, 283, 285n, 287–288
Initiation rites, 24, 169
Introduced games, 67n–68n, 206
  film of, 341
Isaacs, S., 275–276, 320n
Israel, 38, 55, 106–107, 116–117

Joking relationships, 101, 133, 293–294
Jump rope rhymes and games, 36, 91–92,
  178–179

Kardiner, A., 142–145, 179
Kirshenblatt-Gimblett, B., 36, 284–285,
  287, 291, 293, 298, 334
Kluckhohn, C., 10, 20, 24, 35, 156
Kpelle, 37, 108–109, 280–281, 297
Kroeber, A. L., 64, 141
!Kung Bushmen, 37, 129, 129, 130, 130n,
  312, 319–320
  films of children's play, 334–338

Labov, W., 36, 121–122, 294
Lancy, D., 108–110, 281, 297, 333
Langness, L.L., 2n, 58, 61, 79, 248
Language-as-game, 248–249
Laughter and smiling, 53, 309, 312
Leacock, E., 282
Learning games, 278–279
LeVine, B., 119, 182, 184–185
Lévi-Strauss, C., 21, 57, 60, 250, 250n,
  251, 251n
Liminal and liminoid phenomena, 125
Linton, R., 142, 145, 166, 167
Little Hans, the case of, 146–148
Logical types, theory of, 215–219

Loizos, C., 309–310
Lowie, R., 64, 65n
Luba, 37, 166–174, *170, 171*

Macrosphere, stage of, 50, 149, 163
Maintenance systems, 180, *183*
Make-believe, 232, 237, 320–321. *See also*
    Imaginative play; Sociodramatic
    play; Pretend play; Symbolic play
Malinowski, B., 23, 98–99, 101–102, 133,
    153–154
Mancala, 38, 169, 282
Manus, 31, 58, 138–139
Maori, 32, 77–78, *78*, 83
Maretzki, H., 33, 182, 186–*188*
Martezki, T., 33, 182, 186–*188*
Marshall, L., 37, *129–131*
Masansa (children's villages), 169–172
Mbuti Pygmy, 101, 267
Mead, M., 4, 10, 19–23, 31–33, 55, 58,
    60, 77n, 136–140, 160–163, *164*,
    165, 166, 212, 213n, 276, 280n
Mescalero Apache, 35, 228
Metacommunication, 215, 217–222, 225,
    228, 340
Metalogues, 218–219n, 246
Metaphors
    for children, 20–26
    definition of, 21
    for cultural development, 41–42
    for play, 29
    use of by anthropologists, 21, 26, 29,
        325–331
    use of by other researchers, 7, 21n, 26,
        26n, 272, 313–315, 323, 328n
Microsphere, stage of, 50, 149, 163
Millar, S., 201, 333
Miller, S.N., 222–223, 310, 326n
Minturn, L., 31, 182, 190
Mitchell, E., 305–307, 324
Mixtecans, 34, *34*, 182, 191–192, *195*
Moral development, Piaget's stages of, 51
Morgan, L.H., 42, *43*, 59
Murdock, G.P., 179–198

Narratives, 263n, 298–299. *See also*
    Stories
Navaho, 35, 57, 156
Negative feedback, 211
Newell, W.W., 5, 36, 44–45, 67–69
New Zealand, 32, 77, 82–84

Non-human animal play, 309–311, 310n,
    311n, 340
Non-human primate play, 6, 214, 217,
    224, 311, 311n, 313, 316
    primate play face, 220–221
Norbeck, E, 5, 6, 257n, 303, 333
Nydegger, C., 28, *33*, 182, 189–190
Nydegger, W., 28, *33*, 182, 189–190

Oedipus complex, 153–154
    Little Hans and, 147
Operationalism, 181, 302, 323, 329
Operative thought, 269
Opie, I., 38, 87–89, *91*, 126. *See also*
    Classification of rhymes; Class-
    ification of street games
Opie, P., 38, 87–89, *91*, 126
Orchard Town, New England, 182,
    188–189, 192–194, *194*
Order-disorder games. *See* Reversals and
    inversions
Otters, 214–215
    film of play, 340

Pachisi, 5, 62–63, 63n
Paradox, 214–219, 221
Paradoxical statement, 232, 236
Parody, play as, 126–128, 131.
    See also Reversals and inversions;
    Satire
Party games, 36, 92
Patolli, 62–63, 63n
Peers, 193, 237, 245, 304, 311, 320, 355
Phonology, concern with in young
    children's speech play, 285–288
Piaget, J., 22, 50–52, 139, 265,
    268–273, 268n, 276, 299, 332,
    stages of play, 52–60, 54n
Pike, K., 248–249, 299
Pilagá, 34, 150–152
Play as catharsis, 101n, 145, 270–271
Play deprivation. *See* Deprivation/
    Deficiency theories
Play diary, 156–157, 160
Play disruption, 149
Playground movement, 47–48
Playgrounds, 304
Play interventions, 48n, 117–118, 122. *See
    also* Play-tutoring
Play report questionnaire, 203–204
Play socialization, 203–204

Play shelter, 156
Play statements, description of, 237–239
Play therapy, 149, 321
Play-tutoring/training, 118, 122. *See also*
   Play interventions
Playfulness scale, 322
Positive feedback, 211
Practice theory, 100
Pretend play, 229. *See also* Imaginative
   play; Sociodramatic play; Symbolic
   play; Make-believe
Primary institutions, 142, 179–180
Primary message systems (PMS), 222
Projective system
   Freud's concept of, 142
   Kardiner's use of, 142
   Whiting and Child's use of, 180
Propp, V., 261–262, 261n
Psychotherapy, 19n, 212, 219, 246,
   259, 321

Radcliffe-Brown, A. R., 98–99, 101–102,
   133
Rājpūts, 31, 182, 190–192
Raum, O., 23, 104–105
Recapitulation theories, 21–22, 43,
   46–49, 56, 56n, 59
Research situation
   and play, 121, 236–237
   and speech, 271, 271n
Research as play, 323–324. *See also*
   Metaphors
Reversals and inversions, 25, 124–126,
   125n, 132, 225, 245, 265, 295, 330.
   See also Parody; Satire
Ring and wheel games, distribution maps
   for American Indian games, 65, 66
Ritual, play and, 5, 124, 125n, 219
Roberts, J.M., 5, 6, 198–199, 199n,
   200–204, 208–209, 253, 282, 332.
   See also Definition of games;
   Typology of games
Róheim, G., 32, 153–155, 178
Romney, K., 34, 182, 191
Romney, R., 34, 182, 191
Rorschach test, 24, 143, 156
Roth, W.E., 32, 74–76, 75, 76
Russia, 117, 131

Salter, M., 32, 108
Sanga, 37, 166–173

Sapir, E., 135, 249
Satire, play as, 126–128, 130–132, 134,
   296, 330. *See also* Reversals and
   inversions; Parody
Schismogenesis, 211, 213
Schizophrenia, 212, 214–216, 246
Schwartzman, H.B., 5, 25, 33, 37, 232,
   233, 234, 235, 236–245, *240*, 274n,
   289, 333–334. *See also* Definition
   of Play; Play Statements
Schwartzman, J., 224n, 326n
Secondary institutions, 142–143, 179
Sex differences
   in children's behavior, 110–111
   and complexity of games, 112–113
   in play and games, 84–85, 85n,
      111–115
   in infant play, 114
   satire of, 131–132
   and temperament, 140–141
Sex play, 152, 152n, 180, 191
Sibling rivalry, 150–152
Simulative mode, 310
Singer, D., 66n, 118, 318, 320–321, 323–
   324, 332
Singer, J., 66n, 118, 120, 318, 320–321,
   323–324, 332, 333
Singing games, 31, 36, 81, 81n, 92
   film of, 339–340
Six Cultures Project, 24, 31, 33–34, 36,
   182–196, 208
Smilansky, S., 38, 54–55, 116–117,
   120–121
Sociodramatic play, 37–38, 53, 55, 100,
   112, 116–117, 119–120, 229,
   232–245, 273, 276. *See also*
   Imaginative play; Make-believe;
   Pretend play; Symbolic play
Sociolinguistics, 32, 284, 287, 292–293
Sociometric study, 241n
Song games. *See* Singing games
Specific learning, 272, 277–278, 280,
   300
Stevens, P., 294, 333
Stories, 32, 36, 109, 263–265,
   298, see also Narratives
Storyknifing, 36, 298
String figures (cat's cradle), 32, 70, 74,
   75, 76, 92
Structural complexity, 263–264
   classification of games on basis of,
   265–267
Structural-functionalism, 3, 99, 134, 135

Sutton-Smith, B., 4, 25, 32, 36, 55,
    82–85, 112–113, 115, 117,
    124–125, 128, 185, 190, 192–193,
    198–204, 225–226, 259, 261,
    263–269, 273, 275, 296, 332–333.
    See also Classification of games;
    Definition of play
Symbolic play, 53, 55, 269–271. *See also*
    Imaginative play; Make-believe;
    Pretend play; Sociodramatic play

(TAASP) The Association for the
    Anthropological Study of Play,
    6, 6n, 302, 333, 340–341
Taira, 33, 182, 186–187, *188*, 192–194
Taketak, 27–28, 197
Tallensi, 37, 102–104
Tangu, 27–28
Tarong, 28, 33, *33*, 182, 186–190,
    192–195
Taxonomy of play (Hutt), 317
Television, 66n
Teton Dakota, 35, 71
Thailand, 31, 297
Thematic Apperception Test (TAT), 24,
    156
Tick-tack-toe, 200
Tops, 27, 28, 31, *73*, 159
Tindall, B.A., 279–280, 333
Toy preference tests, 111–112
Toys
    and advertising, 307
    construction of by children, 144, *171*,
        187–188, 190
    and play with in experimental context,
        304, 315–317, 319
    ready-made, 189, 193, 193n, 306–307
    realism of, *194*, 307, 307n, 308
    sex-typed, 305–306
    use of by children, 303–304
    See also Dolls-indigenous

Transitional objects, 174–175
Trobriand Island, Trobrianders,
    67n–68n, 124, 153–154, 341
Turkey, 294
Turner, V., 5, 124, 125n
Tylor, E.B., 5, 21, 44, 59, 61–63, 69–70.
    See also Culture, defintion of,
Typology of games (Roberts), 197

Upoko-titi, 78, *78*, 79

Vermont, films of children's play, 334,
    336–337
von Glascoe, C., 34, 253, 255–257, *256*
Vygotsky, L.S., 273–275

Wagner, R., 1, 21, 326, 331
Weiner, N., 210–211, 213
Whiting, B., 21, 24, 181, *183*
Whiting, J.W.M., 21, 23, 179–180, 184
Winnicott, D.W., 174–175
Winning-losing in games, 28, 194, 197.
    See also Competition
Wissler, C., 64–66, *65*
Wolfenstein, M., 16, 17, 290–291
Work-play dichotomy, presence and
    absence of, 4–5, 4n–5n, 42n,
    109, 130, 132, 138, 156, 225n, 327

Yanomamö, films of children's play,
    334–338
Yeke, 37, 166–173
Yoruba, 7, 132
Yucatán, 34, 255–257, *256*

Zaire, 167